FOCUS: GAMELAN MUSIC OF INDONESIA

Focus: Gamelan Music of Indonesia is an introduction to the familiar music from Southeast Asia's largest country—both as sound and as cultural phenomenon. An archipelago of over 17,000 islands, Indonesia is a melting pot of Hindu, Buddhist, Islamic, Portuguese, Dutch, and British influences. Despite this diversity, it has forged a national culture, one in which music plays a significant role. Gamelan music, in particular, teaches us much about Indonesian values and modern-day life. *Focus: Gamelan Music of Indonesia* provides an introduction to present-day Javanese, Balinese, Cirebonese, and Sundanese gamelan music through ethnic, social, cultural, and global perspectives.

- Part I, *Music and Southeast Asian History*, provides introductory materials for the study of Southeast Asian music.
- Part II, *Gamelan Music in Java and Bali*, moves to a more focused overview of gamelan music in Indonesia.
- Part III, *Focusing In*, takes an in-depth look at Sundanese gamelan traditions, as well as modern developments in Sundanese music and dance.
- The accompanying CD offers vivid examples of traditional Indonesian gamelan music.

Henry Spiller PhD is Assistant Professor of Ethnomusicology at the University of California, Davis.

The Focus on World Music Series is designed specifically for area courses in world music and ethnomusicology. Written by the top ethnomusicologists in their field, the Focus books balance sound pedagogy with exemplary scholarship. Each book provides a telescopic view of the musics and cultures addressed, giving the reader a general introduction on the music and culture of the area and then zooming in on different musical styles with in-depth case studies.

Visit the companion website for this new edition:

www.routledge.com/textbooks/focusonworldmusic

This website includes further resources for both instructors and students.

MWHGLECT
09010219

FOCUS ON WORLD MUSIC

Series Editor: Michael B. Bakan

Focus: Music of European Nationalism
Second Edition
Philip V. Bohlman

Focus: Music of South Africa
Second Edition
Carol A. Muller

Focus: Gamelan Music of Indonesia
Second Edition
Henry Spiller

FORTHCOMING

Focus: Music of Northeast Brazil
Second Edition
Larry Crook

FOCUS: GAMELAN MUSIC OF INDONESIA

Second Edition

Henry Spiller

University of California, Davis

Routledge
Taylor & Francis Group

NEW YORK AND LONDON

Figures

Musical Examples on Compact Disc

1 "Gondang Si Monang-Monang," musicians from Parondang, North Sumatra
2 "Gonjing/Sarung Ilang/Gonjing" (for "Rahwana" dance), members of the Panji Asmara troupe
3 *Pelog* and *slendro* (*salendro*) scales
4 *Ladrang* "Pangkur" *pelog barang*, Saptobudoyo Group
5 Music for *memukur* procession, Sekehe Gong Werdhi Suara of Banjar Kedaton, Bali
6 "Jaya Semara," Gamelan Sekar Jaya
7 "Sinyur," LS Giri Harja III
8 "Ujung Laut/Sinyur," Pusaka Sunda
9 "Sinur," Candra Puspita
10 "Lindeuk Japati," Tati Saleh

For additional information on each track, see the Listening Guide, pp. 253–79.

About the Author

Henry Spiller PhD is Assistant Professor of Ethnomusicology at the University of California, Davis. He first encountered gamelan music as a college student at the University of California, Santa Cruz, where he began studying with Undang Sumarna in 1976, and has been involved with Indonesian music and dance as a scholar and performer ever since.

Spiller earned a master's degree in harp performance from Holy Names University and a doctorate in ethnomusicology from the University of California, Berkeley. At UC Davis, he teaches courses in ethnomusicology and directs a Sundanese gamelan ensemble. Before he moved to UC Davis, he taught at California Polytechnic State University, San Luis Obispo, and at Kenyon College in Gambier, Ohio.

Series Foreword

The past decade has witnessed extraordinary growth in the areas of ethnomusicology and world music publishing. With the publication of both the ten-volume *Garland Encyclopedia of World Music* and the second edition of the *New Grove Dictionary of Music and Musicians* (2001), we now have access to general reference resources that ethnomusicologists and world music enthusiasts of even just a few years ago could only have dreamed of. University and other academic presses—Chicago, Oxford, Cambridge, Illinois, Temple, Wesleyan, Indiana, California, Routledge—have produced excellent ethnomusicological monographs, edited volumes, and smaller-scale reference works in ever-increasing numbers, many accompanied by CDs, DVDs, and other media that bring the musics described vividly to life. A host of new introductory-level textbooks for freshman/sophomore-level world music survey courses have come out too, along with new editions of long-established textbooks catering to that market. New instructional resources for teaching these same kinds of introductory survey courses have been created in addition, the Oxford Global Music Series perhaps most notable among them. And the Internet has of course revolutionized everything, with thousands upon thousands of Web-based resources—from superb scholarly and educational resources such as Smithsonian Global Sound (www.smithsonianglobalsound.org) and *Grove Music Online* to the wild frontiers of YouTube and myriad commercial online music providers—all now available from your desktop at the click of a mouse.

Yet for all of this profuse and diverse publishing activity, there remains a conspicuous gap in the literature. We still lack a solid corpus of high quality textbooks designed specifically for area courses in world music, ethnomusicology, and interdisciplinary programs with a strong music component. The need for such texts is greatest where courses for upper-division undergraduate and entry-level graduate students are taught, but it extends to courses at the freshman and sophomore levels as well, especially those enrolling music majors and other students who are serious and motivated.

What has been needed for such courses are books that balance sound pedagogy with exemplary scholarship, and that are substantive in content yet readily accessible to specialist and non-specialist readers alike. These books would be written in a lively and engaging style by leading ethnomusicologists and educators, bringing wide interdisciplinary scope and relevance to the contemporary concerns of their readership. They would, moreover, provide a telescopic view of the musics and cultures they addressed, zooming in from broad-based surveys of expansive music-culture areas and topics toward compelling, in-depth case studies of specific musicultural traditions and their myriad transformations in the modern world.

This is precisely what Routledge's *Focus on World Music* series delivers, with books that are authoritative, accessible, pedagogically strong, richly illustrated, and accompanied by a compelling compact disc of musical examples linked integrally to the text. I am delighted to be part of the team that has brought this exciting and important series to fruition. I hope you enjoy reading these books as much as I have!

Michael B. Bakan
The Florida State University
Series Editor

Preface

While *Focus: Gamelan Music of Indonesia* is not a textbook per se, it is quite useful as either the central text for college-level courses focusing on Javanese, Balinese, and Sundanese gamelan music, or as a supplementary text for courses with wider scopes. It is certainly sufficiently technical for music courses, and the wealth of cultural information it contains makes it a suitable ancillary text for courses in dance, anthropology, cultural studies, and other fields as well. The goal for the accompanying CD was to provide complete examples of most of the genres that the book discusses in detail, especially those that are difficult to obtain elsewhere, and to illustrate technical points made in the book with detailed listening notes that are keyed to the recordings. Of course, teachers and students should supplement their listening experiences with additional recordings; the copiously annotated "Additional Resources" section at the back of the book will provide some guidance in selecting them.

How This Book Is Organized

Focus: Gamelan Music of Indonesia is a revision of a book originally published under the title *Gamelan: The Traditional Sounds of Indonesia* (ABC-CLIO, 2004). For this new edition, I have reorganized the book's contents into shorter, more manageable chapters, which are grouped into three parts. *Focus: Gamelan Music of Indonesia* begins with an introduction to some Southeast Asian musical processes in Part I (Chapters 1 and 2); these processes are, I argue, particularly Southeast Asian because they are intimately related to Southeast Asian geography and history. Part II (Chapters 3 and 4) discusses a sampling of gamelan ensembles and repertories on the Indonesian islands of Java and Bali, all of which bring those musical processes to bear on different social systems with different values. Part III focuses on Sundanese music and dance from the western third of the island of Java. Chapters 5 and 6 present two rather different Sundanese gamelan ensembles (gamelan *salendro* and *degung*), their music, and their social contexts in some depth. At times these discussions present minute technical details; these can be skimmed or skipped by readers more interested in the social and cultural aspects of gamelan music. Chapter 7 explores the role of dance in Sundanese society and addresses issues of change, authenticity, and meaning in the performing arts of West Java; I argue that some of the most traditional sounds of Indonesia are those that do not necessarily fulfill the Western expectation of exoticism. Chapter 8 revisits the musical processes introduced in Chapter 1 and reflects once again on what it means for music to be traditional in a changing world.

New to the Second Edition

The revised edition includes all the material from the first edition, updated to reflect some recent developments and to correct some factual and typographical errors. *Focus: Gamelan Music of Indonesia* continues to be packaged with an audio CD. In addition, there is a companion website, **www.routledge.com/textbooks/focusonworldmusic**, for instructors and students. It includes further resources, lecture notes in the form of PowerPoint presentations, and quizzes for student practice.

A Word About Languages

Out of necessity, this book includes many terms in several foreign languages. Foreign terms are italicized at their first appearance, and thereafter presented in ordinary roman type. Readers may refer to the glossary for brief definitions of these foreign terms. Since there are quite a few words in various Indonesian languages, it is worth taking a moment to mention a few salient facts about some of these languages. Virtually all Indonesians speak the Indonesian national language (called *bahasa Indonesia*, which English speakers usually render as "Indonesian"). Most English speakers can pronounce Indonesian words passably well if they learn a few simple rules. Most of the consonants are pronounced more or less as they are in English, with the exception of "c," which is pronounced "ch," and "g," which is always hard, even when followed by an "e" or and "i." Most Indonesian "r" sounds are rolled (as in Spanish). Indonesians pronounce "a" as English speakers do in the word "father," "e" as in "bed" (or sometimes as in "batter"), "i" as in "pizza," "o" as in "poker," and "u" as in "dude." If the same vowel appears two times in a row, it is pronounced twice with a glottal stop in between. An "h" at the end of a word calls for an audible aspiration (forceful exhalation of breath); a "k" at the end of a word is pronounced as a glottal stop.

Many Indonesians speak a regional language other than Indonesian among their families and friends, saving Indonesian for official situations or to speak to Indonesians from other parts of the country. The two most widely spoken regional languages in Indonesia are Javanese and Sundanese. Both of these languages have a few pronunciation peculiarities. Javanese distinguish between dental "d" and alveolar "dh" sounds; for the dental version, the tongue is right on the upper teeth, while for the alveolar version, the tongue is behind the upper teeth on the alveolar ridge, resulting in a slightly less explosive attack. Javanese make a similar distinction between dental "t" and an alveolar "th"; a Javanese "th" is not pronounced as in "the," but rather more like the "th" in the name "Esther." Sundanese language includes a special vowel that is spelled "eu" and pronounced like the "eu" in French (as in "Pasteur"). A schwa sound, like the "e" in "the," approximates the correct pronunciation; English speakers are not used to saying this vowel except in unaccented syllables, and so find many Sundanese words difficult to pronounce. A Sundanese word that ends in a vowel is pronounced with a glottal stop at the end.

Indonesian, Javanese, and Sundanese (along with many other Southeast Asian languages) belong to the Austronesian language family, and share many words and grammatical constructions between them. They also have borrowed many words from the languages of other cultures with which they have come into contact, including Sanskrit, Arabic, Portuguese, Dutch, and English. Americans are frequently amused to come across an Indonesian word that has clearly been borrowed from English, but whose pronunciation and spelling have changed.

One common feature that many English speakers find startling about Austronesian languages is that they often make no adjustment to a noun to indicate whether it is singular or plural. Thus, the word gamelan might mean "one bronze percussion orchestra" or "many bronze percussion orchestras." Native speakers rely on the word's context in a sentence to figure out the meaning. Readers of this book will also have to rely on context; a sentence beginning with "the gamelan is" obviously is about one gamelan, while "the gamelan are" is clearly about more than one gamelan.

Acknowledgments

If this book is at all successful in achieving its aims, I share that success with countless individuals who have helped me along the way. I am especially grateful for the friendship, help, support, and instruction that two remarkable Sundanese musicians living in the United States—Undang Sumarna and Burhan Sukarma—have lavished on me over the years. My teachers and friends in West Java during my visits there (and their visits to the United States) have generously shared with me their knowledge and feelings about Sundanese music and dance. Otong Rasta, Ade Komaran, Yus Yusdianawijaya, the late Entis Sutisna, and the late Tosin Mochtar each spent hours teaching, playing, and discussing music and dance with me. Members of two *lingkung seni*—the Bandung Zoo's *ketuk tilu* group and The Rawit Group—made me feel welcome as I tagged along to their performances and made a general nuisance of myself. Others who took time to discuss their art with me include the late Abay Subardja, Enoch Atmadibrata, the late Sujana Arja, Irawati Durban Ardjo, the late Nugraha Sudiredja, Ana Mulyana, Nano S., Tjetjep Supriadi, Idjah Hadidjah, Euis Komariah, Hasibun Arief, Salam Mulyadi, Edi Kusnadi, Abdul Rozak, Asep Suparma, Dohot Tarmana, Aep Diana, the late Tati Saleh and members of her group, Tati Haryatin, Ismet Ruchimat, Hardja Susilo, Midiyanto, and Santosa; I am grateful for their time and insights. Endo and Marjie Suanda (along with their entire family) offered me seemingly endless hospitality as well as musicological and cultural insights. Matt Ashworth and Hendrawati provided friendship, a place for *latihan*, and a wealth of valuable contacts. A host of fellow non-Indonesian disciples of Indonesian performing arts have contributed immensely to my own research, including Ben Arcangel, Randal Baier, Andrew Bouchard, Benjamin Brinner, Simon Cook, Michael Ewing, Kathy Foley, Lisa Gold, Richard North, Margot Prado, Rae Ann Stahl, the members of Pusaka Sunda, Suzanne Suwanda, Andrew Weintraub, Sean Williams, and Benjamin Zimmer. While all these individuals (and many more) share the credit for anything that is good in this work, I take full responsibility for all of the misinterpretations or errors that have slipped in.

My research in Bandung in 1998–9 was supported by a Fulbright (IIE) fellowship. I would like to thank the Indonesian Institute of Science (Lembaga Ilmu Pengetahuan Indonesia—LIPI) for facilitating my research, and Iyus Rusliana, former director of the Indonesian Academy of the Arts (Sekolah Tinggi Seni Indonesia—STSI) in Bandung, for sponsoring my stay in Indonesia. I also am grateful to John B. Situmeang and Nelly Paliama of the American-Indonesian Exchange Foundation (AMINEF) for their support in Indonesia. Funding for other relevant research trips was provided by the University of California Berkeley Center for Southeast Asian Studies, the UC Berkeley Graduate Division, the American Association for Netherlandic Studies (AANS), and a Kenyon College Faculty Development Grant. Richard North provided me with much useful information about Cirebonese *gamelan sekaten*. Rob Hodges generously read and commented on the paragraphs covering Toba Batak music. Nano S. provided me with the text for his song, "Lindeuk Japati," along with an Indonesian translation. Tati Haryatin's excellent transcription and translation skills greatly enhanced the listening notes for the "Sinur" track on the CD. The wonderful transcription and translation of an entire *wayang golek* play by Andrew Weintraub and his colleagues (originally published by Lontar Press) provided a similar enhancement for the "Sinyur" track. I would also like to thank Sean Williams for originally suggesting that I write this book.

The editorial staff at ABC-CLIO, including Alicia Merritt, Jane Raese, Carol Estes, and Doug Pibel, did an exemplary job of shepherding this book from its inception to the publication of its original edition. Series editor Michael B. Bakan provided excellent editorial and organizational suggestions on the early drafts as well as specific help and guidance with the sections on Balinese music. For the present edition, Routledge staff, including editor Constance Ditzel, provided valuable guidance in revising the book. Annie Jackson, of The Running Head Limited, greatly clarified the present edition's prose. I would also like to thank R. Anderson Sutton and two anonymous reviewers for calling my attention to a number of factual errors and inconsistencies, which, it is hoped, have been corrected in this edition.

My partner, Michael Seth Orland, has been a source of emotional and moral support since the inception of the project; this book's completion owes much to his constant encouragement and sympathetic ear. His keen readings of many parts of the text provided a much-needed outsider's viewpoint that enhanced the readability and sensibility of many chapters as well.

Finally, I would like to thank the musicians who performed for the recordings that are reproduced on the accompanying CD. Most did not know at the time that their performances would eventually find their way onto this particular compilation; I would like them to know that my goal in reproducing their labors here is not my own personal gain, but rather raising consciousness and appreciation of the excellent work that they do. I am also eternally grateful to those who helped me locate suitable recordings and granted permissions to use them—Florence Bodo and Dedy S. Hadianda, Andrew Weintraub, Nano S., Wayne Vitale, Rae Ann Stahl and Burhan Sukarma, Michael Ewing, Michael B. Bakan, Roger Vetter, Alex Dea, Cathy Carapella, and Philip Yampolsky. I hope that inclusion in this project does justice to their valuable work of disseminating quality recordings.

PART I

Music and
Southeast Asian History

CHAPTER **1**

Southeast Asian Musical Processes

It has been more than thirty years since I first heard the exotic sounds of a *gamelan* ensemble emanating from somewhere in the performing arts building at the University of California at Santa Cruz, where I was a first-year music major. I was sitting in an ear-training class, practicing singing and identifying intervals with my classmates, when all of a sudden an unearthly, ponderous, utterly unidentifiable noise penetrated the walls. It wasn't particularly loud, but it was quite distinctive and strangely compelling; it certainly made a startling contrast with the weak singing sounds my fellow students and I were making. "It sounds like they got the gamelan going," the teacher commented, and I wondered to myself, "what on earth could a gamelan be?" I made it a point to search out the room in which this strange thing was kept, where I discovered that a "gamelan" was a collection of odd-looking percussion instruments. (Somehow, I knew instinctively that the term referred to the whole collection of instruments; I never asked the question I have since heard countless first-timers ask—"which one is the gamelan?") Unlike the musical instruments to which I was accustomed, such as pianos and guitars, with their neat symmetry and manufactured perfection, there was a sort of Fred Flintstone quality about these gamelan instruments—each key and pot was irregularly shaped and sized and attached to the intricately hand-carved stands with uneven nails or rustic-looking ropes. The golden metal from which the keys and pots were made seemed to glow mysteriously. I found the whole package to be invitingly inscrutable; it looked timelessly ancient, mystical, and most definitely exotic.

While I thought the gamelan was quite fascinating, I didn't succumb to its exotic appeal until many months later, when I discovered that a number of fellow students with whom I wanted to be friends played in the university's gamelan ensemble. I didn't realize it at the time, but socializing is also the motivation for many Indonesians who become involved in playing gamelan music. Of course, gamelan instruments don't strike

3

Indonesians as particularly exotic, nor do they find the sounds unfamiliar or strange, but since Indonesians tend to value gregariousness, they often find themselves attracted to the social aspects of playing gamelan.

The parts I learned were not really very difficult, and at first I quickly became bored with them. It gradually dawned on me, however, that the most important question to ask when I learned a new part was not "how interesting can I make my own part?" but rather "how does my part affect all the others?" Over time, I began to conceive my role in the gamelan ensemble as somebody who "fits in" rather than somebody who "stands out."

Gamelan music of all sorts is about playing together with other people in a unified group in which mutual cooperation is rewarded with harmonious music. Expert gamelan musicians use their knowledge and skill not so much to stand out and shine in the group, but to blend seamlessly into the complex musical texture and make everybody shine—an approach to exerting power in all social interactions which Indonesians tend to value highly. I did not realize it at the time, but even from the very beginning of my involvement with gamelan music, the musical processes required to play it were retraining my body and mind to think and act in accordance with these values.

Thirty years later, gamelan music no longer sounds especially exotic to me. In fact, I can't imagine my own life without it. Studying gamelan has taken me around the world, introduced me to a host of fascinating people, and led me to hear and play music in new ways. It is humbling to realize that the musical processes that undergird gamelan music—the conventions and techniques by which it is conceived, composed, played, and heard—have so profoundly formed and shaped my own personality and values. Of course, music and musical activities are among the most meaningful expressions human beings can produce—it should come as no surprise that the music we hear and play affects who we are, what we think, and how we perceive the world around us.

To my mind, what qualifies music as traditional is not how old it is, but rather how well it teaches, reinforces, and creates the social values of its producers and consumers. Traditional music is not something that is stuck in the past; it grows and changes, just as the people who make and listen to it grow and change, just as the values they share with those close to them change (albeit a bit more slowly). Truly traditional music, then, exploits new resources, acknowledges new requirements, and responds to new situations. It provides a place for people to try out new approaches to their existing values, to experiment with new ideas, and to synthesize the new with the old. It is rooted in enduring musical processes—the general ideas about how people organize their musical activities—but is not limited to particular musical instruments, sounds, or repertories. It is easy to forget, amidst the buying and selling of commercial recordings, each of which is the perfected production of superhumanly "talented" artists and advanced technological magic, that musical processes—the doing and sharing of musical activities—have profound meaning and power.

Ever since contact between the Indonesian archipelago and the West began many centuries ago, the Western imagination has been captivated by the region's seemingly endless supply of exotic, even miraculous, things—spices, coffee, and rubber; orangutans and Komodo dragons; the name of the mysterious spy Mata Hari ("matahari" means "sun" in Indonesian; its literal translation is "eye of the day") and a convenient word to describe lunatic behavior ("running amok"); unusual social practices ranging from matrilineal descent reckoning and headhunting to tooth-filing and ritual homosexual acts; the list goes on and on. Is it any wonder that the West expects—even demands—that music from the region be similarly exotic? And in many cases it is. Westerners have long found the bronze percussion ensemble music of Java and Bali—gamelan music—to meet and exceed expectations of exoticism.

This book attempts to move beyond the immediate attraction that the sounds of gamelan music exert on Western listeners and investigate how the music works and how it is meaningful to Indonesian listeners. Most of this book is devoted to describing several kinds of traditional gamelan music from various parts of Java and Bali, with a special focus on Sundanese traditions from West Java. You should not infer from the focus on gamelan that such traditions are the only, or even the dominant, musical sounds in Indonesia. The book is not meant to provide a comprehensive survey of Indonesian music, but rather to explore the musical processes that characterize some specific gamelan traditions as well as gamelan music in general (and, in some ways, many other kinds of traditional Southeast Asian music as well). It is my hope that this introduction will not only make these extraordinary musical traditions seem less exotic and more meaningful to students, but that it will provide them with insights into how all music, regardless of its point of origin, molds individuals and societies; how musical values create, teach, reinforce, and even alter social values; and how musical change is an index of social change.

Although this book's main focus is gamelan (bronze percussion orchestra) music in Indonesia, it is important to establish at the outset that neither the modern nation of Indonesia nor gamelan music developed in a vacuum. Indonesia is a conglomeration of islands, peoples, and cultures; its modern form is the result of a history that involves not only the lands and peoples within Indonesia, but the surrounding areas as well. Ensembles called gamelan are most often associated with the Indonesian islands of Java and Bali, but similar ensembles characterize the musical traditions of the entire region. This first chapter will explore the history of the whole of Southeast Asia to isolate a few musical processes—general ideas about how people organize musical activities—that underlie a great deal of music-making throughout the area, by investigating a selected sample of Southeast Asian musical traditions.

Southeast Asia

Southeast Asia's position on a typical map of the world (see Figure 1.1) is deceiving: down in the lower right corner, it seems to be one of the most remote and marginal places on earth. From this satellite's-eye view, Southeast Asia appears as a misshapen peninsula trailing a chaotic mess of ungainly islands, sandwiched between the more geographically impressive landmasses of China (to the north), Australia (to the south), and India (to the west). Conventional maps of the world arbitrarily place Europe or North America at the center; this Eurocentric vantage makes it easy to dismiss Southeast Asia as an out-of-the-way, insignificant place.

English-language histories, too, tend to be Eurocentric. They concentrate on the rise of civilization in Europe and the spread of European ideas throughout the world while ignoring the achievements of comparable civilizations in Asia, Africa, and the Americas.

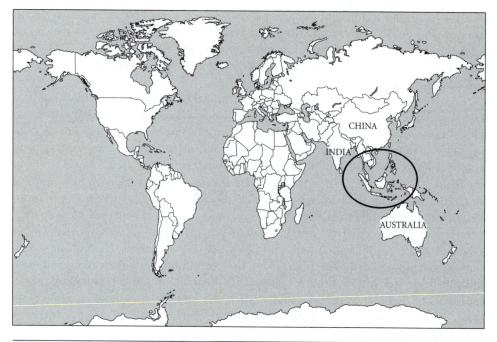

Figure 1.1 Map of the world (Southeast Asia circled).

Such histories generally ignore the cultural accomplishments of Southeast Asian societies, which include the development of many neolithic technologies that contributed to cultural developments throughout the world. Southeast Asia's role in worldwide trading networks before the modern era, too, had far-reaching historical effects rarely acknowledged in modern histories (Lockard 1995: 7–8). In modern times Southeast Asia has been ground zero for conflicts of world-dominating ideologies such as colonialism v. self-determination, capitalism v. communism, and minority rights v. nationalism. The integration of Southeast Asia into the world economy remains an issue of great global concern. That seemingly far-off region has long been, and likely will continue to be, a significant historical, political, and cultural force in the world.

Modern national boundaries in Southeast Asia reflect recent geopolitical realities more than long-standing cultural politics. Most Southeast Asian countries are ethnically heterogeneous; borders are often accidents of history and don't coincide with cultural spheres of influence. Virtually all Southeast Asian nations include a variety of cultural, ethnic, and language groups. Some significant ethnic groups, such as the Hmong in Laos and Thailand, have no nation to call their own. Countries in mainland Southeast Asia include Myanmar (formerly known as Burma), Laos, Cambodia, Thailand, and Vietnam. Southeast Asian island nations include Indonesia, the island city-state of Singapore, the tiny sultanate of Brunei, and the Philippines. Malaysia includes territory on the mainland as well as on the island of Borneo.

Significant geographic obstacles effectively separate Southeast Asia from the rest of the world—expansive, deep oceans (the 6½-mile-deep Marianas trench off the coast of the Philippines is the deepest point in the ocean) mark the south and east boundaries, while some of the highest mountains in the world (the Himalayas) fence off the north and west. The land areas bounded by these natural limits share a hot, wet climate as well as an abundance of water and (once upon a time) thick rainforests. The major islands of Southeast Asia are separated only by shallow seas; as recently as 10,000 years ago, during the ice ages, when much of the world's water was bound up in glaciers, some of the larger islands were joined to mainland Southeast Asia by land bridges; the result of this geographical past is a relatively uniform flora and fauna in the region (Cribb 2000: 7–8).

In contrast, the peoples and cultures of modern Southeast Asia exhibit a staggering variety of languages and customs. The prehistory of the region is rife with waves of settlers from elsewhere, who brought with them markedly different physiognomies and language families. Sometimes the newcomers pushed the previous inhabitants into remote regions, but often they settled on top of existing cultures like sediments in a riverbed. Over the past few thousand years, influential religious missionaries and trade emissaries from India, China, and the Arab world came, followed by European colonial powers. Communities in various places adopted or developed sophisticated agricultural techniques and technologies. Great empires, whose rulers and subjects adhered to major world religions such as Hinduism, Buddhism, and Islam, rose, conquered others, and fell, all the while adopting, adapting, and rejecting languages, ideas, and religions; all along, isolated communities cultivated their own idiosyncratic dialects and animistic religions. This great variety begs the question of whether it is sensible to speak of Southeast Asia as some kind of unit in human terms, despite its geographic unity.

The answer is yes, for two reasons. The first is precisely the common environment: beset by similar environmental challenges, with access to similar resources, it is not surprising that different communities might adopt similar solutions to similar problems. The common exploitation of bamboo as a raw material and the ubiquitous cultivation of rice as a staple food are examples. The second reason is mutual contact among various Southeast Asian peoples and cultures. Different parts of Southeast Asia may be relatively remote to the rest of the world, but they are quite accessible to one another, especially those areas around rivers or bordering the shallow and easily navigable seas. Ideas, innovations, and inventions spread over the region through trade and maritime contact.

Historian Anthony Reid identifies several general social and cultural traits shared by many Southeast Asian cultures which are not characteristic of China and India: "the concept of spirit or 'soul-stuff' animating living things; the prominence of women in descent, ritual matters, marketing, and agriculture; and the importance of debt as a determinant of social obligation" (Reid 1988: 6). Reid also isolates a few more specific practices and technologies shared by many Southeast Asian cultures, including the use of a delicate finger knife to harvest rice, the popularity of cockfighting as a sporting pastime, and music played on bronze gongs (Reid 1988: 6).

This book focuses on bronze gong music, especially on gong music from the Southeast Asian island of Java (one of the many islands that comprise the modern nation-state of Indonesia). The various music cultures of Southeast Asia (including those of Java) incorporate an astonishing variety of ensembles that feature bronze gongs, each one sounding quite different from the others. Nevertheless, they all share some fundamental characteristics. Examining the different musical "surfaces" that emerge when various cultures adopt and develop these shared fundamental music-making principles provides

Figure 1.2 Kubing (jaw harp) from the Philippines (Henry Spiller).

an entry point to an understanding of the general traits of Southeast Asian cultures as well as the historical, political, environmental, and social differences among them. To understand the principles of Southeast Asian music-making is to understand the peoples and cultures of Southeast Asia a bit better.

Ecology, culture, and music

Southeast Asia's environment has had great impact on its residents' economies and ways of life. Ecology has also exerted an enormous direct impact on the region's musical traditions. For example, many varieties of bamboo grow throughout the region, and Southeast Asian cultures have long exploited its unique qualities for many purposes, including making music. Bamboo is already hollow, simplifying the process of making wind instruments, such as flutes, from it. It is quite easy to work with; using simple cutting tools, it is simple to make a *jaw harp* (see Figure 1.2) by cutting a tongue out of a strip of bamboo, or even a simple string instrument by slitting "strings" from the bamboo's skin and inserting sticks as "bridges" to tighten the strings. A technical term for a string fashioned from the same material as its resonator is *idiochord* (*idio-* means "self," and "*-chord*" means string); musicologists generically call this kind of instrument, therefore, an *idiochord tube zither* (see Figure 1.3). Bamboo's naturally sonorous qualities also make it an ideal material for a variety of percussion instruments. Wood is more difficult to manipulate than bamboo, but also provides the raw material for several kinds of musical instruments. Like bamboo, wood is naturally sonorous. A common Southeast

Figure 1.3 Kalinga musician from the Philippines playing the idiochord tube zither called kolibit (courtesy Robert Garfias).

Asian musical instrument consists of a series of tuned bamboo tubes or wooden slabs; the generic musicological term for this kind of instrument is *xylophone*. Some scholars have suggested that the xylophone was a Southeast Asian invention (Miller and Williams 1998: 57).

Organic materials such as wood and bamboo deteriorate quickly in the hot, wet climate of Southeast Asia. Instruments made of readily available materials and requiring little investment of time to make, such as xylophones, jaw harps, and idiochord zithers, are well-suited to this environment because they are easy to replace when they disintegrate. Such instruments have been important components of Southeast Asian music cultures for probably thousands of years, and continue to be prominent in modern times.

Unlike wood and bamboo, bronze holds up quite well in the moist, steamy environment of Southeast Asia. In contrast to natural materials, bronze requires sophisticated technology and expensive raw materials to make and work, but once forged and shaped it is very durable. It is not entirely clear whether the idea for bronze smelting was independently invented in mainland Southeast Asia or imported from China to the north, but ever since a distinctly Southeast Asian bronze tradition developed as long as four thousand years ago the metal has been regarded to have magical properties (see Becker 1988). Perhaps its durability contributed to bronze's perceived mystical power and great value. Among the implements early Southeast Asian bronzesmiths created were so-called bronze drums. Later, bronze became the raw material for a variety of percussion instruments, including gongs, gong chimes (a series of tuned gongs), and metallophones (a series of tuned metal bars). The contrast between bamboo and bronze begins

to illustrate a principle that will assume great significance in the following discussion of Southeast Asian music cultures: the principle of *layering*. Bamboo and bronze belong to distinct layers of material technology that reflect different layers of cultural influence as well. Bamboo represents the technology of the earliest inhabitants of Southeast Asia; direct descendants of these aboriginal peoples have been pushed into marginal areas of Southeast Asia and often maintain traditions different from those of subsequent invaders (Matusky 1998: 594). Bamboo also represents the technology of the first proto-Malays who migrated southward from Taiwan into island Southeast Asia—the areas that are now the Philippines, Malaysia, and Indonesia—and the Southeast Asian mainland. These settlers also brought with them techniques of rice cultivation. Bamboo instruments often are associated with animist Southeast Asian ceremonies that are connected to agriculture and propitiating local spirits.

Bronze technology, on the other hand, first became manifest in mainland Southeast Asia, in what is now Thailand and Vietnam, associated with communities with intensive agriculture, relatively dense populations, and some social stratification. The resources and specialized skill required for bronze technology meant it was available primarily to elite classes. Bronze technology supplements, but does not supersede, bamboo technology; instruments made of bronze might sound different from instruments made of bamboo, but musicians play similar parts on them. They are different solutions brought to bear on the same musical problem: how to produce musical instruments in an environment where everything rots quickly. But while bamboo music is often asso-

Figure 1.4 (Far left) An assortment of early Southeast Asian bronze drums (photo and print collection of the Koninklijk Instituut voor Taal-, Land- en Volkenkunde, Leiden, the Netherlands).

(Left) Motifs from bronze drums showing musical activities (Higham 1989, p. 203, Figure 4.10).

ciated with agriculture, bronze instruments are more often associated with ceremonial music devoted to maintaining an orderly, hierarchical cosmos, as reflected in a social order with higher and lower classes. The expensive resources and specialized technology required for bronze reflect its greater social value and suggest not only a layering of cultural influences, but a layering of social classes as well. Bronze-age Southeast Asian bronze drums (see Figure 1.4) provide an excellent illustration of class distinctions. The technical expertise involved in creating such finely cast implements of such large size (some were as heavy as 200 lbs) suggests specialized artisans working on behalf of upper-class patrons. The drums often are decorated with scenes of lavish rituals featuring musical instruments and elaborate costumes (Higham 1989). Whether the ceremonies were funerals, fertility rites, or celebrations of war victories, there is, according to archaeologist Charles Higham, little doubt that "participation in ceremonials was part of the aristocratic society" in Southeast Asia (Higham 1996: 133).

But bronze technology did not remain limited to the upper classes of stratified societies; it long ago trickled down even to quite isolated cultures. On the island of Mindoro in the Philippines, for example, a small community of Hanunoo lives in the highland areas (into which they were long ago pushed by Tagalog and Bisayan farmers). While much of their music-making employs instruments made from wood and bamboo, they play bronze gongs in ensembles to enliven feasts and celebrations. These bronze gongs are acquired through trade with outsiders, and the Hanunoo consider them to be rare and valuable possessions (Maceda and Conklin 1955).

Very often both bronze and bamboo musical instruments bear names that imitate the sounds they make. The syllable "klung" in *angklung*, for example, captures the resonant quality of the bamboo rattling against the instrument's frame as the player shakes it. The Malay term *gong* is possibly a vocal rendition of the low, ponderous, visceral sound of a large gong. Speakers of Sundanese, one of the regional languages of Java, take the ono- matopoeia one step further: their word "goong" includes two syllables on the "o" sound to imitate the undulating waves of sound that the best gongs produce. The Cambodian, Thai, Lao, and Burmese names for a thick pair of cymbals—*chhing, ching, sing,* and *sì,* respectively—are similarly onomatopoeic.

Subsequent cultural waves in Southeast Asia added more and more layers of tech- nology for Southeast Asian musical instruments. Ideas from the civilizations of India found receptive audiences in the peoples and cultures of Southeast Asia; the develop- ing upper classes especially saw great potential in the notions of social class and kingship that accompanied Hinduism. They adapted the Indian belief that reflecting the organi- zation of the cosmos through a powerful intermediary—a "king" who resided in both worlds and represented an interface between them—would lead to better lives.

Very often the names of these new musical instruments betray their origins. Among the instruments depicted on Hindu monuments are plucked stringed instruments with box resonators; a variety of modern Southeast Asian plucked string instruments, includ- ing *kudyapi* from the Philippines, *kacapi* from West Java, *krajappi* from Thailand, and *hasapi* from Sumatra, have names derived from the same Sanskrit root, *kacchapa,* which can refer to a particular kind of tree (*cedrela toona*); Jaap Kunst notes that the South and Southeast Asian instruments that have related names are all string instruments made from wood (Kunst 1973: 371). Laced drums, too, are probably imports from India (Miller and Williams 1998: 66). Such instruments are not as well-suited to the environment as bamboo and bronze instruments, but their association with desirable Indic ideologies may make worthwhile the extra effort required to make and maintain them.

The Middle East—the source of Islam, one of Southeast Asia's most successful imported religions—also is the source of some new musical technologies. A Persian- Arabic bowed instrument called *rabab* is probably the prototype for various bowed spike fiddles with skin resonators with similar names in Southeast Asia. One of the names commonly given to frame drums (circular wooden frames with skins stretched across one side)—*rebana*—also reinforces the drum's Islamic source; it is, perhaps, derived from the Arabic word "Rabbana," which means "Our Lord!" and is the opening word for many short Arabic prayers (Kunst 1973: 218).

European invaders also contributed musical instruments to Southeast Asian cultures. The violin (one of Europe's most exportable musical inventions) has become entrenched in a number of Southeast Asian contexts and retains its European name (*biyula, biola*). Brass bands, with their connotations of pomp and circumstance, have also found a home among various Southeast Asian peoples.

No matter which layer of cultural influence musical instrument prototypes or names come from, Southeast Asian musicians learned to deploy their instruments in their own ways. Many Southeast Asian music traditions share several fundamental and flexible approaches to structuring and performing music; these approaches may be characterized as *musical processes.* Musical processes are too abstract to be called specific techniques for making or playing music, yet they are not exactly music theory, either. They are, rather, basic paradigms for organizing musical materials at their most elemental levels, and they may result in surprisingly different musical sounds. And an entirely different manifestation of the principle of layers seems to underlie the Southeast Asian musical processes that govern music-making.

Southeast Asian Musical Processes

Vocal music, which strictly speaking requires no technology at all, is a good starting place from which to explore Southeast Asian musical processes. Virtually all Southeast Asian cultures have rich traditions of vocal music, many of which involve the playing of musical instruments as well. There are some genres of song which are common to many Southeast Asian cultures, and these common genres persist through many historical layers of outside influences.

There are quite a few Southeast Asian traditions of epic narrative singing, for example; these typically feature a single singer-storyteller who takes an entire night to spin an episode from a well-known tale through narration and song. In the Kelantan province of Malaysia, a storyteller sings and narrates epic *tarikh selampit* tales, which recount the adventures of a folk hero named Selampit; the bard accompanies himself on a *rebab* (in Malaysia, a three-string fiddle) (Sweeney 1974; Matusky and Chopyak 1998: 420). In *pantun Sunda* from West Java, Indonesia, a storyteller weaves tales from Sundanese mythology, and accompanies himself on a *kacapi* (boat-shaped zither) (Weintraub 1990: 9). Among ethnic Lao in Thailand and Laos, the term *lam* is a generic designator for vocal music with flexible melodies; in *lam nithan*, a solo singer presents epic stories drawn from stories about the Buddha (Miller 1998c: 325, 1998b: 342) to the accompaniment of a *khaen* (Lao mouth organ). Most language groups in the Philippines maintain epic narrative forms that document local histories and local heroes, as well as ancestors and genealogies (Santos 1998: 907). In the lowland, Christianized parts of the Philippines, groups of singers perform the *pasyon* (passion—a poetic rendition of Jesus Christ's crucifixion) during the season of Lent (Canave-Dioquino 1998: 844–5). The content of the stories might change with different layers of cultural influence, but the means of performance—epic singing—remains constant. Dialogue songs, in which participants exchange clever, sometimes sexually suggestive, verses which they might improvise on the spot or have memorized previously, are another widespread genre throughout Southeast Asia. In past times in Central Thailand, men and women in isolated villages sang various kinds of *phleng pün ban* ("songs of the village") to the accompaniment of hand-clapping or percussion instruments (Miller 1998c: 298–301). Northern Thai *saw* repartee songs, on the other hand, are accompanied by a small ensemble of instruments (Miller 1998c: 313), while each of the singers in Lao *lam klawn* dialogue songs has his or her own *khaen*-playing accompanist (Miller 1998c: 325). For *balitaw* songs from the Visayan islands in the Philippines, a woman and a man compete with one another to see who is cleverer at coming up with witty and romantic verses to the accompaniment of a guitar (Pfeiffer 1976: 127; Canave-Dioquino 1998: 851). Cloaking the often intimate sentiments of courtship in song helps to take the edge of embarrassment off meeting and wooing potential mates.

Ostinato and simultaneous variation

Examining the instrumental accompaniment for these vocal forms provides some insight into basic Southeast Asian musical processes. There are two fundamental approaches to Southeast Asian vocal music accompaniment: (1) *ostinato* and (2) *simultaneous variation*. Ostinato is a musical term that refers to a short rhythmic and/or melodic pattern or phrase that is repeated over and over (*ostinato* is the Italian word for "persistent" or "obstinate"). Simultaneous variation suggests performing concurrently two or more melodic lines, each of which is somehow recognizable as a variant of the same basic tune (some musicologists describe simultaneous variation with the term heterophony).

Listeners cannot help but become familiar with an ostinato quickly because it is short and persistently repeated; they soon come to rely on the ostinato's predictability. In this way, ostinato accompaniments provide a solid foundation upon which to build a cohesive vocal performance; no matter what the singer does next, his or her new material remains related to that which came before because it refers to the same ostinato. Using ostinatos as a principle for musical organization is not unique to Southeast Asia; musical traditions all over the world employ ostinatos at times, including Western popular music. For example, the accompaniment to the old Frank Loesser/Hoagy Carmichael hit, "Heart and Soul," which countless children have learned to pound out on the piano, is an ostinato.

Ostinatos are ubiquitous in Southeast Asian musical traditions. In West Javanese *pantun Sunda*, for example, short ostinatos consisting of a few alternated pitches played with a regular pulse provide the sonic backdrop for various kinds of singing and narration (Weintraub 1990: 61–3). In Visayan *balitaw*, the guitar provides a simple chordal ostinato to give shape to the verses (Pfeiffer 1976: 127). In both cases, the ostinato accompaniment sets out a clear rhythmic pulse to give some temporal shape to the singers' melodic phrases. The ostinatos also emphasize a particular pitch or set of pitches, which provides tonal support for the melodies as well. By emphasizing a particular pitch, the ostinato creates the sense that a particular pitch is a tonal center or "home" pitch; by singing phrases that move away from and then return to the "home" pitch, a singer can create a sense of melodic direction and purpose.

In *tarikh selampit* accompaniment, on the other hand, the rebab part does not provide an ostinato; rather, it doubles or imitates the vocal part (Matusky and Chopyak 1998: 420). It is a practical form of accompaniment in that it provides the singer a chance to collect his thoughts and take a breath, while filling in with the rebab. Simultaneous variation also capitalizes on the inherent differences in technique, and thus melodic idioms, that various musical instruments require.

These two styles of musical accompaniment—ostinato and simultaneous variation—are not absolutely mutually exclusive. In the various lam genres from Thailand and Laos, the khaen accompanist provides a steady rhythmic pulse and reiterates a drone pitch—creating a sort of ostinato—while improvising his own versions of the appropriate song melodies (Miller 1998c: 324). Thus, the khaen accompaniment lies somewhere between ostinato and simultaneous variation. And, of course, the two accompaniment styles can be combined; in Northern Thai saw repartee songs, some of the instruments in the ensemble are percussion instruments and provide a rhythmic ostinato, while other instruments are melodic and provide simultaneous variations of the melody (Miller 1998c: 313).

Ostinato accompaniments tend to have a clear, regular rhythmic pulse. They are typically performed on struck percussion instruments or plucked string instruments, which can produce only musical tones that are not continuous—once a tone starts (as a consequence of striking a key or plucking a string), it immediately begins to fade away. For similar reasons, the musical pitches and timbres (tone colors) of ostinato instruments are fixed: unlike a voice, which can produce infinite gradations of pitch and timbre, struck or plucked ostinato instruments produce one single, discrete pitch at a time, and are uniform in timbre. There is, therefore, a marked contrast between ostinatos, with their regular pulse and discrete pitches and timbres, and vocal melodies (and any simultaneous variations), with their variable pitch and timbre and often flexible approach to rhythm. Fixed, regular ostinatos and free, variable melodies represent two layers of musical entities; like oil and water, the two layers do not blend together, and the result is a stratified, layered musical texture. Southeast Asian listeners typically find this dramatic contrast between "fixed" and "free" layers aesthetically pleasing.

The ostinato accompaniments for epic and courtship songs are typically played by a single performer (often the singer himself). Southeast Asian ensemble music often features several ostinato parts played by different performers on a variety of instruments. The way in which the ostinato parts are divided up among the players represents another widespread Southeast Asian musical process: interlocking parts. In addition, it models an important general aspect of Southeast Asian cultures: reciprocity.

Reciprocity and interlocking parts

Anthony Reid includes "the importance of debt as a determinant of social obligation" among the common social patterns he identifies in Southeast Asia (Reid 1988: 6). By debt, he refers to the social bond that grows between partners when they trade goods, services, or favors. Under ideal circumstances, the bond becomes permanent when neither side is entirely certain exactly how much is owed to the other party; the relationship is sustained by an interlocking pattern of giving and receiving. Both parties are "rich" because they share each other's wealth. The social benefits of these mutual reciprocal relationships seem to be greater than the sum of their parts.

Reciprocity also takes the form of mutual cooperation between individuals when it comes to agricultural concerns. The staple crop in most parts of Southeast Asia is rice; rice is a marsh plant that acquires nutrients not from the soil but rather from standing water. As a result, if rice is cultivated in a wet, marshy environment, it can be grown in the same plot year after year without exhausting the soil (Higham 1996: 322–3). The key to increasing rice yields in ancient Southeast Asia was to create irrigation systems that not only simulated marshy conditions, but provided control over the movement of water through the fields to create marshes only when they were needed. Intricate systems of hillside rice terraces, along with the canals and weirs that provide and control their water supply, are a hallmark of intensive agriculture throughout Southeast Asia (see Figure 1.5).

Individual farmers control the flow of water in and out of their fields; those working within these elaborate systems, however, must pay close attention to what goes on upstream

Figure 1.5 Terraced rice fields in Bali (Henry Spiller).

(whence their water comes) as well as downstream (where their water drains). Not only must they make sure there is water available (and somewhere to send it), but they must also make sure that large areas of fields go dry for sustained periods of time to keep pests from getting out of hand (Lansing 1995: 99–101). The key to success is cooperation; the irrigation system is a complex network of individual fields, managed by equal and interdependent family groups (O'Connor 1995: 997). When each family farm times its own needs to interlock with the needs of its neighbors, everybody profits; the yield is, once again, greater than the sum of its parts. Given the great cultural rewards of reciprocity and cooperation in Southeast Asia, it is little wonder that Southeast Asian musicians, too, use interlocking parts to create a musical effect that is greater than the sum of its parts. A simple rhythmic ostinato consists of moments when the musician makes a sound separated by moments of silence. If each of several musicians plays a simple ostinato, but each times his or her part in such a way that its sounds occur when the other ostinatos are silent, the result is a stream of interlocking sounds that join together in the listener's ear to create one single, complex musical result. For audiences accustomed to the idea that intense cooperation is "natural," the results of interlocking musical processes cannot help but seem "beautiful."

Southeast Asian Musical Processes in Toba Batak Gondang Music

A living music tradition practiced in North Sumatra provides specific illustrations of the Southeast Asian musical processes described above. The Toba Batak are one of several ethnic groups living in North Sumatra, sometimes collectively called Batak, who speak related languages and have comparable customs. Toba Batak occupy the area around an enormous lake called Lake Toba, where they subsist mainly through fishing and rice cultivation. Toba Batak reckon family relationships through the male lines, and keep close track of rather distant patrilineal relatives. Several families belonging to an extended lineage might live together in a large multi-family house.

The Toba Batak refer to the traditional system of social, legal, and religious principles that guide the lives of their communities as *adat*; many other cultures in the area use the same term to describe their systems, although the systems themselves might differ. Adat is not cast in stone; it changes over time to respond to different circumstances and needs. At any given time, however, it provides a secure set of guidelines for governing relationships between individuals and families, as well as between ordinary humans and the supernatural world. Music and dance are among the features of community life governed by adat. The characteristic musical ensemble of the Toba Batak, called *gondang sabangunan*, is a symbol of Toba Batak adat. The ensemble includes a set of five tuned drums called *taganing*; two larger drums called *gordang* and *odap*; a gong chime with four suspended gongs called *ogung*; a percussion instrument called *hesek*; and a double-reed wind instrument called *sarune*. According to adat, a performance of gondang sabangunan without its accompanying dancing, called *tortor*, is incomplete.

One customary context for musical activities is a feast, called a *horja*, which strengthens the social relationships between members of a patrilineage, the lineages from which their wives come, and the lineages into which their daughters marry. Other contexts for ritual music-making include pre-funeral ceremonies for deceased family members and sacrificial ceremonies to mark the rice-growing season. Until the mid-nineteenth century, most Toba Batak practiced a kind of religion which paid homage to a variety of deities and ancestor spirits; ceremonial activities involving gondang sabangunan provided a means to communicate with these supernatural beings. Musicians were considered to be experts who could communicate with spirit forces; they were addressed by special titles when performing that showed respect for their important religious function (one such title was *batara guru*, the name of a Hindu deity). The musicians set up to perform on the Batak house's balcony, called *bonggar-bonggar*, which was up above the guests and dancers. This position symbolically aligned the musicians and the gondang sabangunan ensemble with the unseen spirit world.

Unlike many of their neighbors in Sumatra, Toba Batak resisted conversion to Islam. In the 1860s, however, German missionaries made considerable headway toward converting many Toba Batak to Protestant Christianity. Christian missionaries initially tried to eradicate traditional music because of its links to spirit worship; its links to adat, however, made its complete eradication impossible. As a compromise of sorts, Protestant Toba Batak avoid those ceremonies which are specifically associated with spirit worship, and do not participate in adat practices which involve honoring the musicians as mediators with the spirit world (Koentjaraningrat 1975: 62–76; Yampolsky 1997; M. Purba 2002; M. Purba 2003).

The social context of gondang sabangunan reveals this Southeast Asian community's own individualized "layers" of cultural influences. Current Toba Batak adat reflects a syncretic blend of animism (a belief system in which many natural objects are thought to have spirits or souls of some kind), ancestor worship, Hinduism, and (most recently) Christianity. Adat has bent with each succeeding wave of influence without completely breaking.

The ensemble makeup of the gondang sabangunan ensemble, too, exemplifies these

CHAPTER 2

Music and Culture in Southeast Asia

Musical Processes in Social Class, Rituals, and Politics

As we learned in Chapter 1, layers—layers of cultural influences, layers of musical processes—seem to pervade Southeast Asia. Still another kind of layering characterizes some of the more highly organized, state- and kingdom-oriented Southeast Asian civilizations: layers of social classes. Although irrigated rice cultivation at first promotes egalitarian societies, as irrigation systems become larger and more complex, they require more centralized authority to run and maintain them. Stratification of societies begins to develop when some individuals acquire permanent "rights" (such as individual land ownership, for example) to control and authority, as well as the increased wealth and status that go along with such rights.

There is, of course, tension between the egalitarian, consensus-based localized control of irrigation and notions of class-differentiated societies. The emerging elite classes in early Southeast Asian political units generally found ways to justify and exercise their "right" to authority and control that did not directly contradict the egalitarian, cooperation-based economies. Rights to land use were passed from one generation to the next; individuals who could demonstrate a relationship with generations and generations of ancestors, then, could lay claim to authority. Establishing a connection to the unseen and nonhuman spirits who had great influence over the environmental variables that create agricultural success or spell crop failure was another way to accrue status.

As early as the first century AD, traders and missionaries from India traveled to Southeast Asian communities and Southeast Asian sailors visited India (Lockard 1995: 17). The Indian/Hindu notion of "god-king"—which holds that a ruler is in fact an incarnation of a deity—found fertile ground among emerging Southeast Asian elite classes. Establishing oneself as a god-king (or even as a relative of a god-king) consolidates in one fell swoop significant ancestral rights as well as control over the spirit world (Day 1996: 388), imposing a new social paradigm without interrupting the already smoothly running day-to-day practice of agriculture.

These kings exercised their power by acquiring wealth and status from those around them in return for their divine intervention. However, these divine kings were not as politically powerful as one might expect; because prestige was the basis for their rule, their authority extended only as far as their repute. Furthermore, their claim to authority was greatly weakened if their divine interventions failed. Historian Oliver Wolters has compared the way the political units under these god-kings operate to a *mandala*. To Hindus and Buddhists, a mandala is a sacred representation of the universe, often in the form of a diagram consisting of concentric circles. Sacred power and knowledge are at the center of the diagram; through ritual or meditation, one enters at the edge of the mandala and proceeds through the various surrounding layers of circles to the center and the insights that reside there. The king and his spiritual power form the center of a political mandala; his influence emanates in all directions in weakening concentric circles. The center's power depends on its continued ability to affect the circumstances of those under its influence (Encyclopaedia Britannica 2003a). Any small community could be under the influence of several such mandalas; although a king's spiritual prestige and influence might have a long reach, in many ways the people who lived within a mandala led relatively autonomous existences (Reid 1999: 54) as they maintained and regulated their own irrigation systems and community lives.

Acquiring and maintaining prestige, then, became one of the main occupations of god-kings and their courts in mandala polities. Anthropologist Clifford Geertz came up with the concept of a "theater-state" to describe how royal persons (and would-be royalty) sponsored elaborate rituals not only to demonstrate, but to legitimate as well, their divine rights and authority—to the point where the rituals themselves virtually became the source of power (Geertz 1973: 335). God-kings spent their wealth on elaborate rituals to maintain their prestige—the prestige that brought them the wealth they required to sponsor elaborate rituals to maintain their prestige, and so on. In a way, the whole Southeast Asian system of kingship was a cycle of wealth acquisition and outlay that was simply layered on top of the day-to-day economies of the majority.

One of the basic ideas that drives divine kingship is a belief in "parallelism between Macrocosmos and Microcosmos, between the universe and the world of men" (Heine-Geldern 1942: 15). The court cultures that coalesced around Southeast Asia's divine kings sought to make manifest the parallels between the spiritual and real worlds by mimicking the order of the cosmos in the trappings of the court. Maintaining order and symmetry in the real world meant assuring the stability of cosmic order as well. Buildings and temples in the form of mandalas expressed this order and were one expression of the king's pivotal position between heaven and earth.

Musical forms provided another medium for such expressions. In Bali, for example, gamelan music is sometimes interpreted explicitly as an "aural mandala." Balinese treatises associate musical tones with gods, colors, directions, and the like to create mandala structures. The music's rhythmic cycles represent the mandala's outlines; the music's three-section forms map to tripartite structures of head–body–foot and mountain–midworld–sea (Harnish 1998: 740).

The god-kings' musicians took the musical principles that express these ideas of cosmic order and divine authority and layered them over the musical principles that grew out of fundamental Southeast Asian ecological and social principles. The result was an audible metaphor of their divinity and authority; it was music that operated according to the musical processes of their subjects but was governed by the cosmic principles that legitimated the god-kings.

Khmer court music

Some of the earliest mandala polities were organized by the ancestors of the Khmer people who live in present-day Cambodia and southern Vietnam. One of the first organized governments in the area was Funan, which lasted from the third through sixth centuries and boasted elaborate irrigation systems, Indianized ideas of government and the cosmos, and extensive trading networks reaching to Rome and Central Asia (Lockard 1995: 18). A later Khmer kingdom, called Angkor, flourished between the ninth and fifteenth centuries in the area now known as Cambodia. Angkor society was greatly stratified, with a powerful god-king who maintained an extensive network of ritual specialists who maintained his cult. The famous temple complex called Angkor Wat, which the Khmer built in the twelfth century, is an expression of the worldly and heavenly powers of the Angkor monarchs. Angkor's irrigation systems were very efficient, and farmers produced great quantities of rice; this productivity helped finance the prestige-building activities of the royal court.

Rival kingdoms of people living in what is now Thailand eventually led to the downfall of Angkor in the fifteenth century. Among the spoils of their victory over Angkor were musicians and dancers. A Cambodian mandala polity continued on, but with a greatly reduced radius of influence; eventually the kingdom looked to France for protection from its aggressive neighbors. The rival kingdoms, which eventually came to be known in the West as Siam and then Thailand, adopted many of the trappings of the Khmer courts, including music and dance.

Cambodian court music

It is extremely unlikely that Cambodian court music in the twenty-first century is very similar to the music of Angkor, but it does seem reasonable to believe that some of the musical principles underlying the court music of the present reflect the musical values that drove the god-kings' theater-state. Bas-relief stone carvings on the walls of Angkor Wat depict musical instruments that resemble some of the instruments of the modern court musical ensemble, called *pinn peat* (Sam, Roongrüang, et al. 1998: 157). Modern pinn peat music certainly exhibits the Southeast Asian musical processes discussed so far, inflected to express ideas of cosmic order in musical form.

A full modern pinn peat ensemble includes two double-reed wind instruments (*sralai*) of different sizes and pitch levels, two xylophones of different sizes (*roneat ek* and *roneat thung*), a metallophone (*roneat dek*), two circular gong chimes of different sizes (*korng tauch* and *korng thomm*), two drums (*skor thomm* and *sampho*), a pair of small cymbals called *chhing*, and vocalists (Sam, Roongrüang, et al. 1998: 183). The Khmer term *roneat* comes from a word for bamboo strips, but includes any instrument with bars of wood or metal (Sam, Roongrüang, et al. 1998: 163). The word *korng* is the Khmer equivalent of gong; the Khmer gong chimes include a series of tuned gongs laid

			I				like				iced				tea
	I		like		Khmer		tea		I		like		iced		tea
			I		real-	ly	like		drink-	ing	iced		Ang-	kor	tea
I	I	I	I	like	like	like	like	iced	iced	iced	iced	tea	tea	tea	tea

Figure 2.1 Stratified variations on "I like iced tea."

horizontally in a circular frame; the players can use soft or hard mallets to strike the gongs, depending on the desired volume. A smaller version of the pinn peat ensemble includes only one of each instrument type.

The performers on the pinn peat ensemble's melodic instruments play simultaneous variations of a piece's fixed tune. Like the sarune and taganing players in Toba Batak gondang sabangunan ensemble, none of the pinn peat instrumentalists plays a literal rendition of the composition's tune; each plays instead a version governed by the instrument's particular idiom. In the music of Indianized Southeast Asian courts, such as the pinn peat ensemble, however, each instrument's idiom is restricted not only by the particular instrument's physical idiosyncrasies and limitations, but by convention as well. Some parts are thought to lead while other parts follow. Some parts are constrained to move in rhythmically regular, melodically smooth versions of the melody, while others are empowered to indulge in more varied rhythmic motives and more dramatic melodic contours. Some instrument parts are supposed to be more "dense" than others (in this context, calling a part more "dense" than another suggests that an instrumentalist fits more notes—more strokes on the xylophone or gong chime, for example—within the same period of time). The layers of Khmer simultaneous variations are much more distinct from one another than the simultaneous variations we've encountered before, however. Each variation has its own approach to rhythm and density. Figure 2.1 provides an approximate idea of this approach to simultaneous variations by lining up some playful variations on the basic phrase "I like iced tea." If one person recited the basic phrase slowly with a distinct pulse, others could fill in different variants of the phrase while remaining in sync with the basic phrase. The next variation, too, has a regular pulse, but it proceeds twice as fast as the basic phrase, repeats the basic phrase twice but slightly changes its meaning by introducing a new adjective. The following variation, "I really like drinking iced Angkor tea," features both long and short syllables (in the pattern long–short–short) that provide a rhythmic contrast to the regular pulse of the basic phrase. The final variation stutters the basic phrase; it moves more quickly than all the others, but adds no new semantic material. At any given moment, all four voices might be saying completely different words, so they do not blend together very well at all; at the end of the phrase, however, they all arrive together in unison on the word "tea."

Some musicologists call this particular approach to simultaneous variation *polyphonic stratification*; the term evokes a musical texture with "many voices" (which is the literal meaning of the Greek-derived term polyphonic) which are layered on top of each other like strata of sedimentary rock. In such rock formations, clearly delineated sheets of different kinds of rock are layered on top of one another. Although they form a single mass of rock, each layer (or stratum) is clearly defined. When different voices or instruments perform essentially the same melody, but with different idioms, pitch levels, timbres, and densities, each part (or stratum) clearly stands out from the others, even as they all combine into a single "stratified" musical texture.

This stratification is an echo of the social stratification of the mandala kingdoms. The different social classes have different duties, functions, and privileges, and must endeavor to remain stratified even as they act together toward common goals. Individuals are constantly reminded of the reality of social strata, and even the language reinforces class distinctions. Like many Southeast Asian languages, the Khmer language forces individuals to "rank" themselves in relation to the people they talk to by selecting the appropriate forms of address (Sam and Campbell 1991: 30). There is no simple, all-purpose, neutral pronoun equivalent to the English "you" in Khmer; any form of direct address involves an acknowledgment of age, status, and class differences. In languages such as Khmer and Javanese, there are even entirely separate vocabularies to use when addressing royalty; in effect, communication between different social classes requires the use of substantially different languages.

It requires only a few slight inflections to the musical process of simultaneous variation to arrive at polyphonic stratification; those adjustments, however, provide a potent aesthetic analogy for a stratified society and further reinforce the stratification of social classes. The ostinato musical process is likewise modified slightly in Khmer court music to conform better to a mandala concept.

A key instrument in the pinn peat ensemble is also the smallest: the pair of two-inch-diameter cymbals called *chhing*. A chhing player holds one cymbal in each hand and strikes them together. There are two sounds, each with an onomatopoeic name: chhing is an open, ringing sound, while *chhepp* is a damped, choked sound produced by holding the cymbals together after striking them. In most pinn peat pieces, the chhing player sets up an ostinato, constructed of alternating chhing and chhepp sounds, to keep time. Even though there is no appreciable difference in volume between the two strokes, Khmer listeners hear the chhepp (damped) sounds as accented, and the chhing sounds as unaccented. Furthermore, they consider a full rendition of an ostinato to include two iterations of "chhing chhepp"; the first chhepp is heard as having a lesser accent than the second chhepp.

Khmer musicians therefore think of the chhing/chhepp ostinato as a *cycle*—a pattern of hierarchical accents, marked by chhing and chhepp sounds, that repeats. The geometric figure of a circle provides a convenient metaphor for representing a musical cycle; circles are the stuff of which mandalas are made as well. Correlating a cyclical concept with the organizing principle of musical ostinato once again redirects and recontextualizes a Southeast Asian musical process to legitimize a new, Indic approach to cosmic order.

A mandala involves a series of concentric circles; the chhing cycles of Khmer court music, too, exhibit a kind of concentricity. Khmer pieces use one of three different levels of chhing cycles; each level has a cycle with four chhing and chhepp strokes, but the four strokes come faster or slower in the various levels. The first level fits a full cycle—four strokes—into the same amount of time that two strokes occupy in the second level, and that one stroke occupies in the third level. Taken as a whole, then, the musical repertory that encompasses these three levels of chhing cycles represents a sort of time mandala; by working through these varied representations of time, performers and listeners experience the cosmos in an earthly form. Human perception of time does not truly run in a circle, of course, but humans recognize that certain kinds of events do happen over and over again. Day alternates with night in a predictable fashion. The procession of seasons repeats over and over again. And even though individual plants, animals, and people are born and die, the progress of each individual life-form's existence follows the same general cycle as all the others. Musical ostinatos occur in time; extending the circle metaphor just a bit further maps notions of cyclic time onto a cyclic ostinato, and potentially unites the order of the cosmos with music. Music at the court of the god-king, like the god-king himself, is an interface between the spiritual and real worlds (Becker 1979).

The player of the drum called *sampho* leads the pinn peat ensemble; he plays an 8- or 16-beat cycle that corresponds to the chhing cycle. This drum is unusual among Cambodian drums in that musicians consider it to be a sacred instrument, and its construction involves special ceremonies (Sam, Roongrüang, et al. 1998: 168). The basic parts played on the sampho are, like the chhing parts, cyclic patterns that help regulate the ensemble's rhythm; the sampho player controls the ensemble's tempo as well.

Drumming that regulates the ensemble plays an important role in many Southeast Asian ensembles. Typically, drummers coordinate the rhythmic activities of their fellow musicians by subtly inserting cues and signals into the regular cycles of strokes that make up their parts. In this way, drumming models the role of the king—to mediate between the cosmic and the ordinary, to keep worldly matters in sync with the cosmic order. Drumming that regulates the temporal aspects of ensemble music is yet another layer of musical function in Southeast Asian music and represents yet another important musical process.

Although it is unlikely that they did so deliberately, musicians modified fundamental Southeast Asian musical processes to reflect social values. The result was appropriate music for the courts of medieval Southeast Asian god-kings. Ostinatos made up of interlocking parts were reconceptualized as an underlying cycle that could be expanded and contracted like the circles of a mandala. The increasingly specialized parts played on various melodic instruments subtly transformed the principle of simultaneous variation into polyphonic stratification. The addition of a new part, played on Indian-derived drums, served to control the tempo and regulate the cycles and keep them in sync with the cosmos.

Moving from ostinato to cycle, moving from simultaneous variation to stratified polyphony, and providing a single mediating force in an otherwise egalitarian structure —these changes are in some ways only minor inflections of Southeast Asia's persistent musical processes. On the other hand, they express profound cultural changes—social classes, divine kingship, large political spheres of influence. The initial success of Southeast Asian gong-chime ensembles lay precisely in this seeming paradox; by maintaining continuity with older musical processes, the music demonstrated the compatibility of new social orders with time-honored principles. New musical concepts were layered on top of existing musical processes in much the same way that new social classes were layered on top of old ones; the kings merely overlaid the stamp of cosmic order upon existing ecological, agricultural, and economic processes, which continued much as if there had been no administrative change.

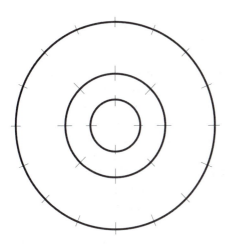

Figure 2.2 Concentric cycles.

Thai court music

The music of Thailand's royal courts owes much to Angkor musical traditions. The Thai ensemble called *pi phat* is clearly related to its Cambodian cousin; it includes a double-reed wind instrument (*pi*), xylophones (*ranat*), gong chimes (*khawng*), cymbals (*ching*), and drums (*taphon*). Like Cambodian pinn peat music, most Thai court music pieces are based on one of three basic rhythmic cycle levels. The expandability and contractability of underlying musical cycles is a recurring theme in Southeast Asian musical traditions. An important musical genre in nineteenth- and twentieth-century Thai music called *phleng thao* specifically exploited the elasticity of underlying cycles. The term *thao* suggests a set of things in graduated sizes (such as a set of nesting bowls, each smaller than the previous one); a phleng thao composition presents the same basic melody in all three of the Thai cycle levels. Performing a tune in a different level is not a matter of simply playing the melody twice as fast or twice as slowly, however. The melodic density of each musician's part (that is, how many strokes or notes are played per arbitrary unit of time) should stay about the same at each level; to spread the melody out into a longer rhythmic cycle, then, requires adding more notes, while contracting the melody into a shorter rhythmic cycle involves leaving notes out.

Figure 2.2 demonstrates this elasticity with a series of concentric circles. Each circle's circumference is twice that of the preceding one. The innermost circle has four equal arcs. The middle circle has eight arcs, each of which is the same size as an arc on the innermost circle; in other words, it requires eight marks to traverse the second circle at the same density of the first. The large outer circle requires sixteen arcs to mark off the entire circle at the same density.

For most Western listeners, a melody with twice as many notes that takes twice as long to play as its "parent" is hardly the same melody at all. Thai listeners, however, pay special attention to the pitches that occur at important structural points, such as at the end of the cycle. When stretching a melody out for a phleng thao piece, Thai musicians take care to ensure that each phrase of the expanded version ends with the corresponding structural pitch of the original at the end of the cycle; this keeps intact the identity of the piece, while allowing for different melodic twists and turns along the way.

A phleng thao piece leads the listeners through all three expansions, giving them the opportunity to marvel at the different qualities and characters each different version imparts to the "same" melodic material. With their metaphorically "concentric" cycles, such pieces seem to be aural mandalas that lead their listeners not only to some better understanding of the cosmic order, but to the secure feeling that the world is in sync with the cosmos. Phleng thao pieces were developed in Thailand in the late nineteenth century (although, as ethnomusicologist Judith Becker points out, the principles of expansion/contraction on which the genre is based are quite old [Becker 1980: 454]). This was a time when the Thai social order faced significant upheaval. Unlike neighboring countries, Thailand successfully resisted overt colonization by European powers, although the Thai monarchs shored up their own independence in part by promoting "modernization" programs from within—learning Western ways and selectively absorbing them (the book and movie *Anna and the King of Siam*, as well as the Broadway musical version *The King and I*, present a romanticized version of this process). Perhaps the musical genre phleng thao was a reaction to these social changes; with its explicit references to the god-king as an interface between heaven and earth, it allowed its aristocratic audience to maintain some semblance of the old order.

Contexts for Music-Making

The previous sections have already mentioned several contexts for music-making, including storytelling, courtship songs, religious ceremonies, and ceremonies in support of the theater-state. In ritual contexts, music serves as a medium with which to communicate with the spirit world, whether that world be in the form of ancestors and place spirits (in the case of Toba Batak) or a Hindu-Buddhist cosmos (in the case of Khmer and Thai music). English speakers use the term "music" to refer to a circumscribed set of specific activities and contexts; very often, there is no exact translation of the term "music" in other languages. Often Southeast Asian performing arts which English-speakers instinctively categorize as "music" inextricably involve activities that do not usually fall within the English-language category of "music"—activities English speakers would characterize as "dance" and "theater" for example. A clear line between ritual music and music for entertainment is similarly difficult to draw in Southeast Asia; very often the same qualities that make music ritually powerful also make them enjoyable as well. When new formal belief systems make ritual music obsolete, artistic activities are often stripped of overt ritual or religious significance and recast as pure entertainment. It is not always clear whether such recontextualizations represent genuine change in meaning, or merely submersion of ritual significance; as time goes on, musical pieces, styles, ensembles, and genres take on multiple meanings.

Ritual

In Southeast Asia, shamanic healing rituals often involve a mystical journey into the spirit world. Musical accompaniment varies from place to place; rituals might involve bamboo instruments, drums, and/or gong ensembles. Specific pieces are generally associated with specific stages of the spiritual journey.

In Cambodian villages, for example, shamanic healers conduct ceremonies called *arakk* to enter a trance state in which the cause of illness is revealed. The ceremony begins with a song that invites a spirit-world teacher to enter the shaman and preside over the ceremony. Once the cause of the illness is understood, the musicians play a special ending piece to thank the spirits and end the ceremony (Sam, Roongrüang, et al. 1998: 193–5). The songs give shape and form to the ceremony. It is quite common throughout Southeast Asia to associate specific pieces with particular functions in a multitude of contexts. In the Tuaran region of northern Borneo, for example, the sound of gong ensemble music creates a ritual space (Skog 1993: 61) where there was no sacred space before. Specific pieces are reserved for particular stages of particular rituals; and so, by playing a particular piece, the musicians consecrate an otherwise ordinary place for the specific ritual purpose. On the eastern Indonesian island of Sumba, descendants of a deceased patriarch expend enormous resources on cutting a huge stone gravemarker. Much of the expense comes from feeding and entertaining the hundreds of relatives and neighbors required to drag a five-ton stone from the quarry to the grave. For these funeral and stone-dragging rituals, musicians perform gong and drum music which includes named gong patterns that can be played only for these occasions (Adams 1981: 80).

Dance and theater

Just as particular pieces are associated with particular ritual purposes, certain musical pieces have specific theatrical meanings. Dance and theater are integral parts of ritual activities involving music. Performances, like shamanic rituals, often are given form and coherence through the use of structural musical pieces, and knowledgeable audiences associate structural pieces with specific theatrical meanings, such as "the play is about to begin," or "a good character is about to enter," or even "now is the time when the audience members may dance."

Western audiences are quite accustomed to using music to shape theater and dance. An opera generally begins with an overture and (as is sometimes said) "ain't over 'til the fat lady sings." Movie soundtrack composers wield an enormous vocabulary of stock musical gestures that can tell viewers as much about what is going on in a scene as the actors' dialogue and actions. And ballroom dancers know instantly upon hearing the first few measures of dance tune whether it is an elegant waltz, a carefree foxtrot, or a sensual rumba, and adjust their movements and dancing style accordingly.

In Khmer court performances, the character of different pinn peat ensemble pieces, each with its own set of associations, helps set the mood for narrative dances. In some cases, there is only one piece in the entire repertory that is appropriate for a particular dramatic situation (Sam and Campbell 1991: 90). In addition, the chhing cycles set the rhythmic framework for the dancers, and the drums provide aural analogs for the dance movements. The Khmer pinn peat ensemble provides music for a variety of music and theater genres. In Cambodian villages, until recent years, pinn peat ensembles accompanied plays with a religious purpose; these were masked plays, intended to gain the attention of the spirit world to prevent illness or bring rain (Sam, Roongrüang, et al. 1998: 190–1).

Among Melayu people in eastern Sumatra, the Malaysian peninsula, and the Riau Islands that lie between those two places, an old-fashioned theater form called *Mak yong* similarly involves structural songs. An ensemble featuring a variety of gongs, drums, an oboe-like instrument, and a rebab (fiddle) provides a musical accompaniment which features typically Southeast Asian layers of musical functions. The musicians perform a special piece which extends a formal welcome to the spectators. Many of the scenes open with songs which the actors sing to introduce their characters' actions and motivations to the audience before they begin their spoken dialogue. Most of the Mak yong songs are specific to the genre and are not performed in other Melayu traditions (Yampolsky 1996: 11, 18–19).

Martial arts

Throughout Southeast Asia, the practice of martial arts (in many places known as *silat* or *pencak silat*) is often accompanied by music. Of course nobody waits for the band to begin if a situation calls for actual self-defense, but the connection of music to movement apparently is so close in Southeast Asian aesthetics that several martial arts traditions include musical accompaniment in practice and demonstrations. Martial arts dances frequently are associated with Islam because they provide sport and entertainment for students in *pesantren* (Islamic schools).

In West Java, for example, Sundanese martial arts practitioners identify two equally important aspects of Sundanese martial arts, called *penca silat*: the *buah* (fruit), namely the practical advantages one gains from studying self-defense, and the *kembang* (flower), which refers to the aesthetically satisfying dance that grows from the practice. The *kendang penca* ensemble that accompanies penca silat practice and exhibitions includes two drummers, a *tarompet* (double-reed wind instrument) player, and a small gong to mark off phrases. Each of the five different named ostinato patterns (generically called *tepak*) is associated with a particular kind of dance or demonstration; there are several for displaying elegant movement combinations, one for humorous routines, and one for sparring and weapons-play.

Cambodian musician and scholar Sam-Ang Sam describes a Khmer boxing match he attended that did not include the appropriate accompanying music as "a dead event. The boxers need the music for movements in preparation for the fight, and also to guide their jumps, kicks, and jabs during the fight itself." There is only one piece that accompanies all Khmer boxing. Its two sections are an invocation to the boxers' teachers, and the fight music. The ensemble includes a sralai, sampho, and chhing (Sam and Campbell 1991: 108).

Entertainment

Clearly, for Southeast Asian cultures, music is a purposeful pursuit; it generally is associated with pragmatic activities (such as healing, worship, and the legitimation of political regimes) in which it serves specific and vital functions. However, purposeful music is often considered to be entertaining as well. In some cases, it is the capacity of a piece to entertain that makes it so powerfully effective; by focusing people's attention on the matters at hand, music creates a space in which social work can be accomplished. Modern globalized culture tends to regard music as a frill, as "mere" entertainment, and as a result, it can be difficult to comprehend how music can be purposeful and fun at the same time.

Musical contexts: Two case studies

A couple of specific examples of music traditions from opposite ends of Southeast Asia illustrate how function and entertainment are intertwined. First we examine gong-chime music from the southern Philippines, where amateur performers participate to amuse themselves through musical interaction and gain an instinctive understanding of how social interactions should be conducted in the process. Then we revisit the gong-chime ensembles of mainland Southeast Asia to explore how their style and meaning have changed in modern times.

Maguindanao Kulintang music

At the other end of Southeast Asia from the Toba Batak and the courts of the Thai and Khmer kings, similar musical processes drive gong ensembles among the Islamic ethnic groups of the southern Philippines. The Maguindanao and the Maranao on the island of Mindanao, as well as the Tausug who dominate the Sulu archipelago, all play variants of gong ensembles they call *kulintang*. The term kulintang (or *kolintang*) refers both to the entire ensemble and to the lead instrument—a gong chime with eight small gongs arranged in a row, which the performer strikes with two sticks.

Although kulintang music is sometimes used for healing ceremonies, kulintang performances in the southern Philippines generally take place in secular, non-religious contexts. The Maguindanao, Maranao, and Tausug have practiced Islam since the fifteenth century. Although gong ensemble music in many parts of Southeast Asia is associated with religious rituals, in keeping with Islamic ideas that music and dance are not appropriate activities for worship, southern Philippine Muslims view kulintang music-making as entertaining. They place value on the opportunity it provides to practice community solidarity, to learn social manners, to express one's self, and to interact with others (Cadar 1996: 99–101).

The forms and processes of kulintang music are consistent with these social aims. As compared to Toba Batak gondang sabangunan music, for example, the individual parts are more equal in the sense that all the instrumentalists have the opportunity to vary their parts and bring their own personal expressions to the group music-making process. In addition, the participants often are given the opportunity to change parts. If there are more players than instruments, for example, people take turns; if one of two interlocking parts is less interesting to perform, groups might play a piece twice to give the two musicians an opportunity to change places. Very often there is a sense of competition between musicians that spices up, but rarely sullies, the sense of group solidarity.

One of the largest southern Philippine Muslim ethnic groups is the Maguindanao; their name means "people of the flooded plain," which reflects the circumstances of their traditional homeland (a river valley) as well as their chief occupation as rice cultivators. Islam became entrenched among the Maguindanao in the fifteenth century, when a Malay missionary from Johore came to the area and established a sultanate (Anon. 2003).

Besides the kulintang gong chime, the Maguindanao version of the kulintang ensemble also includes a pair of hanging gongs with deep flanges call *agung*, a set of four hanging gongs called *gandingan*, a single hanging gong called *babandil*, and a goblet-shaped drum called *dabakan* (Kalanduyan 1996; Dris 2003).

Among the Maguindanao, kulintang performances are mostly for entertainment or secular functions. Sometimes playing kulintang music serves as a courtship activity for men and women; there are conventional ways to flirt by playing in particular fashions on the gandingan and kulintang. While musicians can be hired to perform at functions, families and friends play kulintang music for their own entertainment (Kalanduyan 1996).

Maguindanao kulintang music involves various kinds of improvisation. All of them are based on a firm ostinato foundation; nevertheless, all of the musicians have the leeway to vary their parts. Modern Maguindanao performance practice involves two styles of playing the kulintang, termed simply "old" and "new." In each style of playing, musicians play three different named pieces. Because the actual performance involves considerable improvisation, each of the pieces can sound quite different from performance to performance. Some scholars prefer to characterize the pieces as modes instead because they represent a framework or guidelines for improvisation. What differentiates the pieces or modes (besides their names) are a set of piece-specific rhythmic patterns and accents that drive the improvisation of the individual instrumental variations.

One way of thinking about the southern Philippine approach to musical processes, then, is that it folds the principle of simultaneous variation back onto the principle of ostinato. Kulintang music also reinforces the general tendency for short ostinato patterns to hold pieces together in performance, and for specific ostinato patterns to distinguish musical functions and meanings; among the Maguindanao, for example, a fourth piece or mode is reserved for a healing ceremony (Kalanduyan 1996: 17).

Kulintang performances involve the same musical processes—ostinato, variation, interlocking parts—as other Southeast Asian musics. Once again, however, these processes have been inflected to conform to cultural and social requirements. In the case of Maguindanao kulintang, the social goals of entertainment and social interaction are consistent with the players' improvisatory approach. Compared to Toba Batak gondang sabangunan music, in which several instrumentalists are constrained to play unvarying ostinato parts to ensure the proper progress of the ceremonial activities they accompany, Maguindanao musicians value the personal expressiveness that they bring to the performance of their parts.

Thai and Cambodian "classical" music in the modern world

The term "classical" as a musical adjective has a strange history. In its most basic meaning, classical refers to the aesthetic principles of classical Greece and Rome. Nineteenth- and twentieth-century Western musicologists came to apply the term to works composed by eighteenth-century European court composers such as Josef Haydn, who sought to restore classical ideas of balance, proportion, and rhetorical flair to their compositions; musicologists differentiated these classical compositions from the earlier seventeenth-century labyrinthine baroque court compositions and the subsequent emotionally over-wrought romantic style favored by the European elite in the nineteenth century. In the twentieth century, the designation classical became a catchall category for any music patronized by the Western elite (and subsumed baroque, classical, and romantic).

In democratized European countries, classical music has become a symbol of prestige and status—of social class. Where the social order permits upward mobility, as in the United States, an appreciation for classical music provides an individual with a legitimate claim to "class." Totalitarian regimes, such as the Soviet Union, often coopted classical music to give their own regimes the patina of legitimacy that the music bestowed on their aristocratic predecessors. The musical processes of classical music may be completely out of sync with contemporary social values, but the residual association with class gives classical music its modern significance. In other words, the value of classical music in modern Western societies is the cultural capital it carries and bestows upon anybody classy enough to appreciate it.

The term classical often is applied to Asian court music traditions, including Thai and Cambodian court music. While this may be ethnocentric, there is a certain appropriateness to this usage—not because these traditions adhere to Greek and Roman aesthetic principles, and not because they developed in the eighteenth century, but because they have long been associated with the elite class. Although the cultural values that the musical processes of Thai and Cambodian court music express—social stratification, with a god-king at the apex of this hierarchy—are out of date, these musical traditions provide their new patrons with valuable cultural capital in much the same way that classical music does for Americans.

Cambodia's Prince Norodom Sihanouk established Cambodia as independent of France in 1949 and abolished the monarchy in 1970; his nationalistic program included state support for classical music. One expression of this support was a government-sponsored School of Fine Arts. The existence of a refined, complex artistic tradition gave Cambodia status in international venues and provided a touchstone for crystallizing a nationalist Cambodian identity. Between 1975 and 1979, Cambodia was controlled by the Khmer Rouge, led by Pol Pot, whose interpretation of communist philosophy led those in power to try to abolish social stratification by eliminating all markers of class difference. Their methods involved destroying institutions such as the School of Fine Arts and killing millions of citizens whose status or education were a threat to the project, including musicians and dancers (Sam and Campbell 1991: 52; Miller 1998a: 90).

After the Khmer Rouge regime ended, classical music became an even more potent symbol of Cambodian identity. It remains, however, an endangered species, despite government support and the reestablishment of the School of Fine Arts. Few people have the time or resources to study classical music, and those who do must treat it as an avocation. Most of the established practitioners (some estimates are 90 percent) were killed, so qualified teachers are rare, and contexts for performances are few and far between (Sam and Campbell 1991: 52–3). Troupes of newly trained artists have performed in Cambodia and toured abroad, however; the rebirth of Cambodian classical music from the ashes of the Khmer Rouge represents a potent symbol of hope and tenacity for Cambodian citizens.

In Thailand, too, classical music was patronized and developed in royal households; musicians were royal servants whose livelihood depended on their employers' continued sponsorship. Following the bloodless coup in 1932 that led to the adoption of a constitution and a significant decrease in royal control of the government, these households no longer had the resources to maintain their musical retinues. As David Morton puts it, "with the disintegration of the environment in which the court music flowered, the music, too, was to some degree abandoned" (Morton 1980: 79). According to Terry Miller, the new Thai government actually suppressed classical music between the 1930s and 1950s; perhaps this music was associated too closely with the monarchy's extravagant spending (Miller 1998c: 286).

In the 1960s, however, classical music reemerged, and in subsequent decades found a place in Thai educational programs. The emerging Thai middle class especially expressed renewed interest in classical music. As with classical European music in the United States, the "classy," royal associations of Thai classical music provided a path to upward mobility. Thai classical music's sophistication could compete with the world's other classical musics to serve as an expression of a Thai national identity and pride as well (Myers-Moro 1991: 19).

This change in the music's function goes hand in hand with changes in its meaning. According to Terry Miller,

> though most Thai do not choose to listen to classical music (preferring, instead, the sounds emanating from radios and televisions), people acknowledge the propriety of having classical music in conjunction with ceremonies and rituals and representing their culture to the outside world (Miller 1998c: 286–7)

In other words, the majority of people do not necessarily listen to, or even hear, classical music on a regular basis; rather than the music processes themselves creating meaningful experiences, a decontextualized concept of the music as a whole has become an abstract symbol of a Thai identity.

But Thai music still teaches cultural values; some Thai citizens choose to learn and perform classical music, usually as a hobby (Morton 1980). One of the cultural values one encounters in the study of classical music is acquired by interacting with a teacher. Learning to play an instrument involves the student's assimilating a particular kind of respect for and submission to a teacher as they work together one-on-one. Modern students, of course, do not have the time or the inclination to apprentice themselves to a teacher as they might have done in the past. Students often use cassette machines to record their lessons; the tapes they make become an extension of the teacher. Pamela Myers-Moro relates a story about an older musician who actually bowed to the tape recorder that played a recording of his teacher. Technology provides a means to mediate between old and new values (Myers-Moro 1991).

In democratic Thailand, classical music's main function is to be a symbol of Thai identity and a marker of class, good breeding, and upward mobility. The primary professional occupation open to serious students is to become a music teacher. Classical music is, in a sense, a self-replicating tradition; one of its main functions is to train new teachers. Both Thai and Cambodian classical musics developed to reflect and legitimate social stratification and divine kingship. These values are at the very heart of the musical style, as modeled by stratified polyphony and cyclic rhythmic organization. In both cases, classical music is at best only tenuously connected to contemporary social values, and, indeed, in many ways, directly contradicts notions of democracy and equality.

Over the years, however, these classical traditions acquired new layers of meanings. They came to represent a kind of sophistication originally limited to the elite but now accessible to the middle class as well. They came to represent stability and continuity with the past—something to hold onto in rapidly changing social conditions. They came to represent "traditional" values and a shared identity which people could mobilize to make sense of their new situations, and it is these new layers of meaning that provide a context for the continued practice of classical music.

These new layers of meaning lie atop the older meanings and older values; they cover them but do not eliminate them. Traditional Thai and Cambodian values no longer explicitly include rigid social stratification or the divinity of leaders, but social stratification is still a fact of life in modern Southeast Asia. In a sense, laying denotations of national unity and democracy over classical music perfectly models how democratic and nationalist values interact with de facto class divisions. By regarding the whole of classical music as a symbol of nation and culture, it is possible to overlook the implications of the music's specific musical processes, just as it is possible to overlook the systemic inequalities and injustices that continue to plague modern nations.

Summary

The peoples and cultures of Southeast Asia are quite varied. Different historical, cultural, and political realities have shaped rich, unique societies throughout the region. Nevertheless, Southeast Asia is unified by a common environment, a set of shared historical occurrences, and by the similar solutions different groups apply to common problems. Historian Craig A. Lockard points out that Southeast Asia's integrity as a "region" is comparable to that of the "continent" of Europe. Like Southeast Asia, the peninsula at the western end of Asia known as Europe is separated from its immediate neighbors by formidable mountains, deserts, and seas. A variety of distinctive cultures developed within the confines of Europe, on the fringes of "great" civilizations. Nevertheless, there are enough commonalities among the peoples of Europe to consider Europe to be a discrete region (Lockard 1995: 12).

Common solutions among different cultures in Southeast Asia include several fundamental musical processes, which are organically related to environmental and cultural raw materials. The easy malleability of bamboo and wood predispose these materials to be useful in musical contexts. Ecological and cultural factors conspired to make bronze a high-status, ecologically appropriate material for musical instruments. The sonorous potentials of these materials favored some musical processes—processes with layers—over others. Processes such as ostinato, simultaneous variation, interlocking parts, and the layering of contrasting fixed and free parts are consistent with indigenous Southeast Asian environmental resources and cultural values. Layers of musical organization reflect, too, the layers of human cultures in the region. Newcomers to the region brought their own musical technologies and processes, which often were laminated onto existing musical styles. Southeast Asian musicians adopted and adapted imported instruments to fit into their ensembles. Inflections of existing processes, such as reconstruing interlocking ostinatos into expandable cycles and elaborating simultaneous variation into polyphonic stratification, acknowledged new value systems without completely discarding the old.

Over the course of months, years, and centuries, musical styles and genres accrue their own special meanings. New meanings are layered on top of old meanings, enabling a single musical genre to simultaneously convey many different messages. Court music traditions, whose musical processes can be viewed as embodiments of kingship and social inequality, can become symbols of democracy and nationalism. Gong music meant to propitiate local place spirits can find a place in Christian worship. In Southeast Asia, aesthetic activities such as music shape and reinforce cultural values, which are themselves, like the musical processes that model them, determined by responses to environment and politics.

coast of mainland Southeast Asia and the islands of Polynesia. This prehistoric movement of people is called the Austronesian expansion. It seems likely that these invaders, who reached Java in approximately 2000 BC, displaced or assimilated any existing populations. Ironically, the "original" Austronesians in South China and Taiwan were themselves displaced by the dominant Northern Chinese; their descendants survive today only as marginal aboriginal populations on Taiwan (Diamond 1999: 334–53). The subsequent history of Java and Bali involves wave after wave of foreign invasions; these later invaders, however, did not displace the Austronesian descendants as they had displaced their predecessors. Instead, they assimilated with the Austronesian Javanese. These later invaders contributed ways of thinking and strategies for living rather than genetic material; each new wave imprinted new ideas and concepts on top of the old ones.

Some of these early visitors, probably from northern Vietnam, brought bronze objects and technology in about 300 BC (Hood 1980: 122), and possibly rice cultivation technology as well (Koentjaraningrat 1975: 11). Among the artifacts associated with this wave were items that archaeologists call "bronze drums" because they appear to be tools for producing sound (Hood 1980: 122), and perhaps for making rain (Kunst 1973: 105). By 300 AD Javanese metalworkers had developed the imported technology of bronze casting and forging and created new types of artifacts, including bronze gongs with central knobs on them (Hood 1980: 122).

Hindu missionaries from India first arrived in the fourth (Koentjaraningrat 1975: 13) or fifth (Kunst 1973: 106) centuries AD. Javanese rulers soon adopted the trappings of Indian culture, including a concept of kingly rule that identified the monarch as a descendant of the gods whose primary responsibility was to preserve cosmic order by imitating it in the administration of his kingdom (Koentjaraningrat 1975: 16; Osborne 1985: 22). Indian Buddhist ideas also came to Java during the first millennium; over the course of time, the Javanese blended characteristics of Hinduism, Buddhism, and Javanese animistic practices into a uniquely Javanese religious system (Wright 1978: 5–6). For example, uniquely Javanese versions of the Hindu epic stories *Ramayana* and *Mahabharata* emerged, which were not only recast in Javanese tongues but supplemented with new Javanese characters.

The last Hindu-Buddhist kingdoms on Java were Pajajaran (1333–1579) in West Java and Majapahit (1293–1514) in East Java. Islam first took root in Java along the north coast; Islamic teachers adapted existing arts to help spread the new religion to other parts of Java. Islamic north coast kingdoms managed to overthrow Majapahit, forcing Hindu aristocrats into exile on Bali. Another Islamic kingdom, called Mataram, rose to dominate Java in the sixteenth century; the royal courts of the powerful Mataram empire, based in Central Java, developed music and arts as symbols of their power and influence.

A European presence in Indonesia began with Portuguese traders in the early sixteenth century. It was Dutch colonial powers, however, which eventually dominated the spice trade from the island of Java. The Dutch maintained Mataram's aristocrats as local administrators for their colony, but factionalized them; out of this internal bickering grew several different royal courts. While the aristocrats of Java emulated many of the trappings of European royalty, they also cultivated practices that distinguished them from their European overlords. The different Central Javanese courts, in fact, stripped of any significant political power, competed with one another primarily in the arena of the arts. People in outlying areas, far from the center, emulated these court arts, and adapted them to suit local needs and purposes.

During World War II, the Dutch were displaced from their role as colonial masters of the Indonesian archipelago by the Japanese, who took control of many parts of Southeast Asia. Indonesian nationalists took the opportunity of Japan's defeat in World War II in 1945 to declare an independent Indonesian nation. Although the Dutch attempted to regain control, Indonesia's independence was widely recognized, and by 1949 the Dutch withdrew.

The boundaries of modern Indonesia do not coincide with any particular cultural or linguistic divisions; they are artifacts of Dutch control. Indonesia's national motto, *Bhinneka Tunggal Ika* (Old Javanese for "unity in diversity") encapsulates the modern Indonesian nation's strategy for instilling a sense of common patriotism in a conglomeration of cultures brought together originally only by the circumstance of Dutch colonization.

The linchpin of a pan-Indonesian culture is the national language (which English-speakers call Indonesian, but which Indonesians call *bahasa Indonesia*). Virtually all Indonesians speak this national language, which is used in schools, government offices, and mass media. It is one very important manifestation of the "unity" part of the slogan. The "diversity" part of the motto is reflected in the fact that Indonesian is a second language for most Indonesians, who typically speak some regional language as their first tongue. There are hundreds of these regional languages, which very often reflect older political, social, and cultural boundaries, allegiances, and identities. In Central and Eastern Java, the areas once dominated by the Majapahit kingdom, most people speak the Javanese language. In many parts of West Java, especially those areas formerly under the control of the Pajajaran empire, the dominant language is Sundanese. On the north coast, between West and Central Java, where a distinct political entity emerged with the coming of Islam in the fifteenth century, many people speak a Javanese dialect known as Cirebonese. In some isolated pockets of East Java, locals speak a dialect of Javanese, called *bahasa Osing*, that most speakers of standard Javanese can barely understand. The language around the national capital city of Jakarta is a mix of Malay and a host of local languages, reflecting the diversity of its residents, many of whom relocated to the Jakarta area in search of economic opportunities.

Origins of gamelan

In his book *Music of the Roaring Sea* (Hood 1980), ethnomusicologist Mantle Hood weaves a fanciful fictionalized account of how a Javanese chieftain might have acquired and developed an ensemble of bronze drums in 300 BC. Hood's fictionalized chieftain was initially terrified by the supernatural sounds he heard emanating from the ships of an invader; eventually, however, he found a way to vanquish the invader and seize the bronze drums (along with the musicians who played them) as his own. Hood suggests that the bronze drums' obvious supernatural power, along with several very practical uses to which they were put as signaling devices, led to their adoption and development on Java, and eventually to the cultivation of bronze instrument making and the creation of modern gamelan music.

However it happened in reality, bronze percussion ensembles have played an important role in the cultures of Java and Bali for thousands of years. In kingdoms all over

Figure 3.3 Bossed (knobbed) gong; a large Central Javanese gong ageng surrounded by a number of smaller kempul (Henry Spiller).

how the instruments are played (they are hit with some sort of hammer or mallet) as well as how the instruments are made (they are hot-forged and hammered into shape).

Instruments

Some Javanese musicians divide bronze gamelan instruments into two basic categories: *pencon* (or *penclon*; instruments composed of bossed or knobbed gongs) and *wilahan* (instruments with bronze slab keys) (Kartomi 1990: 89; Sorrell 1990: 28–9; see also Sutton 1999: 640–1).

Knobbed gong (pencon) instruments

Generally speaking, a gong is a metal percussion instrument that has a circular flat surface; sometimes the edge of the surface is turned over to form a "lip" or a "flange." Usually flat gongs do not have a definite pitch; an example is the large flat gong that is some-times played in symphony orchestras, called a *tam-tam*. When hit, a tam-tam makes a raucous, jangling sound; most people would find it impossible to hum or sing a single

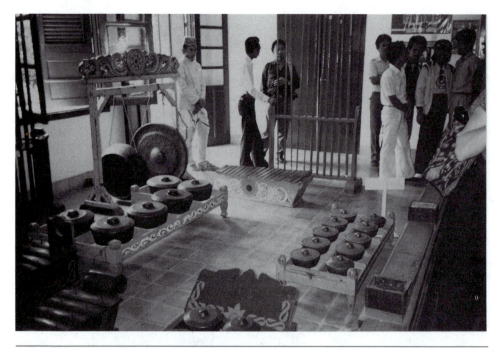

Figure 3.4 Gong chimes in Museum Prabu Geusan Ulun in Sumedang. Left: jengglong; right: bonang (Henry Spiller).

pitch that emerges from the tam-tam. Southeast Asian gongsmiths learned a long time ago that adding a raised knob called a "boss" to the center of the flat circular surface helps to focus the gong's pitch (see Figure 3.3); musicians hit the gong on the boss with some sort of padded mallet to produce a sound with a pitch that is much more clearly identifiable than that of a tam-tam. In Indonesia, the term *pencon* (or *penclon*) refers to these bosses and to gongs that have such bosses. A variety of Indonesian musical instruments are made from one or more bossed gongs. Gongs can be suspended horizontally from ropes and struck from the side, or laid vertically on their flanges over ropes and struck from above. The thickness of the gong's various surfaces, along with its size and weight, determine its pitch; the softness or hardness of the mallet with which it is struck affects its timbre (the quality or "color" of the sound). Sometimes the lips of Indonesian gongs are very deep, and the instrument looks more like an overturned kettle or pot. A bossed gong instrument may consist of a single large (or small) gong. Very often, however, a series of gongs with different pitches is arranged on a frame to create a *gong chime*, which usually is played as a melodic instrument (see Figure 3.4). Sometimes the players of gongs and gong chimes stop a gong's vibrations after striking it by firmly pressing the mallet back onto the boss, or by touching it to damp the vibrations.

Slab key (wilahan) instruments

Slab key instruments consist of four to fifteen or more rectangular metal bars (called "keys" in English and *wilahan* in Indonesian) arranged left-to-right, from largest to smallest (so that the lowest pitch is on the player's left and the highest pitch is on the

Figure 3.5 Keyed instruments from a Cirebonese gamelan accompanying topeng. Left to right: peking, saron, saron (courtesy Michael Ewing).

player's right) on top of some sort of stand or frame. The frame also usually provides some sort of resonating chamber—an enclosed space under a key that helps to amplify the key's sound by reflecting and reinforcing its vibrations—as well. Musicians hit the keys with a mallet or hammer; the timbre depends in a large part on the hardness or softness of the mallet. Because the keys are made of metal, the resulting sound can ring on for quite some time. For this reason, most of the time musicians also stop or damp the sound of the ringing key by firmly pinching or touching the key until it stops vibrating (see Figure 3.5).

Bossed gong and slab key instruments in Java and Bali come in a variety of types, shapes, sizes, and pitch levels, with different numbers of keys or gongs and ranges, different kinds of resonators, and different playing techniques, all of which result in a surprising variety of timbres. In gamelan ensembles, the keyed and gong instruments of various sizes and shapes are given some semblance of a uniform appearance by mounting them on stands with shared decorative motifs and paint colors.

Sundanese and Javanese musicians sometimes emphasize the integrity and unity of these sets of instruments by bestowing a proper name upon them. Each set of gamelan instruments has a unique character based on its sound as well as its appearance. In the courts of Central Java, gamelan names often begin with the honorific title Kyahi (often translated into English as "The Venerable" or "Sir") followed by a poetic combination of words rich with symbolic associations, for example, Kyahi Guntur Madu ("The Venerable Rush of Honey"). Some gamelan names evoke the particular quality of the ensemble's collective voice, such as Kyahi Udan Mas ("The Venerable Golden Rain"). A gamelan originally from Cirebon, but now kept in the Museum Sonobudoyo in Yogyakarta, is named

Figure 3.6 Kyahi Mega Mendung (Cirebonese gamelan in the Museum Sonobudoyo in Yogyakarta) (Henry Spiller).

Kyahi Mega Mendung (see Figure 3.6). This poetic image—dark storm clouds—evokes not only the gamelan's sound, but its appearance as well. The instrument cases have intricate carving based on one of Cirebon's emblematic *batik* (wax-resist dyed cloth with intricate patterns) motifs, also called *mega mendung* (see Figure 3.7); it symbolizes lifegiving rain (Tim Yayasan Mitra Budaya Indonesia 1982: 149), and also provided its original owner, a princess from Cirebon who married into a Yogyanese royal family, a nostalgic reminder of home. In West Java, gamelan names often include the more intimate honorific "Si," such as Si Manis ("Dear Sweet One"), or Ki. One of the most important qualities that distinguishes one set of gamelan instruments from another is its tuning. Instrument makers carefully tune each instrument in a gamelan to match the others, and it is only rarely possible to exchange instruments between gamelan. Despite this uniqueness, individual gamelan tunings follow the general outlines of one of two main tuning systems.

Tuning systems

Something must set the air into vibration for humans to hear a sound; the quality of sound that depends on how fast or slowly something vibrates is called *pitch*. Westerners generally relate pitches to one another not by thinking of them as "faster" or "slower," however, but rather as "higher" or "lower." When one pitch vibrates exactly twice as fast as another pitch, a curious thing happens; although one pitch is perceived to be much higher than the other, the two pitches are nevertheless heard to be somehow "the same." The musical distance delimited by these two pitches is called an *octave* in the West.

Figure 3.7 Mega mendung batik motif
(Source: *Batik Patterns*. Boston:
Shambhala Publications, 1999).

Although there are arguably an infinite number of discrete pitches within the span of a single octave, most musical systems do not make use of all of these infinite pitches. Musicians and listeners limit themselves to a much smaller set of discrete pitches, along with standards for varying and adjusting those pitches (these standards are generally called *intonation*). We typically evaluate musicians by how accurately they conform to our expectations for intonation (there are few judgments that challenge a performer's basic musicianship skills more than declaring, "She plays out of tune"!).

The human voice, along with some instruments (such as a violin), is capable of producing infinitesimal gradations of pitch; other instruments, however, are permanently set to a limited number of discrete pitches. Each key on a piano, for example, is tuned to exactly one pitch more or less permanently. Although there are eighty-eight keys on a standard piano, there are only twelve keys (and twelve discrete pitches) within each octave span on the piano. The relationship among the pitches to which those twelve keys are tuned is the piano's *tuning system*. The term for the distance between any two pitches is *interval*. Because the interval between any two adjacent piano keys is tuned to sound exactly the same as the interval between any other pair of adjacent keys, we can call the piano's tuning system a *twelve-pitch equidistant tuning system*; in other words, the octave is divided into twelve intervals, each of which we perceive as being the same size as the others.

A tuning system provides a basic pitch vocabulary, but not all the pitches need to be included in every piece. The keys on a piano, for example, can be divided into two basic categories: "white keys" which are the larger keys in front, and "black keys" which are narrower, shorter, and further back. Much conventional Western music uses only a subset of these keys at any given time; the piano's "white keys," of which there are only seven per octave, represent one of the fundamental subsets of pitches that Western music uses; one possible term for a subset of a tuning system is *scale*. The piano's white-key scale has two different sizes of intervals; the larger intervals are twice as large as the smaller intervals (because the larger intervals are the sum of two of the intervals created by the twelve-pitch equidistant tuning system). We therefore can call this subset of piano keys a *seven-pitch non-equidistant scale* (it is more commonly called a *diatonic scale*, however, which denotes a particular kind of seven-pitch non-equidistant scale in which there are two small intervals and five large intervals, and the small intervals are not close to each other).

One system for measuring and comparing intervals is called the Ellis "cents" system, developed by the nineteenth-century phonetician Alexander Ellis. He began with the piano's twelve-pitch equidistant tuning system and mentally divided each of the intervals into 100 infinitesimal pieces, called cents. Thus, a complete octave contains 1,200 cents. The pitch difference in a one-cent interval is too small for most human ears and brains to perceive, but most people can distinguish between two notes that are a few cents apart. Expressed using cents, the two small intervals of the piano white key scale are each 100 cents; the five large intervals are each 200 cents.

Javanese tuning systems

Like the keys of a piano, each of the gongs or keys on bronze gamelan instruments is tuned more or less permanently to a discrete pitch. Most bronze ensembles in Java and

Bali are tuned to a variant of one of two main tuning systems, called *pelog* and *slendro* (spelled *salendro* in the Sundanese language). Pelog is a seven-pitch non-equidistant tuning system; that is, the intervals between the seven pelog pitches vary in size from very small (about 90 cents) to very large (more than 400 cents). Slendro is a five-pitch equidistant tuning system; that is, the intervals between the five slendro pitches are approximately the same size (1,200 cents divided by 5 equals 240 cents).

The white keys on any piano are tuned exactly the same as on all other pianos, because all piano tuners use a single standard to tune each note. There are standards both for determining the pitch of each note (for example, the standard pitch for the key labeled "A" near the middle of the piano keyboard is 440 vibrations per second) as well as for the intervals between each note (how much higher or lower one note is, compared to another).

Javanese gamelan tuners, however, do not adhere to a single standard, either for pitch or for the size of intervals, but instead strive to give each set of gamelan instruments they tune a unique version of slendro or pelog. Because the instruments are always played as a set, unlike Western instruments which are interchangeable from one ensemble to another, intonation differences between gamelan sets present few practical problems. Those who listen to gamelan music, in fact, appreciate the intonation differences between one gamelan and another. Each set of instruments imparts its own subtle character into all the pieces the musicians play on it. The exact boundaries between what sounds acceptably "in tune" and what sounds "out of tune" are difficult to nail down, and are the subject of much passionate discussion among Javanese musicians.

So, although both the piano white keys and pelog are seven-pitch non-equidistant tuning systems, they are really quite different. That being said, it is possible to internalize a crude approximation of how the pelog tuning system sounds by comparing it to a piano's diatonic ("white-key") scale. Many people can sing a diatonic scale using traditional *do re mi fa sol la ti do* (and those who cannot do so already can learn quickly by watching the first half-hour of the Rodgers and Hammerstein musical *The Sound of Music*). Remember, however, that this represents a very crude approximation. If there is one certainty about Javanese tunings, it is this: The *do re mi* diatonic scale sounds absolutely *awful* as pelog.

Music in Cirebon

Gamelan sekaten in Cirebon

Cirebonese gamelan sekaten are tuned to a version of this basic seven-pitch pelog scale. And, like most gamelan ensembles, gamelan sekaten include both wilahan and pencon instruments. The pencon instruments include two large hanging gongs (called *gong*), a large one-row gong chime called *bonang*, and a small, horizontal gong called *ketuk* or *kajar*. The wilahan instruments are of two sizes; the larger, lower-pitched ones are called *demung*, while the smaller, higher-pitched one is called *titil*. The ensemble is filled out with a flat, unbossed gong called *beri*, *cret*, or *kecrek*. There also is one non-bronze instrument: a large drum called *bedug* (Kunst and Kunst-van Wely 1923: 35; North 1988: 4, 5) (see Figure 3.8).

The names of many Indonesian musical instruments are onomatopoeic in that they

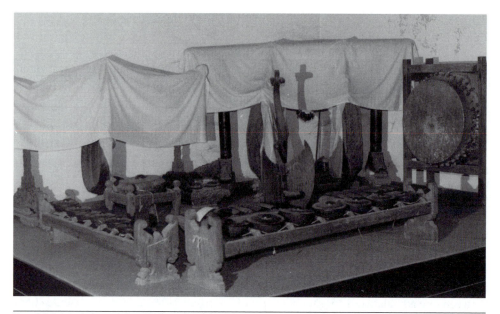

Figure 3.8 Sekaten instruments from the Kraton Kasepuhan (photo and print collection of the Koninklijk Instituut voor Taal-, Land- en Volkenkunde, Leiden, the Netherlands).

are verbal imitations of both the timbre of the instruments and the style in which they are played. The name "gong," for example, is a verbal imitation of the sound a large, low-pitched gong makes when it is struck and allowed to ring. Similarly, the second syllable of the name "ketuk" (that is, "tuk") evokes the sound a higher-pitched gong makes when struck and damped. The "i" vowels and "t" consonants in the name "titil" suggest the delicate, high-pitched, and relatively fast-moving melody of the instrument it describes, while the "u" vowel and "m" and "ng" consonants in "demung" capture the more grandiose sound of the larger keyed instrument. "Cret" and "crek" imitate the crashing sound of the cymbal-like kecrek, while "dug" captures the thumping quality of the large bedug drum's booming low voice.

Even when they are played all together at the same time, each instrument's unique voice and individual sonic personality are clearly audible. As is the case with much gamelan music, Cirebonese gamelan sekaten pieces have several distinct layers; each layer has a different musical function. The distinctive timbres of each of the instruments (as reflected in their names) contribute to the listener's ability to perceive and distinguish the various layers. The following discussion will illustrate the basic layers of gamelan music using a Cirebonese gamelan sekaten piece as an example by constructing, layer by layer, a "timeline" for the piece. By virtue of their majestic sound and especially honored status, the large gongs are assigned the role of regularly marking off the passage of rather large chunks of musical time; the timeline in Figure 3.9 represents one such chunk that is thirty-two seconds long. It is quite difficult for humans to accurately measure a chunk of time as long as thirty-two seconds without somehow dividing it into smaller, more manageable units. The ketuk's sharp attack and quick decay make it an ideal instrument for marking off appropriately smaller units of time. In the timeline, the ketuk sounds on

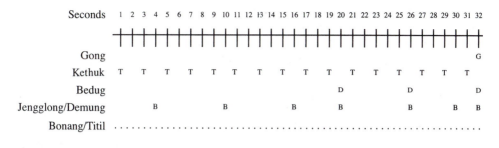

Figure 3.9 Colotomic timeline for "Lagu Sekaten."

the odd-numbered seconds—sixteen times before the gong stroke. Together, these two instrumental sounds act as a foundation for the other instruments' parts; they quite literally lay out a timeline for the other instruments. Ethnomusicologists sometimes call this sort of foundation or timeline, in which regular time periods are delineated by punctuating sounds, a *colotomic form* or *colotomy*. These terms are based on the Greek word for a unit of rhythm (*colon*) and the Greek-derived suffixes for something that cuts or divides into sections (*-tomy* or *-tomic*).

Most gamelan ensembles also include instruments other than bronze percussion instruments. Cirebonese gamelan sekaten includes a large drum, called bedug, which is struck in a less regular pattern than the colotomic bronze instruments; its strokes are concentrated near the gong stroke. This quickening of activity toward the end of the time period helps build expectations about the impending gong stroke and shape the arbitrary time period into a musical phrase with a beginning, middle, and end. Judith Becker calls this kind of drum pattern a *configurative* drum pattern because of its role in creating a sense of musical direction (Becker 1968: 180). This is a common role for drums in gamelan music.

In some gamelan ensembles, drums provide other functions beyond this configurative role as well. It is usually the responsibility of the drummer in a gamelan ensemble to coordinate all the rhythmic activity—speeding up, slowing down, beginning or ending a piece, or transitioning to some other piece. In addition, drum patterns often accentuate and enhance any kind of movement that the gamelan may accompany, such as dance or puppet manipulation, by providing an aural analog for the dancers' or puppets' gestures. Some ethnomusicologists compare the drummer's role in a gamelan ensemble to that of a conductor in Western orchestral music, because a drummer, like a conductor, sets the tempos and helps the other musicians coordinate their parts. Unlike a conductor, however, a drummer in a gamelan ensemble leads with aural signals rather than hand-waving; the mark of a good drummer is his unobtrusiveness, not his flamboyance.

The remaining instruments play simultaneous variations of the piece's melody (n.b.: the melody's rhythm is notated in Figure 3.9, but not its notes). The lower-pitched instruments (jengglong and demung) play versions of the melody that are very simple—only seven notes in the example. The versions played by the higher-pitched instruments (bonang and titil) are, by comparison, very elaborate. They are considered to be different versions of the same melody because they land on the same pitches at regular time intervals. The simplified version, played by the lower-pitched instruments, includes only the melody's most essential contours. The more elaborate versions, played by the higher-pitched instruments, have a lot more notes, but follow the same essential contour as the simpler version.

The two parts might be compared to a person walking a dog. The human is likely to move ahead at a steady pace, while a dog typically will race ahead, run back and forth, or linger behind for a moment before racing on ahead again. The dog's mileage is significantly greater than the human's, but both walk the same path, cover the same ground, and arrive at the same destination at the same time; the difference is that the human walks like a human and the dog walks like a dog. Similarly, the jengglong player and the bonang player perform the same melody and arrive at the same melodic junctures at the same time, but the jengglong part proceeds like a jengglong part (slowly) and the bonang part proceeds like a bonang part (more quickly, covering more musical ground).

The musical texture that results from the simultaneous presentation of different versions of a single melody moving at different densities can be called *polyphonic stratification*. As discussed in Chapter 2, the term polyphonic suggests multiple parts, while stratification suggests that the parts are layered on top of each other like strata of rock in geological formations where clearly delineated sheets of different kinds of rock are layered on top of one another. The different parts—the various "strata"—played on Cirebonese gamelan sekaten instruments can be grouped into four functional layers: (1) foundation/colotomic; (2) simplified/abstracted melody, (3) elaborated/varied melody, and (4) drum patterns that shape the phrases, coordinate rhythmic activity, and synchronize the music with other activities such as dance. These four functions combine to create a stratified musical texture. Sekaten pieces, like many gamelan pieces, are cyclical in the sense that the pattern represented by the timeline can be repeated many times (in theory, indefinitely). Due to their ceremonial nature, sekaten pieces are, in fact, cycled many, many times during a performance. To ensure that the musicians get a chance to rest, one of the musicians keeps track of how many cycles have been performed with the aid of a board with twenty-five holes drilled in it (like a cribbage board). After three gong cycles, a peg is advanced one hole; when the peg gets to the twenty-fifth hole (seventy-five cycles!) it is time to end the piece and take a break (Dapperen 1933: 157).

When it was founded, Cirebon had only one *kraton* (royal palace) and one ruler. Over the years, the kingdom was split several times. The first such split, in 1677, divided the kingdom between two brothers and resulted in two kraton: Kasepuhan (which means "the elder") and Kanoman ("the younger"). (Currently there is a third kraton in Cirebon, known as Kacerbonan.) The original set of gamelan sekaten instruments was divided between the Kasepuhan and Kanoman palaces at the time of the split; the bonang and saron went to Kasepuhan, while the gongs went to Kanoman. Each kraton completed its set with newly forged instruments (North 2002).

Gamelan sekaten is associated with a festival called Garebeg Maulud or Sekaten, which honors the anniversary of the birth of the prophet Muhammad. Sekaten takes place during Muslim "holy week," which is the 6th to the 12th of the third Javanese month Maulud (equivalent to the Islamic month Rabi ul Awal) (Sumarsam 1980: 54; Sutton 1999: 644). In Cirebon, the sekaten festival involves a ceremony called *panjang jimat*, in which all the palace heirlooms (including the gamelan instruments) are brought out of their storeroom in the kraton and washed. The water is coveted for its magical properties (Dapperen 1933: 156; Vetter 2001: 79; North 2002).

Figure 3.10 Kraton Kanoman's sekaten gongs, wrapped in white cloth (courtesy Michael Ewing).

The Kanoman palace's gamelan sekaten is played for this festival, which draws a large crowd (Falla 1985: 38; North 2002). The Kasepuhan gamelan sekaten is played for different, but also Islamic, occasions: to celebrate the Islamic holy days Idul-Fitri and Idul-'adha (North 1982a; Suanda 1999: 687; North 2002). In contrast to the large crowd that the Kanoman palace draws for the prophet's birthday, the Kasepuhan occasion is for the palace residents and guests only (North 2002).

The significance of the gamelan sekaten instruments and pieces lies mostly in their status as symbols of history, royal legitimacy, and continuity with the past. When people play and hear them, they are more concerned with the fact that the instruments have a distinguished history, still exist, and are being played than they are with specifically aesthetic qualities of the sounds. This does not mean that the sounds are not important—they are a potent symbol of all the history, power, and significance that stand behind the instruments. It means, rather, that the sounds are judged by standards that are different than those to which most Westerners are accustomed. Nobody composes new pieces for these ensembles because the meaning of music lies not in novelty or freshness, but rather in the venerability of the prescribed repertory and the ceremonial act of playing them yet once again.

For similar reasons, no efforts are made to keep the instruments perfectly tuned; although intonation adjustments might enhance the music's aesthetic value, they might also diminish its symbolic potency and detract from its venerability. Furthermore, the scraping and filing and pounding that tuning bronze gamelan instruments involves might damage or break the old bronze keys and pots. Only when the instruments are in danger of total disintegration do the musicians cease playing them; the original heirloom gongs from the kraton Kanoman have been unplayable for some time, and replacement gongs are played for performances. The original gongs are still revered as heirlooms, however, and are maintained very carefully, wrapped in white cloth and cleaned every year, to slow down any further deterioration (see Figure 3.10) (Dapperen 1933; Soepandi 1976: 26).

Gamelan sekaten provide a palpable link with the past, and contribute to the prestige and authority of Cirebonese royalty even in modern democratic Indonesia. The sound of the gamelan is an integral part of the celebration soundscape—an essential sonic backdrop for proper observance of the festival. People can experience the past through the sight and sound of these heirloom ensembles, which are believed to have arrived in the present unchanged. These ceremonial ensembles provide their Javanese listeners with a sonic channel to history; they provide outsiders with a glimmer of understanding of gamelan music's symbolic power (cf. Vetter 2001: 67).

Music in Cirebon today

The gamelan sekaten ensembles of Cirebon are more significant as relics than as instruments of a dynamic music culture; some of their meaning lies in the perception that they have not changed for centuries. But gamelan ensembles play an important role in modern Cirebonese music as well. Modern gamelan music still retains a symbolic component—the people of Cirebon believe that the traditional arts are the legacy of the nine saints, and most artists claim to be descended from the Islamic saints Pangeran Panggung and Sunan Kali Jaga (Suanda 1999: 687)—but people tend to judge the sounds of most music not by how "traditional" it is, but by how well it serves their artistic needs and satisfies their aesthetic desires.

Village gamelan

Although gamelan are a symbol of aristocracy and power, they also provide music for village ceremonies and entertainment. In fact, many of the artists who perform for the palaces live in the tiny agricultural villages that surround the city of Cirebon. Village musicians may not be able to afford instruments made out of valuable bronze; a more economical substitute is iron.

Historically, villages around Cirebon maintain their cohesiveness partly through the shared celebration of important events in the lives of individuals ("life-cycle" events such as marriage, circumcision, etc.) as well as through annual celebrations. Because the lives of most villagers are centered around the growing of rice, the annual ceremonies emphasize the agricultural cycle. Cirebonese villages typically celebrate five annual festivals: *sidekah bumi* (blessing of the earth, before the farmers begin to work in the fields); *ngunjung* (giving thanks to Allah and to ancestral spirits); *kasinoman* (a ritual for youth); *mapag tambra* (after planting and weeding), and *mapag Sri* (welcoming the rice goddess as the crop matures) (Suanda 1999: 688).

Villagers see no contradiction in having a good time at these celebrations despite their deep and serious meanings; small children get to indulge themselves with special treats for the eyes, ears, and mouths, young people turn their attention to meeting and wooing potential boy- and girlfriends, and adults enjoy a break from their usual routines. The atmosphere during such celebrations is always *ramé*, which means crowded, full of bustle, with lots of eye-catching sights and ear-catching sounds bombarding the crowds from all sides. The performing arts make an inestimable contribution to this lively atmosphere. Modern Cirebonese gamelan include instruments similar to those of the archaic ensembles as well as additional instruments. Typical village gamelan ensembles include saron of various sizes, two-row bonang and other horizontal gong chimes, and hanging gongs in three basic sizes. Like modern gamelan ensembles from other parts of Java, they include non-bronze instruments as well, including *gambang* (a wooden xylophone) and *kendang* (two-headed barrel-shaped drums). Cirebonese gamelan also features a bamboo flute (*suling*) and singers.

Topeng

Dancing with masks to the accompaniment of gamelan music is an especially time-honored custom in north-coast communities in Java. Masked dance performances called *topeng* continue to be characteristic of Cirebonese village celebrations in the twenty-first century. Topeng performances combine music, theater, and dance into a day-long performance which combines philosophy, entertainment, political comment and satire, and sometimes even magic into one multimedia package. In the village style around Cirebon, topeng is primarily a solo dance form. The main dancer, called the *dalang topeng*, directs a troupe of musicians and dancers and performs most of the solo dances him- or herself. Dalang topeng (like many other artists in Cirebon) usually come from artistic families and learned the art and craft of topeng from an older relative. While dalang topeng take great pains to preserve and perpetuate some elements of their family's heritage, they also introduce changes and innovations which they believe will enhance their performances without sullying their tradition. Each family has developed a unique style, and dalang topeng compete with one another for invitations to perform. The characteristics discussed below represent a shared body of custom, but it is difficult to say anything truly definitive about such a dynamic performing tradition.

Topeng performances center around the presentation of four (sometimes five) solo dances; each dance features a different character and a different mask (see Figure 3.11). The masks alone suggest characters with contrasting personality traits and tendencies. The characters have names drawn from a variety of epic stories known throughout Java, and at times the topeng performance is narrative, but for the most part the characters represent abstract character types which emphasize personality traits that audience members can recognize in themselves. By experiencing the dances, people come to know something about each character trait as well as something about themselves. A topeng performance typically lasts about 8 or 9 hours, from 8 a.m. until 5 p.m. The four or five main dances are interspersed with a variety of other performances, including *bodoran* (standup and physical comedy by the troupe's clowns) and sometimes even *tayuban* (men's social dance), as well as speeches and breaks for prayers.

A dalang topeng brings the characters of the masks to life by adding appropriate movement and music. The dalang topeng "improvises" the dance—improvises in the sense that the exact form the dance takes is not known until the performance is under way, but not

Name	Mask color	Facial features	Character
Rahwana	red	bulging eyes, large mustache, protruding gold teeth	greedy, lusty king
Tumenggung/ Patih	purple/ brown	round eyes, manicured mustache	aggressive prime minister
Rumyang	pink	narrow, downcast eyes, laughing mouth	mature sweetness
Samba/ Pamindo	white/ cream	narrow, downcast eyes, laughing mouth	adolescent exuberance
Panji	white	narrow, downcast eyes, delicate mouth	extremely refined and centered

Figure 3.11 Five topeng masks, their features, and their characterizations (Henry Spiller).

Figure 3.12 The late dalang topeng Sujana Arja dances "Rahwana" (Henry Spiller).

in the sense that the dancer does whatever he or she feels like doing. Each dalang topeng has perfected a large repertory of dance movements, along with the knowledge of how to fit them to the musical accompaniment in limitless combinations. The musicians know the basic framework for each dance, as well as the musical pieces that go with each section of the dance. The dalang and the musicians share a sophisticated set of signals and conventions that allow them to put together a long, complex dance piece on the spot.

This approach to performance—the spontaneous realization and elaboration of relatively simple frameworks through the application of conventional formulas—is common throughout Java and Bali and applies to music, dance, and other arts as well. In effect, performers store pieces in their memories in a compressed form, along with information about how to decompress them during performance. This process partly explains how Indonesian artists can perform richly textured and nuanced music and dance for hours without consulting musical notation or overloading their memories.

An example drawn from the Cirebonese village topeng repertory will illustrate one aspect of this compression/decompression process. "Rahwana" is typically the final dance of the performance. The mask associated with this dance is red, with bulging eyes and a thick moustache. The color and features suggest a coarse, rude individual. The dance movements—fast, full of wild energy and sharp contrasts—reinforce these traits (see Figure 3.12).

The outline of the "Rahwana" dance, like the other topeng dances, involves four main sections, which are named after their basic tempos: (1) *dodoan* (slow), (2) *tengahan* (medium slow), (3) *kering* (medium fast) and (4) *deder* (fast). Each section is associated with a special piece of music, with a specific colotomic form (i.e., a specific pattern of instrumental sounds that act as a foundation for the other instruments' parts). For each section, the dancer knows a variety of possible movement units called *jogedan*, which she can repeat a variable number of times, as well as a variety of transitional movements, called *alihan*, which provide a bridge between two movement units. Within each section, the dancer can present some or all of the movement units in whatever sequence seems appropriate at the moment. Each movement unit fits in with the musical accompaniment in a prescribed manner, however, so the dancer must take care to be synchronized with the music. Furthermore, the transitions can occur only at particular points within the musical pieces (Suanda 1988).

To further connect the dancer with the accompanying music, the ensemble's drummer plays the drum pattern that, by convention, matches the specific movement units the dancer performs at any given moment. These drum patterns often provide an aural analog to the dance movement as well—by matching a strong step with a solid, low-pitched drum stroke, for example, or by accompanying a slow, sustained movement with a tremolo.

The four musical functions that different gamelan sekaten instruments perform are also evident in the gamelan ensemble that accompanies topeng. One way to understand the musical and choreographic structure of the pieces that accompany the different sections of "Rahwana" is to consider their colotomic forms—the foundation part that is outlined by the large hanging gong and other time-keeping instruments. In a gamelan for topeng, the main time-keeping instruments include *gong* (large hanging gong), *kempul* (smaller, higher-pitched hanging gong), *kebluk* (still smaller gong laid horizontally on a frame), *kenong* (gong chime with five to seven high-pitched horizontally laid gongs), and *jengglong* (similar to kenong except one octave lower in pitch). Once again, the second syllable of each instrument name suggests the way it sounds.

Figure 3.13 shows the foundation parts played by the time-keeping instruments for the *kering* (medium-fast) section (a piece called "Sarung Ilang"); Figure 3.14 shows the parts played for the *deder* (fast) section (a piece called "Gonjing"; both these pieces can be heard on Track 2 of the CD that accompanies this book). The part for each of the time-keeping instruments is provided separately; the line labeled "composite" shows how the various parts fit together to create a single musical line consisting of a rapid alternation of different instrumental timbres. One can sing a reasonable approximation of the composite colotomic form by reciting the composite line with the appropriate syllable from an instrument's name in rhythm (that is, "bluk" for B, "pul" for P, and "gong" for G).

The colotomic forms of the two pieces are almost exactly the same; the main difference is tempo (the deder piece, "Gonjing," is twice as fast as the kering piece, "Sarung Ilang") and the number of kenong/jengglong strokes (approximately one per two seconds in both pieces, which translates to eight strokes for "Sarung Ilang" and four strokes for "Gonjing"). In some topeng troupes, the gong player omits one of the gong strokes from the "Gonjing" cycle.

The dancer, however, does not simply dance twice as fast (which would probably be impossible anyway—even the best dancers can step and jump only so fast). Rather, a movement unit in the faster deder section takes up the same amount of elapsed time as a movement unit in the kering section—say, for example, four seconds. That means that the dancer can fit only two repetitions of a four-second movement into one musical

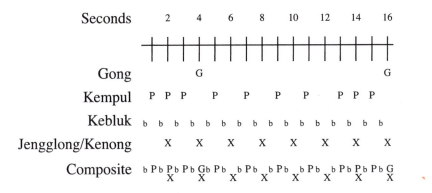

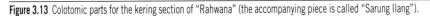

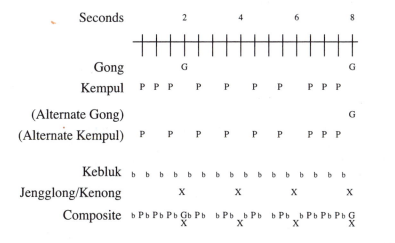

Figure 3.13 Colotomic parts for the kering section of "Rahwana" (the accompanying piece is called "Sarung Ilang").

Figure 3.14 Colotomic parts for the deder section of "Rahwana" (the accompanying piece is called "Gonjing").

cycle in deder, whereas four repetitions could fit into one kering cycle. Four full repetitions might be tedious, however, so the dancer might add more transitional movements to break things up; a common strategy is to insert a special dance and drum pattern just before the gong stroke. For similar reasons, the dancer must initiate the transitional movements at a different point in the cycle of the deder than in the kering to wind up doing the correct thing at the appropriate time; in this case, the drum and dance pattern actually straddles a gong stroke (see Figure 3.15).

Rather than memorizing these possible sequences by rote, however, the dalang topeng thinks only about doing the particular jogedan and about the characteristics of the accompanying pieces. The details of exactly how many times to repeat the jogedan and when to insert the alihan movements emerge in the process of performance. Because the transition movements are typically tied to gong strokes in the accompanying piece, opportunities to change jogedan come more frequently in the later, faster sections of a dance than in the earlier sections, adding to their excitement.

This brief overview of the process of a topeng performance does not begin to do

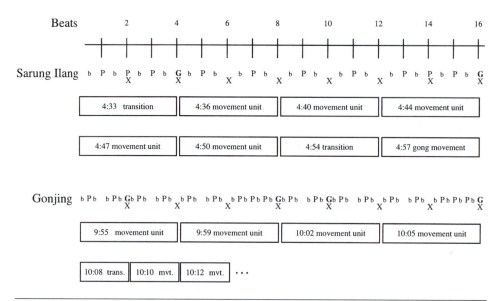

Figure 3.15 Comparison of kering and deder choreography (timings refer to appropriate moments of Track 2 of the CD that accompanies this book).

justice to the complex and subtle artistry such performances involve. It does, however, introduce some basic tenets that underlie Javanese performing arts. In essence, there are two elements at work: (1) the abstract, conceptualized outline or framework of a piece, and (2) the knowledge of how to flesh out the framework in real time. In the case of Cirebonese topeng, the abstract outline of a topeng performance involves a sequence of four (or five) dances; each dance has four sections; each section has a particular musical piece and a generalized sequence of jogedan. To perform the dance, dalang topeng rely on their knowledge of how to repeat, connect, and vary their repertory of jogedan within the constraints created by the hierarchy of frameworks.

In a sense, this approach to performance models the way in which individuals perceive the structure of the universe and their place within it. Anthropologists Gregory Bateson and Clifford Geertz have suggested that Javanese and Balinese people conceive the universe as a "steady state"—a fixed structure through which individuals move on fixed axes. In this conception, the day-to-day events of people's lives are generated by underlying patterns that do not change. This conception does not negate the individuality of a person's experience, or suggest that a person's actions do not affect his or her fate. It does mean, however, that the uniqueness of each individual's experience is thrust into the background, while its sameness is brought to the foreground (Bateson 1963; Geertz 1973). Geertz explains:

It is not . . . their existence as persons—their immediacy and individuality, or their special, never-to-be-repeated, impact upon the stream of historical events—which are culturally played up, symbolically emphasized: it is their social placement, their particular location within a persisting, indeed an eternal, metaphysical order (Geertz 1973: 390).

By finding an individual path in real time through a fixed performance structure—by bringing a sense of "now" to a performance through the deployment of a mastery of the infinite possibilities that the structure of topeng dance enables—a dalang topeng demonstrates the relationship between the individual and the rest of the universe. By portraying several archetypal characters, the dalang topeng suggests that a variety of paths can be negotiated through the cosmos, depending on one's predispositions. By watching, learning, and appreciating the aesthetic outcome of the dalang topeng's journey through the performance, the audience members not only absorb the different character templates available to them, but come to understand the relationship of the individual to the cosmos as well.

Because of their mastery of the relationship between the world of humans and the cosmos, as demonstrated through the performance of topeng, dalang topeng are regarded as individuals who can intervene on behalf of humans in spiritual and supernatural matters. One of the things the sponsor of a topeng event considers when choosing a dalang topeng is how much spiritual power the dalang can bring to bear on the occasion. Mothers might interrupt a dalang topeng's dance to implore him to bless their newborn infants, or even to ask for inspiration in naming the child. Dalang who have demonstrated great supernatural abilities can demand higher fees.

For their part, dalang topeng take their status as intermediaries between the cosmos and the everyday world quite seriously. Their goal is not simply to dance beautifully; the fates and futures of babies, individuals, and even entire communities depend on their skillful and artistic dancing. On a performance tour of the United States, one dalang topeng, about to step on the stage to dance in front of thousands of New Yorkers at Lincoln Center, was asked if he was nervous. He responded that he was not—because there was nothing "important" about the particular performance—nobody's life or future was at stake.

This chapter has introduced some of the basic concepts that underpin the gamelan music of Cirebon and demonstrated how the Southeast Asian musical processes discussed in Part I are manifest in unique ways in both the heirloom gamelan sekaten ensemble and contemporary village gamelan and topeng performances. As we shall see in the next chapter, gamelan music traditions in Central Java, East Java, and Bali have much in common with the gamelan music of Java's north coast, yet they also bear the stamps of the unique ways in which the layers of history have settled in each particular place.

CHAPTER 4

Gamelan in Central Java, Eastern Java, and Bali

For a variety of reasons, gamelan music in Cirebon appears to have changed more slowly and less dramatically than it has in other parts of Java and Bali (Wright 1978: 16; Suanda 1999: 686). Some scholars look to Cirebon for insight into gamelan music of the Hindu, Buddhist, and early Islamic kingdoms of medieval Java. The gamelan music of Central Java, on the other hand, has clearly undergone significant transformations over the past several centuries, and sounds quite different from Cirebonese gamelan music.

Central Java

The four Central Javanese kraton are similar to the kraton in Cirebon in many ways. The Central Javanese rulers trace their ancestry to the powerful Islamic kingdom of Mataram, which arose in the sixteenth century; the influential leader Sultan Agung consolidated power and territory, vanquished the remaining Hindu-Buddhist kingdom in Java (that is, Pajajaran) and even dominated the powerful north-coast Islamic states. Like the royal families of Cirebon, the rulers of these four princedoms own gamelan instruments that establish their legitimacy as heirs to earlier empires, including sekaten ensembles as well as other ceremonial gamelan with rich histories.

Over the years the original Mataram kingdom was split several times in response to rebellions and conflicts over succession. Dutch colonial powers wielded significant influence in the creation of some of the kraton; one of their goals was to constrain the power and influence of Central Javanese rulers by establishing rival rulers in close proximity to one another. By the eighteenth century there were two major kraton, one in the city of Surakarta (also known as Solo), and the other in the city of Yogyakarta. The ruler of the Kraton Solo holds the title of Susuhunan, while the Kraton Yogyakarta's ruler holds the title Sultan. There is a minor kraton in each of the two cities as well: the Mangkunegaran in Surakarta and the Paku Alaman in Yogyakarta.

Unlike the Cirebon rulers, however, the rulers of each of the four Central Javanese kraton had significant financial resources at hand, as well as a keen desire to upstage the other three kraton and flaunt their prestige. Because of the Dutch control of the political situation, there were only limited opportunities for competition; during the nineteenth and early twentieth centuries, a primary arena for this competition was development and patronage of the arts.

The American painter and dancer Hubert Stowitts, who spent about a year living, studying, and painting in the various Central Javanese kraton in 1927–8, provides a vivid account of the courts' rivalry at that time in his unpublished book on Javanese dance and theater (Stowitts n.d.). The palaces were, he wrote, "hot houses of Oriental intrigue and mystery" (Stowitts n.d.: vi–11). According to Stowitts, the Sultan, Susuhunan, and minor court princes wore Dutch uniforms when they visited one another to circumvent the demands of Javanese etiquette that would force them to acknowledge each other's rank and status. The rulers mounted lavish musical and theatrical productions to celebrate important occasions, vied with one another to see who could produce the most elaborate spectacles, and trained their heirs to be patrons of the arts.

We have already seen how the possession of gamelan instruments is a symbol of legitimacy and power. It is not too difficult to imagine how cultivating and refining the music played on these gamelan instruments might enhance the power and status that the instruments already conveyed. For one thing, gamelan music aestheticizes the structure of the universe; the predictable colotomic forms order time into cycles that mirror the progress of time and space. In addition, the performance of gamelan music, as we have seen, models the relationship of individuals to the cosmos.

Furthermore, the stratified musical texture of gamelan music mimics the organization of Javanese kingdoms in sonic form. The adjective "stratified" also describes a social structure; a "stratified" society is one that divides its population into different classes, each with different roles, duties, and privileges. In stratified societies, classes do not mix very often, but social order depends on each class fulfilling its designated role and maintaining the status quo. By regarding the exaggerated musical stratification in gamelan music as beautiful, listeners are predisposed to accept social stratification as the natural order of things. Finally, gamelan music provides a means for displaying wealth and prestige (by having music playing) while further reinforcing a stratified social structure by limiting access to that prestige (only those with specialized knowledge and etiquette can fully appreciate the subtleties of the music).

The ancient ceremonial gamelan of the Central Javanese courts, like Cirebonese gamelan sekaten, include only bronze percussion instruments (with the exception of the large drum called bedug). Such ensembles, and the music played on them, sufficiently represent medieval Javanese ideas of cosmic order and stratified society. In their quest for prestige and political influence in a rapidly changing world, however, Javanese royalty and the musicians they patronized found ways to reconcile more modern musical approaches with the older ideas. In doing so, they modeled a justification for their own continued existence.

A modern Central Javanese court-style gamelan ensemble (see Figure 4.1) is really two different ensembles combined into one. It includes a full complement of the bronze percussion instruments similar to those found in gamelan sekaten—large hanging gongs,

Figure 4.1 Gamelan ensemble in the pendopo (pavilion) of the Kraton Surakarta (Henry Spiller).

gong chimes and keyed metallophones of various sizes, and drums. In the modern Central Javanese style, these "loud-sounding" instruments are complemented by a "soft-sounding" ensemble that consists of male and female singers, a bowed stringed instrument called *rebab*, a bamboo flute called *suling*, a wooden xylophone called *gambang*, a plucked zither called *celempung*, and a keyed metallophone called *gender*. At times, the loud-sounding instruments play alone; at other times, only the soft instruments play. Sometimes the entire forces—loud and soft instruments, as well as singers—all play together.

The soft-sounding chamber ensemble represents a different approach to musical structure than the loud bronze ensemble. These soft instruments' indistinct attacks, coupled with their penchant for blurring one note into the next, make them less suitable for marking off time in the way that bronze gamelan instruments do; at the same time, these instruments are capable of producing subtle nuances of melodic ornamentation that are unavailable on bronze instruments. While the bronze instruments and the colotomic forms they outline evoke the cyclic qualities of time and the cosmos and emphasize the repetitive nature of events, the soft instruments—especially the voices, with their capacity for language and stories—evoke instead the linear qualities of time in which each moment is unique and never to be experienced again.

In performance, the "linear" soft-sounding ensemble is made to conform to the cyclic framework outlined by the bronze instruments. The combination of the bronze and chamber ensembles can be interpreted as a metaphor of the juxtaposition of old Javanese ideas about cosmic order and kingship with newer political approaches introduced by Islam and Europeans. In modern Javanese gamelan music the new musical approach is layered on top of the old approach, but is subordinate to it, and thus perpetuates the prestige and status of the old approach. In a subtle way, then, this updated gamelan music models Javanese royalty's hopes for a new political reality, in which any new approaches to government and authority are firmly grounded in and subordinate to the more old-fashioned concepts of Javanese kingship.

Throughout the nineteenth century and into the twentieth, Javanese aristocrats culti-vated this new approach to gamelan music. Each of the kraton maintained its own staff of trained and dedicated musicians and other artists, who developed increasingly sophis-ticated approaches to music, theater, and dance. There was much cross-fertilization between the four kraton as well; princes and princesses from kraton families married one another and often took instruments and musicians to their new homes as part of their dowries and retinues. Over the past two centuries, a highly sophisticated, modern style of Central Javanese court gamelan has emerged; although there are subtle differ-ences between the various palaces, there is much in common as well.

Musicians outside the courts emulated these palace styles as best they could. Begin-ning in the 1920s, some kraton aristocrats decided to share training in the arts with Javanese outside the palace and opened schools for outsiders. These were attended not only by Javanese commoners, but by an occasional foreign student as well. Following Indonesian independence, these court styles became part of a national, as well as a spe-cifically Javanese, heritage; government-sponsored performing arts academies have become centers for innovations and training in the performing arts as well since their establishment beginning in the 1970s.

Central Javanese gamelan music involves both of the two Javanese tuning systems: *slendro* (a five-pitch equidistant tuning system) and *pelog* (a seven-pitch non-equidistant system). Often a set of gamelan instruments includes a pair (or several pairs) of each instrument—one member of each pair tuned to slendro, the other to pelog. A single musician is assigned to both instruments; when the piece is cast in pelog, he plays the pelog instrument, and when the piece is in slendro, he plays the slendro instrument.

Like Cirebonese sekaten and topeng gamelan music, Central Javanese gamelan music has four different "functional" layers: (1) colotomic foundation layer; (2) simplified/abstracted melody, (3) elaborated/varied melody, and (4) drum patterns.

Colotomic parts

Once again, the foundation layer is provided by the interlocking pattern created by several gongs and gong chimes of various sizes and timbres. The most important of these instru-ments is the *gong ageng*, an extremely large hanging gong. The sound of a good-quality gong ageng is awe-inspiring; these large and heavy instruments produce a pitch so low that it is as much felt as it is heard; furthermore, they are constructed and tuned so that the pitch and volume oscillate (Javanese refer to this quality as *ombak*—ocean waves). The overall effect is quite visceral; it is little wonder that the Javanese often consider a good gong to be a repository of spiritual power, and even give them proper names and royal titles.

Gamelan music tends to be "end-weighted"—listeners hear the rhythms, melodies, and elaborations all propelling toward an inevitable and satisfying close. This end-weightedness is made explicit by the colotomic instruments. Strokes of the large gong mark the endpoints of the main cycles of Central Javanese gamelan music. The sound of a large gong takes quite a long time to die away, and its sound is never damped. For shorter cycles, a smaller type of gong is often played instead of the large gong to mark the ends of cycles; this smaller gong is called a *gong suwukan* (or sometimes *gong siyem*). While its pitch is still rather low, it is not as low and visceral as that of a gong ageng, and its pitch is often more distinct. For this reason, a set of gamelan instruments may include several of these smaller gong suwukan with various pitches; a gamelan rarely includes more than one or two large gongs, however.

A second part of the foundation layer is played on a gong chime called *kenong*. Each kenong pot is a large gong with a very deep lip laid horizontally over ropes in a stand. Although the pots are large, their pitch is very high because of their shape and density, and their sound rings for some time. The second syllable of the instrument's name ("nong") is an onomatopoeic representation of its sound. A modern set of kenong typically includes a pot tuned to each pitch of the tuning system—that is, five for slendro, seven for pelog— although it is possible to get by with as few as one kenong.

Kethuk provides a third instrumental sound in the foundation layer of Central Java- nese gamelan music. As the second syllable of its name ("thuk") suggests, its sound is not as high-pitched as kenong, and does not ring for a long time. A kenong player hits the kenong with the mallet and immediately removes the mallet so that the instrument can ring; a kethuk player, on the other hand, lets the mallet return to the boss after it is hit so that the sound rings only for a short time and is then damped. Often the musician lets the mallet bounce on the kethuk, resulting in a sort of dribbling sound. Central Java- nese colotomic forms also frequently include the sound of *kempul* (one or more hanging gongs, smaller than gong suwukan), and a *kempyang* (a small, high-pitched kethuk-like gong, or sometimes a pair of such little gongs). Figure 3.3 showed one large gong ageng (front right), a smaller gong suwukan (rear right), and two kempul (left).

Central Javanese forms

While there are many Central Javanese gamelan pieces, they all make use of a fairly small number of patterns of interlocking gong, kenong, kethuk, and other colotomic instru- ments. Just as construction workers, when building a concrete structure, start with a wooden form into which they pour cement and rocks, composers of gamelan music begin with a colotomic template or mold into which they "pour" the melody and elabo- ration. In English, a musical template of this kind is typically called a *form*; college music students learn about the classical sonata form, and almost everybody is familiar with the verse–chorus–verse–chorus form of most popular songs. Central Javanese musicians regard each of the standard colotomic patterns that undergird gamelan pieces as a form. Each form has a name and is defined by its distinct interlocking pattern of gong, kenong, kethuk, kempyang, and kempul strokes.

For example, the form called *ladrang* serves as the foundation for many Central Javanese pieces. It is usually described as a phrase that is thirty-two beats long, with a stroke of the large gong marking the last beat. Figure 4.2 provides a representation of the ladrang form's colotomic parts. The timeline across the top of the figure marks off each of the phrase's thirty-two beats; the single large gong stroke is notated with a "G" in the figure. The other colotomic instruments divide this phrase into increasingly smaller segments. Kenong strokes (indicated with "N" in the figure) divide the thirty-two-beat

Beats	1	2	3	4	5	6	7	8	9	10	11	12	13	14	15	16	17	18	19	20	21	22	23	24	25	26	27	28	29	30	31	32
Gong Ageng																																G
Kenong								N								N								N								N
Kempul			W								P								P								P					
Kethuk		T				T				T				T				T				T				T				T		
Kempyang	Y		Y		Y		Y		Y		Y		Y		Y		Y		Y		Y		Y		Y		Y		Y		Y	
Composite	Y	T	Y	W	Y	T	Y	N	Y	T	Y	P	Y	T	Y	N	Y	T	Y	P	Y	T	Y	N	Y	T	Y	P	Y	T	Y	N/G

Figure 4.2 Colotomic patterns for the Central Javanese form ladrang.

phrase into four equal phrases of eight beats each. Kempul strokes ("P") divide each of the resulting eight-beat kenong phrases in half; the kempul stroke in the first kenong phrase, however, is usually omitted (its absence is called *wela*—"W" in the figure). Note that there are eight beats between each kempul stroke. Kethuk strokes ("T") fall between kenong and kempul strokes (every four beats), and kempyang strokes ("Y") fall on the remaining beats (every two beats).

Each part is absolutely regular—a gong stroke every thirty-two beats, a kenong stroke every eight beats, a kempul stroke (or a wela) every eight beats, a kethuk stroke every four beats, and a kempyang stroke every two beats. A musician could conceivably play his part simply by keeping track of his own pattern—by counting to thirty-two, or eight, or four, or two, depending on his instrument.

It is not just the number of beats in each instrument's phrase that is important, however, but the relationship of each part to the others. Each instrument's regular pattern is offset from the other instrument parts so that the composite pattern formed by all five instruments includes some sort of sound on every beat. The musicians and the listeners hear each beat marked by the sound of one of the instruments; they also hear the sound patterns that emerge as the various instrument timbres interlock; these sound patterns group the beats into larger units of time.

When marked with the varying instrumental timbres of a colotomic form, each moment begins to take on more significance. What started out as a simple pulse—a sequence of undifferentiated beats, each of which is exactly the same as the previous one and the next one—becomes a cluster of unique moments, each of which is palpably more or less accented than the moments that precede and follow it. The hierarchy of sounds transforms the beats into a hierarchy of moments in time that seem to lead inevitably and predictably to the most significant beat (and sound) of all—the beat marked by the visceral sound of the large gong. And then it starts all over again. A key characteristic of Central Javanese forms (and of most gamelan music) is *cyclicity*. The sound of the large gong marks not only the end of one phrase, but the beginning of the next phrase as well. Gamelan pieces typically begin and end with a stroke of the large gong.

Ladrang is only one of several forms that underlie Central Javanese gamelan pieces. Most of the other forms (such as *lancaran*, *ketawang*, and *gendhing*) exhibit the same general characteristics, such as a hierarchy of beats and recurring patterns of sounds, but the details—the number of beats in a phrase, which colotomic instruments are included, the relationship between the various instrumental timbres—are different.

The term *gendhing* has two senses in Central Javanese music; in its most general sense, it refers to any gamelan piece with a cyclical foundation—in other words, it means something similar to the English word "piece." Its more specific meaning refers to large-scale forms with 64, 128, or 256 beats in each phrase marked by a gong stroke. Gendhing have two distinct sections (*merong* and *inggah*), each with its own colotomic form. Sometimes the inggah section of a gendhing is a piece in ladrang form.

Not all Central Javanese gamelan pieces are cast in these regular forms. One important class of such pieces are called *pathetan* or *sulukan*. These pieces have no regular beat, and typically set a mood. Pathetan are instrumental versions of these pieces, which a few of the musicians might perform before or after the performance of a gendhing. Sulukan are the same pieces supplemented with a vocal part that typically is sung by a *dhalang* (puppetmaster) to set a mood or a scene in a theatrical performance. Another set of pieces has regular meter, but their colotomic forms are less symmetrical. These pieces, called *ayak-ayakan*, *sprepegan*, and *sampak*, can be started and stopped on a moment's notice and are quite useful for accompanying action scenes in dramatic performances.

Abstracted melody layer

A large body of Javanese pieces has in common the colotomic forms described above. What distinguishes one piece in ladrang form from all the others is its melodic character. Some Javanese musicians assert that each gamelan piece has its own essential melody that musicians conceptualize, but which is not explicitly played on any of the instruments; rather, this abstract "inner melody," coupled with the musicians' understanding of the idioms of each instrument, guide their choices about exactly what to play. The parts that emerge from this process are derived from the inner melody, but are not the inner melody itself (Sumarsam 1975). Thus, all of the different parts that gamelan musicians play are different manifestations—simultaneous variations—of a single essential melodic outline. Many of the musical traditions examined in previous chapters, notably Toba Batak gondang music, exhibit a similarly abstract approach to melody and variation. Other Javanese musicians, however, point to one particular part, played by several instruments together, as the basic melodic outline for a piece. This part is called *balungan* or *balungan-ing gendhing*, which means literally the "skeleton" of the piece. From this point of view, the other instruments play parts that elaborate upon this basic melodic outline.

Balungan

The balungan part is played on several different instruments. *Saron* is a generic term for a keyed instrument with six or seven keys that covers one octave of either the slendro or pelog tuning system. The saron family of instruments in Central Java includes several sizes, each with a different range. The keys of the large *saron demung* are tuned one octave lower than the corresponding keys of the medium-sized *saron barung*, which are, in turn, one octave lower than those of the small *saron panerus* (also known as *peking*). Many gamelan include two or four instruments of each size. While each instrumentalist has

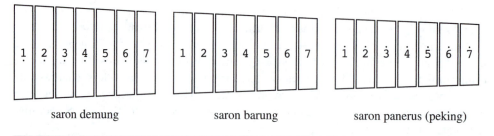

Figure 4.3 Comparison of three sizes of saron.

only one octave's worth of pitches at his or her disposal, taken as a group the three saron sizes cover three full octaves (see Figure 4.3; in the figure, the seven pitches of the pelog tuning system are numbered 1 to 7 from low to high. A dot below the number indicates that the pitch is in the low octave; a dot above the number indicates that the pitch is in the high octave; no dot indicates a pitch in the medium octave). The players of the large and medium-sized saron instruments often perform the balungan part together—each plays exactly the same keys on his or her particular instrument; the result is, of course, that the balungan part is sounded in octaves, because a key on the large saron is an octave lower than the corresponding key on the medium-sized saron. If the essential melody goes beyond the range of an instrument—for example, if it ascends from a 6 up to a 1—the saron demung player simply replaces the pitch that he does not have (in this case, the 1 in the medium range) with a pitch in a different octave that he does have (in this case, 1 an octave below; see Figure 4.4). The saron barung player has the essential melody's 1, but not its low 6; he uses the 6 an octave higher in place of the 6. Although the

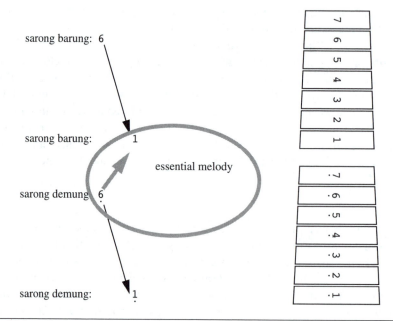

Figure 4.4 Composite of two descending balungan parts.

Y	T	Y	W		Y	T	Y	N
3	2	3	7̣		3	2	7̣	6̣
Y	T	Y	P		Y	T	Y	N
7	6	3	2		5	3	2	7̣
Y	T	Y	P		Y	T	Y	N
3	5	3	2		6	5	3	2
Y	T	Y	P		Y	T	Y	N/G
5	3	2	7̣		3	2	7̣	6̣

Figure 4.5 Ladrang "Pangkur."

contour of the essential melody is ascending in pitch (from 6 to 1), each of the instrumentalists plays a descending melody (6 down to 1̣ or 6 down to 1) instead. Because the
parts are doubled at the octave, however, listeners can hear the "correct" melodic contour
emerging from the combination of the two parts—in this case, the saron demung's 6̣ followed by the saron barung's 1 (see the circled "essential" melody in Figure 4.4).

It is tempting to think of the balungan of a piece as the essential melody itself. When
Javanese gamelan music is notated, it is typically the balungan (along with indications
about when to play the colotomic instruments) that gets written down. Many musicians,
especially those trained in the government conservatories, can extemporize parts for
all the other instruments given the balungan part. It is clear from the above discussion,
however, that the balungan parts do not do complete justice to a very significant aspect
of a piece's essential melody—namely, its overall contour (when it goes high and when
it goes low). With regard to rhythm, the balungan part is typically quite regular; that is,
there is a single note for each beat of the colotomic cycle. Some musicians and theorists
group these notes into four-note groupings, called *gatra*. The rhythmic accent of a four-
note grouping falls on the fourth and final note. In other words, a Javanese musician
would count the beats of a four-note grouping as 1–2–3–**4**, with the emphasis on count
4. This represents a significant contrast with most Western musicians, who would place
the emphasis resulting in ascending essential melody on count 1 (**1**–2–3–4). The "end
accent" is further emphasized by the sounding on the four-note grouping's fourth beat of
whichever colotomic marker is most significant in that grouping.

The balungan part illustrated in Figure 4.5 is that of a piece in ladrang form titled
"Pangkur." In this notation, the letter abbreviations for the colotomic parts are provided
on one line; the pitch numbers of the balungan are provided immediately below. Notice
that each note coincides with one of the instrumental timbres of the foundation part.
The melody notes are grouped into four-note groupings; because ladrang is a thirty-two-
beat form, there are a total of eight four-note groupings (two on each line in the figure).

Of course, the balungan instruments, with their one-octave ranges, would not play the notes exactly as notated here. The second four-note grouping of the piece, for example, has a descending melodic contour (3 2 7 6). The player of a balungan instrument, however, would have to ascend from 2 to the (higher) 7 above it, rather than descend from 2 to a (lower) 7; if one heard "Pankgur" performed only on a saron, its melodic contour would differ significantly from the "essential" version. In the recorded excerpt of "Pangkur" on the CD that accompanies this book (Track 4), the balungan part as notated in Figure 4.5 is especially easy to hear when the musicians play it fairly quickly for *kebar* style (2:46–4:34).

Javanese tuning systems revisited

It is difficult to get the sound of a notated balungan melody in one's ear without some practical acquaintance with Javanese tuning systems. This version of "Pangkur" is set in the pelog tuning system, which has seven pitches per octave. As we have seen, it is possible to internalize a crude approximation of how the pelog tuning system sounds by comparing it to a piano's diatonic ("white-key") scale or by using traditional *do re mi fa sol la ti do*. One way to match the solfège syllables with the Javanese numbers is illustrated in Figure 4.6. Remember, however, that this represents a very crude approximation. Another way is to listen to the seven-pitch pelog scale played in Track 3 of the CD that accompanies this book, mentally mapping the Javanese numbers illustrated in Figure 4.6 with the pitches on the CD.

The basic melody for "Pangkur" includes no 1 or 4 pitches; most pelog melodies do not use all seven pitches that the pelog tuning provides; rather, they make use of one of two five-pitch subsets of the pelog tuning system. Sometimes one (or both) of the extraneous two pitches emerge in a piece to provide additional melodic flavor, much in the way that the piano's black keys provide chromatic flavor in Western music in the key of "C." The version of "Pangkur" notated in Figure 4.5 uses the five-pitch subset of pelog consisting of 7–6–5–3–2 (singing the descending melodic line *sol–fa–mi–do–ti* would approximate this scale). The intervals between the five pitches vary from very small to very large. For example, the interval between 6 and 5 is very small (*fa–mi*; similar to what Western musicians might call a "half-step" or a "minor second," about 100 cents), while the interval between 5 and 3, on the other hand, is quite large (*mi–do*; similar to what Western musicians might call a major third, or 400 cents).

The slendro tuning system, like the subset of the pelog tuning system described above, includes five pitches. The intervals between slendro pitches, however, are all about the same size—neither very small nor very large. Slendro is even more difficult to compare to piano keys than pelog because the medium-sized interval that characterizes slendro is equivalent to approximately two-and-a-half piano keys (about 240 cents); in other words, slendro pitches lie somewhere "in the cracks" between piano keys.

C	D	E	F	G	A	B	C
do	re	mi	fa	sol	la	ti	do
3	4	5	6	7	1	2	3

Figure 4.6 Correspondence of pelog with solfège syllables.

slendro	3	2	3	1		3	2	1	6̣
pelog	3	2	3	7̣		3	2	7̣	6̣

slendro	1̇	6	3	2		5	3	2	1
pelog	7	6	3	2		5	3	2	7̣

slendro	3	5	3	2		6	5	3	2
pelog	3	5	3	2		6	5	3	2

slendro	5	3	2	1		3	2	1	6̣
pelog	5	3	2	7̣		3	2	7̣	6̣

Figure 4.7 Ladrang "Pangkur" in slendro.

Some Central Javanese pieces, including "Pangkur," can be performed using either slendro or pelog. The melodic contours stay the same, but the actual pitches change because of the differences between the tuning systems (even if the 6 is the same in pelog and slendro, the 5 will be quite different). To transpose the version of "Pangkur" notated in Figure 4.5 into slendro, all the 7s are changed into 1s (remember that there are no 7s in slendro; see Figure 4.7). Although this transformation changes significantly the melodic contour of each saron player's part—in pelog, the saron part jumps all over the place to hit the 7s, while in the slendro version the part is relatively conjunct—the overall melodic contour that emerges when all the saron-type instruments play together is more or less the same in both tuning systems.

Elaborated melody layer

The parts played by some elaborating instruments are quite closely related to the balungan. The player of the highest-pitched member of the saron family, the *saron panerus*, for example, might choose to perform a part that is the same as the balungan except that each note is played twice and lasts half as long as the balungan part, as illustrated for the first two four-note groupings of "Pangkur" in Figure 4.8. Many of the instruments that play elaborated melody parts have ranges larger than a single octave (unlike the saron); players of these parts attempt to preserve the contour of the "essential" melody. The parts generally are faster and/or more varied rhythmically than the balungan part as well.

saron panerus	3	3	2	2	3	3	7	7	3	3	2	2	7	7	6
balungan	3		2		3		7		3		2		7		6

Figure 4.8 Saron panerus elaboration pattern for ladrang "Pangkur."

Bonang

Bonang is a gong chime with a two-octave range. In modern Central Javanese gamelan, a bonang consists of two rows of small gongs laid over ropes in a frame. Each of the two rows includes one octave's worth of gongs. As was the case with saron, bonang is a generic name for a family of instruments. In most Central Javanese gamelan, there are two members of the bonang family: the lower-pitched *bonang barung* and the higher-pitched *bonang panerus*. There is some overlap in these two instruments' ranges; the upper octave of the bonang barung is in the same range as the lower octave of the bonang panerus.

In contrast to the keys of a saron, which are laid out systematically from low to high (from the player's point of view), the bonang pots are not in numerical order, but rather arranged to make playing the five-pitch subsets of pelog a bit easier. Figure 4.9 depicts the arrangements of the pots from above (imagine that the player sits just below the pot labeled 3 in the figure). The pitches that are not used in the 7–6–5–3–2 subset are placed at the far ends of the instrument, so that the player need not reach too far for the pitches that will be used most frequently. The pots are not permanently attached to the frame, so the musician can rearrange them to facilitate playing another five-pitch subset.

Like the saron panerus part described above, a possible bonang barung part involves playing twice as many notes as the balungan. Instead of simply repeating each note twice, however, the bonang idiom involves a slightly more complicated process. Instead of elaborating a single note at a time, the bonang player elaborates a pair of notes at a time. The first two notes of "Pankgur" are 3 and 2; the bonang player takes those two notes and plays the pair twice: 3–2–3–2. Figure 4.10 shows a fragment of the bonang barung part for "Pangkur." As a general rule, the higher the pitch (and smaller the size) of an instrument, the faster its part will be. The bonang panerus, smaller and higher-pitched than the bonang barung, plays a part that is similar to the bonang barung's, but which has twice as many notes. To accomplish this, the bonang panerus player takes each pair of notes and plays it four times, at times replacing some of the notes with rests (indicated in the notation with a dot; see Figure 4.11).

Figure 4.12 lays out all of the parts discussed above in a graphic form. In the graph, the Y-axis represents pitch and the X-axis represents time. Each instrument's part is represented by a different shade of gray. The figure demonstrates how the saron-family

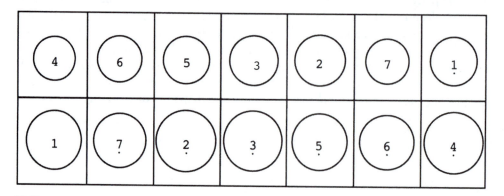

Figure 4.9 Arrangement of Central Javanese pelog bonang kettles.

bonang barung	3 2	3 2	3 7̣	3 7̣	3 2	3 2	7̣ 6̣	7̣ 6̣
balungan	3	2	3	7	3	2	7	6

Figure 4.10 Bonang barung elaboration pattern for ladrang "Pangkur."

bonang panerus	3̇2̇3̇.	3̇2̇3̇2̇	3̇7̇3̇.	3̇7̇3̇7̇	3̇2̇3̇.	3̇2̇3̇2̇	767.	7676
bonang barung	3 2	3 2	3 7̣	3 7̣	3 2	3 2	7̣ 6̣	7̣ 6̣
balungan	3	2	3	7	3	2	7	6

Figure 4.11 Bonang panerus elaboration pattern for ladrang "Pangkur."

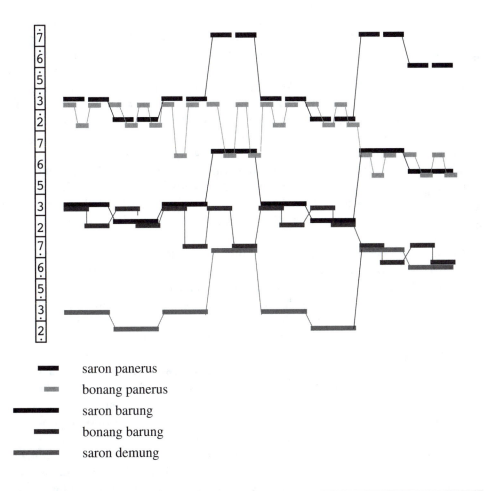

saron panerus
bonang panerus
saron barung
bonang barung
saron demung

Figure 4.12 Stratification of balungan and elaborating parts for "Pangkur."

instruments provide a "skeleton" of melody—the balungan—which the bonang-family parts "flesh out" by adding melodies that not only fill in the spaces suggested by the skeleton, but provide something like "connective tissue" that ties the skeleton parts together.

This graphic representation also illustrates why the word stratification describes the musical texture of gamelan music. Each part has a predictable density—a different number of notes per minute (represented in the figure as a series of thick lines)—as well as a unique timbre (represented in the figure as a distinctive style of shading); thus, each part creates a distinct stratum that remains distinct even as it mixes and crosses the other parts (see Hood 1980: 166–7).

Gender

Another important "family" of musical instruments in Central Javanese gamelan is the *gender* family. In general, the term gender refers to a keyed instrument with keys much thinner than those of a saron-family instrument. These thin keys are suspended in air with cords rather than merely laid on a frame; as a result, the keys can vibrate more freely than the keys of saron-family instruments. Each gender key has its own resonating tube, which is tuned to the pitch of its corresponding key in such a way that it artificially prolongs the length of time that the key vibrates. Musicians play Central Javanese gender with very soft mallets; the combination of the soft attack and the long sustain makes the sound of a gender-family instrument more reminiscent of an organ than a bronze percussion instrument.

The largest member of the gender family, usually called *slenthem*, has six or seven keys; musicians typically play the balungan on the slenthem, using a playing technique that is essentially the same as saron technique. The slenthem's range is one octave lower than that of the saron demung (and, in fact, it is the lowest-pitched melodic instrument in a Central Javanese gamelan ensemble); it adds yet another shade of definition to the balungan part.

The other two members of the gender family, the lower-pitched gender barung and the higher-pitched gender panerus, have fourteen keys each covering three octaves. The gender tuned to pelog include only five of the seven pelog pitches; that is, they are set up to represent one of the five-pitch pelog subsets. For this reason, there typically are two pelog gender barung included in a set of gamelan instruments; one tuned to the 7–6–5–3–2 subset and the other tuned to 6–5–3–2–1. There are likewise two pelog gender panerus.

Unlike a saron player, who hits the keys with a single mallet held in his right hand and damps the sound of the keys by pinching them with his left hand, a gender player holds a mallet in each hand and plays two semi-independent melodic lines, one with each hand. The same hand that plays a key is also responsible for damping the key. Gender players use their understanding of a piece's essential melody to put together a part composed of stock phrases. The stock phrases themselves are often called *cengkok*. The word cengkok can mean "melodic pattern," "melody," "melodic style," or even the "process of melodic movement" (Sumarsam 1995: 230–1). One way gender barung players might conceive of a particular stock phrase is to think of it as an idiomatic way (that is, a *gender*-specific way) to get from one important place in a melody to the next. They may know several equally appropriate ways to get there, or they may decide that one way is more appropriate than the others. They may also decide to add or subtract a few notes, vary the rhythm, or otherwise modify the part to suit the character of the piece or the mood of the moment.

One consideration that gender players take into account in creating their parts for a particular piece is the piece's *pathet*. Pathet refers to a Javanese musical system in which the different notes in a tuning system (or five-pitch subset) have different emphases. Most listeners accustomed to the conventions of Western music are aware that some notes feel more stable than others. Try humming the "Happy Birthday" song, but leave off the last note (the note that coincides with the song's very last "you"); the melody sounds as if it has been left up in the air. That last note in the melody is the "home base" (called a *tonic*) of the musical system in which "Happy Birthday" is cast (the musical system is conventionally called a *major key* or *major mode*). The note that sounds up in the air is one of the pitches that is de-emphasized in the major mode; that is why it sounds incomplete to end there. The general term for musical systems of this kind is *mode*.

There are three slendro pathet, all of which make use of the same five slendro pitches; the difference between the pathet is the musical emphasis (or de-emphasis) assigned to each of the five slendro pitches. In other words, some pitches are made to sound more stable than other pitches; a pitch sounds more stable if it occurs consistently at the most rhythmically important spots such as the ends of phrases. A pitch becomes less stable-sounding if it is avoided at these spots. In *pathet manyura*, the pitches 6 and 2 feel the most stable, while pitch 5 is the least stable. In *pathet sanga*, in contrast, pitches 5 and 1 are the most stable, while pitch 3 is the least stable. The third slendro pathet, *pathet nem*, like pathet manyura, makes 6 and 2 feel stable; pitch 1 (rather than pitch 5) is the least stable in pathet nem, however.

There are also three pelog pathet, each of which includes five main pitches, which are selected from the seven available pelog pitches. The five main pitches for *pathet barang* are 7-6-5-3-2 (omitting 4 and 1). The five main pitches for *pathet lima* are 6-5-3-2-1 (omitting 7 and 4); the five main pitches for *pathet nem* also are 6-5-3-2-1. In pathet lima, pitch 4 is sometimes used as an alternative note to pitch 3; in pathet nem, pitch 4 is an alternative to pitch 5. The pelog pathet also emphasize certain pitches within their five-pitch subsets and destabilize others.

The word pathet, in Javanese, means "to restrain" (Lindsay 1979: 25), suggesting that pathet is a means for limiting and constraining the choices that musicians make. The different pathet also have different moods and feelings associated with them. Modal systems throughout the world associate particular moods and feelings with different modes. When hearing conventional Western music, for example, competent listeners tend to hear a song cast in the major mode (such as "Happy Birthday") as "happy." Songs cast in minor modes (such as Chopin's famous "Funeral March," for example) are generally perceived as "sad." (For an extremely melancholy experience, try recasting "Happy Birthday" in the minor mode.) The emotional moods evoked by the Western modal system are, of course, not nearly so cut-and-dried as "happy" and "sad"; there is no doubt, however, that the extramusical content of modal systems is quite powerful for listeners.

These extramusical associations are particularly important when gamelan music accompanies *wayang kulit* (shadow puppet theater). Wayang kulit performances feature an enormous cast of puppet characters cut out of buffalo hide, carved with intricate patterns and painted with bright colors, mounted on a stick. All of the puppets are manipulated by a single puppeteer, called a *dhalang*, who also provides all the voices and narration, sings the *pathetan* (mood songs), and gives the gamelan cues. The dhalang puts the puppets against a translucent cloth screen, on which an oil lamp (or, more typically in modern Central Java, an electric light bulb) is shining. When viewed from the other side of the screen, the puppets cast evocative shadows that help bring a sense of life to the show. The performance can be viewed from either side of the screen. Wayang kulit performances typically last all night; the dhalang extemporizes the details of the story based on a general outline he has mastered, much in the same way a Cirebonese dalang topeng crafts a unique dance choreography each time he or she performs.

In a wayang kulit performance, each pathet is associated with a different portion of these all-night performances. Slendro pathet nem pieces dominate the first third of the performance (from about 9 p.m. until midnight) and impart a sense of impending and growing tension. Slendro pathet sanga pieces accompany the scenes from the middle part of the performance and give them a profound, sometimes even peaceful, feeling. The action and excitement picks up in the last part of the show (about 3 a.m. until dawn), partly because of the feelings and moods associated with the pieces in slendro pathet manyura which accompany this part of the performance. Gender players know many pathet-specific patterns, which they deploy with an understanding of the extramusical feelings that different pathet impart to listeners. In wayang performances, the gender player constantly plays pathet-specific phrases, called *grimingan*, in the background even when the other musicians are silent. This "noodling" keeps the pathet—and thus the mood—in everybody's mind as the show progresses.

Vocal parts

Central Javanese gamelan music often includes singers. At times, an unaccompanied male vocalist sings a long, unaccompanied, virtuosic introduction, called *bawa*, to a gamelan composition. More typically, however, a group of men, called *gerong*, sings as a chorus in unison. Much Javanese music also features a female vocalist called *pesind-hen*. Although there may be several pesindhen performing with the group, usually only one sings at any given time. The parts played on bronze gamelan instruments, in keeping with the idiom of struck percussion instruments, tend to be melodically straightforward and rhythmically regular. The sung parts, in contrast, exhibit a kind of rhythmic freedom and melodic floridity that would be difficult to imitate on percussion instruments. Even the men's choral parts, which are the least florid vocal parts (in part to facilitate singing them together as a group), seem to float on top of the percussive texture of the bronze gamelan instruments like rushing water swirling around a rocky streambed.

The words that the pesindhen and gerong sing are very often stock poems that can be sung with many different gamelan pieces. Traditional Javanese poetry, called *tembang*, is always sung rather than recited. Different poetic forms have specific melodies associated with them. The piece described above, ladrang "Pangkur," actually shares a name with a Javanese poetic form (*pangkur*); a singer who wants to perform a poem cast in the pangkur form fits the words and lines of the poem to a standard pangkur melody that she already knows. Because the poetic forms specify the number of lines in each verse, as well as the number of syllables in each line, singers can use a single melody to set any poem cast in that form. The essential melody of "ladrang Pangkur," like other Central Javanese pieces with names that reference poetic forms, may be somehow derived from one of these stock melodies for reciting poetry (Sumarsam 1995: 205–11); the texts set to "Pangkur," however, are often in different poetic forms. The version of the balungan for "Pangkur" that is notated in Figures 4.5 and 4.7 doesn't provide enough musical "space" for an entire verse of poetry in the pankgur form; instead, the singers use stock texts in another form called *salisir*. Salisir verses are a sort of riddle in which the first two lines give clues to "mystery" words, and the second two lines somehow play with the "mystery" words suggested by the first two lines to express a moral, a lesson, or an adage. For example, a commonly sung salisir verse is:

> Parabe sang smarabangun
> sepat domba kali Oya
> aja dolan lan wong priya
> geremeh nora prasaja

The first line alludes to an historical Javanese prince whose name, knowledgeable listeners will know, was Priyambada, while the second line means "a fish in the Oya river," which suggests the delicious *gurameh* fish. Priyambada and gurameh do not have much to do with one another; they are simply the "mystery" words that provide the raw subject material for the third and fourth lines of the verse. The third line means "don't play around with men"—the word *priya* (Javanese for "men") recalls the name "Priyambada" to which the first line alluded. The final line means "chattering without thinking"—the word *geremeh* recalls the word gurameh alluded to in the second line (Hatch 1997). There's another level of playfulness in this verse as well: The image of a big fish, in conjunction with the word for "man," can be interpreted as a slightly indelicate allusion to the male anatomy (Hood and Susilo 1967: 35). Javanese listeners not only take delight in the clever ways that salisir verses connect seemingly unrelated words, they also appreciate the sound advice (to keep one's head when flirting with the opposite sex, in this case) that they provide, not to mention the subtly naughty allusions they sometimes make.

Other elaborating instruments

Other elaborating instruments in Central Javanese gamelan include *rebab*, *suling*, *gambang*, and *celempung/siter*. *Rebab* is a bowed string instrument with two strings. Its body is made from half a coconut shell over which a thin animal skin is stretched. A long rod pierces the coconut; one end of the rod serves as a neck, while the other end provides a peg that the player can rest on the floor. Two strings are attached to large tuning pegs at the top of the neck, stretched over a bridge that rests on the skin, and fixed to the floor peg. The player bows the strings with a horsehair bow.

    Suling is a bamboo flute with four or five holes. Players typically use separate flutes for slendro and pelog. Like a singer, a suling player times his phrases so that their ends coincide with rhythmically important musical events such as kenong and gong strokes.

Gambang is a xylophone with eighteen to twenty-one wooden keys. Like gender, gambang is played with two mallets; because the keys are made of wood, however, their sound does not sustain and thus they require no damping. Gambang players typically perform very fast melodic patterns.

Celempung is a zither with metal strings, which the player plucks with his thumbnails. There are two strings for each pitch, tuned the same and placed so close together that the player treats the pair of strings as if it were a single string. A typical celempung has about twelve pairs of strings. The celempung idiom is similar to that of the gender panerus.

Drumming

Court-style Central Javanese gamelan ensembles include a variety of different drums. Like Cirebonese gamelan sekaten, Central Javanese ensembles often include a *bedug*—a large, barrel-shaped drum with skin heads attached to each end with large wooden pegs. When a musician hits one of the heads with a padded stick, it produces a very deep and booming sound. Bedug parts are usually quite sparse. Most of the drumming is provided by a different drummer, who has several different drums and styles at his disposal. These drums are generically called *kendhang*.

Kendhang are also two-headed barrel-shaped drums; their skin heads, however, are secured over the ends of the drum's body by a system of rawhide laces, and can be tuned by tightening or loosening the lacings. One head is always larger (and consequently lower-pitched) than the other. Kendhang players position the drum so that they can play one head with each hand. Although a drummer may occasionally use a stick, most kendhang playing exploits the different timbres and techniques that only bare hands can produce.

The drummer plays the most basic drumming patterns on two kendhang: a very large one called *kendhang gendhing*, supplemented by a small one called *ketipung*. Together, this pair is known as *kendhang kalih* ("two drums"). The large drum rests on a stand in front of the drummer, and the small drum rests in the drummer's lap (or on a second small stand) between the drummer and the large drum. The larger, lower-pitched heads are at the drummer's right.

The basic drum parts played on this pair of drums make use of only a few very simple drum strokes, which are sometimes given onomatopoeic names. The drummer plays the two main strokes with his right hand: *pung*—a high-pitched, ringing sound produced by hitting the ketipung with the forefinger; and *dung*—a low-pitched, booming sound produced by hitting the kendhang gendhing with the palm of the hand. He plays the remaining strokes with his left hand: *tak*—a sharp, crisp sound produced by slapping the ketipung with the palm and fingers; and *keteg*—a gentle, barely audible tap on the ketipung.

Many of the colotomic forms of Javanese gamelan music have specific kendhang kalih patterns associated with them. Kendang kalih drum parts are not particularly prominent in the rich texture of gamelan music, but all the other musicians pay close attention to them because subtle signals can be embedded within the patterns. Signals take the form of unobtrusive alterations to the "business as usual" patterns and let the other musicians know that the end of the piece, or a change in tempo, or some other adjustment is imminent.

Most Javanese gamelan include another drum as well, called *ciblon* or *batangan*, played by the same drummer as the pair of drums described above. In size, it is between the pair's large drum and small drum. Ciblon drumming involves a great many more hand techniques and sounds and moves much more quickly than kendhang kalih parts. The name "ciblon" comes from a musical game played in the water, in which participants slap the water's surface to make pleasing sounds; a group of participants can amuse themselves by creating complex interlocking patterns with these sounds. The ciblon drum's rapid sequence of a variety of percussive sounds is reminiscent of the water game. Ciblon drumming is associated with the accompaniment of movement, whether it be dance or puppet manipulation. This movement-oriented style of drumming is commonly included in strictly instrumental performances as well, however, especially in more modern styles where the excitement and vitality of the ciblon drum patterns add a contemporary flavor to the music.

Modern influences in Central Javanese gamelan music

It often surprises Westerners who hear gamelan music for the first time to learn that its practitioners and patrons often had close dealings with Western colonial officials and Western music. Why, they may ask, is there not more Western influence in gamelan music? The answer is that there is indeed a great deal of Western influence in Central Javanese gamelan music; it is not, however, so much evident in the sound of the music as it is in the cultural trappings and intellectual discourses that surround gamelan music. The Javanese ethnomusicologist Sumarsam (himself an accomplished gamelan musician) points out that the notions of "high culture" and "fine art" are Western ideas that have insinuated themselves into Central Javanese court gamelan music. He further suggests that the twentieth-century fascination with notating gamelan pieces and the rise in emphasis on the balungan part as the essential melody are also artifacts of Western influence. In incorporating these ideas into gamelan music, however, the overall structure of gamelan music and the sounds of gamelan instruments did not change appreciably; once again, gamelan proves to be an extremely flexible forum for combining old and new ideas.

The golden age of gamelan music in the kraton was the end of the nineteenth and the beginning of the twentieth centuries. The various sultans and princes had the financial resources at their disposal to support the arts in an extravagant way. Hubert Stowitts described a three-day performance in Yogyakarta that involved 400 dancers and four combined orchestras (Stowitts 1930: 703); such a massive production was hardly unusual. The kraton maintained a large coterie of musicians, who were organized into various ranks and classifications based on their seniority and abilities. A few of the highest-ranked musicians could even be promoted into the aristocracy.

Kraton performances were held in large pavilions with massive roofs but no walls, called *pendopo*. The high roof, the marble floors, and the breezes kept the pavilions pleasantly cool; their sumptuous decorations, including intricate wood carving and crystal chandeliers, provide an elegant setting for the Javanese nobility's grand artistic productions. The architecture also contributed to the gamelan's sonic effect; the hard floors and cavernous ceiling added a subtle natural reverberation to the sound, while the open sides kept the volume in check. These pavilions often were connected to the verandas of the kraton buildings, enabling members of the royal family to make grand entrances.

One of the legacies of this period was the modern instrumentation of Central Javanese gamelan that combines the "loud" and "soft" ensembles into one large, coordinated
orchestra. Combining these two different approaches to music-making in Central Javanese gamelan music was perhaps a way of modeling the changes of the modern world
in a way that reconciles modern ways with old Hindu-Javanese notions of the universe.
Layering linear musical approaches on top of the cyclical, colotomic foundations of
Central Javanese gamelan music is perhaps a way of legitimating old Javanese systems
of power in a new world. By refining the differences between court music and village
music, the sultans invented something that conformed to European ideals of "fine art" to
maintain their aura of power and prestige under changing circumstances. Subordinating
music that "goes somewhere," such as sung poetry, to fixed colotomic forms that model
the Hindu-Javanese universe's steady state, extols the divine right of rulers to rule and
the persistence of old ideals in the modern world.

World War II and the Japanese occupation of Java brought significant hardships to
Javanese of all social classes. After the war, the kraton continued their patronage of the
court performing arts, but not on anywhere near the same scale as before. The new Indonesian national government, however, stepped in to sponsor Javanese performing arts.
These more recent government-sponsored developments in Javanese gamelan music
continue the trend of modeling social ideals in musical aesthetics. The national radio
station, Radio Republik Indonesia (RRI), promulgated one particular style of court
music (from the Kraton Surakarta) in its broadcasts throughout Java. Musicians from
outside the courts had the opportunity to hear and emulate this refined style as never
before. The RRI musicians made influential recordings that amplified the effect. The
government-run conservatories of music systematized and standardized much of the
lore that surrounds Central Javanese gamelan music, reflecting the processes of standardization and bureaucracy that characterize the Indonesian government's approach to
ruling the country. New gamelan compositions from conservatory-trained composers
often de-emphasize cyclic underlying structures, mirroring the government's position as
a nation in the modern world and relegating the old-fashioned Javanese notions of the
cosmos and kingship to the background.

Since the 1980s, a popular form of Javanese music called *campur sari* (which means
something like "mixing essences") involved a self-conscious combination of Western
musical instruments and approaches with gamelan instruments, sounds, and processes.
The first campur sari experiments in the 1960s involved combining gamelan with old-
fashioned Indonesian *kroncong* (a musical genre characterized by gamelan-like textures
played on Western-derived string instruments such as guitar, mandolins, and cellos in
conventional Western diatonic tunings). More recently campur sari bands have added
elements of other popular Indonesian musics as well as instruments such as saxo-
phones, Latin percussion, and electronic synthesizers. According to Rahayu Supanggah,
Western instruments in campur sari ensembles—especially electronic keyboards—lend
the ensembles a distinctly "modern" image and sound that many Javanese listeners find
desirable (Supanggah 2003: 7). Layering these sonic and visual symbols of technology
and modernity on top of old-fashioned musical ensembles provides Javanese audiences
with a vehicle for coming to grips with the rapidly changing society in which they live.

At some level, all of these Javanese innovations represent attempts to reconcile and merge Javanese ideals, as symbolized by bronze gamelan, with other, outside concepts. It is not only in the realm of music that the past merges with the present; in twenty-first-century Yogyakarta, for example, the reigning Sultan (Hamengku Buwono X) is the governor of the province, while the prince of that city's second kraton (Paku Alam IX) is the vice governor; in Java, the charisma and authority these men acquired by virtue of their status as the hereditary leaders of mandala states translates quite sensibly to a modern democratic system of government (K. Purba 2003). If we remember that many "Javanese" ideals themselves bear the unmistakable stamp of previous Hindu and Islamic influences, it becomes clear that the evolution of Central Javanese music is a replication in miniature of the layers of influence that characterize Javanese society past, present, and future.

Eastern Java

The spread of the Kraton Surakarta's style of gamelan music after World War II affected the kinds of gamelan music heard in the eastern part of Java as well. Although the majority of Eastern Java's residents speak the Javanese language, much of Eastern Java lay beyond the mandala circle of intense influence from the Central Javanese courts. So, even those areas that are ethnically Javanese maintained their own unique regional styles of gamelan music; musicians in some of these regions still cultivated their regional styles alongside the more national Solonese style.

Except for a few minor differences in instrumentation and instrument construction, Eastern Javanese gamelan are quite similar to the court gamelan of Central Java. The repertory of pieces is quite different, however, as are the elaboration techniques that the various instrumentalists use to generate their parts. The parts played on the bonang in Eastern Javanese style are particularly distinct. The drumming, too, sounds quite different. As was the case for gamelan music for Central Javanese wayang kulit (shadow puppet performances), Eastern Javanese wayang music features several pathet (melodic modes) to help set the appropriate mood for the different sections of the performance. The actual pathet system, however, is quite different from the Central Javanese version; Eastern Javanese musicians have different names for their pathet, which have different musical characteristics and are associated with different time periods (Sutton 1991).

One peculiarly Eastern Javanese genre that continues to be especially popular in the region is a theatrical form called *ludruk*. Ludruk casts are all male; some of the actors specialize in convincing transvestite performances. The stories they enact are of historical or topical interest (Sutton 1999). The signature music of ludruk is provided by a slendro gamelan on which the musicians play a uniquely Eastern Javanese repertory; music accompanies an opening dance (called *ngremo*), the characters' entrances and exits, and vocal interludes. The opening dance by itself has taken on the status of symbol of Eastern Javaneseness; just the sound of the accompaniment is enough to conjure the region's separate identity (Sutton 1991).

Eastern Javanese gamelan style makes considerable use of a musical process that is quite common throughout Java and Bali. One way to elaborate or expand a melody is to insert a new note between each of the melody's existing notes; when the inserted note is the same each time, musicians call it a *pancer*. In some Eastern Javanese gamelan

essential melody				3				2				3				5
a: pancer			6	3	6			2	6			3	6			5
b: double pancer	6		6	3	6		6	2	6		6	3	6		6	5

Figure 4.13 Pancer transformation in Eastern Javanese gamelan.

pieces, an essential melody goes through several different transformations, each of which involves the saron players adding a different pancer treatment. Figure 4.13 shows two Eastern Javanese pancer transformations. The first version involves simply inserting a pancer note between the melody's essential notes (see Figure 4.13a); this process lengthens the melody without completely altering its melodic character. A second transformation, called a double pancer (see Figure 4.13b), extends the melody even further; it also lends a new rhythmic twist to the melody. Of course, the other instrumentalists must meet the challenge of coming up with elaborating parts that are suitably long to match the extended melodies (Sutton 1991: 151).

Not all of Eastern Java is populated by Javanese speakers; a few enclaves speak other languages or distinct dialects and maintain cultural traditions quite removed from the mainstream Javanese. One such group is the Osing, from the Banyuwangi area at the far eastern end of the island. The Osing trace their history to the Blambangan kingdom, which was part of the Hindu-Javanese Majapahit empire in the fourteenth century; until well into the twentieth century, the Osing endeavored to maintain a separate identity from the Mataram-influenced Javanese and identified more closely with the Hindu culture of Bali (close at hand across a narrow strait).

One contemporary Osing genre which has gained considerable renown throughout Java is called *gandrung*. Gandrung performances usually last all night; they feature a young, unmarried female singer-dancer, called a *gandrung*, who dances with male guests for a fee. The ensemble which accompanies the singing and dancing includes gongs and gong chimes, drums, as well as a pair of violins, which provide the usual four functional layers of sound. One gandrung instrument—a metal triangle (called *kluncing*) similar to the instrument popular in classroom rhythm bands—is unique to the region (Wolbers 1986).

Regional Javanese styles and genres, such as Cirebonese topeng, Central Javanese court-style gamelan, and the Osing gandrung, are reminders that musical traditions in Indonesia are quite varied in instrumentation, sound, and function, yet they do indeed share many fundamental characteristics and musical processes. Many of the perceived differences in these traditions can be related to the unique historical, political, religious, and social environment of the people who make and consume music; the underlying musical processes produce different results depending on the circumstances in which they are put into practice.

Bali

The tiny island of Bali shares much with Java, its larger neighbor to the west; the two islands are intertwined in history. Many of the underlying musical processes that drive Javanese musical traditions are also evident in Balinese music; yet, Balinese music sounds quite different from most Javanese music, even to uninitiated listeners. Once again, the distinctions stem from the different historical and social circumstances of the Balinese population.

Well over a thousand years ago, the Balinese had already built a society firmly grounded in the principle of mutual cooperation. Early Balinese deified the spirits of the rice that they cultivated and the water that made it grow, and developed complex cycles of rituals synchronized with agricultural cycles. Maximizing the production of rice required the careful monitoring of the flow of irrigation water as it moved from the high mountain lakes, down through the various farming communities, and finally to the sea, as well as the coordination of the different communities' planting cycles. The Balinese made these cooperative efforts a matter of faith by entrusting the administration of the irrigation systems and planting cycles to priests who maintained a complex network of water temples; even in the twenty-first century these priests and temples are an integral part of Balinese agriculture (Lansing 1995). At the same time, each family unit honored its own ancestors and cooperated with its immediate neighbors to make the local community run smoothly.

Indian philosophical ideas of the universe's cosmic cycles, the central authority of god-kings, and the influence of a spirit world on the world of humans gradually were grafted onto existing Balinese cosmological thought as they were brought there by Javanese immigrants late in the first millennium. These religious concepts complemented existing Balinese beliefs, and over the centuries the uniquely Balinese religion emerged, tinged with Hinduism, with multiple ritual cycles to honor ancestors and local spirits, to control community life and agriculture, and to encourage mutual cooperation and social balance. Ritual activities were centered in the many temples that dotted the Balinese landscape, and involved artistic activities of all kinds, including the making of beautiful offerings as well as performances of music, dance, and theater.

Residents of Bali resisted the influx of Islam that swept through Java and other islands in the archipelago and maintained their own religious practices. Some Hindu Majapahit princes from Java who chose to resist Islam found refuge in Bali as early as the thirteenth century (Tenzer 1991: 21), and brought with them into exile their retinues, including musicians, dancers, and other artists. Eventually the Javanese aristocrats (and artists) were incorporated into the highest classes of an increasingly stratified Balinese society (Belo 1970: xiv; Toth 1975: 65; Wright 1978: 6). In keeping with the Hindu-Javanese model of kingship, Balinese royal courts became centers of musical patronage and sponsored the development of a variety of new musical forms to exhibit their wealth and legitimize their high status.

Bali remained isolated from the rest of the world until the Dutch finally took over by force in 1908. Dutch conquest weakened and eventually eliminated the power and influence of the Balinese kings. The Balinese spirit of cooperation, grounded in faith and agriculture, however, had remained strong throughout the centuries, and provided a solid basis for a vibrant Balinese performing arts scene even in the absence of royal patronage. In the twentieth century, Balinese community organizations assumed collective control of the performing arts; once again, the spirit of cooperation provided a solid grounding for a uniquely Balinese culture and enabled the Balinese to adjust to changing circumstances. Balinese scholars sometimes organize the many Balinese musical ensembles that make up the contemporary Balinese music scene into three categories that correspond roughly to the three broad historical periods described above. The ensembles thought to belong to the old (*tua*) period (before the fall of Majapahit and the advent of powerful Balinese Hindu courts) are relatively small and emphasize metal or wood percussion instruments. The middle (*madya*) group includes a variety of large ensembles with drums and gongs that first developed in the royal households. The new (*baru*) ensembles include the various innovations that characterize twentieth-century Balinese music in the post-Dutch period.

Given this history, it may be tempting to think that Balinese music is what Cirebonese or Central Javanese music might have become without the influence of Islam or the West; of course, the development of musical styles is never so simple. It is difficult to determine the exact historical details of if, how, and why Javanese gamelan ensembles were incorporated into the lives of Balinese. Perhaps it is more fruitful to examine instead why Balinese performers and audiences, starting with the same raw materials and models as their Javanese compatriots, have developed such startlingly dissimilar musical ensembles, genres, and styles.

Old period: Gong luang

A few communities in Bali maintain a type of gamelan that is strikingly similar to gamelan sekaten, called *gong luang* (in Bali, the word gong often refers to an ensemble made up primarily of bronze percussion instruments that includes large hanging gongs). Many people believe that gong luang ensembles were brought to Bali from the Majapahit kingdom (Sukerta 1998: 100), and most scholars assign the type to the old category. Although the exact instrumentation varies among the six or so extant gong luang ensembles in Bali, they all include the characteristic instruments of the sekaten ensembles, including hanging gongs, a large gong-chime played by several musicians, and various keyed metal instruments. The gong luang from the village of Tangkas also includes an instrument called *bedug* (Toth 1975: 67), which is similar to the large bedug drum of the Cirebonese gamelan sekaten, but much smaller. Perhaps most significantly, these gamelan ensembles are tuned to a non-equidistant seven-pitch pelog tuning system.

Middle period

A seven-pitch pelog tuning system also characterized the *gamelan gambuh* of the post-Majapahit royal Balinese houses, whose primary purpose was to accompany courtly dance-drama productions that celebrated the stories and exploits of Eastern Javanese heroes. Gamelan gambuh's melody layers were played on soft-sounding instruments— paired *suling gambuh* (large bamboo flutes) and *rebab* (spike fiddle)—over a colotomic framework played on a variety of gongs and gong chimes. Gamelan gambuh's repertories, colotomic forms, and even the hand drumming style have exerted enormous influence on most subsequent Balinese music. Even though gamelan gambuh is rarely heard in the present (a group still performs old-fashioned gamelan gambuh in the Balinese village of Batuan), its characteristic melodies, forms, and aesthetics live on in more modern musical genres.

Among the most impressive ensembles of the middle period were the grand gamelan *gong gede*. These ensembles were enormous, in both sheer massiveness of the individual instruments and the large number of instruments and musicians—as many as fifty—required to play them. Such ensembles provided the core ceremonial music for both court and temple ritual cycles. More streamlined versions of the gamelan gong ensemble continue to provide ceremonial music into the present. Both the instruments and the repertories of gamelan gong also provided models in the twentieth century for the most ubiquitous new period ensemble: *gamelan gong kebyar*.

A variety of other ensembles waxed and waned in the middle period, such as *gamelan Semar pegulingan* and *gamelan pelegongan*, both of which combined melodies and colotomic forms from gamelan gambuh with melodic gong-chime and metallophone instruments similar to those of gamelan gong. These ensembles, too, provided models for more recent twentieth-century gamelan innovations.

Beleganjur

Another musical legacy of the middle period is the portable processional ensemble, called *gamelan gong beleganjur*, which provides a sonic background for a variety of rituals. Because the music was meant to accompany many different ritual events, it had to be flexible as well; musicians were prepared to change the mood of the music (say, from serene to agitated) at a moment's notice to reflect the mood of the processional events. The various instruments—gongs, drums, and cymbals—are all designed to be played while marching.

Like Javanese gamelan music, beleganjur music is organized into four layers: colotomic framework, basic melody, elaborated melody, and drumming. Most beleganjur pieces are set to a single basic colotomic form, called *gilak*. Like Javanese colotomic forms, the unique "fingerprint" of this colotomic form emerges when each of the various colotomic instruments plays its own rhythmically regular part. Because each instrument has its own particular timbre, and because their parts are offset in time from one another, they interlock to produce a richly textured eight-beat cycle in which each beat has its own unique sonic signature. The cycle culminates with a stroke of the largest, lowest-pitched gong (called the *gong ageng*) in the ensemble.

The melodic parts in beleganjur are performed on small gongs; each musician carries and strikes a single gong, and each gong represents one of the four pitches in the tuning system; together, these four pots are called *reyong*. Once again, their individual parts interlock to create an essential melody as well as various elaborations. It is as if the ensemble's multi-gong gong chimes—a lower-pitched instrument to play the essential melody, and a higher-pitched instrument to play elaborating parts—have been broken down into their constituent components, and a single musician assigned to each, to facilitate carrying the instruments.

very fast pulse	1	2	3	4	5	6	7	8	1	2	3	4	5	6	7	8
cengceng strokes	x			x			x		x			x			x	
pulses between strokes	3			3			2		3			3			2	

Figure 4.14 Basic beleganjur syncopated cengceng part (after Bakan 1999: 66).

cengceng 1	x			x			x		x			x			x	
cengceng 2		x			x			x		x			x			x
cengceng 3	x		x			x			x	x			x			
composite	x	x	x	x	x	x	x	x	x	x	x	x	x	x	x	x

Figure 4.15 Interlocking cengceng parts (after Bakan 1999: 66).

Two drummers lead the procession; their interlocking parts give signals to the rest of the ensemble following behind. The drums are reinforced by eight cymbal players, each carrying a pair of cymbals called *cengceng*; it is the strident and clanging sound of all those cengceng that gives beleganjur music its characteristic sound and volume. Sometimes the cengceng players all play the same part, but they frequently play interlocking patterns as well. The interlocking parts of the cengceng are illustrative of a general characteristic of Balinese interlocking parts: each individual part, rather than articulating a regular pulse, is rhythmically syncopated, but the composite of three or more of these syncopated parts is a smooth, impossibly fast regular pulse of percussive attacks.

The basic syncopated part spreads three cymbal strokes out over eight very fast pulses. The time interval between the first and second strokes is three very fast pulses. The time interval between the second and third stroke, likewise, is three very fast pulses. The time interval between the third stroke and the beginning of the next repetition, however, occupies only the two remaining pulses. The whole pattern, therefore, is syncopated, and consists of two three-pulse strokes and one two-pulse stroke (see Figure 4.14).

Each of three cengceng players performs this exact same phrase, but each player takes care to begin on a different pulse than the others. The rhythmic displacement gives each part a different "role": one is the "basic" version (*megbeg*), another is the "anticipator" (*nyandet*), and the third assumes the role of the "follower" (*ngilit*). The composite of the three parts includes at least one cengceng stroke on each of the very fast pulses in the phrase (see Figure 4.15). It would be humanly impossible for a single performer to play the cengceng so fast; in this way, then, the result of this kind of interlocking Balinese playing is greater than the sum of its parts. In practice, cengceng players often elaborate and vary this basic pattern, resulting in even more superhuman-sounding composite results. With several musicians doubling each of the various parts, the effect is magnified even further.

The four players of the small hand-held gongs that make up the reyong often use the same complementary rhythms as the cengceng players. Because each of the gongs is tuned to a different pitch, a fast, rippling melody emerges when the musicians play their interlocking parts. Other instrumental sections in the beleganjur ensemble also exploit similarly cooperative approaches; the two drums, for example, play the "same" part offset in time to produce a dizzyingly intricate composite pattern. Such figurations model the Balinese social ideal of mutual cooperation.

The ear-shattering and pulse-quickening clanging of a gamelan beleganjur at full volume can be quite intimidating. It is no wonder that, hundreds of years ago, beleganjur accompanied Balinese armies into battle. Beleganjur also is associated with cremation and mortuary rituals (Track 5 on the CD that accompanies this book features a beleganjur ensemble playing for a post-cremation purification ritual called *memukur*); in this context, the ensemble accompanies a "battle" between the spirit of the deceased and the spirits who might hinder the soul's journey. The beleganjur ensemble's sounds provide an inspirational source of energy for the living and a sort of sonic ladder for the deceased souls to ascend in their afterlife journeys.

Although beleganjur is a time-honored Balinese tradition, it has not remained the same between the middle and new periods. Much about Bali has changed since the days when these ensembles spurred the armies of rival Balinese kings to fight. Modern beleganjur style is much less flexible than it used to be; groups rehearse diligently to memorize complex arrangements and execute them flawlessly. There is still, however, an emphasis on precision in executing interlocking parts, in which the composite effect is much greater than the sum of the parts. Many innovations in beleganjur music were inspired by musical developments in the new period gamelan gong kebyar groups. These new forms of beleganjur were nourished by the cultivation of a competition style (*kreasi beleganjur*) in Bali's capital city, Denpasar, in the 1980s; their visual appearance has been embellished with dramatic choreography designed to be reminiscent of the movements of ancient Balinese warriors (Bakan 1999).

New period: Gong kebyar

Balinese society, in accordance with its Hindu leanings, remained highly stratified until the twentieth century. Although some prominent kings reigned over various Balinese kingdoms, none of these realms attained the kind of size, power, or influence of the Javanese Islamic kingdoms. Instead, these tiny Balinese kingdoms existed in relative isolation, from one another as well as from the rest of the world, and each developed unique traditions of its own. Music, dance, and theater played a vital role not only in the royal courts, but in the practice of Hinduism by ordinary Balinese; thus, gamelan music in Bali is the legacy of villages as well as palaces.

Dutch rule, beginning in the twentieth century, led to a lessening of Balinese kings' power and influence. Many of their valuable sets of gamelan instruments became the property of the surrounding communities rather than of the rulers. Balinese villagers had long been accustomed to working together to achieve common goals; neighborhood organizations governed the building and maintenance of common resources and areas (such as temples and meeting places). These village organizations, called *banjar*, applied the same organizational principles to rehearsing and performing gamelan music.

Dutch domination also facilitated increased communication between the various kingdoms of Bali. So, when some banjar in North Bali innovated an exciting new modern style of gamelan music based on existing temple gamelan ensembles, remote banjar heard about it, and the innovation spread throughout the island. This new style was dubbed *gong kebyar*. Kebyar means "to burst open" (like a flower) or "to flare up" (like a match). Inspired by this flamboyant new approach to gamelan music, artists from other parts of the island imitated the new style and contributed their own innovations to it.

As a result, in addition to the various regional styles of gamelan music, many of which continue to be performed, Bali is today the home of this peculiarly twentieth-century style of gamelan: gong kebyar. In keeping with its twentieth-century origins, its musical style reflects an increasingly egalitarian Balinese society. Its flashy exuberance is also an important component of Bali's image as an international tourist attraction in the twenty-first century.

Gong kebyar instruments and style

Balinese gamelan ensembles feature the same kinds of instruments as gamelan on Java, but with some different details of construction and ways of playing. Similarly, the musical structure of Balinese gamelan music has much in common with Javanese music, although the sound is very different. The instruments and style of gong kebyar music will serve as an illustration.

Balinese tuning systems, like Javanese tuning systems, are flexible; there are no widely accepted standards, and each ensemble has its own character. As we have seen, the archaic gamelan luang is tuned to the seven-pitch pelog system, which is essentially the same as the Javanese pelog tuning system. Other old-fashioned Balinese gamelan, such as gamelan gambuh and gamelan Semar pegulingan, also feature seven-pitch pelog tunings. As was the case with Central Javanese pelog, most pieces are set in a scale consisting of only five of the seven available pitches. Most pelog gamelan in Bali, including gong kebyar ensembles, include keys for only five pitches per octave, roughly equivalent to the Javanese scale earlier compared to *sol fa mi do ti* (see p. 79), that is, with very small and very large intervals. Other Balinese ensembles are tuned to a slendro scale, again comparable to Javanese slendro. One type of slendro ensemble, called *gamelan angklung*, usually includes only four of the five slendro pitches.

As in Java, the rhythmic structure of Balinese gamelan pieces is manifest in a colotomic framework played on various sizes of gongs. The largest gongs in a gong kebyar ensemble are called *gong ageng*; most ensembles include at least one, but no more than two, large gongs. They sound at the ends of large musical units. Subdivisions of the phrases delineated by the gong ageng are marked with a smaller hanging gong called *kempur*; even smaller subdivisions are marked with a tiny hanging gong called *kemong*. Once again, the names of the instruments are onomatopoeic; the second syllable of an instrument's name provides a good idea of its timbre and relative pitch level.

In Central Javanese and Cirebonese gamelan music, the composite pattern produced by all of the colotomic instruments together outlines a steady beat or pulse, but none of them plays that beat explicitly. In the gong kebyar ensemble, there is an instrument that sounds this basic beat: a small gong laid horizontally on a frame, called *kempli*. Many other Balinese ensembles include similar instruments, with different names, to perform this function as well.

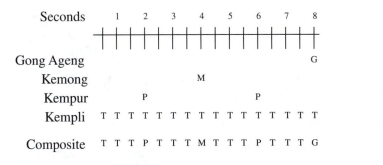

Figure 4.16 Gegaboran colotomic form (after Tenzer 1991: 43).

There are quite a variety of colotomic forms upon which Balinese gamelan pieces are based. Upon hearing music with a familiar colotomic form, a Balinese listener may immediately get a particular feeling associated with that colotomic form. The structure outlined in Figure 4.16, for example, is called *gegaboran*, and underlies pieces that accompany a graceful feminine offering dance called *gabor*. Music with this structure may therefore suggest the feeling one gets from experiencing a delicate female dance even when no actual dancing takes place (Tenzer 1991: 43).

In Bali, saron-family instruments—keyed instruments in which all the keys share a common trough resonating chamber—are relatively uncommon. Although old period ensembles such as gong luang do include saron-family instruments (an alternate name for gong luang is *gong saron*), as do some middle period ensembles such as gong gede, new period ensembles include no saron-family instruments. There is a much greater variety of gender-family instruments, however. As in Java, each key of a gender-family instrument is suspended over its own resonating tube. In Bali, only gender-family instruments played with two mallets, using a technique comparable to Central Javanese gender technique, are actually called gender; other gender-family instruments, which are played with a technique similar to Central Javanese saron technique, have other names. A gong kebyar ensemble includes several sizes of gender-family instruments, each with a different musical function. Like Javanese music, all the gender parts for a piece are based on a common melody; Balinese call this main melody *pokok*. The larger, lower-pitched gender-family instruments play more abstract versions of the pokok melody, while the smaller, higher-pitched instruments play more elaborated versions of the melody or figurations based on the melody.

One striking characteristic of many Balinese ensembles is that the keyed instruments come in matched pairs. The instruments in a pair are virtually identical except for one important detail: the keys of one instrument are tuned to be slightly lower in pitch than the keys of the other. When the corresponding keys on the two instruments are struck at the same time, the ear perceives not two dissimilar notes, but rather a single note that seems to shimmer and dance because it oscillates quickly between louder and quieter. This effect is the result of an acoustical phenomenon known as *beating*. The sound waves excited by the two keys interact with one another—sometimes strengthening each other so the ear hears more sound, sometimes canceling each other out so the ear hears less sound. These variations in volume happen very quickly (several to many times per second). If the two

Figure 4.17 Balinese gong kebyar ensemble in temple courtyard, *c.* 1920 (photo and print collection of the Koninklijk Instituut voor Taal-, Land- en Volkenkunde, Leiden, the Netherlands).

pitches are relatively close, the result will be a fast shimmer; two pitches that are a little bit further apart will create a more leisurely undulation.

The lowest-pitched gender-family instrument in a gong kebyar ensemble has only five keys (one octave's worth of pitches) and is called *jegogan*. A gong kebyar ensemble includes a pair of jegogan. Each is struck with a soft mallet; together, they produce a deep, undulating, sustained sound. The jegogan part is very abstract and includes only the most important notes of the pokok melody; it moves very slowly. There is also a pair of *calung*, often called *jublag*, the next lowest-pitched instrument; they also have five keys, are struck with soft mallets, and provide the most elemental version of the pokok melody.

The remaining gender-family instruments have more keys than the lower-pitched instruments (covering about two octaves); their hard wooden mallets produce a much brighter, metallic timbre. These instruments are collectively called *gangsa*. The lowest-pitched gangsa is called the *ugal*; the ugal player is the leader for the entire gangsa section. Although the ugal's range of pitches overlaps that of the calung, their parts sound quite distinct because of the different mallets with which they are played. The ugal part is a more elaborate and decorated version of the pokok melody. Figure 4.17 shows a Balinese gong kebyar ensemble.

The parts played on the remaining gangsa in gong kebyar ensembles—*pemade* (one octave higher than the ugal) and *kantilan* (one octave higher than the pemade)—are often sophisticated interlocking parts called *kotekan*. We have already seen that the various colotomic instruments in gamelan ensembles play parts that may be said to be complementary to one another because each part plays during the silences in the other parts so that the ear and brain are compelled to hear them as a single musical entity. This technique of interlocking parts applies to other levels of music as well. Much Javanese and Balinese music features interlocking parts between two instruments that sound the same. Kotekan are interlocking parts, characteristic of gong kebyar and several other Balinese gamelan styles, that combine to create the illusion of a single melodic line that often sounds faster than any single human could possibly play. The ethnomusicologist Hardja Susilo once said about Balinese music that "half the group plays as fast as they can, and the other half plays as fast as they can, in between" (quoted in Vitale 1990: 14 fn. 10).

Kotekan requires two performers; they perform their parts on instruments of similar range and timbre (sometimes the two players perform their parts together on a single instrument). The two parts are coordinated so that the second part fills in the gaps left by the first part so that those listening hear a single musical line. Composer Wayne Vitale suggests the following analogy:

> One might imagine . . . the text on this page being read by two narrators, one of whom pronounces only the letters a through m, and the other n through z, yet fitting those sounds together so perfectly that we hear them as one speaker (Vitale 1990: 2).

Typically, although not always, each of the two parts that combine in kotekan is limited to one or two pitches (that is, one or two gangsa keys) only; limiting the number of keys each player has to worry about frees them to play their parts faster and more accurately. Because each of the two parts includes one or two pitches, the entire kotekan can encompass as many as four pitches. There are a number of techniques for fitting the two parts together. The particular kotekan style described in the following paragraphs is called *kotekan empat* and is among the more complicated approaches to kotekan available. The word "empat" means "four" and describes the number of pitches in the composite pattern that emerges from the combination of the two parts.

Figure 4.18a illustrates one of the two parts of an interlocking kotekan pattern—the upper part, called *sangsih*. The two bars along the graph's Y-axis represent the two keys that the player of the sangsih pattern will use; they are labelled "sh" (sangsih-high) and "sl" (sangsih-low). The graph's X-axis is marked off into thirty-two pulses (the length of the kotekan pattern); a black square beneath a beat's number indicates that the sangsih player hits that key for that pulse. The graph illustrates that the sangsih part is composed of two- and three-note "bursts" separated by a pulse of silence. Figure 4.18b illustrates the other part—the lower part called *polos*. The two Y-axis keys are labelled "ph" (polos-high) and "pl" (polos-low). The polos part, like the sangsih part, is composed of short "bursts" (one- and two-note bursts in this case) separated by a pulse of silence. Figure 4.18c shows the two patterns combined. All of the silent pulses in the sangsih part coincide with a note in the polos part, and vice versa. The result is that a note is being played by at least one of the two players for every pulse; rather than hearing little bursts of notes separated by silences, the listeners hear one long, unbroken sequence of notes. In this particular kotekan pattern, the composite pattern starts with a series of four-note ascending melodic figurations; toward the middle it shifts to four-note descending

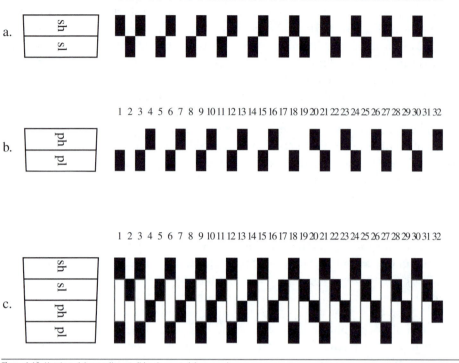

Figure 4.18 Kotekan. (a) sangsih part; (b) polos part; (c) composite.

figurations. Some kotekan patterns, such as the kotekan empat pattern illustrated in the figure, include pulses where both musicians play a note; the result is an even richer sonority (in the graph, the two notes' boxes are connected by a gray line).

It is not too difficult for each player to perform the short one-, two-, and three-note bursts at breakneck speed; the composite of the two, however, would be impossible for a single musician to perform quite so rapidly. The two musicians must coordinate their patterns precisely, however, for the composite to emerge clearly. Which pitches each player hits depends on the notes of the main melody. As in Javanese music, the figurations dance above and below the main melody, but meet up with it at rhythmically significant junctures. In order to end up on the right pitch, the players must begin their patterns on the correct keys. As the melody moves higher and lower, so do the kotekan patterns.

The kotekan technique emphasizes skill in coordination to produce a whole that is greater than the sum of its parts. Because these patterns require such precision, there is no room for improvisation; the parts are carefully worked out in advance and rehearsed until the musicians can execute them without flaw or hesitation. Like the lower-pitched gangsa, the higher-pitched gangsa on which kotekan patterns are played come in pairs to achieve the shimmering acoustical effect. That means there must be a pair of instruments for each of the two parts that interlock to create kotekan, resulting in a total of four gangsa of each pitch range.

Gong kebyar includes a couple of gong chimes as well. Like Javanese bonang, these gong chimes consist of small pot-sized gongs suspended on ropes stretched across a wooden frame. Unlike Javanese bonang, however, all the pots are arranged into a single row, in order with the lower pitches to the player's left. The *trompong* is the lower-pitched of the two gong chimes; it has about ten pots, in approximately the same range as the ugal. A single musician uses two mallets to play a decorated version of the main melody. Trompong is an old-fashioned instrument, and is included only in pieces where this hint of nostalgia is desired. Because the instrument is so long, the trompong player's movements are athletic, almost dancelike.

A *reyong* is pitched higher than the trompong. It usually has twelve pots and requires four players: two for each octave. The two lower-octave musicians play interlocking kotekan parts similar to those played on the gangsa. The two upper-octave musicians play the same kotekan patterns an octave higher. For each kotekan pattern, each player controls two pots. As the kotekan patterns move up and down the scale following the main melody, which two pots are controlled by which musician is continually changing and overlapping. The quartet must coordinate not only their musical parts, but also their body movements to avoid collisions.

All of this shimmering and interlocking creates a rich, busy, exciting sound. Balinese gamelan ensembles usually include some kind of cymbals to add even more noise and excitement. The quality of the sound of Balinese cymbals is suggested by their name: *cengceng*. Although some ensembles include pairs of handheld cymbals similar to the crash cymbals in a symphony orchestra's percussion section, most Balinese cymbals are relatively small, and a complete set of cymbals includes six or more. The player holds two of these small cymbals (one in each hand) and strikes them against the remaining cymbals, which are mounted on a wooden floor stand. With two hands alternating, an energetic cengceng player can play very quickly.

In keeping with the predilection for interlocking parts, gong kebyar ensembles often feature two drummers who play interlocking parts. The drummers are responsible for starting and stopping pieces, controlling the tempo, and providing an interface between the gamelan musicians and dance, theater, or puppet manipulation. Track 6 on the CD that accompanies this book presents a gong kebyar piece that illustrates all of these musical features.

The island of Bali is home to many, many different kinds of gamelan ensembles. Bali's historical separation into small autonomous areas ensured that each region developed and maintained its own particular set of traditions. Communities still take great pride in maintaining the special ensembles and musical styles that are unique to their localities. As a result, the Balinese music scene is a riot of instruments, ensembles, repertories, and contexts. The Balinese people's devotion to the practice of Hinduism engendered many opportunities for the performances of distinctive music and dance traditions in the context of religious rituals. More recently, Bali's status as a destination for international "cultural tourists" has created still more contexts for musical activities.

The development of modern Balinese gong kebyar demonstrates how gamelan music has changed to reflect changes in Balinese society. Gamelan organization is like social organization. The fast interlocking parts mirror the close cooperation that villagers have cultivated to keep their communities running smoothly. When the royal courts disappeared, an existing village institution—the banjar—stepped in to assume ownership of gamelan instruments and patronage of gamelan music. Once again we see that the same underlying musical structure, with colotomic, melodic, elaborating, and drumming functions, provides a flexible framework for making music that suits the needs and desires of its audiences.

Gamelan in the West

The social functions and underlying processes of music traditions shape the actual sounds that listeners hear; Indonesian musical aesthetics are intimately tied to Indonesian social values. The sounds of gamelan music have fallen on European ears ever since the first European explorers came to Java; beginning with the earliest contacts, Europeans were struck by the unfamiliarity of the music they heard. Some early visitors found the music to be unpleasant, such as Christoph Frick, who commented in 1676 about "some Javians coming down in a small Boat, making a mighty noise with some little Bells" (Frick 1929: 141) and John Barrow, who described "drums and squalling flutes" in 1806 (Barrow, Truter, et al. 1806: 223). Others found the music merely strange; in 1795, Charles Thunberg said that the gamelan instruments he heard "have not a bad effect at a small distance" (Thunberg 1795: 308), a sentiment echoed in 1828 by J. R. Logan, who commented, "at a little distance the sound is not unpleasing, though very monotonous" (Logan 1853: 235).

The records from the first Dutch ship to sail to the East Indies in 1595–7 include some fascinating drawings of music and dance activities. According to its old Dutch caption, the illustration in Figure 4.19 shows performers dancing to the accompaniment of an instrument consisting of metal plates played in the manner of an organ, "singing a song, rhyming, arms and legs twisting, and the whole body turning, like dogs who come crawling out of their nests" (Rouffaer and IJzerman 1915: plate 25). These reactions, ranging from negative to indifferent, are not surprising, considering that European social values were quite at odds with the Javanese values that shaped the music these intrepid writers heard.

Toward the end of the nineteenth century, however, many Europeans (and Americans in the European tradition) became fascinated with the exotic sounds of music from the colonies. Gamelan ensembles from Java made appearances at several of the grand international "world's fairs" or "expositions" that various cities hosted during this time. Some composers in the European tradition who were disillusioned with the Romantic musical idiom championed by the likes of Liszt and Wagner, which focused on forward-moving harmonic progressions and endless melodies, were eager to explore new sound possibilities. Claude Debussy, for example, was interested in sonorities—blocks of sound that didn't necessarily lead the listener anywhere, but which were beautiful moments in and of themselves. Among modern fans of European "classical" music, Debussy's encounter with Javanese gamelan music at the 1889 Paris Exposition is the stuff of legend; while it is not clear exactly how deeply he delved into the inner workings of gamelan music, the sounds he heard had a definite effect on his compositional thinking. It is important to remember, however, that Debussy's fascination with the timbres and sonorities of Javanese gamelan music had nothing to do with the music's actual meaning; rather, he found the sounds—excised from the web of social significance which gave them their form—to fit serendipitously into his own social and aesthetic world.

Figure 4.19 Early illustration of Javanese music and dance (Rouffaer and IJzerman, 1915: plate 25).

A number of Europeans and Americans traveled to Java and Bali to experience the performing arts there in the first half of the twentieth century. Many of these individuals were attracted to the Asian arts in general, and Indonesian music in particular, because they seemed to embody both a spirituality and a sense of permanence that they felt were missing from modern Western expressions; the connection of the arts to people's daily lives was another attraction. Very often these expatriate Westerners felt compelled to somehow "translate" these ineffable qualities which they perceived in Indonesian arts into Western forms. The Canadian composer Colin McPhee, who lived in Bali for a number of years, used Balinese materials extensively in his compositions; some of his works are little more than transcriptions of Balinese pieces for Western instruments. For these artists, the appeal of Indonesian music lay primarily in its social values; they sought to transplant some of these values into their own cultures. Quite often, however, the values they saw were merely the values they wanted to see; from their vantage point as colonial masters, they often misinterpreted the privileges of the Indonesian nobility as a kind of utopian egalitarianism.

Following World War II, European and American ethnomusicologists took an interest in preserving gamelan music in Indonesia and promoting it in the West. The influential ethnomusicologist Mantle C. Hood, a specialist in Central Javanese gamelan music, advocated "bimusicality" (the musical equivalent of "bilingualism") as an approach to cross-cultural understanding through music. He put his principle into practice by acquiring gamelan instruments for the UCLA music department (where he taught at the time) and inviting Javanese musicians (such as Hardja Susilo) to teach his students to play them. As Hood's students started ethnomusicology programs at other schools, they often included gamelan instruction as a part of the program. These ensembles continue to thrive in the setting of American higher education for a variety of reasons. They are visually stunning and aurally arresting, and so attract much attention; many of the instruments are relatively easy to learn to play; and the ensembles accommodate fairly large numbers of students. Because there are few Americans of Indonesian heritage, and most Americans know very little about Indonesia, there is little chance that ethnic identity politics might mar the students' innocent enjoyment of their gamelan music. At the beginning of the twenty-first century, possessing a set of gamelan instruments is a collegiate status symbol among American institutions of higher education.

Easy access to gamelan instruments, and to the Indonesian musicians who were brought to teach on them, provided American and European composers in the second half of the twentieth century with a wealth of compositional material. Some composers, such as James Tenney and Richard Felciano, used the instruments themselves as resources, without trying to imitate Indonesian musical processes. Other composers were intrigued by the musical processes they either read about or learned from Indonesian teachers, and incorporated them into their compositions.

The career of the composer Lou Harrison (1917–2003) straddled virtually the entire twentieth century and covers most of the approaches described above. He first heard live gamelan music at one of the last of the great international expositions (the San Francisco Golden Gate Exposition in 1939). He experimented with applying the Indonesian musical processes he read about in books and transcriptions to the pieces he composed for conventional Western instruments. Later in his career, he spent time studying Javanese, Balinese, and Sundanese music with Indonesian artists who visited California, and began to compose for gamelan instruments (some of which were imported from Indonesia, and some of which he built with the help of his longtime partner, William Colvig).

Harrison eschewed the normal twelve-pitch equidistant "equal temperament" tuning system that dominates contemporary Western music; he advocated a return to tunings in which the various intervals are not equidistant, but in which some pitches are carefully tuned so that the combination of some pitches is more acoustically "pure" than equal temperament will allow. Harrison was convinced that Javanese slendro and pelog tunings were somehow related to the "pure" tuning systems he advocated for Western music, and he retuned his own gamelan instruments to such tuning systems. In this regard, Harrison, like many of his predecessors, imposed his own fantasies of the exotic onto Indonesian music. Some of Harrison's most affective pieces combine solo Western instruments (horn, violin, and harp for example) with gamelan accompaniments—these compositions are, in effect, mini-concertos which place the Western instruments in a position of superiority in relation to the gamelan instruments. Although Harrison's motivations for adapting Indonesian musical instruments and processes were unquestionably ethical, such pieces can also be interpreted as making the power imbalance between colonizers and their native subjects seem aesthetically beautiful—well beyond the putative end of colonialism!

Indonesian National Music

The gamelan music of Java and Bali has spread well beyond its islands of origin; and just as gamelan musical processes model Javanese and Balinese social and political values, appropriations by Westerners of gamelan music relate to Western value systems. Gamelan music has been appropriated much closer to home as well, in the service of Indonesian nation building. The nascent Indonesian government promoted a single national language (*bahasa Indonesia*); the same nationalists who supported a single national language, however, were divided about a national music. Some nationalist leaders supported hybridized music, with Western scales but Indonesian roots (such as *kroncong*, which accompanied songs in the Indonesian language with guitars, violins, and ukuleles). Others proposed that the best regional musics in Indonesia should be promoted as national music. The government eventually adopted a policy supporting "peaks of culture" from various regions; in other words, the "best" music and dance from each region would receive government support; music traditions that espoused values that the new government deemed questionable would be sanitized or eliminated. Central Javanese court gamelan, with its lofty aristocratic values, represented one such peak.

Of course, governments do not always have the final say in what music becomes popular and what music does not. Government arts policy has led to the preservation and support of various cultural peaks. It has not, however, prevented the creation of hybrid musics. In Cirebon, for example, a style of music called *tarling* emerged in the 1970s and has been enduringly popular. The word tarling is derived from the names of the two main instruments in the ensemble: gui*tar* and su*ling*. Early tarling songs featured gamelan-like parts played on the guitars, supported by gongs and drums, with a *suling* (bamboo flute) melody floating above it.

Throughout Indonesia, a musical genre called *dangdut* is extremely popular. Dangdut songs are sung in the Indonesian language, and the musical accompaniment combines elements of Indian film music and Malay popular styles from the early twentieth century, with hints of international rock and roll. Although many people once looked down on dangdut music as "low class," in recent years its respectability has risen considerably; in some ways, it is assuming the status of the de facto Indonesian national music.

Despite these innovations, however, gamelan music remains an important expressive form for many Sundanese, Javanese, and Balinese people. It is performed side-by-side with more cosmopolitan and more Western-sounding styles. Many Indonesians see no contradiction in continuing to cultivate musical styles with very different sounds. Gamelan music in Java and Bali provides a model of traditional society in sonic form. Gamelan's primarily metal instruments evoke the power—both material wealth and spiritual potency—symbolized by bronze and exemplified by god-kings. The four layers of functions (colotomic foundation, melody, elaboration, and drumming) mirror a stratified social organization as well as a concept of the cosmos. The way that musicians compress pieces in their memories and expand them in performance mimics an approach to the role of the individual in a steady-state universe.

This is not to say, however, that gamelan music is inflexible. Regional variation in gamelan music in Java and Bali demonstrates how these principles are manipulated, adjusted, and changed to meet new social needs and absorb outside influences.

Developments such as tarling and *campur sari* (combination of electric guitars and keyboards with gamelan instruments) demonstrate once again the flexibility of gamelan instruments and musical structures. By manipulating the various structures and processes of gamelan music, musicians and listeners are able to experiment with the structure and processes of their own lives and social relationships.

PART III

Focusing In:
Identity, Authenticity,
and Tradition in Sundanese
Music and Dance

CHAPTER 5

Gamelan in West Java

Part II introduced some Indonesian musical processes associated with gamelan music in Cirebon, Central Java, East Java, and Bali, and demonstrated how the same processes result in different musical sounds depending on historical circumstances and social values. The following chapters will examine yet another region—West Java—and some of the Sundanese music that thrives there. The Sundanese people have been embroiled in the same historical forces that shaped the rest of Java; in many ways, however, they have been at the margins of Javanese history. Chapters 5 and 6 cover two Sundanese gamelan styles; Chapter 7 will examine modern developments in Sundanese music and dance.

Sundanese History and Music

The mountainous interior of the modern Indonesian province of West Java is populated primarily by people who speak the Sundanese language. They call the highland areas of West Java "Parahyangan"—the land of the gods. A more common name, "Priangan," was first applied to the region when it was taken over by the Central Javanese kingdom of Mataram (Lubis 2000a: 77), and probably derives from the name Parahyangan. The Priangan includes two high plateaus (about 2,400 ft [731m] above sea level) surrounded by high volcanic peaks (up to 5,700 ft [1,737 m]). The Sundanese are the second largest ethnic group in Indonesia (about 30 million people in 2000), outnumbered only by the Javanese in Central and Eastern Java. The Sundanese-dominated part of West Java also includes some of the lowland areas surrounding the interior mountains and plateaus, but does not include Jakarta, the capital of Indonesia, or the areas surrounding it.

Although Sunda is an old word, and a minor kingdom called Sunda existed in West Java during the eleventh century, it is not completely correct to use Sunda as a place name. Strictly speaking, the term refers to a group of people (the Sundanese) rather than to a particular place (Ekadjati 1995: 8), and in Indonesian languages the word typically is used as an adjective, not a noun. The term *urang Sunda*, for example, means Sundanese people, *basa Sunda* means the Sundanese language (Koentjaraningrat 1972: 54), and *tanah Sunda* or *tatar Sunda* means the Sundanese homeland (Lubis 2000a). In English, it seems sensible to use Sundanese as an adjective, and refer to places with names such as West Java (the Indonesian province that includes the Sundanese-dominated areas as well as some Javanese-dominated parts along the north coast) or the Priangan (the traditional name for the Sundanese highlands). A newer term—Pasundan—has been attached to the region by some in the past century, usually with overtones of asserting a separate, Sundanese self-determination in response to a strong Indonesian republic.

The Priangan was a cultural backwater for most of recorded history (Wessing 1978: 8). Early Hindu kingdoms in West Java (such as the aforementioned Sunda kingdom) were small and not based on trade and wet-rice cultivation like more powerful states in Central Java and Sumatra. As a result, the Sundanese area was a remote region away from centers of civilization, often serving as a buffer zone between larger powers. The area's only major Hindu kingdom, Pajajaran, arose after the collapse of the powerful Srivijaya empire in Sumatra in 1333 AD. The Central Javanese Majapahit kingdom claimed sovereignty over Pajajaran, but Pajajaran did not acknowledge Majapahit's authority; the Pajajaran rulers managed to retain control over a fairly large area.

A Javanese poem called the *Kidung Sunda* describes a fourteenth-century incident that illuminates the conflict. As the story goes, the Prime Minister of Majapahit, Gadjah Mada, arranged for the young king of Majapahit, Hayam Wuruk, to marry the princess of Pajajaran to acquire sovereignty over Pajajaran. When the wedding was about to take place, the Pajajaran faction insisted that the new bride be treated as a queen; Gadjah Mada, however, insisted that she would be nothing more than a concubine. Instead of a wedding, there was a gruesome slaughter; the nobles of Pajajaran refused to submit to Majapahit and Gadjah Mada's forces slew them all. Although Gadjah Mada is now regarded as an Indonesian national hero because of his early efforts to unite the Indonesian archipelago, he represents for the Sundanese an oppressor—a symbol of domination of the Sundanese by outsiders.

The Priangan has been under the political control of non-Sundanese for many hundreds of years. Pajajaran may have survived its run-in with Majapahit and Gadjah Mada, but it finally fell to powerful Islamic city-states on Java's north coast, and eventually came under the control of Central Java's Islamic Mataram kingdom in the seventeenth century. Mataram governed its Sundanese subjects by setting up political units, called *kabupaten*, governed by Sundanese aristocrats called *bupati* (ministers) who were loyal to Mataram. (The political unit roughly equivalent to a US county still is called a kabupaten in modern Indonesia.) These bupati emulated the grand style of their Mataram superiors, and acquired many trappings of status and power from the east, including bronze gamelan ensembles. European colonial powers (first the Dutch East Indies Company, then Britain, and then the Netherlands) followed Mataram's lead in administering their West Javanese territories (including the rich tea plantations) through the established authority of Sundanese bupati.

The Dutch administration, hoping to prevent the establishment of a strong Indo-

Figure 5.1 Tembang Sunda ensemble featuring vocalists Teti Affienti (left front) and Tintin Suparyani (right front), with accompanists Gan-Gan Garmana (kacapi; left rear), Iwan S. (suling; center rear), and Cucu S. (kacapi rincik; right rear) (courtesy Sean Williams).

nesian republic after the Japanese occupation ended after World War II, promoted the establishment of a semi-independent state in West Java called Negara Pasundan (Sundanese Nation). Led by traditional Sundanese aristocrats who cited hundreds of years of history as precedent, Negara Pasundan sought to assert Sundanese sovereignty over their traditional homeland (Cribb 1984; Sjamsuddin 1992). The movement ultimately was unsuccessful, however, and the Sundanese-dominated areas are now an integral part of the Indonesian nation.

Despite the imposition of authority from outside, legends and stories of Pajajaran have been kept alive in the Sundanese imagination into the present, often through the medium of epic narrative songs called *pantun*, and several musical instruments and traditions are considered to be indigenous to the Priangan, including *kacapi* (zither), *tarawangsa* and *rendo* (bowed lutes), and *angklung* (bamboo rattle). One uniquely Sundanese modern musical genre, called *Cianjuran* or *tembang Sunda*, is closely associated with the memory of Pajajaran. In keeping with this association, its songs often speak of the distant past and its accompaniment features indigenous Sundanese instruments such as kacapi and suling (bamboo flute) (see Figure 5.1). The sound of a kacapi is sometimes intensely nostalgic for Sundanese listeners, even though they may not know exactly what they are yearning for.

An isolated enclave of Sundanese people called the Baduy maintain many indigenous Sundanese musical traditions. According to popular mythology, the Baduy, who live in the mountainous area southwest of Jakarta, are the descendants of Pajajaran aristocrats who managed to escape the conquest of the court in 1579. Although this origin is unlikely, the Baduy do indeed regard themselves as guardians of Sundanese lands and traditions, and modern Sundanese look to the Baduy as models of indigenous Sundaneseness. Baduy practice dry-rice farming instead of the wet-rice cultivation that characterizes the rest of West Java; wet-rice farming techniques, including the complex irrigation technology they require, are part of the legacy of Mataram. Baduy religious and ceremonial life revolves around the agricultural cycles of planting and harvesting rice (Zanten 1995). There are about 5,000 Baduy, living in about forty-five villages. A few of the most isolated villages are particularly stringent in their preservation of traditional practices; residents of these villages are called the Inner Baduy. They are insulated from the outside world by the Outer Baduy. Inner Baduy men typically wear a white head-cloth, while Outer Baduy men wear a distinctive blue-and-black patterned headcloth.

During the rice-planting season, Baduy men play *angklung* music, both for entertainment and for rituals. An angklung is a bamboo rattle consisting of a rectangular bamboo frame in which two or three bamboo tubes, tuned to various octave equivalents of a single pitch, are suspended. The player holds the bottom of the frame firmly with the left hand while steadying the top of the frame with the right hand. By vigorously shaking the bottom of the frame, the player causes the suspended tubes to vibrate, creating a pleasing tremolo sound with a clear pitch. The ritual performances chronicle the villagers' interactions with the goddess of rice—first they awaken her with angklung music, then they celebrate her engagement to be married to the earth. Several weeks later they play once again to protect the goddess and the earth from disease. The Baduy angklung ensemble includes nine angklung of various sizes, each tuned to a different pitch. Each angklung is played by a single musician (except for the two highest-pitched angklung, which are both played by a single musician). The ensemble also includes three drums. The participants sing and dance to the accompaniment of the angklung ensemble.

Since the sixteenth century, being Sundanese has involved conforming to the expectations and standards set by ruling outsiders while maintaining some sense of "Sundaneseness." Until the twentieth century, Sundaneseness was mainly the concern of an aristocratic class (called the *menak* in Sundanese) who interacted in various capacities with the foreign overlords of West Java; commoners were keenly aware of class differences between themselves and the Sundanese menak, but less aware of non-Sundanese ways of living in the outside world.

Gamelan ensembles were one artifact of outside rulers that Sundanese aristocrats adopted and made their own; developing uniquely Sundanese styles of gamelan music served as a way to emulate foreign rulers while delineating a specifically Sundanese identity. Gamelan music eventually spread to the lower classes as well and is an integral part of Sundanese music. Gamelan is so well integrated into Sundanese culture that even the self-consciously old-fashioned Baduy—at least the Outer Baduy—play gamelan music. The Inner Baduy avoid instruments made of metal, and even the Outer Baduy restrict the time of year in which gamelan music may be played to the months between the end of the harvest and the beginning of planting. The Baduy gamelan is similar to modern Sundanese *gamelan salendro*, suggesting that Baduy gamelan is a relatively recent innovation.

The recognition of a history that is separate from the rest of Java is the key element of a modern Sundanese identity. The legends of the aristocrats of Pajajaran as well as the maintenance of traditional Sundanese ways by the Baduy contribute to a sense of Sunda-

Figure 5.2 Diatonic angklung ensemble (courtesy Sean Williams).

neseness. Angklung has become a veritable symbol of Sundanese culture. In the 1930s, it occurred to a Sundanese musician named Daeng Sutigna that an angklung ensemble was similar to a Western handbell choir (Perris 1971). In a handbell choir, each musician is responsible for two or three bells; by watching the music and the conductor, each musician knows when to play a particular bell. A well-rehearsed handbell choir interlocks the individual parts to produce sophisticated melodies and harmonies.

Daeng Sutigna's clever idea was that angklung, tuned to a diatonic scale, could replace the handbells to provide an inexpensive means for music instruction in West Java's emerging educational system. In diatonic angklung music, Western approaches to musical organization have replaced the four functional layers that characterize gamelan (and traditional angklung) music. As in a handbell choir, several musicians divide up the notes of a melody between them. Some special angklung include bamboo tubes tuned to the different notes of a chord, so that a few special angklung can provide a chordal accompaniment. Sometimes very large, low-pitched angklung provide a bassline; sometimes a string bass is added to the ensemble to provide the bass. Diatonic angklung groups (see Figure 5.2) perform arrangements of once-popular Western tunes, such as the "Blue Danube Waltz," as well as renditions of Indonesian popular songs and diatonicized Sundanese folk songs.

Diatonic angklung music may not sound as exotic to Western ears as gamelan music, but it still exemplifies Sundanese (and Javanese) values. The instruments are constructed from bamboo—a material that is intimately connected with the land and the cultures of Java. And although the musical organization departs from the four functional layers that characterize much Javanese music, the group's organization maintains one of the most significant Javanese musical processes: interlocking parts.

Nevertheless, a variety of gamelan ensembles derived from Javanese models are an integral part of that unique Sundanese identity as well. Although gamelan ensembles came to West Java as symbols of outside authority and power, in the ensuing centuries an astonishing variety of regional styles and repertories have flourished. Throughout these centuries

Sundanese musicians have adapted those aspects of foreign cultures that appealed to them, including not only gamelan, but ensembles with Western instruments, such as brass bands (Heins 1975; Yampolsky 1994a) and string bands (Harrell 1974: 12). The borrowings always take on a distinctly Sundanese flavor. Their foreign origins are obvious, but so is their Sundaneseness.

Archaic gamelan ensembles

It seems likely that the gamelan instruments that arrived in West Java from Mataram would resemble the ceremonial gamelan that are the valued heirlooms of the Central Javanese and north-coast palaces—namely, *gamelan sekaten* (see Chapters 3 and 4). While there are very old gamelan that do resemble gamelan sekaten in the Priangan, they are not the property of the palaces (that is, the kabupaten in the Sundanese case), but rather are the valued community property of a handful of small villages. Such ensembles are called *goong renteng*, among other names.

Some scholars speculate that goong renteng ensembles were played in the courts of the Pajajaran empire. When the north-coast city-states conquered Pajajaran, some stories tell us, they took the heirloom goong renteng instruments from Pajajaran to the courts of Cirebon, where they have come to be called *denggung*, and where they are still housed and played on special occasions. Cirebon royalty regards these ensembles as "foreign" (i.e., Sundanese) (North 1982a; North n.d.). Others suggest that renteng-like gamelan instruments came to West Java only after Mataram took control of the Priangan, and that the Sundanese villages came into possession of goong renteng instruments as "hand-me-downs" from the kabupaten, which may have replaced them with more up-to-date instruments as tastes and fashions changed (Heins 1977: 142).

In either case, it seems likely that these old sets of instruments represent some kind of window into the past. A few villages maintain these old instruments, and in keeping with their probable shared heritage with sekaten ensembles, many villages bring them out for the celebrations of Maulud (the prophet's birthday). As the ensembles grew older and hoarier, they became increasingly venerated. Some goong renteng ensembles are believed to possess remarkable powers; playing the ensemble in Lebakwangi (not too far from Bandung), for example, often brings rain.

Each of the surviving goong renteng ensembles differs from the others in significant ways; over the years, some ensembles have lost or added instruments and assigned different names to similar instruments. For example, the goong renteng in Lebakwangi includes a large one-row *bonang*, a *saron*-like instrument with many keys called *gangsa*, a gong without a *pencon* called *beri*, a drum, and two large gongs (Soepandi 1977). In Guradog (near Banten), the bonang is called *koromong*, and the saron-type instrument is called *selukat*. The ensemble at Cigugur includes mostly the same instruments, but the saron-like instrument is called *cecempres*, there is no beri, and there is an additional *kenong*-like gong chime called *panglima* (Soepandi and Atmadibrata 1976). A set from Leuwiliang (near the city of Sukabumi) adds a double-reed wind instrument called *tarompet* (Sastramidjaja 1978). The sets of instruments in Cikebo and Cileunyi (near Tanjung Sari) have even fewer instruments: a bonang-type instrument called *kokuang renteng*, two gongs, and drums (Soepandi and Atmadibrata 1976; Soepandi 1977). Figure

Figure 5.3 Goong renteng instruments (Henry Spiller).

5.3 is a photograph of goong renteng instruments formerly housed in the Museum Negeri Sri Baduga in Bandung.

There are some common features of these unique ensembles—features that characterize other archaic gamelan, such as sekaten, as well. They all feature a one-row gong chime (named bonang, koromong, or kokuang renteng), a pair of gongs, and drums. Many include a saron-type instrument (gangsa, selukat) as well. They all feature pelog-like tuning systems.

Most of these ensembles have a limited repertory of pieces; in keeping with the ensembles' venerated status, musicians make efforts to avoid modifying the pieces they play. Nevertheless, as each generation of musicians passes along the repertory and style to the next, inadvertent changes and innovations creep in. Sometimes musicians remember the names of pieces that used to be played but which have been forgotten. As instruments break, go out of tune, or become too fragile to play, the musicians make adjustments in what they do. As a result, each of the goong renteng ensembles features a truly unique sound, playing style, and repertory. This uniqueness reflects the identity of the community that owns the instruments and is invested in its history, and is manifested as well in the variety of terminology and piece names associated with each ensemble.

Like the gamelan sekaten in Central Java and Cirebon, the meaning of goong renteng music lies chiefly in its symbolism—the instruments themselves are tangible signs of the ancestors, while the sounds represent a perceptible, yet ineffable, link to the past. Although people recognize the significance of goong renteng music, they are rarely able to articulate exactly how it acquires its potent meaning. One particularly verbal musician, however, once provided ethnomusicologist Ernst Heins with a detailed account of the music's significance in the village of Lebakwangi.

Much of the message, the musician explained, arises out of the names of the pieces; each title suggests a web of meaningful connotations and associations. The specific sequence in which the pieces are played, then, provides its listeners with a sort of abstract allegory or philosophy. The title of the first piece, for example, is "Sodor" (literally "lance," but also suggesting "to thrust out" or "to present"); as a gift, then, the piece honors those in attendance and attracts their attention. Each subsequent piece title suggests a quality to strive for or advice for good living; its position in the sequence and relationship to the other titles further contribute to a coherent philosophy of life. The sum of all the pieces represents a lesson in how to conduct oneself with honor, humility, and dignity (Heins 1977: 124–32). It is not enough merely to recite, list, or know the piece titles, however; the discipline of playing and, most importantly, hearing the pieces unfold over time is an integral part of conveying their meaning (Zanten 1997).

Music for Dance and Theater: Gamelan Salendro

During the period of Mataram control, many Central and Eastern Javanese people moved to West Java, bringing with them Javanese culture, including wet-rice cultivation, batik (wax-resist dying), gamelan, dance, and wayang (Heins 1977: 15). Even today, in the small city of Sumedang, the old kabupaten building, now the Prabu Geusan Ulun Museum, proudly exhibits several sets of heirloom gamelan instruments as symbols of its rich history.

Gamelan history

After the fall of Pajajaran in 1579, one of its vassal states, the kingdom of Sumedanglarang, appropriated Pajajaran's collection of heirlooms (including the celebrated gold crown of Pajajaran's most famous king, Prabu Siliwangi). By possessing these heirlooms, the ruler of Sumedanglarang, who was named Prabu Geusan Ulun, laid claim to all the lands of Pajajaran. He managed to maintain some semblance of independence for many years, although he never did wrest the fallen Pajajaran lands he claimed from its conquerors. Sumedanglarang eventually fell under the control of Mataram; this new satellite region, combined with other conquered areas, was named Priangan, and its aristocrats became bupati who ruled under the authority of the king of Mataram.

One of the heirloom gamelan in the Sumedang kabupaten, a gamelan salendro with the name Panglipur (actually Panglipur is a court title rather than a proper name), dates from the time when Pangeran Rangga Gede was the bupati (1625–33), shortly after the Mataram takeover. Another heirloom gamelan, named Sari Oneng ("Essence of Longing"), is reputed to have been crafted in Mataram; its presence in Sumedang dates back to the time of Pangeran Rangga Gede's successor, Pangeran Penambahan. In the seventeenth century, these gamelan sets represented the link between the rulers of Sumedang and their Central Javanese overlords and served as symbols of the Sumedang nobility's authority to govern.

At the beginning of the eighteenth century, however, Mataram ceded control of the Priangan to the Dutch East Indies Company as payment for their help with a nasty political problem at home. Although the Company continued Mataram's policy of administering the area through the "native" aristocrats (the bupati), under Dutch control the easy flow of Javanese culture stopped. The ethnically Javanese but culturally distinct areas of Cirebon and Banten, in northern West Java, however, continued to be important influences.

Figure 5.4 Pangeran Surya Kusuma Adinata (also known as Pangeran Sugih), ruler of Sumedang, 1836–82 (photo and print collection of the Koninklijk Instituut voor Taal-, Land- en Volkenkunde, Leiden, the Netherlands).

The bupati nevertheless continued to model themselves and their kabupaten after the royal courts of Central Java. These aristocrats could and did travel east, and kept up with new developments they found there. Sundanese kabupaten flaunted their status and secured their position with gamelan instruments modeled after Central Javanese ensembles. The flow of ideas and fashions between Sundanese and Javanese cultures never completely stopped; newer innovations in Central Java eventually found their way west as well. Thus, the instruments of nineteenth- and twentieth-century Central Javanese gamelan were imported to West Java. Once again, the heirlooms in the Prabu Geusan Ulun Museum provide a window into these developments. Several gamelan from the time of the Sumedang rulers Pangeran Kornel (1791–1828) and Pangeran Sugih (1836–82; see Figure 5.4) take their places of honor beside the older gamelan.

One of the nineteenth-century sets of instruments now in the Prabu Geusan Ulun Museum in Sumedang even helps to tell the story of the Western world's first contact with gamelan music. Inspired by artifacts and tales brought back by adventurers and colonial officials from Africa and Asia, Europeans and Americans developed an intense curiosity about the customs of the rest of world during the late nineteenth century. One means to satisfy their curiosity was international expositions—grand world's fairs which featured exhibits of the latest technology and fashions, and quite often performers and craftspeople from various African, Asian, and American colonies. Dutch plantation owners

JAVA VILLAGE,
MIDWAY PLAISANCE.

Attention of the public is called to the TEAS and COFFEES sold in cups and small packages at the Tea and Coffee Booth. Tea from the famous Sinagar and Parakansalak Plantations. Tea, like coffee, is not Indigenous to Java. The great success following the introduction of coffee culture induced the planters to try the cultivation of tea. The success attending this has been so phenomenal that the Java planters have determined to put this production on the American market, being sure the excellent quality of JAVA TEA will be soon recognized by the American People.

While in the Village do not fail to visit the JAVA THEATRE, a reproduction of the Sultan's Theatre at Solo, directly opposite the Coffee and Tea Booth.

While in the Agricultural Building please visit our TEA, COFFEE, SPICE and FIBRE exhibit in JAVA SECTION, EAST GALLERY.

THE JAVA AMERICAN EXHIBIT CO.

Figure 5.5 Advertisement for the Java Village at the 1893 World Columbian Exposition in Chicago ("Java Village" [advertisement]). *World's Fair Puck* 12 (1893): 143).

exploited the world's fairs as a forum to publicize the coffee and tea products from their East Indies plantations; and they sent gamelan instruments, musicians, and dancers to the expositions to attract the attention of the crowds.

The set of gamelan instruments named Sari Oneng Parakansalak, now housed at the Prabu Geusan Ulun Museum, was forged in Sumedang around 1825; the name Parakansalak refers to the enormous tea plantation near the city of Sukabumi to which it belonged. Although it is now kept in Sumedang, the Parakansalak plantation administrators sent the gamelan, along with contingents of musicians and dancers, to expositions in Amsterdam in 1883 and Paris in 1889. The plantation owners' motives were mainly commercial; they wanted to attract attention to the coffee and tea products they were producing and exporting (see Figure 5.5). It was the gamelan performances at the Paris Exposition that Debussy heard (see DeVale 1977).

The plaque at the Prabu Geusan Ulun Museum claims that this gamelan also was sent to the World Columbian Exposition in Chicago in 1893 (see Figure 5.6). This cannot be true, because that set of instruments still is in Chicago—it was sold to the Field Museum in that city, where it remains to this day. It appears, however, that the Chicago gamelan is, for all intents and purposes, a replica of the Parakansalak gamelan; both gamelan share

Figure 5.6 Parakansalak gamelan and dancers at the 1893 World Columbian Exposition in Chicago (Bancroft 1893: 847).

features that are quite distinctive, especially the saron stands which are carved to look like two-headed lions (see Figure 5.7).

The Chicago group consisted mostly of plantation workers from Parakansalak (the trip to Chicago was a reward for faithful service), but included some Central Javanese musicians and dancers as well. The combined group performed both Central Javanese and Sundanese music on the Parakansalak instruments. It is clear from listening to the nineteenth-century wax cylinder recordings that even though the Sundanese musicians may have been using instruments essentially identical to their Central Javanese counterparts, they had long since developed their own styles of playing these instruments, along with uniquely Sundanese repertories; there is great contrast between the Javanese and Sundanese sections of the cylinders (Spiller 1996).

The specific instrumentation of Sumedang's heirloom gamelan varies quite a bit from set to set; while some of these gamelan are still playable, for most of the performances and classes held at the museum the musicians play a twentieth-century Sundanese gamelan named Sekar Manis ("Sweet Flower"). This not only prevents wear-and-tear on the heirloom sets, but the modern gamelan provides instruments that are more familiar and better suited to contemporary gamelan styles.

Sundanese gamelan tuning

Following Central Javanese models, nineteenth- and twentieth-century Sundanese gamelan could be tuned to one of two distinct tuning systems: salendro (the Sundanese language version of the Javanese word slendro) and pelog. Sundanese salendro and pelog

Figure 5.7 Saron stands carved in the shape of a two-headed lion from the gamelan Sari Oneng Parakansalak in the Prabu Geusan Ulun Museum in Sumedang (Henry Spiller).

are for most intents and purposes identical to their Javanese counterparts. As discussed in Chapter 3, salendro is a five-pitch equidistant tuning system; that is, the intervals between the five salendro pitches are approximately the same size (1,200 cents divided by 5 equals 240 cents). Pelog, on the other hand, is a seven-pitch non-equidistant tuning system; i.e., the intervals between the seven pelog pitches vary in size from very small (about 90 cents) to very large (more than 400 cents).

Although there was considerable overlap in repertory and playing style, Sundanese gamelan salendro and gamelan pelog, as they were known, represented distinct musical genres during the nineteenth and early twentieth centuries; each had its own functions and contexts. Gamelan pelog was appropriate for wayang (puppet theater), while gamelan salendro was appropriate for *tayuban* (aristocratic men's dance) and *kliningan* (listening music featuring female singers). Historical documents from various kabupaten sometimes provide separate lists of the kabupaten's salendro compositions and pelog compositions. Although double gamelan, which include both pelog and salendro instruments, are common in Central Java, Sundanese double gamelan are rare.

In the colonial period, acquiring even one set of instruments was a formidable undertaking outside of aristocratic circles because of the enormous cost; those who managed to do so had to choose between salendro and pelog. Because most of those non-aristocrats looking to own gamelan were dalang (puppeteers), who needed the instruments for their work, pelog was a popular choice. After Indonesian independence in 1949, however, audiences began to demand that female singers appear with gamelan, even gamelan for wayang. Female singers (called *pasinden*) preferred gamelan salendro,

salendro	1	M		2	M		3	M		4	M		5	M		1
sorog	1 S 2		L			3 S 4		M		5			L			1
pelog degung	1 S 2		L			3		M		4 S 5			L			1

Figure 5.8 Intervals of salendro, sorog, and pelog degung.

and gamelan pelog fell out of fashion (some musicians even retuned their pelog instruments to salendro). In the ensuing years, most musicians forgot the pelog repertory and many of the specific style characteristics associated with gamelan pelog.

A key reason that female singers preferred salendro over pelog was that salendro provided them much more flexibility to sing songs in a variety of other Sundanese tuning systems, each of which sets a different mood. These alternate tuning systems, like salendro, basically are pentatonic, and two or three of the pitches in the alternate system actually coincide with the gamelan's salendro pitches (Sundanese musicians call these common pitches *tumbuk*). But the remaining pitches are quite different from their salendro counterparts. By adjusting just a couple of salendro's pitches, the character of all the melodic intervals changes—instead of all equidistant intervals, which make each melodic step sound the same as the others, the alternate systems feature very large and very small intervals in addition to the medium-sized salendro intervals. When performing with a salendro gamelan, a singer can choose from three basic scales: salendro, *sorog* (also called *madenda*), and *pelog degung* (also call *kobongan* or *mataraman*). Figure 5.8 is a representation of the intervallic structures of salendro, sorog, and pelog degung and the relative position of small, medium, and large intervals in each.

Some musicians call these alternate tuning systems, and the practice of using them, *surupan*. Ethnomusicologist Max Harrell characterized sorog and pelog degung as "quasi-pelog" scales because, like pelog, they are characterized by large and small intervals (Harrell 1975: 89). They are, however, five-tone scales, not seven-tone scales like pelog. Furthermore, sorog and pelog degung, unlike pelog, include one characteristically salendro interval—that is, an interval that is approximately 240 cents.

Nowadays, gamelan pelog and gamelan salendro represent a unified musical genre, which some people call *gamelan salendro/pelog* (Supandi 1970: 21; Natapradja 1972: 63; Soepandi and Atmadibrata 1976: 65; Heins 1977: 54), but others call simply gamelan. Recent experiments with instruments that provide the capability to play both salendro and pelog pitches, and which can be played in a variety of the alternate tuning systems as well, reinforce the notion that Sundanese musicians conceive of a single, overarching gamelan "style" that is appropriate for accompanying dance, wayang, and other theatrical productions, and listening music featuring female singers.

Musical terminology

Sundanese musical terminology and musical notation is a labyrinth of confusion and contradiction; the following discussion is most definitely not for the faint of heart! Sundanese musicians name the five pitches of the salendro scale, from high to low, *barang* (or *tugu*), *kenong* (or *lorloran/loloran*), *panelu*, *bem* (or *galimer* or *gulu*), and *singgul*. Sundanese musicians, especially those associated with government-sponsored schools of the arts, sometimes assign numbers to the five pitches of the salendro scale. In direct contrast to the Central Javanese system of numbering pitches described in Chapter 4, in which the number 1 is assigned to the lowest pitch in the scale, Sundanese musicians assign the number 1 to the highest pitch in the scale. Of course, the numbers are repeated in each octave; the note above 1 is 5. Sundanese musicians also sometimes use a syllable system, comparable to the Western *do–re–mi*, called *damina* after the first three of its five syllables (*da, mi, na, ti,* and *la*). The damina system is moveable in the sense that any pitch can be designated as *da*, and the rest of the syllables follow suit; the syllables are assigned to pitches from high to low.

As if salendro were not confusing enough, pelog is a little more complicated. The names of five of the seven pelog pitches are the same as the salendro names. Pelog has two additional pitches: one, called *bungur* or *liwung*, lies between kenong (2) and panelu (3); the other, called *sorog* or *petit*, lies between barang (1) and the singgul (5) in the next octave above it. As was the case with Central Javanese gamelan, Sundanese pelog pieces tend to emphasize five-pitch subsets of the seven pelog pitches, so it makes sense that the five pitches with names in common between salendro and pelog would keep the same numbers. Bungur, because it is "less than 3" (that is, between 2 and 3), is notated as 3– (even though it is higher in pitch than panelu). Similarly, petit, because it is "more than 5," is designated as 5+ (even though it is lower in pitch than singgul). These various naming systems are summarized in Table 5.1; note that pitches go from top to bottom in the table, in accordance with the way Sundanese musicians conceptualize their scales. Musicians use similar systems to describe the pitches in the various surupan as well.

Assigning damina syllables to pelog scales involves determining which five-pitch subset is in use, which of those five pitches should be *da*, and working from there. Sundanese theorists recognize three named subsets of pelog: *pelog jawar* (barang, kenong, panelu, bem, singgul); *pelog liwung* (barang, kenong, bungur, bem, singgul); and *pelog sorog* (barang, kenong, panelu, bem, sorog). For pelog jawar, barang is da; for pelog liwung, bem is da; for pelog sorog, panelu is da (see Table 5.2).

If all of these systems of pitches, scales, subsets, names, and numbers seem hopelessly confusing, that is because they are in fact hopelessly confusing. There is little standardization among Sundanese musicians and theorists regarding concepts of tuning system and scale, pitch names, or notational systems. Some, but certainly not all, of the alternate pitch names have already been mentioned. To some musicians, the word *laras* means tuning system, as in "laras salendro" or "laras pelog"; but it might also refer to the various five-pitch subsets of pelog, such as "laras pelog sorog." Others will use the term surupan to refer to those pelog subsets, confounding those who use surupan to describe the alternate tuning systems that can be combined with salendro. And some musicians, especially when working with pelog or the alternate scales sorog and pelog degung, will use a moveable numbering system in which the number "1" is always associated with da—throwing off those who regard the numbers as permanently associated with particular keys or gongs on their instruments.

Nevertheless, most musicians manage to communicate with one another—mostly by avoiding notation altogether. Musicians are generally familiar with the variety of terms in common usage, and can determine from the context what their fellow musicians are talking about. In fact, some musicians take great delight in arguing endlessly about the exact meanings of particularly contentious terms. Perhaps the fluidity and ambiguity

Table 5.1 Salendro and pelog naming and numbering systems.

Sundanese salendro pitch name	Sundanese pelog pitch name	Sundanese damina syllable	Sundanese number	Javanese number (see Chapter 4)
—	sorog/petit	(leu)	5+	7
barang	barang	da	1	6
kenong	kenong	mi	2	5
—	liwung/bungur	(ni)	3–	4
panelu	panelu	na	3	3
bem/galimer	bem/galimer	ti	4	2
singgul	singgul	la	5	1

Table 5.2 Salendro and pelog naming and numbering systems.

Sundanese pelog pitch name	damina for pelog jawar	damina for pelog liwung	damina for pelog sorog	Sundanese number	Javanese number
sorog	(leu)	(ni)	na	5+	7
barang	da	na	ti	1	6
kenong	mi	ti	la	2	5
bungur	(ni)	la	(leu)	3–	4
panelu	na	(leu)	da	3	3
bem	ti	da	mi	4	2
singgul	la	mi	(ni)	5	1

in terminology actually contributes to the rich flexibility of Sundanese musical practice. Certainly when they are playing together, Sundanese musicians rely on their ears to guide them. It is only when music is written down—when it is excised from the context in which it usually embedded, and cast in stone—that confusion might arise.

Learning to play gamelan

For most musicians, playing gamelan music in West Java is not a very lucrative proposition. While it is true that some musical specialists, such as female singers and dalang (puppeteers), sometimes earn considerable fees for their services, and that there are some salaried civil service positions available for qualified performers, the majority of rank-and-file musicians earns only a pittance for their services. Even musicians who are "professional" musicians in the sense that they are always paid for their work almost always have to find some other sources of income.

Obviously, few are drawn to the performing arts because of the financial rewards; most people who become musicians do so because something compels them to do so. Sundanese people recognize three compelling forces that lead individuals to the arts: family lineage (*keturunan*), tendency or aptitude (*bakat*), and desire (*kemauan*). Those rare individuals with all three have almost no choice but to make performing the focus of their lives; it is quite possible, however, to become an excellent musician with just two, and a competent musician with only one.

Family lineage puts budding artists in an environment in which they learn the nuts and bolts of music and other performing arts the same way they learn to speak—by osmosis, before they are even aware that they are learning anything. Musical activities in West Java are dominated by musical families, in which many family members are accomplished artists. It is not unusual to see the young children (even adopted children) of established performers do prodigious technical feats at a very young age. Such children often receive relatively formal instruction from their older relatives, which gives them quite an advantage over students from non-artistic families.

Undang Sumarna, who has taught thousands of American students the basics of Sundanese gamelan music during his long tenure teaching at the University of California at Santa Cruz, is an example of a musician from an artistic family. He learned how to play gamelan, as well as the intricate skills of drumming for dance, from his grandfather, Abah Kayat. Several of Kayat's brothers were accomplished musicians, and they all belonged to a troupe of musicians who staged dance performances (Spiller 1993). Not all of Undang's siblings became musicians, however; Kayat recognized in Undang an additional quality—a knack, or an aptitude, for memorizing the complex drum patterns that accompany dance movements and understanding how they fit into the musical structure. So Kayat singled Undang out for intensive instruction (at times encouraging Undang to practice by inflicting mild corporal punishment). Undang's family connections also provided him with the visibility he needed to find employment as a drummer.

Burhan Sukarma, whose style of playing the *suling* (bamboo flute) set new standards of style and excellence in the 1970s and 1980s when he was a staff musician at the Bandung branch of Radio Republik Indonesia (RRI), and who has played for countless commercially released recordings, is an accomplished musician who did not come from an artistic family. The main thing that compelled him to pursue music was an overwhelming desire, which led him to seek out and "hang around" accomplished musicians. By making himself welcome by doing favors and acting agreeable, he could observe and imitate their actions. He also collected cassette recordings of musicians whose playing he admired and tried to copy their performances during his private practice sessions. Unlike Undang, Burhan did not receive any musical training as a young child; he began his musical studies in his teens. By dint of his dedication and talent, however, the established musicians noticed his advancing skills and welcomed him into their ensembles.

Most people would agree that Burhan and Undang both came equipped with a special knack for musical performance; a compelling family background (in Undang's case) and an overwhelming desire (in Burhan's case) reinforced the knack and led them to master some of the more difficult instrumental skills. There is a place in Sundanese gamelan music, too, for people with nothing but an overwhelming desire to play. Very often, such musicians are drawn to the social life that playing with a gamelan group entails;

a working troupe travels together from place to place, enjoys considerable hospitality from its employers, and builds strong bonds of friendship with fellow troupe members through constant close contact. Kathy Foley quotes a gamelan musician as saying "if you are a musician, you always have friends" (Foley 1979: 85). The magical, lively, and glamorous world of gamelan performance provides a welcome respite from the daily grind of home and family.

It is possible to learn the basics of playing gamelan by sitting on stage with musicians during their performance; this is, in fact, the way that many musicians acquired their skills. Gamelan performances are rarely so formal that a few extra people on stage pose any problem. Musicians sometimes bring one of their children (or a neighbor's child who has an interest) along for the ride, and expose the young one to the excitement of playing gamelan. Older individuals with the desire to learn can mill about in the background, ingratiating themselves with the musicians and getting a close-up view of the various instrumental parts and techniques. Eventually, a musician might leave the stage, creating an opportunity for a budding musician who is brave enough and knows the part well enough to try playing it. A mistake will result in mild, long-lasting, but good-natured derision from the musicians. The error will do little to mar the performance irreparably, but it's not likely that the humiliated student will ever make the same mistake again.

Much gamelan "rehearsal" is actually accomplished during performances; what makes for good performances is the precision with which the musicians work together. Musicians do sometimes get together for practice sessions, called *latihan*, outside of performances. Sometimes a latihan is intended to prepare for a particular performance. More often, however, latihan are meant to provide an opportunity to learn or improve one's skills; those who would like to learn more about playing music find latihan a useful exercise. The root word, *latih*, has the sense of "becoming accustomed to." Only rarely do latihan participants stop and spot-rehearse something; rather, they play through pieces as if they were at a performance, and in doing so they become accustomed to performing. Sometimes, accomplished artists host a latihan for aspiring musicians who would like to learn from them; in such cases, the participants are expected to discreetly pay their teacher.

Thus, in any gamelan group, there will be some master musicians, some merely competent players, and sometimes even rank beginners. The instrumentation, style, and structure of gamelan music facilitate these multiple tiers of skill levels. Some of the instruments require vast stores of knowledge and great dexterity to play, while others are relatively simple. Prospective musicians begin with the easier instruments and progress to the more difficult ones as their family position, aptitude, and desire allow.

Gamelan salendro instrumentation

In its most basic form, Sundanese gamelan includes nine performers who play instruments that are often quite similar to the Central Javanese gamelan instruments described in Chapter 4. The core Sundanese gamelan instruments are described below.

> *Goong*—a large knobbed gong that is vertically suspended from a frame and struck with a thickly padded stick. The low-pitched, deep, undulating sound is not damped, and the specific pitch is unimportant.

Figure 5.9 Gamelan salendro instruments. *Left to right*: gambang (in back), gendang, rebab, two saron, and part of the panerus gong stand visible in back) (Henry Spiller).

Kempul—a knobbed gong that is smaller and has a higher pitch than goong. It is suspended from the same frame as goong, and it is struck with the same padded stick by the same musician. The performer usually damps the sound of kempul after it has been struck, usually with one hand which is inside the back of the instrument; this hand also prevents the instrument from swinging too much. As with goong, specific pitch is unimportant.

Saron—six- or seven-keyed metallophone, the keys of which are laid over a common trough resonator (occasionally individual but untuned resonators) hollowed out of a single block of wood. The musician strikes the keys, one at a time, with a light wooden hammer (*panakol*). The player damps the sound by pinching the vibrating key with his free hand. Sundanese gamelan usually include two saron.

Panerus—six- or seven-keyed metallophone, the keys of which are laid over a box resonator (that is, not hollowed out of a single block of wood, but rather a box made of boards). The playing technique is the same as that of saron. Panerus is tuned one octave lower than saron, has thinner, broader keys, and produces a softer, mellower sound.

Bonang—gong chime with ten small knobbed gongs supported horizontally in two rows on ropes stretched in a frame. The player uses two thinly padded sticks to play and damp the gongs. The lower octave is in the same range as panerus; the higher octave is in the saron range. The total range is two octaves.

Gambang—xylophone with eighteen to twenty-one wooden keys placed over a box

Figure 5.10 Gamelan salendro instruments. *Left to right*: two saron, panerus, kenong (Henry Spiller).

resonator. The musician plays with two padded disks attached to thin sticks. No damping technique is required. The range is approximately three and a half to four octaves.

Gendang—set of two-headed, barrel-shaped drums.

Rebab—spike fiddle with two brass strings and a skin-covered resonator, played with a horsehair bow. Unlike the other gamelan instruments, which are a set and incompatible with instruments from other gamelan, all rebab are compatible with any gamelan. Sundanese rebab players generally bring their own instruments to performances. A modern rebab is made so that it can be dismantled and carried in a small briefcase. The rebab strings are tuned to the pitches barang and bem.

Pasinden—female vocalist. Although not really an "instrument," per se, the pasinden's vocal part is comparable in some ways to the other gamelan instruments' parts. Some female vocalists prefer to be called *juru kawih.*

Other instruments can be added to this basic ensemble, provided the instruments themselves are available and additional performers beyond the core nine are there to play them. These optional instruments are described below.

Kenong—gong chime with one to six large, high-pitched knobbed gongs laid horizontally over ropes in a frame. The gongs are tuned to pitches in the gamelan's tuning system.

Figure 5.11 LS Rawit Group from Soreang, with pasinden Lia Mustika (Henry Spiller).

Jengglong—gong chime with three to six gongs. Jengglong is similar to kenong, but the gongs are flatter and tuned an octave lower.

Peking—metallophone similar to saron but tuned an octave higher.

Rincik—gong chime similar to bonang but tuned an octave higher.

Kecrek—stack of iron plates which is hit with a wooden hammer to make a noisy, jangling sound.

Ketuk—small gong laid horizontally and hit with a padded stick.

Figures 5.9 to 5.11 show various Sundanese gamelan instruments and personnel. Although many of these instruments are quite similar to their Central Javanese counterparts, the names and construction details of some instruments are significantly different. Sundanese call the large gong goong (pronounced go-ong to suggest the instrument's undulating quality); a Sundanese goong is often polished to a bright sheen, in contrast to most Javanese gongs, which are left with the black patina they acquire in the forge. Sundanese kempul, in contrast, are often left black, while Javanese kempul are almost always shiny. The Sundanese rincik is for all intents and purposes the same as a Central Javanese bonang panerus. The Sundanese word rincik, when applied to musical instruments, means high-pitched, but in other contexts it also has connotations of delicately falling rain or a creeping vine that intertwines itself with whatever supports it—appropriate metaphors for the fast, cascading figurations played on instruments called rincik. The Javanese impart similar implications to the word panerus, which comes from the root word *terus*, and suggests following along or accompanying something else (Soeharto 1992: 110), or continuing, and they also apply the term to the highest-pitched instrument in an instrument "family" (e.g., saron panerus, bonang panerus, gender panerus).

Some of the name and construction differences point to significant differences in musical aesthetics and playing styles between Sundanese and Javanese gamelan. In the Sundanese language, the word panerus has similar implications as it has in Javanese and Indonesian languages. The instrument that Sundanese call panerus, however, most closely resembles a Central Javanese saron demung—the lowest-pitched member of the saron family; in other words, it seems to have exactly the opposite implication that it carries for the Javanese. In Sundanese gamelan style, musicians typically play relatively fast-moving, decorated parts on this low-pitched saron-type instrument, in contrast to the relatively slow parts associated with the saron demung in Central Javanese gamelan style. Sundanese panerus tend to have thinner keys and a larger resonator box than their Javanese counterparts, and Sundanese musicians typically use a soft, sometime padded mallet to play the panerus rather than the robust Javanese wooden hammer; as a result, the Sundanese panerus has a softer, more delicate sound than the Javanese equivalent. It appears that the Sundanese panerus is not so much a member of a "family" as it is an individual instrument with its own unique function in the ensemble.

Like Javanese, Sundanese prefer the sound of gamelan made of bronze (*perunggu*), but a considerably less expensive alternative is iron (*beusi*). Instrument stands (*ancak*) often feature elaborate carvings and bright paint (most often blue, green, blue-green, or red; brown, and natural finishes also are common) with gold highlights.

Musical organization

Sundanese gamelan music features the same four functional layers as the Cirebonese, Javanese, and Balinese gamelan music described in Chapters 3 and 4: (1) colotomic foundation; (2) simplified/abstracted melody, (3) elaborated/varied melody, and (4) drum patterns that shape the phrases, coordinate rhythmic activity, and synchronize the music with other activities such as dance. Once again, these four functions combine to create a stratified musical texture; in Sundanese gamelan style, however, the layers are not always as clearly articulated as they are in Central Javanese and Balinese music. The four layers also chart a budding musician's path to learning to play gamelan music. The colotomic layer is perhaps the easiest to learn because many different pieces share the same colotomic forms. Once students have mastered these formal basics by successfully playing the goong and kempul, they can move on to learning the abstract, essential melodies for various pieces by playing the kenong. Most students advance to playing instruments such as saron, panerus, and bonang, which require mastering some elaboration techniques. Only a few musicians progress beyond these instruments to learn to play rebab and gendang.

Instruments that have a primarily colotomic function include goong, kempul, kenong, jengglong, and ketuk. Melodic Sundanese gamelan instruments can be divided into two categories: (1) percussion instruments with fixed pitches (that is, each key or pot is tuned permanently to a single pitch that cannot be altered during performance) and small ranges, and (2) non-percussion instruments with no fixed pitches (that is, the instrument can produce a multitude of pitches) and large ranges. These can be referred to as "fixed" and "free" instruments, respectively. The fixed instruments are percussion instruments, and they are limited to pitches in the salendro tuning system. As percussion instruments, their sound, once started, can be stopped (damped) but not sustained. The fixed instrument category includes kenong, saron, panerus, peking, bonang, and rincik. The free instruments are rebab (spike fiddle) and the singers. The singers and the rebab player delight in producing minute variations in pitch and timbre and taking advantage of the control they have over the duration and volume of their sounds.

The gambang (wooden xylophone) is somewhere between a fixed and a free instrument. While it is a percussion instrument, its sound can be sustained (in a manner of speaking) with a tremolo technique in which the player rapidly repeats a note to suggest a sustained tone. The gambang's range—almost four octaves—is much wider than the other fixed instruments. Unlike the rebab and pasinden, however, with gamelan salendro gambang is limited to the salendro tuning system. The four layers are completed by the gendang (drums) player who, of course, provides the drumming element.

Colotomic layer

Sundanese colotomic parts are like Central Javanese colotomic parts in that a long cycle marked by a gong stroke is divided into increasingly shorter units by strokes on instruments with distinctive timbres. In theory, kenong strokes divide the gong phrases into smaller sections. In practice, however, the instrument kenong is not always included in the gamelan ensemble; nevertheless, listeners "hear" the implication of kenong strokes, even if the instrument itself is not audible.

Again in theory, a kempul stroke marks the midpoint of phrases marked with kenong strokes. In practice, Sundanese kempul parts are rarely so simple. Kempul players consistently add an extra kempul stroke or two just before striking the goong. Occasionally the kempul player performs a more complicated pattern of strokes or leaves out a few strokes (cf. Foley 1979: 56).

Theoretical ketuk strokes come halfway between (theoretical) kenong and (theoretical) kempul strokes. In practice, a ketuk is rarely played at all, or even present; the bonang often (but not always) plays the ketuk's colotomic rhythm. The absence of kenong and ketuk in many gamelan, the melodic as well as rhythmic role of kenong in current practice (see below), and the liberties players take with kempul parts minimize the roles of these instruments as colotomic markers in Sundanese gamelan style. In Sundanese gamelan music, the colotomic functional layer is always implicit but rarely explicit; either the instruments that would play them are absent, or else the basic colotomic parts are embellished beyond their role as regular time markers.

The goong strokes, however, are an important aural marker for Sundanese musicians and listeners. Perhaps the most glaring mistake a musician can make is forgetting to play the goong, or playing it at the wrong moment. A misplaced goong stroke will inspire visible discomfort in the other musicians. One musician sees the "meaning" of gamelan music as the working together of the various musicians toward a common goal, namely the stroke of the goong. He sees the goong stroke as the payoff, the reward for working hard and cooperating. The goong stroke is *enak*—"delicious" (Otong Rasta, pers. comm., 6/19/99; see also Weintraub 1993). Kathy Foley reports that "players say that the sounding of the deep-toned goong is as necessary and inevitable as death is to life" (Foley 1979: 55).

Core melody

Sundanese musicians "encode" gamelan pieces in their memories as abstract melodic outlines that capture the essential, identifying features of a piece without instrument-specific features. Many Sundanese gamelan pieces are conceptualized as a simple sequence of pitches called *pola lagu* ("pattern for a piece/song"), *tugu lagu* ("piece/song pillar[s]") (Soepandi 1985: 166), or *arkuh lagu* ("song skeleton/frame"). These terms suggest that the sequence of pitches provides a pattern or an outline for the musicians to follow—a framework for them to fill in. The individual pitches in the sequence, which musicians sometimes call *pokok*, *posisi kenong*, or *kenong*, act as musical "pillars" that provide a sturdy framework on which the musicians can hang their individual parts. In its most essential form, a piece's core pattern may consist of as few as two "pillar" pitches.

To perform the pieces, musicians flesh out the pillar pitches with instrument-specific melodic motifs—a process some musicologists call realization. Sundanese realization techniques differ from musician to musician, family to family, and group to group. One performance of a piece can sound very different from another performance; nevertheless, Sundanese listeners recognize the particular pattern of pillar pitches and know which piece they are hearing. The most common pieces of this sort are known collectively as *patokan*. In the Sundanese language, the root word of patokan (*patok*) has to do with boundary markers, again suggesting that the pieces provide an outline for the musicians. The individual pitches quite literally show the musicians the "boundaries" of the piece as they navigate their way through the music.

In performance, a piece's pillar pitches occur at regular time intervals; the time interval between pillar pitches may be quite short or rather long depending on the circumstances of the performance. To generate a part, an instrumentalist chooses from a personal repertory of motifs that rhythmically and melodically lead to and coincide with the appropriate pillar pitch at the appropriate time.

Elaboration

In Central Javanese gamelan, an entire group of instrumentalists (on the various sizes of keyed instruments in the saron family) play the *balungan* ("skeleton")—a part that many regard to be the core melody—while other musicians elaborate the core melody. In Sundanese gamelan, the parts played on all the melodic gamelan instruments (with the possible exception of the kenong) involve some kind of elaboration upon the piece's core melody. Core melody is an especially abstract concept in Sundanese music, but it represents the mental boundary markers that keep all the musicians playing together.

The piece "Sinyur" (heard on Tracks 7 and 8 of the CD that accompanies this book), for example, consists of four essential pillar pitches. Two of the four pillar pitches are goong tones, meaning that they coincide with strokes of the large goong; these are indicated with circles in the following notation.

$$1 \;\; ⓐ \;\; 1 \;\; ③$$

In performance, these pillar pitches are evenly spaced in time, and the cycle of pillar pitches is repeated for as long as the piece needs to be played. The musicians fill in the

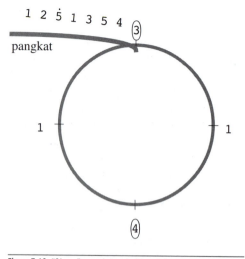

1 2 5̇ 1 3 5 4

③

pangkat

1   1

④

Figure 5.12 "Sinyur": pangkat and pillar pitches.

spaces between them with instrument-specific melodic motifs. Perhaps a better way to graphically illustrate a piece's pattern is by arranging the pillar tones in a circle, as in Figure 5.12. The gray circle represents the musical time that the musicians fill with their instrument-specific realizations. To begin the piece, one musician (typically the saron player) plays a short introductory melodic phrase, called a *pangkat*, that leads to one of the pillar pitches marked by a goong stroke. The introductory phrase notated in the figure is the one that the lead saron player provides at the beginning of "Sinyur" as performed by LS Giri Harja III (Track 7 on the accompanying CD, from 0:00 to 0:06). Once started, the piece proceeds clockwise around the circle until a drum signal indicates that it is time to end; the musicians draw the rendition to a close at a goong stroke, so that the sound of the goong is the last thing people hear.

Often the first step in realizing a patokan piece involves somehow increasing the number of pillar pitches in each gong phrase to four or more. Musicians can derive the extra pitches in several ways. One way is to simply repeat the preceding pillar pitch (see Figure 5.13). Another way is to add a *pancer* pitch between each of the essential pillar pitches. In Sundanese, the word pancer means "middle point" or "center"; as a musical term, it suggests choosing a consistent pitch to insert halfway between existing pitches. In choosing a pancer for a piece, musicians avoid using any of the pitches already in use; in the case of "Sinyur," the pitches 1, 3, and 4 are already in use, so the choices for pancer are 2 and 5 (see Figure 5.14).

This expanded outline—the pillar pitches plus a pancer—is an appropriate part for a kenong player to play. In most modern gamelan, the instrument kenong (if present) includes gongs tuned to each pitch in the tuning system. The pitches played by the kenong player often are the pillar pitches of the piece's outline. Perhaps this is why many Sundanese musicians refer to the pillar pitches themselves as "kenong" regardless of whether the instrument kenong is included or played in the ensemble. The part played on the kenong is perhaps the most complete version of the essential melody of any of the parts.

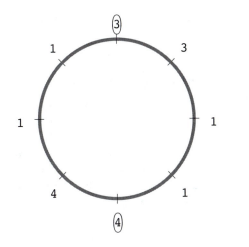

Figure 5.13 "Sinyur": deriving additional pillar pitches.

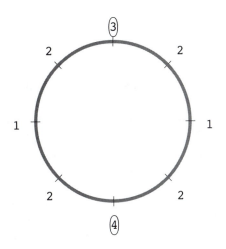

Figure 5.14 "Sinyur": deriving additional pillar pitches with a pancer.

The LS Giri Harja III musicians chose pitch 2 as their pancer for the performance recorded in Track 7 of the accompanying CD; for the first two full iterations of the cycle of "Sinyur," the kenong player's performance of the pillar pitches as notated in the figure is clearly audible. Table 5.3 maps the CD timings to the kenong strokes on the recording. Note that the tempo speeds up considerably in the second phrase of the first iteration, only to slow down again at the beginning of the second iteration.

The goong player (who also plays the kempul) subdivides each kenong phrase in half with a kempul stroke. It is customary to add an extra kempul stroke before the goong, usually as notated in Figure 5.15. This basic goong/kempul pattern represents an extremely common colotomic form in Sundanese music.

The most basic part that a bonang player in a Sundanese gamelan could provide would

Table 5.3 Timings for pillar pitches in "Sinyur."

Pangkat, first goong		(pangkat)		③
CD timing				0:05
First repetition				
pillar pitches	2	1	2	④
CD timing	0:08	0:11	0:15	0:17
pillar pitches	2	1	2	③
CD timing	0:19	0:21	0:23	0:26
Second repetition				
pillar pitches	2	1	2	④
CD timing	0:29	0:33	0:36	0:40
pillar pitches	2	1	2	③
CD timing	0:44	0:48	0:51	0:54

duplicate the colotomic rhythm that a ketuk player would provide—that is, subdividing the time segment between kenong and kempul strokes. Because the bonang also is an elaborating instrument, the bonang part has a melodic role as well; it anticipates the upcoming pillar pitch by sounding it in the ketuk rhythm (see Figure 5.16).

Because the kenong player is "filling in" the extra pillar position with a pancer, however, there is a delicious clash between the pitch that the bonang part anticipates and the pitch the kenong actually plays; these clashes are resolved by the time the original pillar pitches come around, however (see Figure 5.17).

The two saron in a Sundanese gamelan are identical, but they rarely play the same part. The lead saron player (saron I) can choose from a variety of realization styles to come up with a part. The saron II player usually constructs a part whose notes fall between the saron I part's notes both rhythmically and pitchwise so that the two parts interlock; Sundanese musicians call these interlocking figurations *caruk*.

The players of the other "fixed" instruments, namely panerus, peking, and rincik, follow similar procedures to create their parts. Each instrument has its own idiom, which predicts how slow or fast its part should proceed and what kinds of melodic twists and turns it should take. The musicians have quite a bit of latitude within these idioms; the only truly hard and fast rule is that all the instrument parts come together at the pillar pitches. In between the pillar pitches, they weave a rich fabric of pitches, melodies, timbres, and textures. In addition, there is a variety of realization styles for each instrument, which in different combinations allow for almost limitless moods to emerge from the ensemble. The two saron might choose to play lightning-fast, delicate interlocking motifs to provide an appropriate accompaniment for a singer. The saron players might switch to a less florid style to accompany quick-moving action in a dance or puppet show. In such a situation, the bonang can play aggressive melodic figurations to enhance the new mood. LS Giri Harja III's performance of "Sinyur" (Track 7 of the CD that accompanies this book) includes many such realization style changes as the ensemble first accompanies a puppet's aggressive and energetic dance (the first three minutes of the recording) and then, without stopping, continues to accompany some narration (at 2:55), followed by a lyrical solo sung by the pasinden (at 3:43).

"Fixed" instrument parts generally move along in strict rhythm; regardless of whether a fixed instrument part moves quickly or slowly, it is usually quite even and consistent. The idioms of the rebab player and the singers are "free" in the sense that their rhythm can be quite elastic compared to the other gamelan instruments. They often arrive at pillar pitches slightly before or after the fixed instrument parts. The free parts include long-held notes as well as quick-moving melodic fragments. Singers and rebab players also deploy an arsenal of ornaments, such as trills, slides, and vibratos, to further elaborate their already florid parts.

When performing with gamelan salendro, rebab players and singers often further enhance the contrast between their free parts and the fixed instrument idioms by using a different tuning system (sometimes called *surupan*) than the fixed instruments. Alternate tuning systems, such as sorog and pelog degung, are "superimposed" over the gamelan's tuning system so that there are two or three pitches in common with the fixed instruments' salendro tuning. The contrast between the rhythmic and melodic characteristics of fixed and free instrument idioms is a major part of Sundanese musical aesthetics.

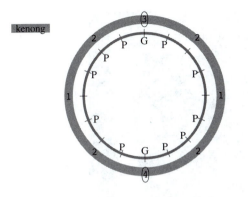

Figure 5.15 "Sinyur": goong and kempul parts.

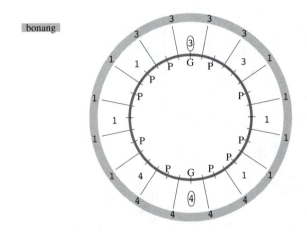

Figure 5.16 "Sinyur": bonang part.

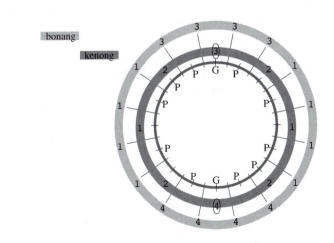

Figure 5.17 "Sinyur": bonang part with pancer.

Figure 5.18 Otong Rasta playing rebab; his left hand shows the sorog hand position (Henry Spiller).

The alternate tuning systems that rebab players and singers superimpose over salendro are differentiated by the intervals between their five principal pitches. While there are subtle differences between the intervals, they all can be characterized as small, medium, or large. Salendro includes only medium intervals. Both sorog and pelog degung have two small intervals, two large intervals, and one medium interval (refer back to Figure 5.8 on p. 121 to see these tuning systems compared).

Perhaps the simplest way to conceptualize how these alternate tuning systems can be combined with salendro is to examine how a rebab player produces the various alternate tunings on his instrument. Although the rebab has two strings, most of the notes are played on only one of them; this string is tuned to the pitch barang (i.e., pitch 1). A rebab player stops the string with his forefinger (f), middle finger (m), ring finger (r), and pinkie (p) to produce the various pitches on the rebab (see Figure 5.18). Most typically, the performer keeps his hand in one of three positions along the neck of the rebab at any given time. Between the four fingers and three hand positions, it is possible to produce notes over a range of approximately two octaves.

To play in salendro, the rebab player positions his hand in such a way that his four

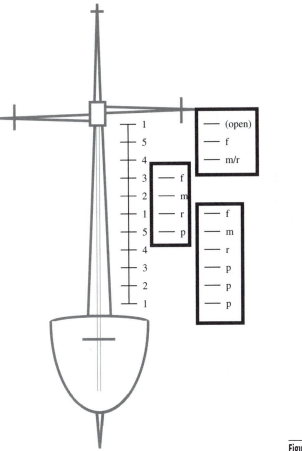

Figure 5.19 Rebab fingerings for salendro.

fingers touch the strings so that the distance between each finger is approximately the same (in reality, because of the physics of vibrating strings, each distance is slightly different; conceptually, however, the distances between the fingers are the same). Figure 5.19 illustrates where each finger must touch the string in each of the three hand positions to produce a salendro pitch. The hand positions overlap to a certain extent; some pitches can be played in more than one hand position. The three highest salendro pitches are played by sliding the pinkie up and down from the highest position.

Unlike salendro, which features only medium-sized intervals, the other surupan include mostly large and small intervals. To play a small interval, the rebab player can squeeze any two adjacent fingers very close to each other. Large intervals are more problematic; because of the anatomy of the human hand, it is difficult to separate the middle and ring fingers far enough to produce a large interval. It is quite easy, however, to stretch the pinkie out to reach a large interval, and not impossible to place a large interval between the forefinger and middle finger. Sorog fingerings, therefore, feature hand positions that place the large intervals between the ring finger and pinkie or between the forefinger and middle finger, as illustrated in Figure 5.20.

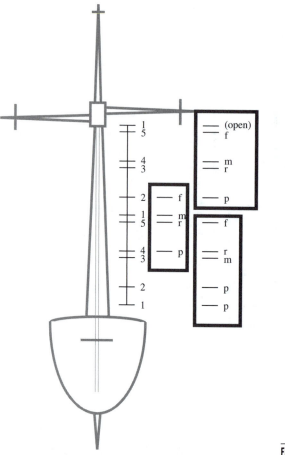

Figure 5.20 Rebab fingerings for sorog.

In fact, in the minds of many rebab players, sorog is characterized primarily by a particular hand position in which there is a medium interval between the fore- and middle fingers, a small interval between the middle and ring fingers, and a large interval between the ring finger and pinkie. In Figure 5.20, this characteristically sorog hand position was the middle hand position. By moving this characteristic hand position to other places on the string, a rebab player can produce other sorog scales, with different pitches in common with salendro. Because the small, medium, and large intervals follow a different pattern in pelog degung, rebab players use different hand positions for these surupan as well, as illustrated in Figure 5.21.

When playing in sorog or pelog degung, some of the rebab's pitches are the same as the gamelan's salendro pitches, and some of them are not; there are, however, always at least two, and often three, pitches in common (tumbuk) between salendro and sorog. Rebab players choose a surupan in which the gamelan piece's pillar tones match up with the surupan's common pitches. The pillar pitches for "Sinyur," for example, are 4, 3, and 1; whatever surupan the rebab player chooses must include the salendro pitches 4, 3, and 1 so that the rebab part will match up with the gamelan at the pillar pitches. In Track 7 on

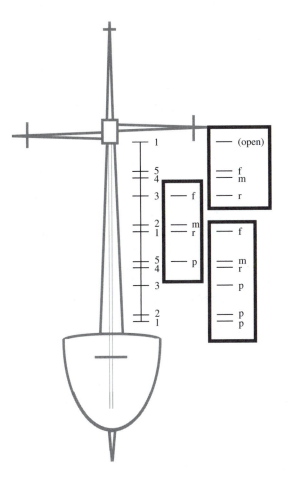

Figure 5.21 Rebab fingerings for pelog degung.

the CD that accompanies this book, the pasinden and rebab player perform almost exclusively in sorog, creating considerable dissonance at times, but they always return to the pillar pitches at the appropriate times.

At least one female singer, called a pasinden, performs with the gamelan; if there are more than one pasinden, they take turns. The male instrumentalists sometimes sing as well, and it is increasingly common to include a male soloist, called *wiraswara* or *juru alok*, whose only job is to sing. He typically fills in the musical spaces left by the pasinden, or responds to her vocal lines. Pasinden and wiraswara often set stock phrases or poems to the melodies they sing. While performing, pasinden often consult a small notebook with texts written in it. Some of the melodies they sing have particular texts associated with them, but in many cases they select words that somehow relate to or enhance the situation at hand.

Pasinden do not sing constantly; there is ample opportunity to breathe between phrases. Rebab players, however, do play almost constantly and fill in the gaps where the singers breathe or rest for a while. When rebab and pasinden are performing simultaneously, they perform in the same tuning system, and make an effort to choose similar figurations; the result is a texture of simultaneous variation.

The use of alternate tuning systems, the pitches of which may be dissonant with the rest of the gamelan, by rebab player and singers, as well as their elastic rhythm and florid idioms, help them to stand out in the texture of gamelan. These clashes are part of the aesthetic appeal of Sundanese gamelan music. The clashes that characterize Sundanese gamelan music are comparable to the combination in Central Java of loud and soft styles; however, Sundanese exaggerate the contrast between free and fixed idioms far beyond those of Central Javanese loud and soft styles.

Musical forms

Chapter 4 briefly outlined some forms for Central Javanese gamelan music; these were differentiated by the different ways in which the colotomic parts interlock, among other characteristics. While there is great disagreement among Sundanese musicians about how to classify formal structures in Sundanese gamelan music, there are two broad categories upon which most people agree: (1) *lagu alit* ("small pieces"), also called *lagu leutik, sekar alit, rancagan,* or *rerenggongan,* and (2) *lagu gede* ("great pieces"), also called *sekar ageung.* Some people use a third category, *lagu tengahan* ("middle pieces"), for pieces that do not fit conveniently into the other categories.

In their most basic form, lagu alit have positions for four pillar pitches. If the goong phrase has fewer than four identifying pitches, additional pillar pitches may be derived through techniques such as adding a pancer. "Sinyur" is an example of a lagu alit.

In performance, musicians often expand (or contract) the time interval between pillar pitches in lagu alit. The terms *sawilet, dua wilet, opat wilet, dalapan wilet,* and *kering* refer to such expansions. Musicians can determine which *wilet* treatment to use by listening to the drummer, who will play particular drum patterns to indicate how much musical time there is to fill before the next pillar pitch. The basic treatment of lagu alit is called *sawilet* ("single wilet"); upon hearing sawilet drumming, for example, the saron I player knows that he has plenty of time to play a four-note pattern for each pillar pitch. He may also decide to play eight-note patterns, but he will be aware that these patterns will be very fast. The term "wilet" refers to the flexible measure of musical time that separates the occurrence of pillar pitches.

A different drum pattern would cue the musicians to play the lagu alit in *dua wilet* ("double wilet"); the musical space between the pillar pitches is approximately twice as long as it is in sawilet. The saron player knows that he has plenty of time to play eight-note patterns for each pillar pitch (of course, he could decide to play very fast sixteen-note patterns as well). In dua wilet, the kenong player might decide to play more notes by adding an additional pancer. The same expansion processes apply to *opat wilet* ("quadruple wilet"). *Dalapan wilet* ("octuple wilet") is a possibility as well. *Kering* literally means "dry" but refers to a much faster treatment of the piece. Sundanese musicians sometimes call kering *satengah wilet* ("half wilet"). Wilet expansions occur only in multiples of two—there is no possibility for "triple wilet," for example.

In LS Giri Harja III's performance of "Sinyur" in Track 7 of the CD that accompanies this book, the drummer gives a cue after the goong stroke at 3:16 that tells the musicians to switch to four wilet at the next goong stroke. The musicians immediately begin to slow down to put more time between the pillar pitches; by the next gong stroke at 3:34, they are playing in four wilet, and the kenong player begins to add extra pancer pitches to stretch out the phrases. The next goong stroke is a full forty seconds later, at 4:14; up to this point, the goong strokes had been about ten to fifteen seconds apart.

No matter what the wilet treatment, the average pulse or melodic density of each instrument's part remains more or less consistent—a musician produces notes at about the same pace regardless of wilet. It is the number of notes between each pillar pitch that changes, not the tempo of the melodic parts. To effect a transition from one wilet treatment to another, as the drummer slows down (or speeds up) the pulse to signal a new wilet treatment, an instrumentalist slows (or quickens) his pace until it becomes unidiomatically slow (or fast); at that point, he changes abruptly to the new density, which likely will be a bit fast (or slow) for a moment, until the drummer settles completely into the new rhythm. Within each wilet treatment, the drummer can indicate to the musicians to go faster or slower, however.

In many cases, musicians give a different name to a lagu alit when it is played in four wilet. The different name usually refers to a song, played by rebab and pasinden, that is superimposed over the lagu alit in four wilet. The song "Golewang," for example, goes with a four-wilet version of "Sinyur." If the rebab player and pasinden perform "Golewang," the four-wilet version of "Sinyur" that accompanies it is called "Golewang" as well. A lagu alit also can be treated in four wilet without superimposing a song over it, in which case the rebab player and pasinden improvise (as LS Giri Harja III musicians do for "Sinyur" in Track 7 of the accompanying CD). Songs also can be superimposed over lagu alit in other wilet treatments as well; the lagu alit retains its essential identifying features, such as number of goong phrases in the cycle and identifying pillar pitches.

Not all gamelan pieces are defined solely by a simple succession of pillar pitches. There also is a repertory of longer pieces with set melodies, of which all the musicians play simultaneous variations. Lagu gede or sekar ageung are such pieces with very long goong phrases. As always, the colotomic instruments mark a metric foundation for the piece.

Gamelan Style

The style of Sundanese gamelan salendro (and other Sundanese music) is characterized by the layered presentation of contrasting elements. In addition to the four functional layers that characterize Javanese and Balinese gamelan music in general, Sundanese musicians delight in layering tuning systems (sorog or pelog melodies with salendro accompaniment), approaches to rhythm (the regular rhythm of the fixed gamelan instruments with the freer rhythm of the rebab and pasinden parts), and even different pieces. The tension between these contrasting elements, as well as the resolution of that tension when the elements converge at pillar pitches and the strokes of the goong, are important factors in Sundanese aesthetic appreciation.

CHAPTER **6**

Sundanese Gamelan Degung

The Sundanese gamelan salendro/pelog described in Chapter 5 is quite similar in terms of its instrumentation to gamelan from Central Java. The gamelan ensemble called *degung*, on the other hand, is uniquely Sundanese in the form of its instruments as well as in its sound and style.

From Aristocratic Courts to Urban Popular Music

In urban parts of modern West Java, one is likely to encounter a degung ensemble at a wedding or any other social celebration, at civic and private receptions of all sorts, and even in hotel lobbies—anywhere an atmosphere of elegance and Sundaneseness is desired. Degung's elegant connotations derive from its origins as the gamelan ensemble of the Sundanese aristocracy; since Indonesian independence, however, Sundanese musicians have found ways to adapt degung to play pop music as well as the austere *klasik* (classical) aristocratic pieces. These musical developments contribute to degung's increasingly democratic and egalitarian status even as it retains an aura of "class."

The word degung apparently is an old Sundanese term for referring to gongs and gong ensembles. It is similar in this sense to the Balinese use of the word *gong* to refer to ensembles that include large hanging gongs (cf. Soepandi and Atmadibrata 1976: 64). In this sense, the words degung and gong are essentially synonyms for the word gamelan. In the twentieth century, however, the term gamelan has come to refer to all gamelan-like ensembles throughout Indonesia. It is not uncommon to hear degung referred to as gamelan degung, even though such usage is, strictly speaking, redundant. Since the term degung has also come to refer to the particular tuning system of the ensemble, however, the term gamelan degung also can be interpreted to mean "a gamelan ensemble tuned to degung."

Summarizing the work of the Sundanese theorist R. M. A. Koesoemadinata (see Weintraub 1997), Max Harrell characterized the degung ensemble's scale as a "quasipelog"

143

Figure 6.1 Degung instruments: peking (left), jengglong (at rear), bonang (front) (Henry Spiller).

scale because, like pelog, it is characterized by large and small intervals, but, unlike pelog, pelog degung is a five-tone, rather than a seven-tone, scale (Harrell 1975: 879). The pelog degung scale is further differentiated from true pelog because some of its intervals sound like slendro intervals; as discussed earlier, the degung tuning is compatible with salendro gamelan instruments when rebab players and singers use it.

Musicians name the five pitches of pelog degung with the same names they use for salendro (that is, from high to low, barang, kenong, panelu, bem, and singgul). Unlike salendro and true pelog, which are not easily represented by the Western pitch system, however, pelog degung's intervals are relatively close to intervals that can be played on a piano. If the barang is equivalent to a "G" on the piano, the other pitches would be fairly close to the pitches outlined in Table 6.1. Sundanese musicians sometimes number the five

Table 6.1 Degung tuning

Sundanese number	Sundanese pitch name	Western pitch equivalent
1	barang	G
2	kenong	F#
3	panelu	D
4	bem	C
5	singgul	B

Figure 6.2 Degung instruments: bonang (left), panerus (right), goong/kempul (rear right) (Henry Spiller).

pitches of the pelog degung scale. Once again, Sundanese musicians assign the number "1" to the highest pitch in the scale.

Compared to the gamelan ensembles of Central Java and Bali, degung is quite small. A basic degung consists of only a few bronze instruments—bonang, two saron-type instruments (panerus and peking), goong, and jengglong—supplemented by a bamboo flute called suling and a set of drums called gendang. As few as six or seven musicians are enough to perform most pieces.

The degung's bonang consists of fourteen pots arranged in a single row. Each pot is a small bossed gong. As is characteristic of all bonang-type instruments, the pots are laid with their bosses facing up over ropes that are stretched in a wooden frame. In the degung bonang case, the frame often is divided into two sections, which are placed to form a V-shape. The bonang player sits inside the V, facing its point. By twisting the torso to face either right, center, or left, the player can easily reach all the pots with either hand. Some bonang frames include three sections rather than two, which are arranged in a U shape (as is the case with the bonang degung illustrated in Figure 6.1). Each of the two mallets is a wooden stick about one half inch in diameter. About half of the stick is padded with a thin layer of rubber and then wrapped in yarn or cloth. To play a note, the player holds the bare wood section of the stick in the hand and hits the boss of one of the pots with the padded portion of the stick. The pot's sound can be damped by firmly pressing the padded portion of the stick onto the boss of the vibrating pot. When playing melodies, bonang players often alternate left and right hand strokes so that each note can be damped with one hand while the other plays the next note. One characteristic feature of the bonang's sound is the soft but audible sound of damping, which lends an air of understated rhythmic complexity to the bonang idiom.

Each of the two saron-type instruments in a basic degung ensemble has approximately twelve to fourteen keys (the precise number may vary from gamelan to gamelan). The two instruments have different pitch ranges. The lowest pitch of the panerus (which some people call *demung*) is typically an octave below the lowest pitch of the peking (also called *titil* or *cempres*). Because each instrument has so many keys, there is considerable overlap between the two instruments' ranges; the upper keys of the panerus have the same pitches as the bottom keys of the peking. As is the case with most saron-type instruments, a panerus or peking player hits the keys of the instruments with a wooden hammer, which is held in the right hand, and damps the ringing sound of the metal keys by pinching them with the left hand (see Figure 6.2).

Jengglong is a gong chime with six gongs. In degung ensembles, the individual gongs often are suspended vertically from a frame, presenting a vertical wall of shiny gongs to the performer, who strikes them with a pair of padded mallets. The sound of jengglong gongs can be damped in the same way that bonang pots are damped, although they are sometimes left ringing. Jengglong also can be mounted on a U-shaped horizontal frame.

In very old degung ensembles, the jengglong player used the largest and lowest-pitched jengglong pot to provide the kind of phrase punctuation usually played on large hanging gongs. Most modern degung include a separate gong, much larger than the jengglong gongs and hanging in its own frame, to provide this punctuation. Once again, this large gong is called by the Sundanese word *goong*.

Sundanese people are fond of creating "folk etymologies" called *kirata* that purport to explain the derivation of everyday terms, but which actually provide metaphorical insight into the clusters of ideas surrounding the term. In a kirata, each syllable of the word in question is attributed to another word; the words are then arranged to create an obscure sentence that somehow illuminates the significance of the word at hand. A group of degung experts report a kirata for the word degung: It is a shortening of the phrase "deg ngadeg ka nu Agung," which means "we must always be pious toward God." The name thus reminds people that the sound of the degung ensemble is an example of something exalted (Tjarmedi, Suparman, et al. 1997: 11).

The famous Dutch ethnomusicologist Jaap Kunst reported in the 1920s that another name for the instrument now called jengglong was degung, and that it was this particular instrument that gave the ensemble its name (Kunst 1973: 366, 387). Very few people call this instrument by the name degung in the present. It does seem likely, however, that it was the presence of a degung/jengglong that differentiated the old degung ensembles that were present in some of the Sundanese kabupaten from other archaic ensembles such as goong renteng and sekaten.

The exact chronology of the development of degung ensembles in Priangan is hazy. Perhaps ensembles similar to degung were played in the courts of the Sundanese Hindu-Javanese kingdom of Pajajaran. Evidence of this is indirect, consisting only of stories associated with heirloom instruments in the kraton of Cirebon. Three of the Cirebonese kraton own sets of instruments called denggung; these are dated back to the fifteenth century and are reputed to have been acquired when Pajajaran was conquered (North 1988: 4; Ricklefs 1993: 37). The repertory consists of only eight pieces, of which contemporary musicians know only two (Wright 1978: 2–22).

Degung (and denggung, for that matter) may also be descendants of the gamelan

Figure 6.3 R. H. A. A. Wiranatakusumah, bupati of Bandung (1920–31; 1935–45) (photo and print collection of the Koninklijk Instituut voor Taal-, Land- en Volkenkunde, Leiden, the Netherlands).

instruments originally brought to the Sundanese courts by Mataram conquerors when they delegated their governing authority to an already existing Pajajaran aristocracy. Playing the instruments and music of Mataram in the former courts of Pajajaran would have provided a very clear sign both of Mataram's domination and authority over the aristocrats, and of these aristocrats' delegated authority over the Sundanese.

Over the course of two or three centuries, more modern forms of gamelan ensembles became popular among the bupati. Several of the kabupaten, however, maintained sets of degung instruments. For much of its existence, degung consisted only of the bronze instruments described earlier (bonang, saron, jengglong, and goong) along with a drum or two. It is not clear, however, exactly what sort of music these instruments provided; the instruments may have been played to welcome the bupati's guests or to provide background music to the aristocrats' various leisure activities (such as hunting and sailing). Although degung's patrons were all aristocrats, the musicians themselves were not; rather, they were servants brought in from the surrounding communities.

Degung music retained its exclusive association with the upper class well into the twentieth century. In 1921, a group of Sundanese aristocrats and Dutch civil servants collaborated on an extravagant theatrical production. The performance was to be presented at a meeting of the Java Instituut (a Dutch organization interested in Javanese culture) in Bandung. One of the meeting's themes was the problem of reconciling traditional Javanese and Sundanese values with those of the modern world. One hidden agenda of the meeting was to articulate a particularly Sundanese identity to the Dutch and other foreign visitors, who were more familiar with Javanese and Balinese cultures.

The bupati of Bandung, R. H. A. A. Wiranatakusumah (see Figure 6.3) collaborated with another well-known Sundanese aristocrat, P. A. A. Djajadiningrat, to come up with a production that would showcase Sundanese culture in the context of an increasingly modernized Dutch-controlled Indonesia. They decided to base their drama on a Sunda-nese legend called "Lutung Kasarung" rather than on one of the more conventional Indian epic stories. They also decided to use uniquely Sundanese musical forms—including degung—for the drama's accompaniment in lieu of the more typical gamelan salendro/pelog ensembles that accompanied upper- and lower-class theatrical productions.

The Bandung kabupaten's music director was a highly regarded musician named Idi. (Although Sundanese and Javanese aristocrats have long, flowery names such as Djajadin-ingrat, as well as initials that indicate their rank and lineage such as R. T. A., ordinary Sundanese individuals sometimes have a single name.) Idi elected to use an expanded degung ensemble to accompany the production. He added a bamboo flute called *suling* to provide the more florid melodies that people were used to hearing for theatrical music, as well as gendang drums which were essential for accompanying movement. The ordinary suling was designed to play in a register and at a volume that was not quite appropriate for degung. A special suling, which came to be called *suling degung*, was developed that was smaller, higher-pitched, shriller, and louder than normal bamboo flutes. Because it would need to play only the five pitches of the pelog degung scale, suling degung were made with only four finger holes (in contrast to the usual six holes that facilitate playing a variety of scales). Gendang were essentially the same drums that Sundanese musicians used to accompany all sorts of theatrical movement and dance—one large barrel-shaped drum called *gendang indung* ("mother drum") and one small barrel-shaped drum called *gendang leutik* ("small drum") or *kulanter*.

The addition of these two instruments greatly enhanced the ensemble's range of expression; this expanded instrumentation quickly became the norm for degung ensembles in the kabupaten. People in other parts of West Java heard the new instru-mentation when Idi's group traveled to various cities to provide accompaniment for a silent film version of "Lutung Kasarung."

This enhanced degung ensemble was still the exclusive domain of the kabupaten. Not long afterwards, however, degung was exported outside the kabupaten for the first time to provide entertainment at a wedding. Subsequently, an independent degung group, named Purbasasaka and led by a kabupaten musician named Oyo, was formed to play at events outside the kabupaten. To retain some sense of the aristocratic privilege, their aristo-cratic patrons prohibited them from playing particular signature kabupaten pieces, such as "Palwa" and "Layar Putri" (Soekanda 1991; Tisana 1997: 28–9; Swindells 2004: 25). Idi and his colleagues composed a number of pieces that were just different enough from the forbidden pieces to satisfy their patrons, but similar enough to evoke the same feelings of prestige among their new non-kabupaten audiences. These pieces remain the core of the degung repertory, and often are called *lagu klasik* ("classical pieces").

Lagu klasik

Idi is credited with having composed the lion's share of the lagu klasik repertory during the 1920s; only a few pieces, such as "Ayun Ambing" and "Lalayaran," predate him. A number of other influential degung musicians in succeeding generations, such as Ono Sukarna, U. Tarya, and Entjar Tjarmedi, contributed lagu klasik as well. For a piece to become a lagu klasik, however, it must become widespread enough so that it takes on a life of its own and becomes decoupled from its composer. Sometimes a lagu klasik is attributed to several different composers; it is a true sign that a piece has "made it" when people begin to forget exactly who composed it.

It is not simply age and fame that transform a piece into a lagu klasik; the designation of lagu klasik suggests a particular musical style as well. These pieces are characterized by irregular formal structures, a texture in which all the instruments play simultaneous variations of the melody, a few stock melodic phrases that show up in many pieces, and simple drum parts played with sticks.

One of Idi's pieces, "Ujung Laut," illustrates several characteristics of degung lagu klasik. For one thing, it has been in the public domain long enough that several different versions have emerged. Although they all share the piece's main identifying melodic phrases, the different versions occasionally take a different melodic turn, or repeat a phrase more or fewer times than the others. The version described here is that performed by Burhan Sukarma, who was a musician with the government-run radio station, Radio Republik Indonesia (RRI) degung group in the 1960s and 1970s, and currently lives in San Jose, California, where he directs a degung group called Pusaka Sunda ("Sundanese heirloom"); Pusaka Sunda's recording of "Ujung Laut" is included as Track 8 on the CD that accompanies this book.

One way to look at the form of "Ujung Laut" is to divide it into three phrases, each of which ends with a stroke of the large goong. Each of the phrases in Burhan Sukarma's version has a different number of beats (the numbers in parentheses are the timings for each phrase from the rendition of "Ujung Laut" on the CD).

> Phrase 1: 64 (0:11–0:40; 2:08–2:37; 4:02–4:33)
> Phrase 2: 80 (0:40–1:15; 2:37–3:10)
> Phrase 3: 120 (1:15–2:08; 3:10–4:02)

Each phrase has its own characteristic shape. Phrase 1 begins on a very high note, which is sustained for the first sixteen beats, and then takes the next sixteen beats to meander downward a full octave, where it hovers for another sixteen beats before taking the final sixteen beats to descend once again to a very satisfying cadence at the goong stroke (see Figure 6.4).

Phrase 2 can be divided into four subphrases. The second subphrase is a repetition of the first—a meandering descent. The third is almost another repetition, except that it abruptly ascends at the end instead of descending. All three of these subphrases occupy sixteen beats. The fourth subphrase takes up the remaining thirty-two beats; it is a thrilling descent to the goong stroke, and is a stock cadential phrase found in many other degung lagu klasik. Burhan Sukarma calls this phrase "Palwa B"; he remembers it as the second phrase ("B") of another lagu klasik piece called "Palwa," and uses this name as a shorthand to refer to the phrase when it appears in other pieces.

Phrase 3 has three subphrases; the first two are exactly the same, and each occupies forty beats. This subphrase rises precipitously, then descends again, only to rise again at the very end. The third subphrase begins similarly and also occupies forty beats, but ends slightly differently than the other two by descending to a satisfying low ending.

A schematic summary of the phrase outlines of "Ujung Laut" (see Figure 6.5) illustrates its irregular formal structures. Other lagu klasik are also irregular, but each has its

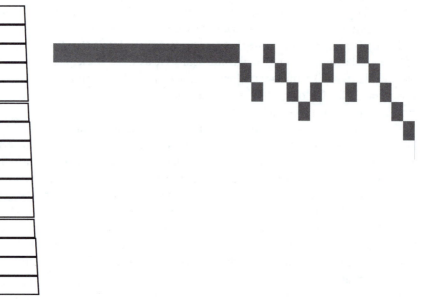

own peculiar irregularities; the form outlined in Figure 6.5 is unique to "Ujung Laut." These irregular phrase structures present a striking contrast to the relentlessly regular quadratic structure of most other gamelan music.

The bonang plays a particularly prominent role in the lagu klasik style. Most often the bonang player provides the pangkat for the piece; in fact, the exact same bonang pangkat opens quite a few lagu klasik. Once the piece has begun, the bonang player provides a particularly florid version of the main melody, sometimes playing runs, sometimes playing octaves, and always adding rhythmic interest with creative damping techniques. The panerus plays essentially the same melody as the bonang, but without the syncopation or rhythmic variety. If the varied rhythms of the bonang part are akin to wrinkles in a piece of cloth, the panerus part is a "smoothed over" version of the same melody—it moves along with notes of even time values, as if all of the rhythmic variety had been "ironed out." The cempres part, on the other hand, dances around the bonang part with even more

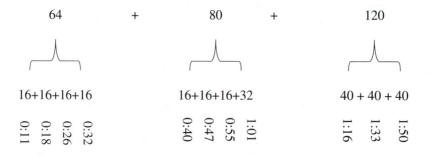

Figure 6.5 "Ujung Laut": phrase structure (with CD timings).

32 33 34 35 36 37 38 39 40 41 42 43 44 45 46 47 48 49 50 51 52 53 54 55 56 57 58 59 60 61 62 63 64

Figure 6.4 "Ujung Laut": melodic contour of phrase 1.

rhythmic intricacies. The suling, too, plays essentially the same tune, but with soaring sustained notes, dramatic trills and vibratos, and a certain rhythmic freedom added in.

Modern degung

Despite the gradual erosion of degung's exclusivity, degung was little known except among the upper class before the 1950s. In the 1950s, the local Bandung station of RRI began to broadcast degung music. In keeping with the nationalist goals of the government-run RRI, much of the radio station's programming was in the national language because the government wanted to promote the use and understanding of Indonesian. There was also, however, a local programming component in the national programming agenda. The Bandung station maintained a number of Sundanese music ensembles and a staff of Sundanese musicians to provide this local component. RRI Bandung also produced a Sundanese-language broadcast, for which degung provided the theme music (the signature piece was "Ladrak"). This practice had the effect of associating the sound of degung with a particular Sundanese ethnic identity in a national Indonesian context. It was at this time that non-aristocratic people began to build and acquire degung instruments and develop new repertories and contexts for degung performance (Entis Sutisna, pers. comm., 3/23/99).

One modern use of degung music is, in a sense, a direct outgrowth of the original theatrical drama that led to the formation of the modern degung ensemble. Since the 1920s, multimedia Sundanese theatrical productions involving music, dance, and theater called *gending karesmen* provided a medium for entertainment and artistic experimentation.

The 1921 "Lutung Kasarung" performance, with its innovative use of Sundanese music, provided a model for subsequent productions. A gending karesmen created by Wahyu

Figure 6.6 Upacara adat performed by LS Rawit Group (Henry Spiller).

Wibisana in 1958 included a well-received section that reminded viewers of the part of a Sundanese wedding ceremony where the groom is escorted into the bride's home (Tisana 1997: 31). In the intervening fifty years it has become increasingly popular to include a gending karesmen–like performance, based on this 1958 production, in Sundanese wedding ceremonies (Bratawidjaja 1990). The popularity of this wedding performance has increased in part because of the broadcast of such wedding productions on television (pers. comm., Otong Rasta, 3/26/99). This special wedding performance is most typically called an *upacara adat*, although that term more generally refers to any traditional ceremony (*upacara* means "ceremony," and *adat* refers to traditional laws, customs, and values). In fact, some sticklers for accuracy suggest that the wedding performance is better described as *upacara khusus* ("special ceremony") because it is clearly not adat, but rather something quite new (pers. comm., Entis Sutisna, 3/23/99).

Typically, a professional group called a *lingkung seni* (arts circle), often abbreviated "LS," provides all the music and entertainment components for a wedding, including the upacara adat. Figure 6.6 shows part of LS Rawit Group's upacara adat; members of the troupe carry umbrellas and dance to the accompaniment of degung music as they escort the groom and his party to the bride's home (where the wedding celebration will take place). Lingkung seni are usually managed by a charismatic, business-savvy person, who often is a well-known artist in his or her own right (Williams 1998: 722). These arts entrepreneurs serve as musical agents or brokers, making and maintaining the connections required to provide a variety of performances for their clients. Lingkung seni provide one-stop shopping for most or all of a host's performance requirements, usually own all the musical instruments and costumes, and have a stable of performers on call for the performance genres they provide.

Sometimes, however, the degung portion of an event might be provided by an amateur group, most often a group of women who rehearse together as much for social enrichment as for musical enjoyment. When they perform, the women take great care to dress up in elaborate, matching outfits, makeup, and hairstyles. These groups are called *gamelan ibu-ibu* (women's gamelan); although there are still some such groups (the group pictured in Figure 6.1 and Figure 6.2 was photographed in 1999), their popularity peaked in the 1960s and 1970s.

Since the 1950s, the degung ensemble's repertory has expanded to include all sorts of musical styles. Many of the new developments in degung involve the addition of singing—an inappropriate addition in the minds of some traditionalists, but popular nevertheless. The musicians at RRI Bandung first added a female chorus to their degung ensemble in the 1960s (Cook 2007).

Speakers of the Sundanese language use two words to describe singing. *Tembang* refers to a very formal style of singing refined poetry, while *kawih* connotes an earthier style of singing in which the words are usually simple couplets. While users of these terms tend to exaggerate any actual measurable stylistic differences between tembang and kawih, the terms do mark off some conceptual categories. Tembang-style singing in West Java is associated with the aristocracy and involves complex poetic forms imported from the courts of Central Java (such as the *pangkur* poetic form discussed in Chapter 4; in Central Java the generic term for this sort of poetic form is *macapat*, while in West Java these forms are known collectively as *pupuh*). Kawih, on the other hand, is associated with the common people.

One particular style of such Sundanese courtly tembang singing from the kabupaten of the city of Cianjur earned a wide reputation throughout the Priangan for its beauty and refinement, and was imitated in other parts of West Java as well. Most people called this style of singing *Cianjuran*, referring to its place of origin. Cianjuran involved solo vocalists, both male and female, who intoned poems that described the legends of the Pajajaran kingdom with florid, unmetered melodies to the accompaniment of a suling and a plucked string instrument called *kacapi*. As the Cianjuran style became known outside of Cianjur, the genre expanded and changed as musicians imitated it and experimented with new ideas. In recognition of this influence that spreads well beyond the city of Cianjur, this style of singing is often referred to as *tembang Sunda*.

One innovation involved adding a kawih song to the end of a tembang poem. The kawih songs were usually lighter in terms of subject matter as well as with regard to musical style. While the tembang poetry and their accompaniments tended to be in free rhythm—that is, without a steady pulse or regular meter—kawih songs were often accompanied by ensembles that played with a steady pulse and a clear meter. While both men and women studied and sang the serious tembang songs, only women sang the lighter kawih songs. Because these kawih songs were quite literally added on to the end of tembang songs, they became known among tembang aficionados as *panambih* ("additions") or *lagu ekstra* ("extra songs").

To accompany kawih songs, the instrumentalists tried to imitate the sounds and textures of a gamelan ensemble. The kacapi players developed a way to imitate both the drum patterns and colotomic instruments with the left hand, while providing a core melody and some elaboration with the right. To further enhance this imitation gamelan, tembang ensembles began to include a second, smaller kacapi called *rincik* which was played only during panambih and provided another layer of gamelan-like melodic elaboration.

A significant portion of the tembang Sunda repertory is cast in the pelog degung scale (one of three tembang Sunda scales). Given the rising popularity of panambih songs, which were accompanied by plucked string instruments and suling imitating the sound of a gamelan ensemble, and given the existence and increasing popularity of a real gamelan ensemble which, although it was not associated with vocal music, was tuned to the same scale as many panambih songs, it was probably only a matter of time before somebody decided to try singing panambih songs to degung accompaniment. The result was called *degung kawih*.

For degung kawih, degung musicians play somewhat different parts than they do for lagu klasik. In effect, they imitate the idioms of gamelan salendro using the degung instruments. The bonang player, for example, typically chooses the ketuk-rhythm octave style of playing characteristic of gamelan salendro rather than the more florid melodic style of the lagu klasik. The panerus and peking players, who usually provide melodic renditions of the main melody when performing lagu klasik, might choose to imitate the two saron of a gamelan salendro ensemble and play interlocking parts for a degung kawih song. They take advantage of the fact that the ranges of the panerus and peking overlap, and confine their interlocking parts to the sections of their instruments that have the same pitches. The drummer switches from the simple, austere stick drumming that characterized lagu klasik to a more florid style of hand drumming called *tepak melem*.

Sometimes extra instruments are added to the ensemble to enhance the effect. Kempul, for example, is an instrument that characterizes gamelan salendro but is missing from degung; some degung ensembles include a kempul, which the goong player plays for degung kawih songs. Although it is possible to imitate the sound of two interlocking saron with panerus and peking, some ensembles include a matched pair of six- or seven-key saron to provide the interlocking parts for degung kawih.

Some Sundanese musicians were enamored with the sounds of the Western popular music they heard, and looked for ways to combine these new ideas with their own music. In the 1950s, for example, the influential musician and composer Koko Koswara (more familiarly known as Mang Koko) created Western-inspired songs for his popular gamelan salendro groups (Ruswandi 2000: 12), as well as Sundanese instruments with diatonic tunings. He felt that, above all, music should appeal to its audience, and should use both traditional and non-traditional means to do so (Ruswandi 2000: 29). Many of Mang Koko's songs have become standards; just about any Sundanese child or adult can sing "Badminton" (about Indonesia's most popular sport) or "Pahlawan Bangsa" ("National Heroes"—a patriotic song).

Mang Koko's protégé, Nano S., alarmed that the younger generations seemed to prefer to abandon gamelan music and other traditional Sundanese forms completely in favor of imported popular music, innovated hybrid forms that he hoped would captivate their young listeners. Nano S. took advantage of the similarity between the degung tuning and Western diatonic scale to compose melodies that could be accompanied either by *ban* (a Western-style combo with keyboard, guitars, and drums) or by degung. His enormous hit from 1986, entitled "Kalangkang" ("Silhouette" or "Reflection"), is just as likely to be heard performed with degung or gamelan salendro accompaniment as it is to appear on a karaoke CD with synthesized orchestral accompaniment (see Williams 1989–90). Although it has a varied, catchy melody that is difficult to identify as either pelog or sorog, "Kalangkang" is easily accompanied by a basic gamelan piece pattern that is so simple and basic it is known as "Catrik" ("student/disciple").

Many Bandung musicians refer nostalgically to the decades of the 1970s and 1980s as *zaman kaset*—the golden age of cassette recordings. During those years, a local recording industry arose in West Java, centered in Bandung, that catered to a market interested in purchasing modern Sundanese music, often with a traditional twist. Cassette technology was inexpensive both for producers and consumers, and business boomed. The musicians wistfully remember that they were reasonably well paid for their services in addition to the opportunity to participate in ground-breaking, experimental projects.

Many of the cassettes produced during these years featured some sort of innovation, and some of the recordings achieved enduring popularity. One degung cassette, entitled *Sangkala Degung*, performed by Grup Gapura, became popular not only among Sundanese listeners, but in other parts of Indonesia as well. Even today, a tourist walking down the street in Bali is likely to hear the sounds of degung emanating from a storefront. (*Sangkala Degung* was also released in the United States by ICON Records in 1985.)

Although the golden age of cassettes is over in West Java, Sundanese musicians are still experimenting with traditional music. In the 1990s, a young musician named Ismet Ruchimat, along with several friends, released recordings featuring a diatonic degung ensemble performing renditions of international hits. *Degung Dedikasi*, as one cassette was titled, featured soaring suling versions of such hits as The Eagles' "Hotel California" and John Lennon's "Imagine." In his more recent projects, Ismet begins with concepts from Sundanese music. The musicians he works with come primarily from the government-sponsored college-level school of the arts (Sekolah Tinggi Seni Indonesia [STSI]) in Bandung, so they all have experience with Sundanese music; by exploiting the conventions of Sundanese gamelan music, such as using a simple outline to generate a variety of complementary instrumental parts, Ismet is able to coordinate the musicians quickly and confidently (Shelley 2002). In 1997, the group took the name CBMW; their album *Rhythmical in Sundanese People* included a variety of fusion projects that combine elements of Sundanese, Balinese, and Western musical traditions in fresh, innovative ways. One of the tracks, entitled "Sambasunda," made a big splash, and since 1998 the group has been known as Sambasunda; under that name they continue to appear in concerts all over the world. (The track entitled "Sambasunda" has been released by The World Music Network in the United States on a compilation CD entitled *The Rough Guide to Indonesia*.)

Gamelan in Modern Sundanese Life

To Western ears, Sundanese gamelan music sounds mysterious and exotic. To Sundanese ears, accustomed to hearing it in the course of everyday life, gamelan music sounds anything but extraordinary. In fact, to many young Sundanese especially, it sounds hopelessly old-fashioned. Many young people consider it to be something relevant to their parents or grandparents, but not especially meaningful to them. It strikes them as outdated, unsophisticated, and even hokey, especially when compared to imported and domestic popular music—metal, rap, *dangdut*, and *pop Indonesia*, among others. Many of the musical experiments described above appeal to these listeners because they successfully bring local flavor to international tastes or (vice versa) bestow some cosmopolitan panache on familiar sounds.

Perhaps an appropriate analogy would be most young Americans' attitudes toward accordion music. The very timbre of an accordion is enough to turn many Americans off—some people find it hard to take any accordion music seriously. On the other hand, the sound of an accordion can trigger deep feelings of nostalgia, even in the most jaded young Americans, reminding them, for example, of carefree times watching the *Lawrence Welk Show* on TV with their grandparents. Some young people find themselves inexplicably drawn to accordion music despite their peers' general disdain. And there are even those who parlay the accordion's hokiness and nostalgia into something hip, new, and exciting. In all cases, the sound of the accordion evokes complex reactions in its American listeners, carrying the baggage of generations of different meanings.

It is the same with gamelan music in West Java. So, even among folks who do not particularly care for it, there is a place for gamelan music. It is customary for Sundanese families to host a ceremonial event called a *hajat* to mark significant events in their lives. At its most basic, a hajat is simply a communal meal; the hosts share food with their neighbors to bring about a state of well-being. Making sure that things go well is especially important around the time of significant life-cycle events (Wessing 1978: 63). Particularly important events, such as a boy's circumcision or a child's marriage, call for particularly lavish hajat. The ultimate goal of the hajat is to bring together many guests, provide them with food, and create a *ramé* ("lively") atmosphere. And, indeed, enormous numbers of people receive invitations and attend. There is usually some form of entertainment throughout the party to increase the ramé quotient. Most guests stay just long enough to acknowledge the honorees, eat some food, and enjoy a bit of entertainment; they then leave to make room for other guests. Ideally, the hajat will be crowded and lively throughout the day.

Hosting a big hajat at home requires the cooperation of at least a few immediate neighbors. Usually the hosts transform the area around their house, including the houses and yards of the neighbors, into a completely different world for the hajat. Somehow, a fairly large gathering area must be carved out of the street, terraces, and yards; this may involve temporarily blocking traffic and removing fences, doors, and even windows. There is always a raised stage area, covered with an awning if necessary, for the entertainers. Usually several kitchens are mobilized to prepare and serve the constant supply of food for the guests. For a wedding, one room in the host's house is completely redecorated—draped with sumptuous cloths and refurnished with grandiose carved furniture—to serve as a receiving room. In Bandung, many people hire a hall in which to host their hajat. Often, certain ceremonies are still performed at home, in the presence of a select group of guests, before moving the party to the hall, which provides stages, furniture, catering, and room for hordes of guests.

Some hajat involve entertainment all day and all night. Hajat are one of the primary venues for *wayang golek* (rod puppet theater) performances, which begin in the evening and last all night. Sundanese wayang golek is similar to Central Javanese wayang kulit:

Figure 6.7 Wayang golek stage (Henry Spiller).

A single puppeteer called a dalang manipulates puppets, provides all the narration and dialogue, and gives cues to the gamelan ensemble that accompanies the play. In wayang golek, however, the puppets are not flat leather shadow puppets, but beautifully carved and painted three-dimensional wooden rod puppets (see Figure 6.7; Track 7 on the accompanying CD is from a performance of wayang golek). Wayang performances remain popular among all classes and ages of Sundanese because a good dalang finds ways to make the stories (usually episodes from the Indian epics the *Mahabharata* and the *Ramayana*) relevant to people's lives. The dalang appeals to the senses and the intellect at many levels—he waxes philosophical, he produces withering political commentary, and he makes jokes that range from crude to subtle. And, if spectators become bored during the seven-hour performance, they can always watch the musicians, especially the female singers, or talk with their friends, or buy something to eat.

Gamelan music is an integral part of a wayang performance. The gamelan begins to play long before the dalang appears on the scene, to keep spectators entertained and to create the ramé atmosphere that characterizes successful events. As the play proper begins, the gamelan plays a standard sequence of pieces to accompany the dalang as he sets up the first scene on the puppet stage—a couple of banana logs laid across a frame, into which the dalang can stick the puppets. Then, the gamelan accompanies him as he narrates the *murwa*, an opening narration, and sings the opening songs that set the mood for the first scene. As the play progresses, the gamelan is always there to accompany the puppets' dances and fights, and to usher them on and off stage. At times, the dalang takes a cigarette break, and cues the ensemble to play music for the crowd's entertainment. Such pieces always feature the pasinden—the female singers who are often as popular as the dalang himself.

In recent times, other venues (and shorter time frames) for wayang have become possible, and even all-night performances have become shorter. Sometimes political parties, government agencies, or private companies will sponsor a wayang performance to attract attention to a political candidate, publicize new policies, or to celebrate a company milestone.

Tayuban—a kind of dance party with gamelan accompaniment—were popular hajat entertainments in the 1960s and 1970s. In the 1980s, performances featuring *jaipongan*—another dance genre featuring gamelan salendro (see Chapter 7)—edged tayuban out. Some hosts began to prefer a lower-key approach and hired a group to perform tembang Sunda and *kacapi-suling*. And certainly some people preferred something a bit more modern, such as karaoke, *ban* (rock band), or *dangdut* (see Chapter 7).

With all these possible entertainments from which to choose, some people began to insist on choosing them all. For a wedding celebration, a lingkung seni might be asked to provide an upacara adat in the morning, followed by degung kawih, followed by a jaipongan performance, followed by dangdut dancing in the late afternoon. Alternatively, the hosts might request a comedy performance, or a wayang, or a karaoke singalong, or pop tunes.

Filling these requests often places significant demands on the lingkung seni—they may have to bring a set of degung instruments, a gamelan salendro, and a keyboard and other band instruments for dangdut, not to mention all the musicians required to play these styles. One means that some lingkung seni employ to minimize the number of instruments they have to carry is a *gamelan selap*—a special gamelan that includes extra keys and gongs that enable the instruments to play in salendro, pelog, degung, and other surupan as well. The word *selap* means to put something in between other things; in a gamelan selap, the extra keys required to produce the degung tuning are positioned in between the various salendro keys, taking advantage of the fact that degung and salendro have several common pitches. The addition of two or three extra keys, for a total of seven or eight per octave, would result in a gamelan that can be played in salendro and degung. Most gamelan selap include a couple more keys—a total of ten per octave—to provide a reasonable approximation of some of the true pelog scales, such as pelog jawar, as well. The extra saron keys are apparent on the gamelan selap played by LS Rawit Group in Figure 5.11 (on p. 128).

The specific tuning for gamelan selap requires a little bit of compromise and a great deal of skill and cleverness to find the exact pitches that seem to sound in tune in several different contexts. Figure 6.8 shows the layout of the saron from the gamelan selap owned by the dalang Asep Sunandar Sunarya, as documented by Andrew Weintraub; which keys the players select to perform in the various surupan is indicated in the figure. When performing in salendro and the salendro-derived surupan, which can be conceptualized as consisting of small, medium, and large intervals, the musicians play adjacent keys to achieve a small interval; they skip one key to produce a medium interval; and they skip two keys for a large interval.

Of course, the instrumentalists must remember to skip keys when they are playing familiar pieces—it takes a little time to become accustomed to playing on a gamelan selap. Instruments such as the bonang, for which the players learn and remember their realization techniques as kinetic patterns, present special problems. It is possible to remove the keys and pots that are not needed at the moment, and some musicians do this if they

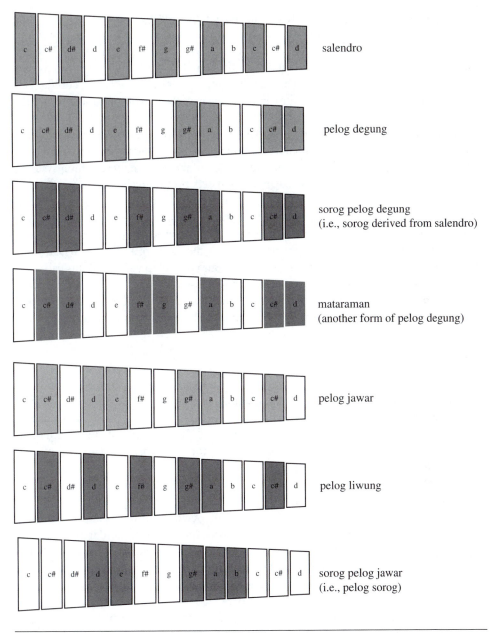

Figure 6.8 Saron layout for gamelan selap (after Weintraub 1997: 124).

know in advance that they will not need to switch tuning systems quickly. It also should be stressed that some listeners find some of the tunings produced by gamelan selap to be somewhat out-of-tune—beyond the limits of conventional tuning variation.

On the other hand, having all of these tunings available at once allows for some spectacular musical effects. The lingkung seni who use gamelan selap typically have one or two show-stopping pieces in which they change tunings several times, leaving their audiences breathless and disoriented as if they had just ridden a thrill ride. Groups can respond to requests for songs that might otherwise have been difficult because of tuning incompatibilities between the song and the gamelan. And superstar wayang golek troupes, for whom the use of gamelan selap became standard in the 1990s, could create vivid theatrical effects by adjusting the tuning of the gamelan accompaniment to suit the mood of the dramatic scene.

The idea of gamelan selap is not particularly new. R. M. A. Koesoemadinata, a Sundanese music theorist, developed gamelan instruments that could play in several surupan as early as the 1930s; he used them to work out his ideas about Sundanese tuning systems. All those extra keys and pots made such gamelan sets prohibitively expensive. In addition, musicians were accustomed to a certain standardization of gamelan instruments; for the most part, musicians found gamelan selap instruments intimidatingly difficult to play. The recent rise in popularity for gamelan selap after so many years of disinterest is probably connected to a variety of developments, including the desire of audiences to hear more variety, the rise of all-purpose lingkung seni who could provide a variety of musical entertainments, and the relative wealth of a few very successful arts entrepreneurs who could afford the increased cost of gamelan selap instruments and felt that the impressive display that all that bronze provided enhanced their status and popularity (Weintraub 1997).

Summary

Whether they think Sundanese gamelan music is hopelessly old-fashioned or find it to be moving, exciting, and invigorating, most Sundanese audiences take the sound of Sundanese gamelan for granted. It is something quite ordinary—one of those things people are simply used to. The significance of gamelan music—as a symbol of Sundanese identity, as a model for Sundanese values, as a link to the Sundanese past—is simply not something that they consciously consider.

Nevertheless, gamelan music cannot help but have these meanings for Sundanese audiences. Along the lines of the precedent set by ancient goong renteng music, the fact the gamelan is played—and heard—is enough. Seeing the shapes and hearing the sounds of the instruments connects individuals with the events of Sundanese history—degung evokes the aristocrats of Pajajaran, gamelan salendro speaks of the assimilation of ideas and customs from Mataram and Central Java, as well as domination first by the Dutch and then by the Indonesian national government. Hearing the scales called pelog degung and sorog clash sweetly with salendro as the rebab player and pasinden superimpose these uniquely Sundanese surupan over the imported Central Javanese tuning recalls how a unique Sundanese identity persists despite centuries of outside domination. Perceiving a distinctly Sundanese sound emerging from ensemble music that shares a common underlying musical structure with other parts of Indonesia emphasizes that the Sundanese share a heritage with the rest of the nation. Combining the old instruments and sounds with new ones models the ways that modern Sundanese cope with a changing world and explore what it means to be Sundanese, Indonesian, and citizens of the world—all at the same time.

CHAPTER 7

Identity, Authenticity, and Tradition
in Sundanese Dance Music

Throughout Indonesia, gamelan music often serves as an accompaniment for dance or other movement-oriented performances (such as wayang). This chapter explores the relationship between Sundanese dance and music, and how Sundanese individuals manipulate music and dance as units of cultural meaning to make sense out of the circumstances of their own lives. Exploring the continuities and changes in Sundanese tradition illuminates the significance of the performing arts not only in Indonesia, but everywhere else as well.

There is a long-standing close relationship between Sundanese music, especially drumming, and dance; most commentators on Indonesian dance cite the prominent drumming as a distinguishing characteristic of all Sundanese dance music. The presence of an aural analog for movement elements is a deep-seated component of a Sundanese dance aesthetic; any movement, it seems, requires an audible reaction.

An ancient village ritual dance (described in Soepandi and Atmadibrata 1976: 71–5; Atmadibrata 1980: 212) illustrates a practical consideration in this aesthetic connection. In *dog-dog lojor*, a ceremony following the harvesting of rice, the farmers make music while carrying their harvested rice to the storage area. Bundles of rice are tied to either end of poles which the harvesters carry on their shoulders. The rice on the pole becomes a musical instrument called *rengkong* that makes a rhythmical squeaking sound when carried properly. The sound of the rengkong is a natural consequence of their swinging motion—an audible reaction. Several *dog-dog* (single-head drums), each played by a marcher, provide a rhythmic accompaniment that interlocks with the sound of the rengkong. The drum sounds coordinate the actions of the farmers; the sounds also elevate the level of excitement and incite the marchers to have a good time while getting the work done.

But music and dance are not just about good times; they play a much more important role in Sundanese communities. Music and dance provide a context in which moral values can be learned, practiced, and challenged; the aesthetic dimension of music and dance, however, makes this engagement with values unconscious. Learning how to move "beautifully" or "naturally" is really learning how to move in a way that is consistent with social norms. Practicing dance trains these social values into the bodies of the participants. Music (and drumming) that motivates good movement is judged to be aesthetically pleasing—good music.

Much Sundanese music and dance has its origins in ceremonial and ritual activities connected with the planting and harvesting of rice. In the distant past, villagers found ways to increase the likelihood of a successful agricultural cycle. Their methods were not limited to practical farming techniques; they also developed rituals to encourage the nature spirits, which they believed animated the earth, rice, and rain so vital to their success, to work in their favor.

They considered the sky, and the rain which fell out of it, to be masculine, while they conceived the ground, and the rice which grew out of it, as feminine. In rituals, a village woman represented Dewi Sri—the rice goddess—while the village men played the part of the sky and the rain. They hoped that their erotic dance movements, which were a metaphor for a fertile growing season, would ensure agricultural success (Sumardjo 1999). Thus, important beliefs about cosmology, cultivation, and culture were learned and reinforced in the process of dancing.

Over the centuries, however, the Sundanese have had to contend with other systems of values, which sometimes deemed the erotic nature of these village ceremonies to be unacceptable. Dance and music then became arenas for exploring these clashing values. Once again, the aesthetic nature of these activities masks the important cultural work that goes on; new forms are thought simply to be better or more beautiful if they successfully model a new, modified system of values.

Changes in Sundanese music and dance over the past hundred years or so illuminate this process. An examination of a variety of music and dance traditions in West Java, along with the social changes that motivated their development, shows how these aesthetic activities represent a trying-on for size of different sets of values. The focus in this chapter is on six significant genres—*ketuk tilu, tayuban, tari kursus, bajidoran, jaipongan,* and *dangdut*—which cut across Sundanese geography and history, but which are unified by a consistently Sundanese approach to connecting dancing and drumming.

Village Ceremonial Dance: Ketuk Tilu

Even in the twenty-first century, Sundanese village life follows the yearly cycles of weather patterns and their effects on agriculture. The basic outlines of the rituals associated with the beginning of the planting season and the harvest—men dancing as a group with a single female dancer—have continued in various forms for hundreds, perhaps thousands, of years, in village dance events. Although the details of the dance events differ from village to village and from generation to generation, a few basic characteristics remained fixed. The female role became the responsibility of a professional female entertainer who sang and danced to the accompaniment of a simple musical ensemble. The ensemble always included drumming, and the drum patterns were closely coordinated with dance movements. The ritual's main participants—male dancers—continued to be men from the community, who let the drumming animate them to dance freely.

Figure 7.1 Three ketuk as seen from above; goong (right) and rebab (left) also are visible (Henry Spiller).

Ketuk tilu is an umbrella term that modern historians of Sundanese dance usually apply to these village dance events. The word *ketuk* usually refers to a small knobbed gong, and *tilu* means three in Sundanese; the name ketuk tilu, therefore, means something like "ketuks three," and refers to one of the instruments in the musical ensemble—the gong chime with three ketuk (see Figure 7.1). Quite a few dance traditions that fit the general description of ketuk tilu, however, do not include the three-ketuk gong chime; it seems more precise to use the term ketuk tilu to refer to the entire performance context rather than the instrument itself (Sugiharwati 1980: 9; Amelia 1996).

It is difficult to trace with any certainty the history and development of ketuk tilu and related music and dance traditions. Following the lead of the eminent Indonesian dance historian Soedarsono, who describes three periods of Indonesian dance (primitive, feudal, and modern), it is common to describe three main periods of ketuk tilu development: (1) prehistory, (2) a period of popularity beginning in the nineteenth century, and (3) a revival in the 1970s, in the form of *jaipongan*.

The description provided above for prehistoric ketuk tilu dancing is, of course, primarily conjecture. Some people look to the Baduy village celebrations for a window to the past, believing that these isolated Sundanese communities might preserve something of ancient customs. And, indeed, Baduy planting and harvest celebrations involve men dancing in honor of the rice goddess (Zanten 1995). They use *angklung* and drums for accompaniment, however; there are no signs of the female singer-dancer or of the ketuk accompaniment. The ubiquity of these elements elsewhere in West Java, however, attests to their long history.

Figure 7.2 Ronggeng dancing wawayangan at a performance at the Bandung Zoo (Henry Spiller).

As for the second period—nineteenth-century popularity—it is a part of oral history in West Java that ketuk tilu was already well known in 1883, because some people dancing at a ketuk tilu event were killed by a coconut tree felled by the infamous eruption of the volcano Krakatau (Suhaeti 1986: 9; Somawijaya 1990: 15). And combing through the travelogs written by foreign visitors to Java in the nineteenth century reveals quite a few descriptions of music and dance events that could be construed to be ketuk tilu performances, although none of them uses that term specifically.

In keeping with their ritual nature, ketuk tilu events followed a ceremonial protocol. An event began at approximately 10 p.m., and was held outdoors. At the center of the performance space stood an oil lamp with three wicks (and thus three flames) called an *oncor*. The light from the oil lamp circumscribed a performance space, bounded by the darkness beyond, in which the participants—*ronggeng* (female singer-dancers), musicians, and the men—performed. The first part of the event was an opening ceremony, consisting of an instrumental overture, called *tatalu*, played by the musicians. Next, the ronggeng lined up and faced the audience for the *jajangkungan* (literally, walking on stilts), in which they rose up on their toes at goong strokes in the music. The jajangkungan flowed into the *wawayangan* (literally, act like a wayang puppet) section (see Figure 7.2) in which the ronggeng sang and performed solo or group dances. After the wawayangan, the ronggeng sat down again, and the musicians performed the sacred song of invocation called "Kidung" while the leader of the troupe lit incense and prayed for a successful evening.

The transition out of the opening ceremony and into the participatory event followed, to the accompaniment of a song called "Erang." Men from the audience could get up and dance with a ronggeng without paying during this transitional piece. After "Erang," the evening proceeded according to the wishes of the audience; men could request (and pay for) songs to which to dance as well as particular ronggeng with whom to dance. Other men could join the paying dancer on the floor (Soepandi and Atmadibrata 1976: 76–81; Sugiharwati 1980: 36; Somawijaya 1990: 27; Sedyawati and Parani 1995: 308–10; Atmadibrata 1996: 80–1; Fajaria 1996: 35–9).

Male ketuk tilu dancers cultivated a personal style of individualized movements, and the ronggeng's movements followed and "served" her male partner's movements (Somawijaya 1990: 56). When dancing, the men's foot movements were expected to coordinate with the drum patterns, while their hands and the rest of their bodies were free (Sugiharwati 1980: 38). Their goal was to dance freely and spontaneously, but in keeping with the drumming patterns played by the musicians. They based their motions both on the musical rhythm and upon their own desires.

One means men had for following their own desires was by choosing a song whose character and mood were compatible with their own. The man who started the dance got to choose the piece, and he usually selected a form and a song that would enhance the kind of dancing he wanted to do—humorous, acrobatic, artistic, or whatever.

Quite a few ketuk tilu songs are relatively short and simple; their short phrases and simple poetic form provide great freedom for improvisation by the dancer; the singer, too, had considerable freedom in selecting stock verses for these tunes. Some of these tunes had more particular associations; for example, for the song "Buah Kawung" ("sugar palm fruit"), male dancers typically performed *penca silat* movements; the song "Cikeruhan" ("in the style of the village of Cikeruh") accompanied movements meant to be *kocak* (amusing).

There are also a number of songs with complex, asymmetrical forms and special drum patterns, such as "Geboy" and "Paris Wado." Dancers had to negotiate these songs' structural peculiarities in order to coordinate their movements with goong strokes, and thus displayed their own expertise and cleverness. The repertory also includes set pieces, which help delineate the form of dance events, such as "Kembang Gadung," which typically accompanies the wawayangan dance, and "Kidung" and "Erang," which have already been mentioned. Lyrics for ketuk tilu songs are usually in the poetic forms *wangsalan*, *sisindiran*, and *paparikan*. These texts tell of ordinary, every day things, but are considered to be *disilibkeun* (indirectly spoken)—listeners interpret the mundane topics as metaphors for more profound or weighty matters. Ronggeng can call male guests up to the stage by nickname, or make a reference to a particular customer by choosing a text that evokes him.

The example in Figure 7.3 is in the paparikan form, in which each of the two couplets that form the verse addresses completely different subjects, but which nevertheless acquires a relationship through the use of parallel vocabulary and sounds. In this case, the first couplet describes a bat hanging upside down in the darkness. It sets a sinister tone—something slightly threatening (a bat) is close by, yet out of sight. The second

kamana si kalong hideung	*where is the black bat*
teu kadeuleu-deuleu manting	*he can't be seen swinging*
kamana si jangkung hideung	*where is the tall dark guy,*
teu kadeuleu pulang anting	*he can't be seen, wandering back and forth*

Figure 7.3 Ketuk tilu verse (Somawijaya 1990).

couplet relates that one of the dancers has disappeared but remains, out of sight, beyond the pool of light cast by the oncor. The implication is that he is doing something sinister, or at the very least something outside the normal bounds of propriety.

Although ketuk tilu events followed a ritual protocol, the particular sequence of events was subject to the whims and desires of the men who attended them. It was common knowledge that these desires could tempt men to retreat into the darkness with the ronggeng of their choice and convert their ceremonial fertility rite into a flesh-and-blood sexual liaison. Sometimes transgressions of the protocol extended into the performance space as well. A popular ploy for some men was to "accidentally" kick over the oil lamp to extinguish it, and take the opportunity presented by the darkness to grope their partners.

Following each dance of the men with the ronggeng there was a second, men-only dance called *oray-orayan* (literally "moving like a snake," it also is the name of a children's game), in which the paying male dancer led the other men around the performance space in a sort of conga line. This men-only dance was meant to restore fellowship among the men and prevent arguments or fights among the men over ronggeng; in the past, at times such conflicts could turn ugly, and could even become fatal (Salam Mulyadi, pers. comm., 6/15/99, 6/17/99; see also Herdiani 1996: 45).

The various "bad" behaviors in which ketuk tilu fans indulged—drinking, showing off, carousing with women, and fighting with other men—are viewed as natural masculine behaviors. In everyday life, however, men are expected to suppress these urges; it is also considered a masculine attribute to control one's bad behavior. A real man, then, lives a contradiction—he is randy and rowdy while simultaneously behaving with dignity and circumspection—both in the dance space and in real life.

Ketuk tilu events provided a space in which to explore these masculine contradictions as well as to ensure a successful rice-growing season. In fact, the two meanings became inextricably bound up with one another. While the men enjoyed their freedom to indulge in excessive behaviors, including uninhibited drinking, carousing, and fighting, the female singer-dancers, in a sense, took most of the blame for the men's bad behavior. It was, after all, their beautiful appearance and beguiling voices, coupled with the animating rhythms of the drums, that were responsible for the men's stepping outside the boundaries of propriety. Dance events with female singer-dancers and drumming provide a safe place for men to allow their true nature to percolate to the surface—an opportunity to prove that they are "real" men. On the dance floor, they demonstrate their masculinity whether they succumb to temptation or overcome it; if they succumb, they are "real" men, while if they overcome the singer-dancer's temptations, they are powerful men. It is a win–win situation for men, who in real life all too often find themselves in less fortunate circumstances. In either case, dancing also provides them an opportunity for fellowship with their peers—to be men in the company of men.

It is within some people's living memories that ketuk tilu–like events such as those described above were popular throughout the first part of the twentieth century. The ketuk tilu ensemble consisted of the three-ketuk gong chime, a hanging goong (played by the ketuk player), rebab, and gendang, plus the singing of the ronggeng. This minimal ensemble—with only three musicians—provided a stripped-down version of the four functional layers that characterize Indonesian gamelan music. The ketuk and goong provided a colotomic structure; the rebab and ronggeng based their elaborated versions of the melody on some unperformed basic outline, and the gendang player provided the drumming layer. Track 9 of the CD that accompanies this book, the ketuk tilu tune "Sinur," illustrates this texture.

Ketuk tilu events became less common after Indonesian independence (Sugiharwati 1980: 2). Various forms of ketuk tilu–like events are purported to have been outlawed in the 1950s in some localities (Sugiharwati 1980: 9; Azis and Barmaya 1983–4: 5; Somawijaya 1990: 16; Amelia 1996: 60; Sukarya 1997: 3). This decline in ketuk tilu's popularity in the twentieth century was probably precipitated by two significant changes in Sundanese (and Indonesian) life.

First was a burgeoning interest in a more orthodox approach to Islam. Although most of West Java had been Islamic since that religion first spread to Indonesia in the sixteenth century, the practice of Islam in West Java accommodated many pre-Islamic practices and did not greatly affect underlying political or social patterns (Anderson 1972: 58–9). In the late nineteenth century, some wealthy Sundanese were able to make the haj (pilgrimage to the holy city of Mecca), observe how Islam was practiced in the Middle East, and encourage their Sundanese compatriots to adopt more stringent Islamic standards of moral behavior. Because ketuk tilu involved dancing that could be easily construed as lascivious, especially because it was common knowledge that the female performers might be willing to extend their ritual relationship with their male partners into actual sexual encounters, ketuk tilu events came to be seen as irredeemably immoral.

Second, some Indonesian nationalists became interested in forging an Indonesian nation out of the various islands and cultures then under Dutch rule. A key strategy in developing an Indonesian identity involved minimizing people's interest in local traditions and getting them to focus on an emerging pan-Indonesian culture which was based in a large part on more internationally accepted political and social mores. Once again, lascivious dancing with overtones of prostitution did not fit well with these nationalist ideals.

Neither of these movements was anti-agriculture, although they did discourage the spiritual, goddess-centered approach to fertility represented by dance events. Their moral standards, however, definitely were at odds with an old-fashioned approach to masculinity in which bad behaviors were permitted—even encouraged—in the context of dance events.

As a result, the competing social values with which Sundanese men need to contend have become even more complicated. On the one hand, it is their duty to ensure a fertile and successful growing season by dancing with (and possibly having sex with) ronggeng, the ritual representatives of the rice goddess. Furthermore, Sundanese people understand carousing with women to be a "natural" predilection for men. On the other hand, these activities are cast as immoral under any circumstances from Islamic and nationalist points of view (Notosusanto and Weiss 1995: 119), and while it is generally acknowledged that men are born with the urge to carouse, powerful men are expected to curb their natural urges.

At their heart, ketuk tilu events created a safe space to explore these contradictions through the interplay of three key elements: (1) female singer-dancers (ronggeng) and (2) the animating rhythm of drumming, both of which facilitate (3) free improvisatory dancing. In old-fashioned ketuk tilu performances, the three elements emerged one by one: first the drumming (in the tatalu), then the ronggeng (in the wawayangan); finally, the men join in with their free dancing. The ronggeng played the part of the goddess, which brings a sense of the sacred to the proceedings, mitigating any perceptions of wrongdoing. The drumming also relieves the men of any responsibility for their actions by coercing the men into action. Any bad behavior in the free dancing that results from these elements is thus socially acceptable. These three elements—ronggeng, drumming, and free dancing—constitute a core of Sundanese custom that persists into the present, despite the pressures of orthodox Islam and Indonesian nationalism. Many of the developments in Sundanese music and dance in the twentieth century were motivated by attempts to reconcile all these paradoxical sets of values—to find some middle ground in which to be Islamic Sundanese nationalists.

Animating Dancers with Drumming

Before examining some of these more recent developments in Sundanese music and dance, it is necessary to examine more deeply the relationship between dancing and drumming. A key feature of all Sundanese dancing is a close relationship between dance movements and particular drum patterns. It sometimes appears that there is a "cause-and-effect" relationship between dancing and drumming, although it is not always clear which is the cause and which is the effect. At times it seems as if a dancer's body and limbs are encountering invisible barriers that make them stop suddenly; the drum patterns sound like the noises these imaginary collisions create. Sundanese people associate similar sound effects to just about any kind of everyday movement. At the same time, however, it is a common belief that particular kinds of drum rhythms invite movement to go along with them—in effect, drum patterns animate the bodies of dancers, whether the bodies' owners are willing to dance or not.

Drummers and non-drummers alike learn drum patterns by associating spoken phrases with them as mnemonic devices; these phrases in turn come to suggest the movements they accompany. Dancers, when practicing or demonstrating, typically provide their own accompaniment in the absence of a drummer by singing onomatopoeic representations of drum patterns.

Ordinary people as well as musicians vocally imitate the sounds of drum patterns, and some Sundanese claim that Sundanese drums actually speak. Each of the variety of tones and timbres that a drummer can produce on the various drum heads using a variety of hand techniques suggests words or syllables. *Tepak kocak* (humorous drum patterns) suggest a certain movement by quite literally saying it. For example, one well-known drum pattern is heard to say "kadupak pingping, kadupak pingping, gulingkeun gulingkeun (goong)," which means in Sundanese "rub thighs, roll around (ending on the stroke of the goong)." The cause-and-effect relationship here is vague; it is unlikely that these particular drum sounds are specific enough to mimic unambiguously the words. Nevertheless, this linguistic interpretation is clear to most listeners, but only because they have heard it before. It is worth noting that this particular drum pattern has some deliciously lewd implications. The drums not only animate dancers, but they sometimes tell them to engage in otherwise unacceptable behaviors. Sundanese dance drumming can provide a convenient excuse for indulging in questionable activities on the dance floor—"the drumming made me do it!"

There is a circularity inherent in this kind of joke—listeners need to be expecting the drum sounds to suggest movement, and at the same time such jokes reinforce the expectation that sounds and movements are related. An analogous circularity underlies the entire dance–drum relationship in Sundanese music—one must expect the drums to suggest movement, and at the same time coordinating movements to drum patterns reinforces the expectation.

Drum sounds and patterns have the power to evoke movement at many levels of organization. Individual drum sounds can suggest certain accented movements. Short patterns can suggest different types of walking, or ways of moving one's arms while standing. Imitations of drum sounds even characterize entire dance "genres"; the terms *jaipongan* and *dangdut*, for example, are generally acknowledged to be imitations of drum sounds (e.g., Hatch 1985: 218; Tirasonjaya 1988: 293; Soeharto 1992: 27–8; Hardjana 1996: 129; Soepandi, Sukanda, et al. 1996: 49). Each genre's distinctive rhythmic "groove" and the movement style associated with it are essentialized in a short, catchy vocal abbreviation of the drum accompaniment.

Sundanese drums

Three drum types are common in West Java: *dog-dog, terbang,* and *gendang.* Dog-dog are single-head conical drums hit with sticks or bare hands. Terbang, also called *rebana,* are single-head frame drums. Gendang (also called *kendang*) are double-head barrel-shaped drums. Dog-dog are associated with music and dance genres in which the musicians provide their own accompaniment while they parade or dance. Terbang are most often played in ensembles in which the musicians sit down. Gendang are associated with most other kinds of dancing.

Sundanese dance drummers usually perform with one large barrel-shaped drum, called *gendang indung* ("mother drum"), supplemented by one or more small drums, called *kulanter, gendang leutik,* or *ketipung.* Drums of both sizes share the same general appearance and construction. Each drum body is carved from a single piece of wood. The outside may be conical or barrel-shaped; the inside is hollowed out in an hourglass shape. Drum bodies are either stained and varnished or painted. Old drums are left with a worn finish despite the apparent preference for new and shiny appearances; visible wear indicates age and venerability, qualities that are prized (but rarely faked).

Each end of a drum is covered by a skin head that is wrapped around a rattan ring slightly larger than the end of the drum. The rings and heads are placed over the ends of the drums and laced onto the drum with a single long leather cord in a criss-cross pattern. Each of the resulting pairs of criss-crosses is joined by a small braided rattan ring which facilitates tightening and loosening head tension.

One of a drum's heads is typically slightly larger than the other. Sundanese drummers usually rest the smaller end of the drum on a stand to elevate it a foot or so off the floor; in the absence of a stand, a drummer might use a pillow or his leg. Most drummers place their feet in cloth or string loops that are attached to the larger head of the gendang indung. This helps prevent the drum from moving and allows the drummer to change head tension, and thus the drum's pitch, with his heel.

The drummer places various kulanter within easy reach. At least one kulanter is placed

Figure 7.4 Drummer Usep playing gendang set up in a typical arrangement (Henry Spiller).

upright on its larger head near the smaller head of the gendang indung. Some drummers prefer to tilt this kulanter slightly with a special piece of wood made for this purpose which is semi-permanently tied to the drum, or by resting it on the tuning hammer or some other convenient object. The tilting affects the timbre of the drum slightly, since the unplayed head can vibrate sympathetically.

One, two, or three additional kulanter are placed opposite the drummer near the large head of the indung. These may be laid on their sides or placed upright. Usually the drummer hits only one head of each of these kulanter, either the larger or the smaller head. This basic arrangement pattern (see Figure 7.4) may be considered standard; however, each drummer exhibits personal idiosyncrasies of some kind. Although many drummers express preferences for one method or another, few drummers consider alternate arrangements incorrect.

Walking patterns—mincid

Looking closely at one particular drum pattern provides some insight into the Sundanese dance–drum connection, especially if that drum pattern is actually produced by dancers who are playing drums. Several Sundanese ensembles include a cadre of hand-held conical drums called dog-dog (see Figure 7.5). In the comic entertainment form called *ogel* or *reog*, four performers provide their own accompaniment on dog-dog while they dance and tell jokes. Each performer plays a different sized dog-dog; specific interlocking patterns of dog-dog strokes are associated with specific movement patterns

Figure 7.5 Four dog-dog players (courtesy Michael Ewing).

(Soepandi and Atmadibrata 1976: 71–5). In this case, the dog-dog accompaniment also serves as a means for communication and signaling between the performers.

The Reog Mitra Siliwangi troupe from Bandung, for example, play a variety of patterns on their four dog-dog. The drums are called (from smallest to largest) *tilingtit* (#1), *panempag* (#2), *jongjrong* (#3), and *bangbrang* (#4). The #1 player leads the tempo, rhythm, and movements; #2 is lower-pitched than #1, and is played on offbeats; #3 is lower-pitched than #2, and is played on onbeats; #4 is the lowest-pitched, acts as gendang and goong, and may play many variations (Solihin 1986: 14–15). Figure 7.6 shows each dog-dog part for one of the group's patterns.

This particular pattern is for the accompaniment of walking around. It is significant that the patterns played on the panempag and jongjrong (#2 and #3, respectively) are absolutely regular, evenly spaced strokes; but the two patterns are offset from one another so that they interlock. Because the two drums' timbres and pitches are reasonably close to one another, and because their strokes occur sequentially, those listening tend to perceive both drum sounds as a single musical entity—as if they were coming from a single drum—and organize the sounds into groups of strokes. Thus, listeners hear a recurring drum motif—"high–low–high"—emerge; each iteration of the motive is separated by a moment of silence.

This motif can be thought of as mimicking the physical process of taking a step. The first higher-pitched sound represents the muscular impulse to lift the leg. The lower-pitched sound suggests the falling of the foot on the ground. The final higher-pitched sound recalls the release of muscle tension and the impulse to prepare to shift weight to

beat	1	2	3	4	5	6	7	8	1	2	3	4	5	6	7	8
talingtit (#1)		•	• •	•	• •	•	• •				• •	• •	• •	•		
panempag (#2)		•		•		•		•		•		•		•		•
jongjrong (#3)	•				•			•				•				
bangbrang (#4)		x	x x	x x		x	x x	x x x	•		• •	• •	• •	•		x

beat	1	2	3	4	5	6	7	8	1	2	3	4	5	6	7	8
talingtit (#1)			• •	• •	• •	•					• •	• •	• •	•		
panempag (#2)		•		•		•		•		•		•		•		•
jongjrong (#3)	•				•			•				•				
bangbrang (#4)	x •				•				•			•				

beat	1	2	3	4	5	6	7	8	1	2	3	4	5	6	7	8
talingtit (#1)		•	• •	•	• •	•	• •				• •	• •	• •	•		
panempag (#2)		•		•		•		•		•		•		•		•
jongjrong (#3)	•				•			•				•				
bangbrang (#4)		x	x x	x x	x	x x	x	x	•		• •	• •	• •	•		x

Figure 7.6 Dog-dog walking pattern (after Solihin 1986: 25).

the other leg. The pattern's offset from the music's accents suggests indefinite repetition of steps. The result is, at some level, the sound of a body walking (although not necessarily the sound a body makes when walking). The other parts (tilingtit and bangbrang, #1 and #4, respectively) decorate and vary this "walking" motive with syncopated rhythms and a wider variety of drum timbres.

Performance genres featuring dog-dog typically rely on interlocking figurations between the dog-dog drums and a division of labor among them to provide the drumming that animates the movement. The lead dog-dog player uses particular patterns to signal changes in tempo and choreography to the rest of the group. The repeated ostinato patterns echo and embody the movements coordinated with them.

In genres such as reog, each dancer provides a part of his own accompaniment. In ketuk tilu and other dance forms, however, a single gendang player provides all of the various drum sounds while the dancers concentrate on dancing. The set of gendang can produce a variety of pitches and timbres. Although it is a non-dancer who plays the gendang, the nature of the gendang parts is still dance-oriented; particular drum patterns suggest specific kinds of movements, and a specific drum pattern accentuates and supports each dance movement.

The dog-dog pattern described above, and others like it, have come to be associated with walking dance movements. Upon hearing such a pattern, a dancer is compelled to perform such walking movements in time with the drum rhythm. And, upon seeing a dancer perform walking movements, a drummer is obliged to accompany it with an appropriate drum pattern. Many gendang patterns, especially those that accompany walking movements, are reminiscent of interlocking dog-dog patterns; this makes sense considering that a kendang player has at his disposal a set of sound resources similar to that of four dancers playing dog-dog. A drummer can set up the "high–low–high" pattern by playing strokes on two different drums with one hand while providing the variable, syncopated patterns on yet another drumhead with his other hand.

Mincid is a Sundanese term that describes walking in a dance-like manner (Panitia Kamus 1969: 314; Eringa 1984: 501; Tamsyah, Purmasih, et al. 1998: 212), or "stepping— one step or in place" (Natapradja 1975: 106, 108). *Keupat* means a swinging, swaying movement where the hands and arms move back and forth while the feet step in opposition to the hands (Eringa 1984: 398). These walking movements and the drum patterns that accompany them illustrate the circularity and ambiguity with regard to cause and effect. The drum patterns can be explained as caused by the walking movement—resulting from the very steps that the dancer-musicians take—or as actually causing the walking movements.

Drumming in ketuk tilu

Mincid walking patterns are part of ketuk tilu drumming and dancing. Ketuk tilu pieces usually begin with a special section called *nyered* or *nyorong*, which does not vary from piece to piece. Some people even consider this section to be a separate piece (Somawijaya 1990: 52). After nyered, the *lagu* (main song) begins; the repeated cycle may consist of one or more goong phrases. The drumming for the main song can be thought of as having two main sections. In the first, the drumming for each goong phrase of the lagu usually begins with a "stationary" pattern that persuades its hearers to remain poised but inactive, followed by a "moving" pattern that leads to the end of the goong phrase and obliges its hearers to perform active movements that end abruptly with the goong stroke. At some point, after a few repetitions of the main song's cycle, there is a signal to change to the second primary section, the mincid section. The change may be initiated by one of the male dancers (in which case the drummer changes the drumming appropriately) or by the drummer (in which case the dancers follow suit). In mincid, walking patterns of the kind described previously are repeated without break. Although there may be special cadential figures leading to the goong strokes, there are no "stationary" patterns following the goong stroke, and no periods of inactivity. After several more repetitions of the main song, the pulse quickens a bit to the goong, and nyered is tacked on as an ending phrase or as a bridge to another main song. Participants do not dance to the nyered sections.

Each of the two primary sections has its own organization: For the first, moving toward goong strokes is the main organizing principle; in the second, it is walking continuously (mincid). For the moving phrases, dancers are (in principle) free to do whatever they like, as long as it fits the drumming. Fitting the drumming means moving during a flurry of drumstrokes and striking a pose when the flurry ends. During this section, ketuk tilu dancers concentrate on moving their upper bodies and arms, with only occasional steps. Male dancers often strike poses while standing on one foot. If there are steps, they are typically large, and may include jumps. The male dancers usually move away from their ronggeng partners during the goong phrases, only to approach the ronggeng again as the goong phrase comes to an end. Most typically, the movement at the goong stroke involves stepping up to the ronggeng and pretending to kiss or touch her on the accented beat just before the goong stroke; the pose is held through the goong stroke, which gives it emphasis.

The mincid section, in contrast, concentrates on foot movements. Dancers usually perform some kind of stylized stepping for mincid, often with complicated patterns involving steps without weight shifts. Dancers often maintain one hand and arm position over the course of several steps. In these sections, if the drummer plays no cadential figure leading up to a goong stroke, the dancers continue their stepping right through the stroke, as if it were not there.

The conventions of ketuk tilu music and drumming make it easy to learn to dance. Nobody studies this kind of dancing; many men regard this free dancing as part of their natural abilities as men. Of course, they watch and imitate the dance movements of others they admire, and some men even admit to practicing dancing alone by listening to songs on cassettes or radio and dancing along. But learning to fit their movements to the drumming is relatively simple because the structure of the drumming itself is simple. There is considerable variety and freedom to do whatever sorts of movements one wants, as long as they fit the drumming and the song.

Aristocratic Men's Dancing: Tayuban

Men dancing in the company of ronggeng was not limited to the common people in villages; aristocratic men, too, danced with each other and with ronggeng at evening dance parties. For the same reasons that ketuk tilu fell out of fashion—namely changes in moral values that made the rowdier aspects of ketuk tilu dancers' behavior unacceptable—aristocratic men's dancing underwent some significant changes during the first part of the twentieth century. These changes set the stage for many of the innovations in Sundanese presentational dance in the late twentieth century and into the present.

The aristocratic class, called the *kaum menak*, led a lifestyle significantly different from that of Sundanese commoners. For them, the performing arts were an important symbol of status and differentiation because they provided opportunities for displays of wealth and ostentation. The upper class took pains to differentiate their artistic productions from those of the commoners. They held their events in large covered porch areas, rather than outdoors, and danced to the accompaniment of a full gamelan salendro ensemble rather than the minimalist ketuk tilu ensemble. Aristocratic dancers developed rich movement vocabularies and complex choreographies.

While differences of scale and protocol are apparent between upper- and lower-class dance events in nineteenth-century descriptions, it is not until the late nineteenth century that people began to apply different names to these variants of Sundanese men's social dance; the aristocratic version came to be called *ibing tayub* or *tayuban*. Although the trappings of upper- and lower-class dance parties were different, it seems likely that the same female singer-dancers were hired to perform at both. The male guests paid the ronggeng, often in a very public manner—handing them money, placing it in a special bowl, or slipping it into their clothing. In the aristocratic parties, the men typically danced one at a time, often in order of their status and rank. Often, one of the female performers, the host, or the previous dancer chose the next male dancer by presenting him with a dance scarf. Once the chosen man was dancing, others could join in after asking and receiving permission from him. Although tayuban had much in common with ketuk tilu, its roots in any agricultural rituals are much more obscure. While ketuk tilu celebrated masculinity as a metaphor for agricultural fertility, tayuban was about a different kind of masculinity: establishing a man's rank and status relative to the other aristocrats in attendance.

The professional female singer-dancers were the only women dancing at the aristocratic events. Wives and daughters attended the parties, but did not dance; rather, they observed the spectacle of their husbands, fathers, and sons dancing with one another and with the ronggeng. While the female audience members clearly enjoyed watching as the men jockeyed for status, sometimes they became jealous if their husbands crossed some ill-defined line of propriety. At some point in the evening, the female (and foreign) guests would always leave, and the parties reputedly became increasingly wild (Dyck 1922: 65; Brandts-Buys n.d.).

It is often difficult for twenty-first-century readers to understand how dancing skills could acquire so much importance. Since the fall of the Sundanese Pajajaran kingdom in the sixteenth century, the Priangan was part of non-Sundanese political units that delegated authority to govern to the existing Sundanese aristocracy. These aristocrats' authority depended at least partly on their ability to maintain a perception that they were somehow different from and better than their rank-and-file subjects, and therefore worthy to govern; one means to achieve this perception was to cultivate manners and practices—etiquette—that distinguished them from the common people and legitimated their right to rule (Kartodirdjo 1982: 188).

In 1871, the Dutch demoted the Sundanese bupati (Sujana 1993: 49)—they were relieved of many of their hereditary governing responsibilities, some of which were shifted to the local Dutch officials while the rest were assigned to native bureaucrats. While there was no requirement that these bureaucrats have any aristocratic blood, because of their education and status, aristocrats filled many of the new positions, and thus these new bureaucratic positions once again became associated with the existing noble class. However, the Dutch also instituted merit-based promotion within the bureaucracy. Membership in the aristocracy became something neither completely hereditary, nor completely merit-based. There was no longer any official privilege attached to a noble birth; status and respectability could be, and needed to be, acquired and maintained.

It was then possible for someone of common birth to break into and advance among the ranks of the aristocracy. An ambitious fellow could get himself apprenticed at a young age to an aristocratic household or kabupaten, and attempt to win the favor of the master. The candidate did menial tasks and learned office skills, but also learned how to fit into high society. Acceptance and approval in such circles could provide an entry into the bureaucracy as well as the means to advance (Sutherland 1979: 32).

When blood alone no longer determines place in society, other factors become more important. Aristocrats—as well as aspirants to aristocracy—developed even more elaborate etiquette skills. The publication of a number of Sundanese etiquette books in the

Figure 7.7 Tayuban dancer wearing aristocratic pakaian adat (Henry Spiller).

early twentieth century attests both to the importance of etiquette among the kaum menak and to the possibility for upward mobility for those who master the intricacies of etiquette, which according to at least one of those books (the 1908 *Tatakrama Oerang Soenda*—Sundanese People's Etiquette, by D. K. Ardiwinata), involved three aspects: language, dress, and behavior (Lubis 1998: 173).

To address the first aspect, aristocrats cultivated different vocabularies (levels) of the Sundanese language. A speaker's choice of language level situated him or her in relationship to others—a person quite literally spoke "up" or "down" to other people. People of lower rank were obliged to use deferential language when speaking to their superiors, creating a palpable distance between them. People of higher rank were empowered to use cruder vocabulary when speaking to their subordinates. Using these speech levels—and getting away with it—provided a means to quite literally speak one's rank and status.

Details of dress, too, provided opportunities to situate one's self within aristocratic society; by noting the batik patterns, styles of clothing, jewelry, and ornaments it was possible to know at a glance somebody's rank and status. Aristocratic men traditionally wore a *kain batik* (wrapped batik skirt), a shirt and/or jacket of various different styles and cuts, and a headcloth or covering of some sort. The quality and pattern of the batik cloth bespoke a man's rank and taste; the details of how he pleated the ends and wrapped and wore the cloth were also markers of his good breeding. Different kinds of jackets went in and out of style, and men needed both money and taste to keep up with trends. Watches, watch chains, and other jewelry were similar indexes of a man's wealth, status, and good taste.

The final dimension of etiquette was careful attention to one's behavior, or more specifically, one's bodily deportment. The etiquette of West Javanese aristocrats created distance between those affecting upper-class mannerisms and those of lower status (Lubis 1998: 172). In short, becoming an aristocrat involved learning to move as an aristocrat. The *sembah* gesture is an example. In this gesture of greeting, one puts one's hands together as if praying and holds them in front of one's face. Sembah was used in all sorts of situations, such as greeting somebody or receiving something. Ardiwinata, the author of the aforementioned etiquette book, compared the sembah gesture to the "commas and semicolons in a literary work or goong strokes in gamelan music" (Lubis 1998: 174); in other words, its correct usage punctuated graceful behavior and provided a sense of completeness to a man's deportment. Knowing how and when to sembah was a mark of bodily eloquence and style.

Just as the well-dressed aristocrat's clothing eventually became a sort of dance costume for aristocratic dance (see Figure 7.7), the gestures of aristocratic men's dancing doubtless developed as an extension of this bodily etiquette. Many etiquette gestures were incorporated into tayuban dancing, including sembah, *sila* (sitting crosslegged), various styles of walking respectfully, and *ngampil* (carrying a symbolic object solemnly) (Lubis 1998: 173). But, even more importantly, dance events provided a forum in which men could develop and display their skill at looking and moving like an aristocrat.

In fact, being good at dancing became a requirement (Durban Ardjo 1998: 167; Lubis 1998: 246). Men cultivated their skill at dancing, and guarded their reputations as dancers, as part and parcel of the business of being manly in an aristocratic way. The highest-ranking bupati often had a *kostim* (dance character and song) that they preferred to dance in tayuban. There were grave supernatural consequences for somebody who usurped somebody else's kostim without permission.

Upward mobility also required, at some level, the approval of the Dutch overlords. The Sundanese upper classes also adopted things European (as they had adopted things Javanese earlier) during the period around 1900, including drinking whisky and playing cards (Sutherland 1979: 43). Pressures of upper-class European morals, which frowned on overt dalliances with women of ill repute, combined with similar pressures from increasingly orthodox Muslims, led some aristocrats to "clean up" their tayuban events. Most histories credit the Sumedang aristocrat R. Gandakusumah (also known as Aom Doyot; Aom is a title bestowed on the son of a bupati) with modifying tayuban etiquette in several significant ways—including forbidding the ronggeng to stand and dance and relegating them to the role of singer only (Soepandi and Atmadibrata 1976: 84). Other reformers eliminated the consumption of alcoholic drinks as well.

Inconveniently for these reformers, the words tayub and tayuban themselves probably come from an old Javanese word "anayub" (Sumarsam 1995: 35, 27 fn. 43), which meant to drink a fermented beverage (Zoetmulder, Robson, et al. 1995: 1063). Some reformers even came up with new *kirata* (retroactive acronymic etymology) to eliminate this association with alcohol use, such as ma**taya** (dance) plus gu**yub** (together), and mena**ta** (put in order) pagu**yub**an (togetherness); these interpretations put the fellowship aspect of tayuban dancing into the foreground while attempting to cover up tayuban's association with drinking and other bad behaviors (Sujana 1993: 24–5).

Faced with the prospect of being judged on their dancing skills, and deprived of erotic spectacle from the ronggeng, participating men turned to enhancing their own spectacle. One particularly rich resource in the cultivation of increasingly complex dancing was *topeng Cirebon*. As described in Chapter 3, this village theater form featured a solo dancer portraying a variety of characters in an all-day performance. Sundanese dance enthusiasts were intrigued by Cirebonese dance, possibly because its sophisticated movement repertory, characterization, and complex formal structures all provided fresh ways to distinguish one individual's dancing from that of the others. A number of Cirebonese *dalang topeng* capitalized on this interest and made regular trips to the Sundanese parts of West Java. Sundanese dance enthusiasts observed and studied elements of topeng with these visiting dancers and enriched their own dancing with elements of form, style, and gesture from topeng.

Dancing became a competitive activity during this period. Competitions for male dancers, called *konkurs* (from the Dutch term *concours*, meaning competition), were popular in the early part of the twentieth century (Atmadibrata 1998: 3). Competitions provided a context in which standards of dancing excellence were developed and extended. Individuals who excelled at improvisational dancing were asked to teach others their skills, resulting in the founding of organizations devoted to dancing. Members of the clubs studied with these masters and competed in the konkurs.

This "evolved" form of tayuban dancing—a single man dancing alone, without a ronggeng partner, exhibiting his skill with expanded forms and large movement vocabulary from topeng Cirebon—came to be known as *ibing keurseus* because its fans learned to dance by studying dancing systematically in dance courses. "Ibing" is the high Sundanese word for dancing, while "keurseus" comes from the Dutch word "cursus," meaning "course of study." This new name also further disassociated men's dancing from the use of alcohol.

Ibing keurseus rapidly gained popularity among the Sundanese for several reasons. Its aristocratic connotations and its reputation as a means for social advancement encouraged its study by ambitious young people. Beginning in the 1930s, several academic schools began to offer instruction in ibing keurseus (Sujana 1993: 99). The dance clubs had developed systematic teaching methods which were easily transferable to academic settings. The very name "ibing keurseus," with its Dutch origins and vaguely systematic and "scientific" ring, gave the emerging dance genre an aura of upward mobility and modernity adaptable to both aristocratic and democratic models of society. In keeping with the ideals of a wider Indonesian identity, some people began to call the dance genre *tari kursus*—the Indonesian-language translation of the Sundanese phrase ibing keurseus.

Eventually, tari kursus became the base on which what is now called Sundanese classical dance (*tari klasik*) was built. It provided a repertory of dance movements, with specific accompanying drum patterns, and a formal structure for developing dance pieces. It even provided a model for costumes. It might be more difficult to learn and perform than ketuk tilu or tayub dancing, but it was more interesting to watch. Thus, over the course of about fifty years, aristocratic men's improvisational dance morphed from an improvised, social dance form into a kind of presentational dance, and became completely decoupled from the context of the participatory dance events from which it sprang. Tari kursus dances, divested of tayuban's seamier elements and upgraded to be presentational dances, could be shown off to non-Sundanese as examples of high

Sundanese art, alongside similar classical dances from Central Java and Bali, as expressions of the Indonesian nation's motto *Bhinneka tunggal ika* (Old Javanese for "unity in diversity"). Although it is clear that the form, style, and gestures of modern Sundanese classical dance are firmly rooted in men's improvisational dance, differences in context and meaning are profound. The model of paying admission and sitting to watch a performance is fundamentally different from the more established Sundanese ways of experiencing performing arts in the context of a family celebration.

Sundanese men's improvisational dance—both ketuk tilu and tayuban—provided men with an opportunity to establish their masculine identities. Whether one was a farmer or an aristocrat, dancing well and dancing cleverly, without crossing the lines of bad taste or impropriety or seeming too flamboyant or proud, provided a way to enhance a man's status in the sight of other men and in the sight of any women who might be observing. Because of the ritual connotations of men's dance events—the female singer-dancer's association with the rice goddess and of the men's obligation to ensure agricultural fertility by interacting erotically with the female performers—dance events also involved behaviors that generally were frowned upon, such as drinking and womanizing. Establishing a masculine identity, then, involves doing these contradictory activities at the same time through the medium of dance movements. Although negotiating the twists and turns of Sundanese masculinity was a treacherous undertaking, the mechanics of dancing in ketuk tilu and tayuban were relatively easy. Anybody familiar with the drum patterns and the structure of the music could come up with appropriate dance movements. The new presentational Sundanese dances, however, were perceived to be quite difficult to learn; they require special training and courses and specialized knowledge, not to mention special costumes.

Modern Men's Dancing

In the 1960s and 1970s, ketuk tilu performances were increasingly rare, but performances called "tayuban" were popular at Sundanese *hajat* (life-cycle event celebrations) among middle-class, non-aristocratic, urban Sundanese. The hajat host needed to hire a gamelan and invite dancers as guests. The guest dancers received special invitations indicating that they would be called upon to dance, so that they would come prepared to dance and would dress appropriately (i.e., in *pakaian adat*—the kain batik, jacket, and headcloth worn by aristocrats, which were by that time obsolete for most occasions). Several issues with these tayuban performances contributed to a decline in popularity. For one thing, the "feudal" overtones of the event were very apparent; tayuban, after all, was most closely associated with the aristocratic class, and this association was reinforced by the costumes worn by the dancers. By the 1960s, Indonesians were increasingly aware that the existence of an aristocratic class was not compatible with the nation's democratic ideals. Another reason was that the competence required to dance tayuban—all the specialized movements, the specific order of movements, and how to fit the movements into musical structures—had become esoteric knowledge. Most of the invited dancers performed choreographed tari kursus dances, further intimidating the average participant because of the specialized knowledge and technique required to perform them. In other words, the pressures that had brought about the "cleaning up" of tayuban resulted in a populace that was no longer interested in watching—much less performing—tari kursus.

Ketuk tilu, too, is rarely encountered any more in Priangan, but there are a couple of troupes that still perform occasionally. One group performs every other week in the Bandung Zoo; their show is billed as a "cultural performance," the goal of which is to preserve ketuk tilu as a cultural artifact and educate zoo visitors about this old-fashioned style of Sundanese dancing. The ronggeng are, for the most part, very old, as are the male dancers. Although the audience is encouraged to participate, few spectators join in the ketuk tilu dancing. The zoo audiences are aware that ketuk tilu is an old form of Sundanese folk art which involves ronggeng and amateur male dancers, but they are not acquainted with the particulars of ketuk tilu music and dance. The zoo performances are called *ketuk tilu buhun*; *buhun* means "ancient" and thus reinforces this distance. For Bandung residents, then, ketuk tilu and tayuban have entered into the realm of esoteric folklore.

Bajidoran

Although ketuk tilu and tayuban fell out of favor in the Priangan, dancing with ronggeng has remained popular in some parts of West Java. The area around the cities of Karawang and Subang (north of Bandung) are especially well known for dance events involving professional female singers and dancers facilitating the participation of men from the audience. In many surface details, these modern dance events do not much resemble the austere, reconstructed versions of ketuk tilu as performed in the Bandung Zoo or tayuban at hajat. From a broader perspective, however, modern men's dancing in Karawang and Subang has much in common with ketuk tilu and tayuban. In the earlier part of the twentieth century, ketuk tilu troupes are reported to have followed dalang around to steal their audiences; some people speculate that the assimilation of the ronggeng into wayang performance practice as the pasinden (seated, non-dancing female singer) was a strategy on the part of wayang golek dalang to overcome their newfound competition by assimilating it (Foley 1979). More recently, as ketuk tilu events became difficult to find, fans starting going to wayang golek performances and asking the pasinden to dance for them. The pasinden became the focus of the performance, often at the expense of the wayang's ostensible main focus, that is, the storytelling. Dalang Tjejtep Supriadi from Karawang describes how some dalang encouraged this practice because it contributed to their own popularity (Suganda 1996), but other dalang sought to impose standards on wayang performance that would prohibit dancing by female performers (cf. Weintraub 1997: 176–82). In response, some female performers began performing in a new kind of group, which presented music drawn from wayang and ketuk tilu repertories for listening and dancing (Dahlan 1996: 2, 34–5).

These performances were at first called *kliningan*. In the past, kliningan referred to a small ensemble for accompanying kawih singing (see Hermantoro 1991). *Klining, kilining*, or *kilinding* is an obsolete instrument resembling a Central Javanese gender (Soepandi 1985: 111). A newer name for these performances is *bajidoran*, because the male fans who come to the performances came to be called *bajidor*. In Subang and Karawang, this term has been in use to describe male dancers since the 1950s (Junengsih 1997: 15). Mas Nanu Muda provides a kirata for the word—**ba**risan **ji**wa **dor**aka (a row of sinners)—and relates that it was originally used as a joke among bajidor themselves, but eventually came

Figure 7.8 Bajidor dance below the stage where sinden dance under colorful lights (Henry Spiller).

to be applied to the entire musical genre (see also Suganda 1998; Muda 1999: 14). There are a number of variants of this kirata, including **ba**risan **ji**wa **dur**haka (row of rebels) (Suganda 1996) and **baji**ngan **dor**aka (sinful, evil men; *bajing* is a flying squirrel, which has approximately the same meaning as the American slang "rat" when applied to a man). Mas Nana Munajat Dahlan corroborates his brother Nanu's explanation, but supplements it with a second, completely different kirata for bajidoran: **ba**njet, tan**ji**, dan bobo**dor**an (*banjet* is a dance/theater form; *tanji* refers to Sundanese music performed on Western brass instruments, and *bobodoran* suggests humorous movement—clowning around). He explains that this kirata accounts for the similarities of bajidoran to banjet and tanji with regard to the dance, music, and drum patterns, as well as the humor that pervades bajidor events (Dahlan 1996: 5). Other possible sources for the term bajidor might include the Portuguese *bailador* (dancer) and the Hindu *bayadere* (*devadasi*, female temple dancers).

What most of these tales about the origin of the terms bajidor and bajidoran have in common is that they capture the free masculine energy that characterizes the events. The story of the development of bajidoran demonstrates how persistent the idea of men's free dancing facilitated by ronggeng and drumming remains in the Sundanese imagination despite the pressures of conflicting value systems. For various reasons, ketuk tilu and tayuban dancing fell out of favor; but the same underlying pattern of social relationships and meanings found an outlet in other forms of music and dance. Although ketuk tilu and tayuban are for most intents and purposes extinct in Priangan, kliningan/bajidoran groups are thriving in northern West Java; there are more than 100 groups in the Subang area alone (Dahlan 1996: 39; Junengsih 1997: 6), and perhaps as many as 1,000 female singer-dancers around Subang and Karawang (Suganda 1998).

The groups in Subang typically include ten to fifteen female singer-dancers called *sinden*, accompanied by a large gamelan salendro, including several gendang players, performing on a very high stage (approximately five feet above the ground). The bajidor often show up to any performance that features their favorite sinden. The performance sponsors do not necessarily know the individual bajidor personally, but they welcome their attendance and even provide them with alcoholic drinks (which the regular guests do not receive) to encourage them to dance. To avoid the appearance of impropriety, however, the men dance on the ground in front of the high stage, which provides them only limited opportunities for physical contact with the sinden (see Figure 7.8).

One form of physical interaction is called *egot*. A bajidor stands in front of the stage, sometimes on a wooden box placed there for this purpose, and his chosen sinden kneels in front of him. They join hands and swing them back and forth in time to the music. The sinden expect the bajidor to tip them generously and often. After a few minutes of egot, the sinden breaks contact, and will not reengage until the bajidor tips her.

Like ketuk tilu, bajidor dancing requires only a basic understanding of a few musical conventions and the mastery of a few simple dance drumming patterns. Once again, there are two main grooves associated with bajidor dancing: standing/moving patterns and walking patterns. Whereas ketuk tilu involves several different standing/moving patterns, some of which are associated with special phrases in particular songs, most of the stationary patterns in bajidoran are based on a single framework, called (when it is given a name at all) *bubukaan* ("opening") or *pola ibing* ("dance pattern"). Once again, the walking patterns are called *mincid*. A typical bajidoran song alternates between these two grooves.

The gamelan accompaniment for bajidoran dancing is usually a *lagu alit*—those "small pieces" described in Chapter 5 in which the musicians base their parts on a simple sequence of pillar pitches that occur at regular time intervals. Usually the pieces are performed in *dua wilet* ("two wilet"—a rhythmic treatment that specifies how much time there is between pillar pitches; see p. 140). The pola ibing pattern divides each goong phrase into several parts; each part involves a frenetic flurry of drumming, followed by a complete stop of activity (and silence from the drums). The pola ibing is an important foundation of jaipongan as well; these patterns can be heard on Track 10 ("Lindeuk Japati") of the CD that accompanies this book.

The first drum phrase in the pola ibing is the opening movement, called *bukaan*; its end coincides with the goong phrase's first pillar pitch. This phrase is notated in Figure 7.9 using the drum syllables that a drummer or dancer might sing to represent the drum pattern; the reader can produce an approximation of what the pattern sounds like by setting an even beat (referring to the beat numbers above the drum syllables) and singing the syllables indicated in the boxes in time with the rhythm. The "ng" sounds at the end of syllables suggest a ringing drum sound, while the "k" sounds correspond to sharp, slapped drum sounds. A "p" or "t" at the beginning of the syllable suggests a higher pitch, while a "b" or "d" sound suggests a lower pitch. Extra consonants ("l" or "r") inserted after the initial sound suggests a drum roll or flam. Notice that the drum is silent for the first seven beats of the pattern; there is then a flurry of activity culminating with the rising drum figure "bang-dut."

The next phrase also begins with a seven-beat stretch of silence, followed by some stepping movements. This pattern is called *jalak pengkor* (lame bird) because it suggests foot movements that limp along, spending more time on one foot than the other. The

	1	2	3	4	5	6	7	8
							pang	pak

	9	10	11	12	13	14	15	16
ter	pak blang	pak blang	pak ting	prak	ting	pong	bang	dut

Figure 7.9 Bajidoran pola ibing: bukaan.

	1	2	3	4	5	6	7	8
								blang

	9	10	11	12	13	14	15	16
pak	pak	blang pak	pak	trupak		tung ping	baba bang	bang dut

Figure 7.10 Bajidoran pola ibing: jalak pengkor.

	1	2	3	4	5	6	7	8
				dong	pak ting	tung pong	bang	pak

	9	10	11	12	13	14	15	16
				dong	pak ting	tung pong	bang	pak

Figure 7.11 Bajidoran pola ibing: capang.

	1	2	3	4	5	6	7	8
	tung ping	ber pak pak	bang				dut

	9	10	11	12	13	14	15	16
ting	pong	dut	ting pong ber	pak		tung ping	dong BAP	(G)

Figure 7.12 Bajidoran pola ibing: cindek and ngala genah.

pattern ends with the same rising figure that ends the bukaan flurry. The syllables for jalak pengkor are illustrated in Figure 7.10.

A moment of silence follows jalak pengkor, but not as long as the moment that followed the bukaan movement. The next flurry of activity, called *capang* ("sticking out sideways with upward points"), begins with the fourth beat of the phrase and is characterized by triplets—evenly spacing three drumstrokes over the time usually allotted to four—which give the phrase a feeling of building tension. The capang flurry is played twice during the third phrase, as illustrated in Figure 7.11.

All of the tension that has been built up by the juxtaposition of flurries of activity and silence and the triplets will be released in the last phrase. The final flurry of activity, *ngala genah* ("look for something delicious"), is prepared by a short movement called *cindek* ("inevitable") or koma ("comma"), as illustrated in Figure 7.12. Ngala genah ends with a strong accent one beat before the goong stroke; the goong stroke itself is met with silence and stillness.

Bajidor dancers are free to translate these drum patterns into movement however they wish. Very often the movements they choose are funny; sometimes, but not always, the humor is intentional. I have seen a dancer move to the pola ibing looking like the movie version of Frankenstein's monster—never bending his elbows or knees, and keeping his gaze blindly straight ahead. Another bajidor dancer has earned a certain measure of fame by moving only his facial muscles, following the dictates of the drum flurries by making ridiculous grimaces in time to the patterns. For improvised dance, the aesthetic goal is to dance with freedom—to appear unconstrained by conventions or restrictions. Dancers do attempt to synchronize their movements with drum patterns, but this is not regarded as a restriction so much as an axiomatic, defining characteristic of dance.

There are some general tendencies in the choices that most men make for the various flurries in the pola ibing. Men tend to adopt a stance in preparation for the first flurry (bukaan). This stance, called *adeg-adeg* (support post; see Figure 7.13), involves placing one foot back and one foot forward (both turned out about 45 degrees from center), with the back knee bent and taking most of the body's weight. The dancer's trunk leans back a bit, his gaze is downcast, and his arms are relaxed. When the bukaan drum flurry begins, the dancer gestures with his head, arms, and torso, leaving his feet on the ground. He may change directions, and most of the gestures could be characterized as floating and sustained. At the end of the flurry, when the drummer performs the characteristic rising drum motive (bang-dut), there is an abrupt change; the dancer usually makes some sort of a dabbing or punching gesture, after which he stops moving so that his final position becomes a pose. Dancers typically do not move during the times when the drum is silent. Most men do not even hold a pose for these periods; instead, they stop dancing and just stand there until the next flurry of activity begins.

Jalak pengkor and capang involve similar movements (although jalak pengkor typically involves stepping as well). The rising drum motive at the end of each flurry inspires an abrupt change in dance energy—a dramatic gesture followed by a pose. The dramatic stop at the end of the ngala genah cadential pattern inspires a similar, but usually more dramatic, change in energy flow. In contrast to the previous abrupt changes, the shape change of ngala genah movements are also characterized by a pronounced sinking quality, giving it more of a feeling of finality.

Figure 7.13 Abdul Rozak (dancing with ronggeng Rakmi) in adeg-adeg pose (Henry Spiller).

The attraction of dancing might be summed up in the phrase ngala genah (or ala genah). In Sundanese, ala or ngala means "to pick (as fruit)" or "to look for"; genah means "delicious" or "pleasing." Ala genah refers to the final gesture of the pola ibing, specifically to the abrupt stop, accentuated by a loud drumstroke (bap), that comes just one beat before the stroke of the goong. Dancer and choreographer Mas Nanu Muda explains that the pleasing part of ngala genah is getting back in sync together with other dancers at that particular point in a dance. He said that it is nice to dance according to one's own wishes during the lively drumming that leads up to the goong stroke, but that coming back together at the point where the drumming stops before the goong stroke is especially satisfying.

In bajidor dancing, the pola ibing section is repeated several times before the musicians switch to the second groove—*mincid*. For mincid, most men match their foot movements to the drumming, stepping in some patterned way (for example, step-left/close/step-right/close). Depending on their personalities and mood, they might travel only slightly (e.g., back and forth in a "slot") or else move aggressively around the dance arena. The stepping is continuous, providing a significant contrast with the alternation between flurries of activity and stillness that characterize the pola ibing section. Dancers usually supplement their foot movements with head, arm, and torso gestures. Drum cadential figures (and dance movements) that lead to goong strokes in mincid are similar to ngala genah in the pola ibing.

In the 1990s, some bajidoran groups began to include a third rhythmic groove as well—an extremely fast and agitated mincid-like pattern called *triping*. Although the drumming for triping is quite frenetic, most men dance to it rather slowly, swaying their heads from side to side and stepping somewhat erratically. The groove is said to mimic the effects of the drug Ecstasy, with its intense mental acuity and overall feeling of well-being. The name triping is derived from the English term "tripping."

The dancers consider themselves free to dance however they want; the most pleasurable part of dancing for them, however, is the moment when they stop dancing freely and pause for a moment, in unison, and shift their focus from the internal to the external. These pauses in the first groove, of which ngala genah is perhaps the most dramatic example, suggest a sort of checking in with the rest of the dancers—interrupting the introspective, personal sojourn that is improvisational dance to make sure that everybody else is still in the same groove. The dancers' cherished freedom is, in effect, limited quite frequently by these checks—much as their personal freedom to act as they please is held in check by the strictures of society and the limits of good taste. The second groove, mincid, is blissfully free of these reality checks, and the dancers are given the opportunity to really let loose; because they are constantly moving according to the drums, however, once again their perceived freedom is reined in by convention. The familiar framework of female singer-dancer and animating drumming enables this illusion of total freedom in bajidoran.

Jaipongan

Bajidor dancing may be a popular diversion for lower-class men in some parts of West Java, but such dancing still is held in low esteem by upwardly mobile Sundanese. While there are many aspects of such events that raise eyebrows, including the use of alcohol and the men's predilection toward uninhibited behaviors, most of the disapproval is focused on the female singer-dancers. They are seen to encapsulate every thing that is immoral about men's dancing because it is they, people believe, who lead the men into temptation.

Yet, at the same time, even upwardly mobile Sundanese enjoy the opportunity to perform the contradictions of Sundanese masculinity and the fellowship of men that "free" dancing provides. It is no simple matter to change a culture's notions about masculinity, especially when they have been continuously reinforced for centuries by the durable three-part framework of female singer-dancers, animating drumming, and free dancing in a variety of dance events. Once again, it is the female singer-dancers who most reliably symbolize these associations with men's dance events. Give them too big a role, and the music becomes sleazy; push them too far into the background, and the music becomes uninteresting.

Jaipongan, a music and dance form that became popular in West Java in the late 1970s, seemed to strike exactly the right balance with regard to the female singer-dancer's role. By maintaining all that was up-to-date and exciting about bajidor music and dancing, and by keeping female performers in the foreground but sanitizing their roles by emphasizing their status as star performers, jaipongan forged common ground between the participational nature of traditional Sundanese men's dance events and the more modern presentational dance forms pioneered with tari kursus.

A Bandung-based choreographer and record producer named Gugum Gumbira Tirasondjaja claims to have invented jaipongan in the 1970s. As a young man, he says, he was attracted to popular music from the United States and Europe. He was inspired, however, to look beyond imported rock and roll to indigenous Sundanese forms because of an admonition by Indonesia's first president, Sukarno, to eschew foreign influences and look to Indonesian roots for contemporary expressions (Yampolsky 1987; Broughton, Ellingham, et al. 1994: 428). Gugum's account of jaipongan's genesis also suggests that he was dissatisfied with the approach to masculinity expressed in presentational dances such as tari kursus; the virility and authenticity he perceived in rock and roll were among the qualities that made it attractive.

Douglas Myers paraphrases Gugum's thoughts:

> [Gugum] was a young and virile man. He wanted to move. He wanted to express his vigour. Within the range of cultural dances available to him there was nothing which he felt allowed him to express what he wanted to say. The dances were too slow and constrained to allow the movements of the impetuous young man (Myers 1992: 45).

Gugum found what he was looking for in the bajidoran/kliningan music of Subang and Karawang. One particularly famous drummer from Karawang named Suwanda caught Gugum's attention, perhaps because his spectacular virtuosity—his playing was almost superhumanly loud and fast—captured the qualities that Gugum was seeking. Gugum's first jaipongan pieces are masterful combinations of a variety of existing Sundanese music and dance elements. Many of the characteristic drum pattern sequences come from Karawang-style music and dance. The dance movements for his staged choreographies were drawn from a variety of sources, including penca silat (Sundanese martial arts). The first jaipongan hits, such as "Oray Welang," were adaptations of songs from the ketuk tilu repertory.

It is quite unlikely that Gugum's somewhat self-aggrandizing account of the invention of jaipongan is completely true; other creative forces were instrumental in innovating and popularizing jaipongan. While it is true that Sukarno disapproved of Western popular music, and some government officials banned rock and roll from Indonesian radio from the late 1950s until Sukarno's fall in 1965 (Lockard 1998: 77), that was more than a decade before the beginnings of jaipongan in the late 1970s. And several other prominent musicians and dancers contributed important ideas and materials to the development of jaipongan, notably the late Nandang Barmaya. One of the first major public presentations of jaipongan was developed for a presentation at the Third Asian Arts Festival in Hong Kong in 1978; Gugum refined and rehearsed what was then known only as *ketuk tilu perkembangan* (developed ketuk tilu) with a number of artists, including Nandang and the late singer/dancer Tati Saleh.

The contribution of the drummer Suwanda, whose brilliant playing leaps out of the speakers for most of the original jaipongan hits and was an enormous part of their appeal, should not be underestimated. The name "jaipongan" itself usually is connected to the sound of drumming. Although "pong" is a common vocalization of drum sound, the syllable "jai" is not. One story is that the phrase "jaipong" was borrowed from a comedian who deliberately garbled dance–drumming syllables for comic effect. Some people have suggested that the word "jai" is not an imitation of drum syllables at all, but rather the name of a Karawang artist. A few people even claim it is a Chinese word. In any case, Gugum used the new name, and it did not take long for it to eclipse the tongue-twisting term ketuk tilu perkembangan.

Gugum's role in jaipongan's creation and popularization is significant, and it is not limited to dancing and choreography; his artistic vision and business acumen as a recording producer were instrumental to jaipongan's success. Jaipongan's eventual popularity is due in no small part to its dissemination in a medium that emerged in the late 1960s and reached a zenith in the 1970s and 1980s: cassette recordings. Unlike phonograph technology, which never caught on in Java because of the prohibitive expense of both the equipment to manufacture records and the equipment required to play it back, cassette technology provided an economical means both to produce and play back prerecorded music. Furthermore, it came along precisely at a time when the Indonesian middle class, which could afford such simple luxuries, began to grow. Cassette players and prerecorded cassette tapes became cheaply and widely available throughout Java in the 1970s (Manuel and Baier 1986: 99).

Gugum and his wife, singer Euis Komariah, founded a recording studio, in part to sell jaipongan recordings. They named the studio Jugala (a kirata for **ju**ara **ga**ya dan **la**gu, which means "the champion of style and song"), and released a string of jaipongan cassettes in the 1980s.

And not just jaipongan cassettes—in the 1980s, cassettes became the medium for a phenomenal explosion of popular innovations in traditional Sundanese music. Jugala, along with several other companies (notably Hidayat), churned out releases by the hundreds, and accomplished musicians found frequent work in recording studios. Some of these musicians now look back fondly on the *zaman kaset* ("era of the cassette") when they were able to pick up significant extra income by playing for recordings. Many of the cassettes produced in the 1980s are still available for purchase in Indonesia, but not very many new cassettes of traditional music are being produced in Bandung, and those that are released appear to be much more conservative in repertory (perhaps aimed at the tourist or export CD market rather than the local market). Jugala, for example, has not produced many new recordings since 1989 (Euis Komariah, pers. comm., 4/18/2007); however, their existing catalogue of recordings is widely available, and their studios are in constant demand for other recording projects.

In these early jaipongan hits, the roles of female singer and female dancer were both highlighted, but performed by separate individuals. Gugum's choreography was rather athletic, and the singing was quite virtuosic; it would be difficult for anybody to perform both simultaneously. The female performer's two roles are decoupled—separated from one another. Some of Gugum's choreographies were designed for groups of female dancers, whom he deployed on the stage with complex blocking and formations; male audience members were free to ogle the performers as well as appreciate their skill and precision. Other choreographies featured a couple—a man and a woman; in this case, male audience members could experience vicariously the thrills of a truly accomplished man's free dancing through the male dancer (often Gugum himself).

Although choreographed jaipongan dances sidestepped many of the moral objections people had to female dancers, some people still found some jaipongan choreography to be objectionable. A controversy erupted in the Bandung newspaper (*Pikiran Rakyat*, "The People's Thoughts") in the early 1980s over the erotic nature of jaipongan dancing. Discussion centered around "the three Gs," namely *gitek*, *goyang*, and *geol* (Sundanese words for various kinds of hip and buttock movements), and there were calls to ban jaipongan.

Perhaps the controversy was inflamed by some performances by the late Tati Saleh, a gifted singer and dancer whose distinguished career by 1980 already included appearances abroad (at the 1964 New York World's Fair, among other venues), a number of pop hits, and parts in Indonesian films (including one, *Nji Ronggeng*, in which she played the role of a ronggeng). Because she danced with Gugum for many of the early exhibitions of jaipongan, she became associated with jaipongan as a dancer in the minds of many Sundanese. As she was an accomplished singer as well, she would at times combine both roles while performing jaipongan, at first with established groups, and then eventually with her own troupe, LS Tati Saleh Group. Although her credentials as a serious artist were never in doubt, her singing and dancing (and especially the combination of the two activities) were nevertheless perhaps a little too close to an "immoral" presentation for comfort (Tati Saleh is the featured singer of Track 10, "Lindeuk Japati," of the CD that accompanies this book).

The controversy calmed after Gugum released a much tamer, softer, and less overtly erotic jaipongan tune entitled "Serat Salira" ("My Letter"), featuring the mesmerizing voice of Idjah Hadidjah from Karawang. By 1980, Idjah had established a reputation as a pasinden performing with the wayang golek troupe headed by her husband, dalang Tjetjep Supriadi, and had won a prestigious prize for her singing. Gugum placed her under contract with Jugala; over the course of about four years, she recorded approximately forty cassettes of jaipongan and other music. Another of the songs she recorded for Jugala, "Daun Pulus/Keser Bojong" is among the most famous jaipongan songs and choreographies of all (this tune, along with other Idjah Hadidjah songs, was released in the US by Elektra/Nonesuch Records on an album entitled *Tonggeret* [9 79173–2] in 1987, and rereleased in 2003 as *West Java: Sundanese Jaipong and other Popular Music* [Nonesuch Explorer Series 79815]).

Idjah's voice and skill in singing attracted many male fans, but by performing with her husband she avoided many of the bad associations that accrue to female singers. Furthermore, she never danced at all. In fact, she never even performed jaipongan music for live events—only during recording sessions. She and her husband scrupulously avoid any activities that might suggest Idjah is anything but a superstar singer (Tjetjep Supriadi, pers. comm., 6/23/99). She told me that the jaipongan recordings were her least favorite because the frenetic drumming interfered with her vocals.

Jugala was not the only successful producer of jaipongan hits. Cicih Cangkurileung is another hugely successful recording artist, who by her own reckoning has released over 100 cassettes. Born into a family of musicians and dalang, she began to sing in public in her childhood. She assumed the stage name Cangkurileung ("bulbul bird") when she entered a singing contest; at the time, it was common for singers to take bird names (Suganda 1999). Among Cicih Cangkurileung's hits is the very successful song entitled "Adumanis." It is worth discussing "Adumanis" in a little bit more detail, not only because it is quite representative of jaipongan songs, but because its words and music express on many levels the aesthetic values of Sundanese performing arts in general.

The Sundanese-language phrase "adu manis" literally means "sweet clash" or "sweet conflict." As a general principle, Sundanese find great aesthetic value in the close juxtaposition of dissimilar things. People often wear combinations of designs and patterns that most Westerners would regard as simply too busy; Sundanese take great delight in color combinations that would probably strike Westerners as garish. The words of the song "Adumanis" extol the aesthetic principle of "adu manis" on several levels.

First, the lyrics describe jaipongan as a combination of several contrasting Sundanese dance forms—ketuk tilu, penca silat, classical dance, as well as "influences from all over." Then, the words connect jaipongan dance to matters of romance, by suggesting that jaipongan can be a courtship dance involving flirtatious glances. The song proceeds to characterize romantic relationships between men and women as another sort of sweet conflict; the clash experienced by the couple described in the song is especially sweet because their differences have been magnified by a long separation. The song closes by reminding its listeners that the conflict of romance is everybody's common experience; it may never be resolved, but it is indeed sweet.

Most jaipongan tunes begin with a fast introductory section, and "Adumanis" is no exception; this opening section exhibits the aesthetic principle of sweet conflicts in several ways. First comes an opening *a cappella* chorus of men intoning the word "adumanis" in vocal harmony. Then the dynamic drumming that characterizes jaipongan heralds a very loud, boisterous gamelan salendro phrase. After a few bars, however, comes a contrasting section; the tempo is still quite fast, but most of the gamelan instruments drop out, leaving only the delicate sounds of the gambang and rebab to accompany the whispered words "adumanis." The various contrasts—among the voices singing in harmony, and between the loud and soft sections—set the stage for a musical exposition on sweet conflicts.

As is typical in jaipongan songs, the fast introductory section draws to a close with a dramatic slowing in tempo; by the time the goong stroke arrives, the gamelan salendro is playing at a relatively soft volume, at a slow, easy tempo. At this point, Cicih Cangkurileung begins to sing; right away, the ear encounters another sweet conflict—the song's melody is in the surupan pelog degung, which clashes quite noticeably with the gamelan's salendro tuning.

It is not long before the next clash arrives. This time, it is the first flurry of drumming that creates the conflict, its volume and speed contrasting deliciously with the leisurely pace of the song. As the drumming proceeds with the standard pola ibing described earlier, the contrasts between the flurries of drum activity and the silences that separate them emerge as yet another sweet conflict. Every aspect of the song—the words, the music, and the choreography—illuminate the aesthetic principle of "adumanis."

Many, but not all jaipongan songs are self-referential in this way—the words describe some aspect of jaipongan in particular (or music and dance in general). Many other songs address love or romance in some way or another. Some songs tell stories about historical events. For example, Peter Manuel cites a jaipongan song called "Mat Peci" in his section on jaipongan in *Popular Musics of the Non-Western World* (Manuel 1988: 213–19); it describes a Sundanese Robin Hood-style antihero.

The words to another jaipongan hit, "Lindeuk Japati" (see Figure 7.14 and listen to Track 10 of the CD that accompanies this book), do not address dance specifically at all. Yet, they may indirectly evoke the image of a ronggeng dancer. Here the words paint a picture of a woman who seems eager to flirt but who flits away at the last minute without making commitments; the image of a pet dove—sometimes affectionate but always skittish—provides an apt metaphor.

The choreography of "Lindeuk Japati," as manifest in the drum patterns, is typical. Like bajidoran, jaipongan choreographies usually alternate between the pola ibing (with variations) and mincid (walking) sections. Jaipongan songs typically have a noticeably slower

Lindeuk Japati	*Pet Dove*
Lindeuk japati	*Pet dove*
Bangun lungguh bangun deudeuh	*Looks elegant and full of love*
Dihaja dihelaran	*If she's approached*
Harepan beunang kacangkring	*With the hope of capturing her*
Eh . . . ngejat jauh	*Eh . . . she moves far away*
Lindeuk japati	*Pet dove*
Sorot seukeut umat imut	*Shining eyes, quick to smile*
Dicoba dideukeutan	*If she's approached*
Bangun anu ngalayanan	*In the way she seems to invite*
Eh . . . ngejat jauh	*Eh . . . she moves far away*
Kapanasaran ditantang	*Suppressing that embittered feeling*
Ditarekahan sing beunang	*Trying to go and meet her*
Si lindeuk sugan kabandang	*The pet, to be attractive*
Deukeut deukeut dilomaan	*Draws close and gets friendly*
Tapi tetep ngajauhan	*But she always moves away*
Dikitu dikieu	*This way or that way*
Si lindeuk nampik	*The pet always pushes away*
Lindeuk japati	*Pet dove*
Horeng teu gampang kataji	*It's not easy to capture her heart*
Lindeukna ukur pamake	*Her appeal is but a ruse*
Lungguh timpuh pulas deudeuh	*Despite an elegant countenance*
Hatena can puguh daek	*Her heart has yet to be won*

Figure 7.14 "Lindeuk Japati" (composed by Nano S., sung by Tati Saleh, translated by Henry Spiller).

tempo than bajidoran tunes, however. For the most part, complete goong phrases are devoted to one type of phrase or the other. Choreographed jaipongan songs also include a third type of choreographic material, which can be characterized as "alternating" phrases. These are similar to the jogedan phrases of Cirebonese topeng (see Chapter 3) and tari kursus in that they are relatively complex drum patterns that repeat several times; dancers usually repeat the same movements, but alternate the direction they face from right to left and back again for each iteration.

When hearing jaipongan drumming for the first time, it might sound impenetrably chaotic and complicated. The schematic diagram in Figure 7.15 gives some insight into how dancers and musicians conceive and organize jaipongan choreographies; if they already understand the structure of gamelan music and know the principles of the pola ibing and mincid, there is little left to learn. Except for the alternating patterns (only two gong phrases' worth in "Lindeuk Japati"), the drum patterns are variations either of the pola ibing or of mincid.

Through cassettes, jaipongan choreographies, as manifest in the drum accompaniments, became widely available in a fixed form. Cassette owners could listen to these tapes over and over again, memorizing the sequence of drum patterns that made up the choreographies, and putting moves together to go with the drum patterns. In this

Lindeuk Japati / Renggasmara

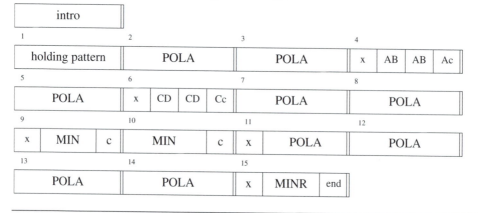

Figure 7.15 Schematic outline of "Lindeuk Japati" choreography. The diagram does not provide the details of the fast opening section; its presence is acknowledged simply with a box labeled "intro." Each segment bounded by a double line represents a goong phrase; each segment may be broken into four equal subphrases. In the goong phrases labeled "holding pattern," the drummer plays a soft drum pattern; it is not meant to be danced to. The jaipongan pola ibing phrase, which takes up an entire goong phrase, is indicated in the figures with the notation POLA. The notation MIN represents mincid; MINR is mincid rangkep—mincid done in double-time. The letter 'x' represents transitional phases; the letter 'c' represents cadential drum patterns leading (usually) to a goong stroke. There is often a transition leading to an alternating pattern, which typically occupies the rest of a goong phrase, ending with a special cadential pattern that accentuates the goong stroke. The repeated units of the alternating patterns are represented with capital letters (A, B, C, and D). The special drum pattern that signals the ending of the piece is labeled "end."

manner, the most popular jaipongan tunes, along with their choreographies, became well-known to many. Proficient dancers often opened dance schools, called *sanggar*, in which they taught all comers their choreographies for the big jaipongan hits; they, too, used the cassette recordings as accompaniment.

Through the medium of cassettes the drum's role became the leader of dancers; the dancers began to follow the drum accompaniment on the cassettes (Suganda n.d.: 9). Cassettes encourage people to dance who might not otherwise be brave enough to get up on stage. They can turn on the tape recorder and find an outlet for their desires, trying out the moves they see other people do, and moving according to the drum patterns in the privacy of their own homes (Somawijaya 1990: 59).

And, once they have perfected their routines, they can perform them in public—at hajat celebrations for weddings and circumcisions. Live musicians are strongly preferred over canned music at hajat, so dancers who hone their routines to the accompaniment of commercial cassettes expect their live accompanists to provide the same (or at least recognizably similar) music and drumming. Jaipongan drummers learn the choreographies from cassettes, too. Some jaipongan drummers develop personal shorthand notation systems that enable them to reproduce a wide selection of jaipongan sequences without having to memorize them all, but many drummers have memorized the most famous jaipongan drum parts.

As was the case with the development of tari kursus, the creation of jaipongan involved contextual as well as technical innovations. Gugum's jaipongan dances were meant to be presentational and were performed on stage, for seated audiences, but they never-

Figure 7.16 A group jaipongan dance performed at the Bandung kabupaten; note that the portraits of the president and vice president of Indonesia seem to gaze down on the dancers approvingly (Henry Spiller).

theless captured some of the thrills that characterize participational dance. The passive audiences could experience vicariously the excitement of dancing with a ronggeng, of dancing like a rogue, and of playing with the double standard of masculinity.

One significant difference between jaipongan and tari kursus was that jaipongan dances, unlike tari kursus dances, featured female dancers prominently. The concept in both genres was to make the female performer more respectable by separating the two roles of singer and dancer. In tari kursus, the female's role as a dancer was eliminated completely, although the ronggeng image was still referenced by a pasinden's singing. In jaipongan, there were two prominent female roles, performed by two separate performers. Although female jaipongan movements are usually characterized as provocative, and Sundanese men frequently ogle the female dancers, some female dancers themselves insist that jaipongan is not sexy at all, and resent any suggestions that it is perceived as such. Female dancers' own image of themselves as artists is at odds with the sexual implications of the ronggeng image. They stress that their movements are rooted in Sundanese tradition, which they imagine is too worthy of respect to have such mundane associations. Female dancers who regard themselves as artists find it difficult to accept the idea that they are objectified by their male audiences; their self-deceptive denial of their sex appeal by invoking the lofty authority of tradition disregards the historical realities of Sundanese female performers (see Figure 7.16).

Gugum's jaipongan dances are presentational dances, meant to be watched. As it is performed by amateur dancers at hajat, however, jaipongan is often reconstituted as a participational dance form. Indeed, in most social contexts, the boundary between

Figure 7.17 A male guest with professional female jaipongan dancers at a wedding (Henry Spiller).

presentational and participational jaipongan is quite fluid. Featured female dancers often find themselves partnered with guests, and guests often pay the musicians to follow them instead of the formal program (see Figure 7.17). One of jaipongan's advantages is that its conventions allow, even encourage, this ambiguity. Thus, jaipongan, unlike tari kursus, provides a way for fans to remain respectable by most standards without having to give up hearing, seeing, and even interacting with a female singer-dancer. In amateur jaipongan dancing, once again, the persistent pattern of free dancing, facilitated by ronggeng and animating drumming, is reasserted.

Jaipongan as "tradition"

When I first arrived in Bandung, the capital of West Java, in 1981, the Sundanese residents were not accustomed to seeing American faces, especially on the various forms of public transportation that I used to get around the city. They typically expressed their curiosity by asking me what I was doing there. "I'm here to study traditional music and dance" became my pat answer, and I became accustomed to the inevitable follow-up question: "Have you learned jaipongan yet?"

What's remarkable about this conversational exchange is that jaipongan, at the time, was not considered by most Sundanese to be traditional, but rather to be a new music and dance craze that was sweeping the region and even gaining national popularity. Unlike other popular music fads, which were characterized by the sounds of a global pop idiom (guitars, keyboards, and simple chord progressions), however, jaipongan looked and sounded distinctly Sundanese. Not only did it involve singing in the Sundanese language, but it involved gamelan salendro music, featured the singing of a pasinden, and utilized dance movements drawn from penca silat (Sundanese martial arts) and traditional dances. Yet there was clearly something about it that set jaipongan outside of most people's understanding of what tradition meant. By asking me—an outsider with a stated interest in Sundanese traditional music and dance—about jaipongan, I suspect that the Sundanese strangers I met were trying to clarify in their own minds exactly how to comprehend the paradox presented by this "modern tradition."

It took fewer than ten years for jaipongan to become transformed from a new innovation into the preeminent form of Sundanese "traditional" performing arts. In 1980 jaipongan was controversial and there were calls to have it banned; by 1990, jaipongan performances could be seen in hotel lobbies, at cultural shows, and in the recitals sponsored by *sanggar* (private studios) teaching dance. Some people even speak of a "'Modern Classic' concert style" of jaipongan (Broughton, Ellingham, et al. 1994: 429). Since the 1990s, presentational jaipongan has become an important part of the curriculum at the government-sponsored college-level school of the arts (Sekolah Tinggi Seni Indonesia [STSI]) in Bandung. STSI students write theses on the fine details of jaipongan style, choreography, and costuming.

One effect of all this official acceptance is to choke off the amateur approach to jaipongan. After all, jaipongan is now something one goes to college to study! It is therefore perceived to be too difficult for the average fellow to master. In addition, jaipongan has come to be seen as an important symbol of Sundanese regional identity; it is therefore perceived to be of use only for expressing how Sundanese culture differs from other regional cultures in Indonesia, and of little use to those for whom Sundaneseness is a given. Sundanese dance, and the uniquely Sundanese-sounding gamelan music that accompanies it, become less relevant to ordinary people the more they perceive them to be not only difficult, but disconnected from their daily lives and concerns.

Dangdut as "traditional" music

City dwellers especially have come to feel that Sundanese-sounding music is incapable of accompanying improvised, self-motivated dancing, and that it is good only for displaying a regional identity. During my stay in West Java, I noted that the further one got from the center of cosmopolitan Bandung, the more likely there was to be amateur male dancing to ketuk tilu or jaipongan music. Dangdut music, on the other hand, inspired dancing among men whether it was in cities or in rural areas.

Dangdut is a popular music phenomenon with a large following throughout Indonesia. Hit songs are recorded by a small number of star performers and promulgated via radio and television. Dangdut music is usually performed using an ensemble that features Western instruments such as guitars and keyboards, as well as a transverse flute (*bangsing* or *suling*) and drums.

As has often been pointed out, the uniquely Indonesian thing about dangdut is its language—but even that is shared to a certain extent with its Malay predecessor, *orkes melayu* (Malay orchestra). It also incorporates influences from Western popular music and Indian film music, which came to Indonesia via mass media (Lysloff and Wong 1998: 104). Dangdut's original popularity in Indonesia is usually attributed to the influential songwriter

	1		2		3		4		5		6		7		8
					dang		dut						dang		dut

Figure 7.18 Dangdut groove.

and performer Rhoma Irama, who consciously set out in the 1970s to create a modern popular music that carried an intelligible message to young people without being too Western in style (Hatch 1985).

Rhoma Irama's songs cover the gamut of topics, from intensely political to shamelessly sentimental. "Qur'an dan Koran," which can be heard on *Music of Indonesia 2: Indonesian Popular Music—Kroncong, Dangdut and Langgam Jawa* (Smithsonian-Folkways, 1991), for example, is pure political commentary—it criticizes modern Indonesians for placing too much stock on Westernization and "progress" while forgetting their religious obligations. The title uses newspapers (*koran*) as a symbol of the West and Islam's holy book (the Qur'an) as a symbol of Islam; the two words' almost homophonic pronunciation makes for a powerful statement. "Begadang," which can be heard on the CD *The Rough Guide to the Music of Indonesia* (World Music Network, 2000), on the other hand, chides people who talk too much without saying anything. Many of Rhoma Irama's songs, however, address the standard topics of popular music—love, romance, and heartbreak.

Dangdut's characteristic dance groove is usually played on a small bongo-like double drum called *tabla* (Hatch 1985: 218) or *calti* and consists of two accented drum strokes, the first of which is low-pitched ("dang") and the second of which rises in pitch ("dut"; see Figure 7.18). On calti, this rising pitch is effected by striking the drumhead and applying pressure with the heel of the hand to tighten the head and raise the pitch. The drum and technique are derived from North Indian *tabla*. These drum sounds came to Indonesia through the medium of Hindi film music (Lockard 1998: 94). Ethnomusicologist Peter Manuel relates the dangdut drum rhythm from a North Indian rhythm called *kaherva*, which was common in Indian film music (Manuel 1988: 211). The emblematic groove can also be played on other drums, including the standard set of Sundanese gendang.

Although it is the superstar performers, such as Rhoma Irama, Elvy Sukaesih, and their successors, who make songs popular and set new trends, live performances of dangdut are extremely popular as well; most of these performances feature singers and musicians who have little hope of attaining superstar status (Yampolsky 1994b: 38). In many circumstances, dangdut music and dancing appear in conjunction with other kinds of music and dance. Most bajidoran groups, for example, supplement their traditional repertories with dangdut songs (Dahlan 1996: 80; Junengsih 1997: vi), when their audiences request them. In and around Bandung, the small-time dangdut singers are known as *artis dangdut* ("dangdut artists"). The moniker "artis"—derived from the English term artist—has a modern connotation, and is mostly used to describe non-gamelan, non-traditional performers.

At Sundanese hajat, the entertainment might include an afternoon or evening dangdut performance, with one or several artis dangdut singing on stage to the accompaniment

Figure 7.19 Artis dangdut Mayanti dancing with male guests at a wedding (Henry Spiller).

of a full-blown orkes melayu with bangsing, keyboard, bass, dangdut drums, and other instruments. The accompaniment could also be a bit more modest—electronic keyboard and drum machine.

Although dangdut stars are just as often male as female, most of the artis dangdut who perform at hajat are young women. At the weddings I attended, the artis dangdut usually chose a man from the audience to be the central male dancer on stage for each song. She interviewed him, or gave him a *goyang* lesson—goyang refers to a sensual rolling hip movement—before beginning to sing and dance. The central male dancer was typically joined by several friends and relatives, who danced with each other while the artis dangdut performed. The artis dangdut also provided amusing, or at least titillating, patter in between her songs.

In other words, in the context of Sundanese performances, dangdut singers act like ronggeng—facilitating men's free dancing. Although their style of dress is modern—typically low-cut dresses or pantsuits made from shiny fabrics in lurid colors, with revealing holes at the midriff and thighs, high platform shoes, thick makeup, and long straight hair—they conform to the ronggeng image in that their clothing and demeanor are unusually sexually suggestive. In addition, they sing and dance, and interact with male guests (see Figure 7.19). In the hajat context, the only significant difference between an artis dangdut and a ronggeng is the sound of the songs (cf. Foley 1989: 60–1).

On the surface, dangdut music and dance may seem a significant departure from traditional Sundanese music, in terms of tonal material (dangdut songs are usually modal or diatonic), ensemble (dangdut is not associated with gamelan music), dance groove (the dangdut dance rhythm is continuous, not segmented and varied like the pola ibing), and language (most dangdut songs are in Indonesian rather than Sundanese). However, there is more in common between bajidoran and dangdut dance grooves than might be immediately apparent. Despite differences in their sonic signatures, dangdut and more traditional musical genres occupy the same musical milieu in West Java and mutually influence one another.

The key strokes in the dangdut drum pattern are the two low-pitched beats. A gendang player executes the second of these strokes with his foot on the drumhead; after striking the drum he increases his foot pressure on the head so that the pitch of the sound rises. This creates the eponymous "dang-dut" sounds. Other strokes may be added for variety, but this essential groove is maintained, and the pattern is repeated over and over again, forming a cycle—a continuously repeating rhythm.

The late distinguished Sundanese musician Entis Sutisna believed that the underlying approaches to rhythm that motivate jaipongan/bajidoran and dangdut are indeed quite different. He distinguished between *wanda klasik* (classic style) and *wanda anyar* (new style). The classic style rhythm is characterized by alternating stillness with dynamic drumming and movement, while the new style rhythm is continuous. In his opinion, it is the *dinamika* (dynamics), referring to the sudden contrasts in the classic style, which distinguishes it from the continuous new style (pers. comm., 5/8/99). In everyday language, modern Sundanese typically distinguish between these two styles of dancing with different words: *ibing* and *joged*. Ibing usually implies classic style—dancing to Sundanese music with starts and stops—while joged suggests new style—dancing to modern, popular music with a continuous groove.

The examples of the jaipongan/bajidoran pola ibing and the dangdut groove support the contention that the two rhythmic approaches are inherently different. But traditional Sundanese dances, such as ketuk tilu, tayub, jaipongan, and bajidoran, include two main sections or grooves; only one of these two grooves is what Entis would call "dinamika." The other groove, mincid, is cyclical and continuous like dangdut. In contrast to Entis's assertion, some people argue that the only difference between jaipongan/bajidoran and dangdut is the accompaniment—dangdut is diatonic and features the "dang-dut" drum rhythm, while jaipongan/bajidoran uses Sundanese scales and drum patterns. As proof, they point out that dancers can and often do use the same dance movements when dancing to dangdut music and jaipongan/bajidoran. In this view, the cyclical, continuous nature of the drumming is not so significant.

Furthermore, there is common musical ground between the pola ibing and the dangdut groove. The rising pitch motive at the end of each of the bukaan and jalak pengkor flurries of activity in the pola ibing (see Figure 7.9 and Figure 7.10 on p. 183), which motivates dancers to strike a pose and wait for the next flurry, is echoed by dangdut's eponymous rising pitch gesture ("dang-dut"). Yet, the dangdut phrase simply continues on with no pause, like mincid. In a sense, it is as if the two different grooves that characterize traditional Sundanese dance accompaniment—the pola ibing and mincid—have been conflated and combined into one short, condensed drum pattern.

According to ethnomusicologist Philip Yampolsky, the aim of men when dancing to dangdut "is apparently to be transported to a state where they are unaware of their surroundings, free of self-consciousness and inhibition" (Yampolsky 1994b: 38)—in other words, precisely the same motivations that ketuk tilu and bajidoran dancers have. The dangdut groove provides the same kind of animation that is implicit in old-fashioned Sundanese drum patterns. Coupled with the charms of a female singer-dancer, it empowers men to dance freely. The persistent idea of men's free dancing facilitated by ronggeng and drumming once again emerges.

The dangdut groove is not the only instance of a continuous approach to rhythm replacing more dynamic approaches. The triping drum groove in bajidoran is another example. In this case, it is the international house music groove that supplies the inspiration. Ironically, a critic for the Indonesian newspaper *Kompas* once argued that jaipongan rhythms were fundamentally incompatible with a house music groove (Anon. 1996); he was quickly proven wrong as triping became an integral part of bajidor music and dance.

Many of the dangdut songs that are popular at hajat include significant Sundanese elements. Many songs are from the subgenre *dangdut Indramayuan* from the northern coastal region of Indramayu; Indramayu ensembles typically include goong, kempul, kecrek (a stack of metal plates hit with a mallet), and gendang. Songs sometimes feature jaipongan-like drum "hooks" and cadential patterns as well, to which dancers always set corresponding dance moves. Dangdut songs become hits via their dissemination through mass media. Like popular music in Europe and America, music videos are an important promotional vehicle for dangdut music. Such videos are broadcast on television in West Java on shows devoted to dangdut and as fillers between other shows.

A number of Sundanese dangdut stars have released songs they describe as *dangdut jaipongan* or, sometimes, *pongdut*. These recordings often feature genuine gendang players, who perform patterns that combine elements of the dangdut groove and mincid patterns, interspersed with dramatic pola ibing-like patterns. Even if the songs do not include gendang in the mix, their videos frequently show a gendang player (drums are the only musical instruments shown) and intercut images of female jaipongan dancers with scenes of more modern dancing. Often, too, a group of men who actively participate in free dancing may be included. Sometimes the song's female singer is even depicted as a ronggeng.

The images in many of these videos suggest that their creators are systematically, if not necessarily consciously, bringing to the foreground the similarities between some dangdut music and Sundanese men's dancing. At times, it seems clear the video producers are actively trying to convince the viewers that dangdut music, or at least some of the more Sundanese-influenced dangdut styles, is functionally the same as other men's dance forms; they accomplish this by cutting back and forth between images of traditional dance, such as ketuk tilu and jaipongan performed by dancers in traditional dance costumes, and more modern hiphop-influenced dangdut dancing by young men and women dressed in the latest unisex fashions. They literally replace one image with the other in the viewer's field of vision, and thus in their conceptions as well.

A song that artis dangdut frequently perform for dance events in and around Bandung, "Kuda Lumping," suggests other ways in which old meanings of Sundanese music and dance are inscribed onto dangdut. The song's title refers to a rural trance ritual in which men mount straw hobby-horses and dance around to the accompaniment of angklung and dog-dog until they enter a trance. While in the trance, they act like horses—eating grass (sometimes eating glass or nails as well) and jumping around.

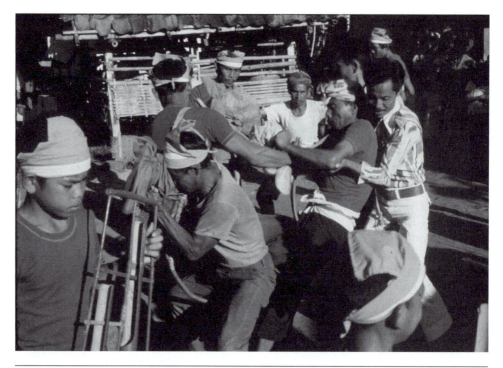

Figure 7.20 Kuda lumping dancers in Ujungberung (courtesy Michael Ewing).

The idea behind the ritual is that spiritual power becomes manifest in a tangible form—a powerful horse entity that takes possession of a human body—and spreads this spiritual power through the community. Kuda lumping is similar to ketuk tilu and other men's dancing events because it suggests that spiritual power, like masculine energy, is wild and uncontrolled in its natural state, yet is ultimately a good thing. Figure 7.20 shows kuda lumping participants, mounted on their hobby horses, going into trance, with two angklung players in the foreground.

The lyrics to Rhoma Irama's song "Kuda Lumping" (as sung by dangdut diva Elvy Sukaesih) provide a rather cursory summary of the event. They describe a performance in which someone mounts a fake horse, goes into trance, and does peculiar things such as eat grass and eat glass. The trance state is described with words—"lupa diri" ("forget one's self")—that Indonesians apply to a state of extreme enjoyment as easily as they do to a trance. This state is, in fact, the very state the male dancers seek when they submit to the animating rhythm of drumming and the charm of a ronggeng. Thus, the song manages to conflate the ideas of kuda lumping's harnessing of spiritual power, men's dancing, and dangdut all into one neat package.

In the chorus, the singer rapidly repeats the words "kuda lumping" several times. The chorus also features a distinctive syncopated drum pattern, with exciting off-beat accents. The repetition of the words suggests the repetitive rhythms that drive kuda lumping dancers into the trance in which they can forget themselves, and invites the dangdut dancers to do the same. The last verse includes a warning not to get too close to the kuda lumping dancers because of the danger of getting caught up in the trance. But, by the time the weak warning of danger comes, it is already too late; the dancers have already taken the opportunity to "forget themselves" by dancing to the strangely compelling chorus.

When I saw male guests dance to "Kuda Lumping," they always interpreted the syncopated drumming in the chorus to be animating drumming; in other words, they left the usual dangdut movements behind and performed gestures that fit the syncopated patterns. As often as not, these included explicit pelvic thrusts that coincided with the drum accents. It was as if the singer was exhorting them to go into trance with her repeated words, and the drums were empowering them to forget their sense of respectability and perform, in public, motions that would in most circumstances be considered obscene. The rest of the guests and the artis dangdut encouraged these lapses of propriety with their positive reactions.

The guests who get up to dance freestyle at these modern Sundanese dance events are mostly, but not exclusively, male. Women who get up to dance freestyle act like men in the sense that they interact with the dangdut singer and with each other. Although free dancing is still a mark of masculinity, it is increasingly a form of masculine energy and power in which women, asserting their changing roles in modern Indonesian life, can share.

Fewer and fewer Sundanese (and even fewer urban Sundanese) are interested in learning or doing traditional dances these days, perhaps because these dances no longer have the capacity to articulate energy and power the way dangdut dancing does. Instead, audiences tend to view traditional dances as objects—something to be seen, and even enjoyed, something that presents a favorable image of Sundanese culture to the world, but not something that contributes to their own lives.

Most people do not interpret their disdain for traditional music and dance this way, however. Typical Sundanese people think that ketuk tilu, tari kursus, and even jaipongan are simply more difficult to perform than dangdut and joged dancing—even though the bodily movements involved are essentially the same. These old-fashioned dance forms have become assimilated into the foggy category of tradition. While most Sundanese endorse their new meanings, through conviction or coercion, it results in the recasting of dance events into presentational, non-participational performances, and Sundanese audiences no longer feel empowered or compelled to join in. Artistic productions that maintain the veneer of traditional forms, but change the underlying meaning to express new values, may be thought of as "invented tradition" (Hobsbawm 1983).

Jaipongan occupies an ambiguous place between authentic tradition and invented tradition—a place where dance is still about performing masculinity, even if some of the relationships between free dancing, female singer-dancers, and animating drumming have changed and people's focus sometimes shifts from participating to watching. Jaipongan belongs to both of these worlds; the ease with which it can slip from one to the other and back again accounts for its phenomenal success as a modern dance genre. In many contexts, jaipongan is synonymous with ketuk tilu; in other contexts, people take great pains to distinguish the two.

Dangdut music resists incorporation into regionalism and nationalism precisely because it has such tenuous regional and national ties. Some of its significant precursors come from outside Indonesia (India, Malaysia, and the West) and its popularity transcends any single region or ethnic group. The character of dangdut music may, in fact, match the "national character" that Indonesians seek (Frederick 1982: 124). Although for many years dangdut was regarded as low-class music for the working poor, in recent years its status has risen considerably; it is now socially acceptable for Indonesians of all economic classes to enjoy dangdut music.

Dangdut's surface details cannot possibly stand for the contribution of a single ethnic group to the diversity of an Indonesian nation. At the same time, dangdut is susceptible to the overlay of regional flavors and colors, and frequently appears in such guises; in this sense, it cannot stand for the unity of an Indonesian nation, either. Because it fills the cracks between national and regional music, consumers are able to do with it whatever they will.

So many Sundanese focus on music and dance that is cast in a decidedly non-traditional idiom—dangdut. Dangdut, then, is subversive in that its fans resist the realignment of music and dance into the discourse of national politics. It is conservative, however, in its incorporation of an entrenched Sundanese pattern involving free dancing, female performers, and animating drumming. For Sundanese men, the whole point of the exercise of movement is to dance one's way into the social matrix, to find a way to physically integrate one's body into the maze of contradictions that make up masculine identities. In traditional dance events, female singer-dancers are objects of desire that inspire the men to behave like "real" men, and the drumming provides a convenient excuse to explain their free behavior.

This traditional pattern of interaction between performers has characterized many different music and dance genres: ketuk tilu, tayuban, tari kursus, jaipongan, and dangdut. In recent times, however, the sounds of some of these genres have acquired new meanings that replace traditional Sundanese values with more modern ones. The new values gain some legitimacy through their association with old-fashioned music. It is ironic that the most direct vehicle with which to accomplish the very traditional Sundanese dance of masculine posturing currently is dangdut music—arguably among the least traditional sounding music in common circulation in West Java. By avoiding—even precluding—the sonic emblems of Sundanese music that have come to represent invented tradition and the values it engenders, dangdut is able to provide a forum for enacting an unassailably authentic approach to Sundanese dance. Viewed in this way, it is clear that the guitars and synthesizers of dangdut should be considered to be among the traditional sounds of Indonesia.

CHAPTER **8**

Music and the Future

The previous chapters have described how a number of persistent, entrenched musical processes are manifest in both the music of the past and the music of the present in Southeast Asia. These processes continue to undergird contemporary musical expressions—even though these modern expressions may sound, on the surface, quite different from older musics. The example of Indonesian music in general, and Sundanese music in particular, illuminates the paradox of musical change: change grows out of continuity, and tradition is as much about the present as it is about the past. As the old saying goes, the more things change, the more they stay the same.

Musical Processes and Layers of Influence

Part I related musical processes such as interlocking parts and ostinatos to the geographic and cultural ecology of Southeast Asia. The hot, humid environment of Southeast Asia is favorable for percussion instruments made of bamboo and bronze. Interlocking parts represent an artistic manifestation of the kind of close cooperation that wet-rice cultivation mandates. An aesthetic appreciation of the composite of interlocking musical parts reinforces a cultural appreciation of the fruits of cooperative living. It is little wonder that ostinatos composed of simple interlocking patterns played on percussion instruments acquired rich significance in such an environment.

The subsequent chapters articulated how subtle inflections of these processes could model inflections in the ecological, ideological, and cultural realities of Indonesians. Ostinatos were already attuned to the cycles of seasons that govern agriculture; it was a small adjustment, then, to associate ostinatos with more sophisticated Indic ideas of cyclic cosmic time. In the courts of Hindu-Javanese god-kings, these cycles grew into enormously complex aural mandalas that made audible these rulers' roles as the interface

203

between the cosmos and the kingdom. The musical processes originally associated with egalitarian cooperation came to support an entirely different social pattern. Just as the new social patterns were laid over older ones, these musical processes produced new kinds of sounds, and acquired new meanings, without completely eradicating their original ones.

Simultaneous variation as a musical process has a similar pedigree. It is easy to imagine the genesis of simultaneous variation arising from the differences in instrumental idioms—playing the "same" tune on musical instruments with different capabilities and idiosyncrasies naturally resulting in melodic variations that highlight the different instruments' idioms. In this guise, simultaneous variation models an egalitarian society in which different voices cannot help but impart their own individual flavor, even when they are expressing the same thing. With only a slight twist, however, simultaneous variation becomes polyphonic stratification, in which each voice has a hierarchical position and a circumscribed role. Some instruments are constrained to play only simple, unvarying parts, while others are empowered to improvise more freely than ever. In this case, the musical texture not only models a stratified, class-conscious society—it helps make the new social order seem linked to the old one.

Layers

As a general rule, what makes music everywhere so powerfully expressive is its capability of sending different—even contradictory—messages at the same time. A simple example: a song about a lost love might combine words that express pleasant memories with a melancholy tune to depict the conflict of happy memories with deep sadness that one might feel in this situation. When we hear such a song, we somehow experience two contradictory feelings—the flush of love and the pain of loss—at the same time. In Southeast Asian musics, rhythmic cycles composed of multiple ostinatos simultaneously express both egalitarian and hierarchical social principles. Polyphonic stratification simultaneously models equal social relations based on reciprocity and social classes based on rigid functional roles. Cloaked in aesthetic beauty, these contradictions acquire a veneer of naturalness and inevitability.

In Indonesian music, the existence of competing, contradictory meanings is particularly clear because of the way the various meanings are layered on top of one another. Just as the layers in a rock formation provide geologists with a static picture of the dynamic geological processes that created the formation, the distinctness of the various layers in Indonesian music provides a window into understanding the complex, competing meanings the music expresses.

Most of the Southeast Asian gong-chime music discussed in the previous chapters makes use of a basic four-layered musical texture. The first layer is usually some sort of cyclic ostinato, generally resulting from the playing of interlocking parts. This colotomic foundation provides a foundation for the next two layers, namely main melody and elaboration (simultaneous variation). A fourth layer—drumming—provides a means to control and coordinate the other layers.

A broad outline of Southeast Asian histories is evident in the instrumentation of many ensembles. Bronze instruments, made using technology that is uniquely Southeast Asian, frequently provide the ostinato parts; drums of Indian design represent another layer. Arabic-influenced bowed string instruments and frame drums recall the coming of Islam to the region, while European-derived instruments recall the colonization of the area. These instruments' unique sonic signatures evoke these historical changes; when heard all together, they create an aural representation of the region's many-layered and dynamic history.

Musical Change and "Tradition"

Thus, traditional Southeast Asian music is the outcome of generations of dynamic historical and social changes; each generation of musicians and listeners takes the music traditions of the past, adds its own stamp in the present, and passes it on to the future. Although there is continuity in the musical processes that undergird each generation's music, the actual sounds might change considerably as the years pass. As opposed to a rigid notion of "tradition" (in quotation marks here to suggest this notion's problems) as a static time capsule from the past in the form of institutions and practices which have not changed from generation to generation, genuine traditions (without quotation marks) are (as Richard Taruskin puts it) "engines of change—perpetual, gradual, regenerative, unstoppable change" (Taruskin 1995: 182). Similarly, "authenticity" (again, in quotes) is conceived as a quality that stems from an unwavering dedication to the preservation of rigid traditions. There is a temptation to regard anything that seems modern as non-traditional and inauthentic because it seems self-evident that modern things are at odds with these rigid principles of "tradition" and "authenticity."

However, the very sounds that seem to represent "tradition," as we have seen, are themselves the products of generations of change. "Traditional" Cambodian, Thai, and Indonesian gong chime ensembles literally model in sound the rise and fall of kingdoms and the ups and downs of history. It is only from our perspective, far away from these events in both time and space, that they seem static at all. The sounds are not traditional in the sense that they represent something from the past carried unchanged into the present, but rather traditional in the sense that they are the ever-shifting summation of the past reconfigured for the present. As time goes on, each present moment's configuration is absorbed into the summation as the sounds and processes are reconfigured for the future and a new generation.

Although the particular sounds of any traditional music are at first merely the direct consequence of the particular musical processes that created them, over time the sounds acquire meanings of their own, independent of the processes that created them. For example, the ponderous colotomic formal structures of Central Javanese gamelan music described in Chapter 4 were at first sonic expressions of the Javanese king's position as the interface between the cosmic universe and the tangible world. By representing the cosmic order in sound—specifically by organizing different ostinato cycles so that they coincided in auspicious ways—the king's music effectively imposed cosmic order onto his own realm to ensure its harmonious existence. The process—layers of ostinatos—that modeled cosmic order produced a particular kind of musical sound. Over time, the sounds themselves came to be associated with royal courts, god-king theater-states, and stratified societies.

In Southeast Asia, in more recent times, the associations between gong-chime music and political authority have become less specific; people connect these sounds not with a particular king or social order, but rather with a more generalized sense of national or ethnic identity. Ironically, sounds that originally modeled a social organization with a god-king at its center can come to represent a modern, democratic nation-state that rejects the very notion of hereditary rule by divine right. In this way, traditional sounds take on new meanings that may contradict the original processes that formed them.

According to Benedict Anderson, modern nation-states are "imagined communities" in which large groups of unrelated strangers collectively imagine some sort of close kinship with one another to forge a unified political entity—a "country" (Anderson 1991). Unlike the historical Southeast Asian mandala states, in which a ruler's influence spread only as far as his personal connections, modern nation-states rely on a government's capability to create a sense of unity among a large group of people who can never have personal connections to one another. In the present, the classical music traditions of the kings of mandala states can represent abstractly the past glories and achievements of successful empires with charismatic leaders of legendary proportions. An appreciation of classical music, then, forges an imaginary link between each stranger in the present with that glorious past. This imagined shared heritage strengthens the sense of connection that strangers feel with one another in the present, and reinforces their sense of an imagined community. Often newly formed Southeast Asian countries place a great emphasis on preserving and democratizing the classical music traditions of the royal courts, with the intention that these traditions will foster a sense of national identity, unity, and pride.

For comparable reasons, the communist Khmer Rouge regime, led by Pol Pot, which controlled Cambodia in the late 1970s, sought to systematically eradicate classical music. They recognized that the musical processes involved in court music were sonic representations of the stratified social order that they presumably sought to eradicate completely to create a truly communistic social order. For Pol Pot, effecting a complete break with the non-communist past necessitated the elimination of all traces of the musical traditions connected with it, and quite a few court musicians were among the millions of victims of the Khmer Rouge genocide.

New meanings for old music

These recontextualized classical music traditions, however, are not the musical forms of the past; rather, they have changed considerably from their original court forms to fit these new situations. Javanese gamelan provides an example. To most Western ears, the gamelan music promulgated by the Indonesian government-sponsored music institutions sounds foreign and exotic enough, primarily because of its strange and unfamiliar musical instruments, scales, textures, and timbres. It is tempting to equate this strangeness with antiquity and changelessness—to imagine that gamelan music has survived the centuries unchanged and represents a living fossil. The preceding chapters have described, however, many of the ways in which gamelan music has indeed changed over time. Truly ancient forms of gamelan, such as the austere sekaten ensembles described in Chapter 3, are quite different in sound and concept from the nineteenth- and twentieth-century court music of Central Java (discussed in Chapter 4); the musical processes of these two ensembles express the very different social meanings that they embody.

Furthermore, it is possible for the values that underlie musical processes to change without drastically affecting the musical surface. In the case of gamelan music, Western-ers and Javanese alike often marvel at the apparent resilience of gamelan music in the face of relentless Western influence. They are amazed that despite the propensity of Central Javanese sultans and princes to adopt the trappings of their Dutch overlords—including crystal chandeliers, card games, and even ballroom orchestras and dances—their gamelan music did not come to sound like Western music. Of course, such individuals are falling into the trap of using surface details—musical instruments and tuning systems—as the measure of resilience and continuity with the past. While ethnomusicologist Sumarsam agrees that "there was no significant musical syncretism between gamelan and European music" (Sumarsam 1995: 241), he also points out these surface details are not as signif-icant as the underlying concepts that support them. Sumarsam documents significant changes in the processes and values that govern gamelan music, and charts how Western ideas such as music notation and fixed compositions, as well as a notion of high and clas-sical arts, had profound effects on Javanese gamelan music in the Javanese courts during the nineteenth and twentieth centuries; these effects are even more pronounced in the gamelan music taught and performed at the Indonesian government-sponsored music institutes. Although it is not necessarily immediately apparent to casual Western listen-ers, modern Javanese gamelan music places much more emphasis on a fixed melody (the balungan described in Chapter 4) and less emphasis on simultaneous variation.

Sundanese degung (see Chapter 6) provides another example. In this case, the aristo-cratic sound of the small degung ensemble came to stand for a Sundanese regional and ethnic identity within a larger Indonesian national framework. The instrumentation and tuning system of the ensemble became the hallmarks of a uniquely Sundanese sound, facilitating all sorts of experiments in musical form, style, and repertory. Although the overall sound of degung retains an air of Sundaneseness, a wide array of new musical processes, borrowed from other Sundanese and Indonesian genres as well as from imported musical forms, have found their way into the degung tradition. In contem-porary West Java, degung music has the means to provide a tangible expression of each Sundanese person's multiple identities as individuals of Sundanese descent, residents of West Java, citizens of Indonesia, and global consumers.

Old meanings for new music

Dangdut music and dance also provide means to explore multiple identities, but coming from a very different angle. In this case it is not the sounds that are linked to the past, but rather the underlying musical processes. As discussed in Chapter 7, the musical sounds of dangdut themselves are global in nature, combining features of global pop, Indian film music, and Malay elements. Although dangdut's sonic signature is inher-ently international, it also lends itself quite easily to localizations; by incorporating local instruments into the mix, or tweaking the melodies, harmonies, and vocal styles, dangdut can take on distinctly regional characters.

Perhaps more significant, however, is the manner in which Indonesian dangdut fans have taken the modern sounds of dangdut and layered them over old-fashioned musical processes. The driving "dangdut" drum pattern that gives the genre its name is, of course, a simple ostinato that hearkens back to the earliest kinds of Southeast Asian music-making—despite this particular ostinato's distinctly Indian roots. The close connection between the dangdut rhythm and dance movements in the minds and bodies of dangdut fans is a manifestation of yet another long-standing Indonesian musical process—a connection between drumming and dance, and the ability of drum sounds to animate human bodies.

The response of Balinese musicians and artists to tourism provides still another variation on the theme of recontextualization. Chapter 4 outlined anthropologist Clifford Geertz's explanation of pre-twentieth-century Balinese kingdoms as "theater-states," in which rulers sponsored elaborate rituals not only to demonstrate, but to legitimate as well, their divine rights and authority—to the point where the rituals themselves became the source of power (Geertz 1973: 335).

The Balinese kings are long gone, but the elaborate rituals and performances retain a prominent place in Balinese life. Although they remain meaningful to Balinese people as religious, spiritual, and pragmatic practices, they also have acquired a new function: as tourist attractions. Since the early part of the twentieth century, when the island acquired a reputation for artistic spectacle, Bali has been a popular destination for cultural tourists—foreigners looking to sample the novelty of unfamiliar, but attractive and compelling, cultural practices. A variety of new performances aimed at the tourist market have become staples of Balinese arts—the core of this new tradition. In this sense, tourism is the new god-king of the Balinese theater-state because it becomes both the cause and the effect of continued artistic activities.

If nations are imagined communities, then conceiving the much larger global village requires even more dramatic leaps of imagination. A number of global music genres have proliferated throughout the world via mass media. In the twenty-first century, three-minute pop songs, with standard verse–chorus–verse format, along with MTV-style videos replete with beautiful people, colorful costumes, elaborate dance routines, and lightning-fast image cuts, are universally recognized artistic forms. Pop songs and videos provide a convenient unit of global musical exchange—instantly understood by millions of people in hundreds of countries all over the planet.

A global pop song fits well into the workings of global capitalism because it can be conceived and traded as a commodity, especially when fixed into a tangible object in the form of sheet music or a recording. At the same time, however, a song's significance remains latent until it is performed—spun out in real time, with real people watching and/or performing. And each time it is played or performed, a song can acquire new meaning and new value. In this way, a global pop song confounds global capitalism, because it is the performance in real time, rather than the object itself, that has real value. The first years of the twenty-first century have been marked by bitter arguments over copyright laws—what it means to own a song, how the owners of songs should be compensated for their use, and who has the right to control distribution of recordings.

Global and Local Meanings

It is perhaps for this reason that the global musical economy has yet to completely wipe out local musical styles. Perhaps because the leap of imagination required to truly conceive a global community is simply too great, people tend to group themselves into much smaller, localized communities within the global context; without some attention to local interests, people tend to feel out of place, disenfranchised, and disconnected. Musical expressions provide one means for such groups to construct viable identities within local, national, and global contexts. Vital musics play with the local, the national, and the global to negotiate stances that combine local, national, and global identities together into a workable balance.

As long as Southeast Asian communities are based on mutual cooperation and emphasize local control with a loose, almost spiritual guidance from above, Southeast Asian musical processes (which derive from ecological and cultural histories), including ostinato, interlocking parts, and layering, will continue to be relevant, regardless of the surface sounds they produce. And, as long as those processes guide and undergird musical activities, musicians and listeners alike will come to cherish as beautiful the underlying values manifest in the processes.

The traditional sounds of Southeast Asian gong-chime ensembles, such as Sundanese, Javanese, and Balinese gamelan music, on the other hand, have acquired meanings of their own which can play an important part in the construction of local, regional, ethnic, national, and even inter- and transnational identities. The project of modern nation-states is to foster a sense of community among large groups of people who have no real interpersonal connections to one another in order to solidify and strengthen a strong central governmental authority. The unique surface sounds of the music of various Southeast Asian mandala governments—which ironically developed to make manifest in sound a central loose authority over intense local cooperation—can be and have been redeployed by modern nation-state governments to provide a sense of shared history and destiny among otherwise unconnected groups of people.

The coexistence of these two contradictory, yet strangely complementary, approaches to musical sounds—one in which traditional musical processes result in a variety of new musical surfaces, and the other in which existing traditional musical surfaces are separated from the processes that created them and endowed with new meanings—creates a rich, many-layered, ever-changing musical soundscape in Southeast Asia. In Indonesia, a consideration of these two approaches helps to make sense of a culture in which ancient, ceremonial gamelan music, modern pop songs with gamelan accompaniment, and dangdut songs with guitar and synthesizer accompaniment can exist side by side. Because they have roots in the past, meaning in the present, and possibilities for the future, all of these varied musical expressions are indeed the traditional sounds of Indonesia.

Glossary

adat Indonesian traditional system of social, legal, and religious principles; traditional laws and customs

adeg-adeg basic Sundanese men's dance position

agung in Maguindanao *kulintang* ensembles, a pair of hanging gongs with deep flanges

ala genah final drum pattern in *bajidoran* drumming's standard pattern; also called *ngala genah*

alihan transitional movements in Cirebonese *topeng* dance

angklung Sundanese bamboo rattle; also a kind of four-pitch Balinese gamelan

angsel special kind of drum pattern and dance movement in Balinese *gong kebyar*

arakk Cambodian shamanic healing ceremony

arkuh lagu pitch framework for a Sundanese piece or song (also called *pola lagu* or *tugu lagu*)

artis Indonesian term denoting a performing artist

artis dangdut *dangdut* singer

ayak-ayakan a type of Central Javanese piece

babandil in Maguindanao *kulintang* ensembles, a single hanging gong

bahasa Indonesia the national language of Indonesia; "Indonesian"

bajidor Sundanese male dance fanatics

bajidoran Sundanese dance events catering to *bajidor*

bakat Indonesian (and Sundanese) term meaning tendency or aptitude

balitaw Visayan island dialog songs from the Philippines

balungan skeleton or framework of a Central Javanese gamelan piece; also called *balunganing gendhing*

balunganing gendhing *see balungan*

ban Indonesian word for band; Western-style combo with keyboards, guitars, and drums

bangbrang largest *dog-dog* in a *reog* ensemble

211

bangsing transverse flute associated with *orkes melayu* and *dangdut* ensembles

banjar Balinese village organizations of people working together to achieve common goals

banjet north-coast Javanese dance/theater form

barang a Sundanese pitch name (equivalent to *tugu*)

batangan in Central Javanese gamelan, a medium-sized *kendhang*-style drum; also called *ciblon*

batik wax-resist technique for dyeing cloth

bawa unaccompanied vocal introduction to a Central Javanese *gendhing*

bedug in Central Javanese gamelan or in *gamelan sekaten*, a large barrel-shaped drum with skin heads attached at each end with large wooden pegs

beleganjur Balinese ceremonial marching ensemble with gongs, drums, and cymbals

bem a Sundanese pitch name (equivalent to *galimer* or *gulu*)

beri in Sundanese *goong renteng* or in *gamelan sekaten*, a flat, unbossed gong (in *gamelan sekaten*, also called *cret* or *kecrek*)

besi Indonesian word for "iron"

Bhinneka Tunggal Ika Indonesia's national motto (Old Javanese for "unity in diversity")

biola Malay term for Western violin or similar instruments; also called *biyula*

biyula *see biola*

bobodoran Sundanese word for clowning around

bodoran Cirebonese term for clowning around

bonang in Central Javanese gamelan, a generic term for a family of horizontal gong chimes with ten to fourteen pots arranged in two rows; in Sundanese *degung*, fourteen-pot horizontal gong chime arranged in one row on a V- or U-shaped frame; in Sundanese *gamelan salendro*, horizontal gong chime with ten to fourteen small knobbed gongs arranged in two rows; in *gamelan sekaten*, large one-row gong chime

bonang barung in Central Javanese gamelan, the lower-range *bonang*

bonang panerus in Central Javanese gamelan, the higher-range *bonang*

bonang renteng large, one-row gong chime in Sundanese *goong renteng*; also called *koromong* or *kokuang*

bonggar-bonggar balcony of a Toba Batak house

buah literally "fruit"; the practical, self-defense aspect of *penca silat* (as opposed to *kembang*, "flower," the performing aspect)

buhun Sundanese word meaning "ancient"

bukaan opening drum pattern in *bajidoran* drumming's standard pattern

bungur a Sundanese pitch name in *pelog* (equivalent to *liwung*)

bupati administrative official in charge of a *kabupaten* (administrative unit equivalent to a county)

calti small, bongo-like double drum used for *dangdut*; also called *tabla*

calung second-lowest-pitched gender-family instrument in a Balinese *gong kebyar* ensemble; also a Sundanese bamboo musical instrument

campala a wooden hammer used by a Sundanese *dalang* to give signals to the gamelan; he holds the *campala* in his right hand and gives signals by knocking it against the wooden chest in which he keeps his puppets

campur sari Javanese and Sundanese musical styles involving a combination of Javanese and Western instruments

capang third drum pattern in *bajidoran* drumming's standard pattern

caruk Sundanese interlocking technique

cecempres *saron*-like instrument in Sundanese *goong renteng*

celempung in Central Javanese gamelan, a zither with metal strings; also called *siter*

cempres in Sundanese *degung*, fourteen-key metallophone (also called *titil* or *demung*)

cengceng in Balinese *beleganjur*, pair of cymbals; in Balinese *gong kebyar*, a set of six or more cymbals played by a single player

cengkok Central Javanese term for melodic pattern, melody, melodic style, or process of melodic movement

chhepp damped, choked sound produced on Cambodian *chhing*

chhing pair of small cymbals in Cambodian *pinn peat* ensemble; also the open, undamped sound produced on the instrument

Cianjuran Sundanese sung poetry (also called *tembang Sunda*)

ciblon in Central Javanese gamelan, a medium-sized *kendhang*-style drum; also called *batangan*

cindek Sundanese dance gesture; also called *koma*

colotomic form a musical foundation or timeline in which regular time periods are delineated by punctuating sounds; also called colotomy

colotomy *see* colotomic form

cret in *gamelan sekaten*, a flat, unbossed gong (also called *beri* or *kecrek*)

dabakan goblet-shaped drum in Maguindanao *kulintang* ensemble

dalang Cirebonese, Balinese, or Sundanese puppet master (*see also dhalang*)

dalang topeng Cirebonese *topeng* (masked) dancer

dalapan wilet eight *wilet* (*see wilet*)

damina Sundanese system of assigning syllable names to the pitches in various *surupan*; the five syllables (from high to low) are *da mi na ti la*

dangdut popular Indonesian music and dance style with a characteristic drum groove that makes the sounds "dang-dut"

deder fast-tempo section of a Cirebonese *topeng* dance

degung a uniquely Sundanese gamelan ensemble in the *pelog degung* tuning system

demung in *gamelan sekaten*, the larger, lower-pitched keyed metallophones; *see also panerus*

denggung type of heirloom gamelan in Cirebonese palaces

dhalang Javanese puppet master (*see also dalang*)

diatonic scale a seven-pitch non-equidistant scale in which there are two small intervals and five large intervals; associated with Western-style music

disilibkeun Sundanese for indirectly spoken

dodoan slow-tempo section of a Cirebonese *topeng* dance

dog-dog Sundanese single-head conical drum

dog-dog lojor a Sundanese ceremony following the harvesting of rice

dua wilet two *wilet* (*see wilet*)

egot kind of interaction between a male fan and a female singer-dancer in Sundanese *bajidoran*

enak Indonesian word meaning delicious, enjoyable

frame drum wooden frames with skins stretched across one side

galimer a Sundanese pitch name (equivalent to *bem* or *gulu*)

gambang Javanese, Cirebonese, or Sundanese xylophone, usually with about eighteen to twenty-one wooden keys laid over a trough resonator

gamelan Indonesian ensembles consisting primarily of bronze percussion instruments

gamelan angklung type of Balinese gamelan ensemble with a four-pitch *slendro*-like tuning system

gamelan gambuh type of middle-period Balinese gamelan ensemble

gamelan gong gede large middle-period Balinese gamelan ensemble

gamelan ibu-ibu all-female gamelan groups

gamelan pelegongan type of middle-period Balinese gamelan ensemble associated with *legong* dance

gamelan sekaten in Central Java and Cirebon, type of ceremonial gamelan ensemble; also called *gamelan sekati*

gamelan sekati *see gamelan sekaten*

gamelan selap special Sundanese gamelan with extra keys and gongs that enable the instruments to be played in *salendro*, *pelog*, *degung*, and other tuning systems

gamelan Semar pegulingan type of middle-period Balinese gamelan ensemble which included metallophones and gong-chimes and played repertory derived from *gamelan gambuh*

gandingan in Maguindanao *kulintang* ensemble, set of four hanging gongs

gandrung Eastern Javanese (Osing) dance genre featuring a young, unmarried female singer-dancer (who also is called a *gandrung*)

gangsa family of gender-family instruments with multiple octaves of keys in Balinese *gong kebyar* ensemble; *saron*-like instrument with many keys in Sundanese *goong renteng* (also called *selukat*)

gatra four-note groupings in Central Javanese *balungan* melodies

gegaboran Balinese colotomic form for accompanying *gabor* dance

gendang in Sundanese ensembles, set of two-headed barrel-shaped drums (*see also kendang*, *kendhang*)

gendang indung "mother drum"; large Sundanese two-headed barrel-shaped drum

gendang leutik small Sundanese double-head barrel-shaped drum; also called *kulanter* and *ketipung*

gender in Cirebonese, Javanese, and Balinese ensembles, a generic term for a family of keyed instruments with thin keys suspended over resonating tubes

gender barung in Central Javanese gamelan, the medium-pitched member of the *gender* family, with fourteen keys

gender panerus in Central Javanese gamelan, the highest-pitched member of the *gender* family, with fourteen keys

gendhing term for several Central Javanese colotomic forms

gending karesmen multimedia Sundanese theatrical productions; sometimes characterized as Sundanese opera

geol one of the "three Gs" (with *gitek* and *goyang*) that describe various Sundanese dance movements emphasizing a female dancer's hips and buttocks

gerong in Central Javanese gamelan, a male chorus

gilak a basic colotomic form for Balinese *beleganjur* music

gitek one of the "three Gs" (with *goyang* and *geol*) that describe various Sundanese dance movements emphasizing a female dancer's hips and buttocks

gondang hasapi Toba Batak string ensemble that imitates musical structure of *gondang sabangunan* using stringed instruments called *hasapi*

gondang sabangunan Toba Batak drum and gong ensemble

gong round percussion instrument, usually with a broad surface that vibrates and a narrow flange or lip

gong ageng in Central Javanese gamelan or Balinese *gong kebyar* ensemble, an extremely large hanging gong

gong chime a series of gongs with different pitches, usually arranged on a frame

gong kebyar type of Balinese gamelan ensemble with a five-pitch *pelog*-like tuning system

gong siyem in Central Javanese gamelan, a hanging gong (smaller than *gong ageng*); also called *gong suwukan* or *siyem*

gong suwukan in Central Javanese gamelan, a hanging gong (smaller than *gong ageng*); also called *gong siyem* or *siyem*

goong in Sundanese gamelan *salendro*, *degung*, and *goong renteng*, a large hanging gong (in *goong renteng*, there are typically two *goong*)

goong renteng Sundanese ceremonial heirloom village gamelan

gordang in Toba Batak *gondang sabangunan*, large drum

goyang one of the "three Gs" (with *gitek* and *geol*) that describe various Sundanese dance movements emphasizing a female dancer's hips and buttocks

grimingan *pathet*-specific phrases improvised by a *gender* player as a background for a Central Javanese *dhalang*'s narration and dialog during a *wayang kulit* performance

gulu a Sundanese pitch name (equivalent to *bem* or *galimer*)

hajat Sundanese ceremonial event to mark life-cycle milestones such as weddings and circumcisions

hasapi Toba Batak instrument with two plucked strings

hesek rattle in a Toba Batak *gondang sabangunan* ensemble

heterophony the musical texture that results from simultaneous variations

horja Toba Batak ceremonial feast

ibing Sundanese dancing to traditional music with rhythmic starts and stops

ibing keurseus Sundanese solo male dance based on *tayub* dancing; also called *tari kursus*

ibing tayub Sundanese aristocratic men's dance (*see tayuban*)

idiochord tube zither string instrument, often made from bamboo, in which the strings are cut from the bark of its wooden resonator

inggah the second of the two sections of a Central Javanese *gendhing*

interval the musical distance between two pitches

intonation standards for varying and adjusting pitches

jaipongan modern Sundanese music and dance genre with *gamelan salendro* accompaniment

jajangkungan *ketuk tilu* dance in which *ronggeng* rise up on their toes

jalak pengkor second drum pattern in Sundanese *bajidoran* drumming's standard pattern

jaw harp mouth-resonated musical instrument whose sound is produced by plucking a semi-rigid tongue of bamboo, wood, or metal

jegogan lowest-pitched *gender*-family instrument in Balinese *gong kebyar* ensemble

jengglong in Sundanese *degung*, gong chime with six low-pitched gongs, suspended vertically or arranged horizontally; in Sundanese *gamelan salendro*, horizontal gong chime with three to six gongs, flatter and tuned an octave lower than *kenong*

joged Sundanese dancing to modern-style popular music with a continuous groove

jogedan dance movement units in Cirebonese *topeng* dance

jongjrong second-largest *dog-dog* in a Sundanese *reog* ensemble

juru alok male vocalist in a Sundanese gamelan; also called *wiraswara*

kabupaten Indonesian administrative unit approximately equivalent to a US county

kacapi Sundanese zither

kacapi-suling Sundanese instrumental genre utilizing the accompanying ensemble for *tembang Sunda*, that is, two *kacapi* and a *suling*

kain batik a length of *batik* cloth

kakawen mood song, sung by the *dalang* to set a scene, in Sundanese *wayang golek*

kantilan gangsa one octave higher than a *pemade* in Balinese *gong kebyar* ensemble

kasinoman Cirebonese ritual for young people

kaum menak Sundanese aristocratic class

kawih in Sundanese usage, an earthy and freely ornamented style of singing

kecrek in Sundanese gamelan, stack of iron plates hit with a wooden hammer; in *gamelan sekaten*, a flat, unbossed gong (also called *cret* or *beri*)

kemauan Indonesian term for desire

kembang in Indonesian and Sundanese, literally, "flower"; the aesthetic, dance aspect of Sundanese *penca silat*

kemong tiny hanging gong in Balinese *gong kebyar* ensemble

kempli small gong laid horizontally on a frame in Balinese *gong kebyar* ensemble

kempul in Central Javanese gamelan, a gong chime consisting of several small hanging gongs; in Sundanese *gamelan salendro*, a small gong suspended from the same frame as the *goong kempur* smaller hanging gong in Balinese *gong kebyar* ensemble

kempyang in Central Javanese gamelan, a small, high-pitched *kethuk*-like gong, or a pair of such little gongs

kendang Javanese, Balinese, Cirebonese, and Sundanese two-headed barrel-shaped drums (in Sundanese, more typically spelled *gendang*; in Javanese, spelled *kendhang*)

kendang penca ensemble that accompanies Sundanese *penca silat* (martial arts), consisting of two sets of *gendang*, a small hanging gong, and a double-reed wind instrument called *tarompet*

kendhang in Central Javanese gamelan, a two-headed barrel-shaped drum with heads secured with rawhide laces

kendhang gendhing in Central Javanese gamelan, a large *kendhang*

kendhang kalih in Central Javanese gamelan, "two drums"—combination of *kendhang gending* and *ketipung*

kenong in Central Javanese gamelan and Sundanese *gamelan salendro*, a horizontal
  gong chime with one to six large, high-pitched gongs; a Sundanese pitch name
  (equivalent to *lorloran* or *loloran*); a main "pillar" pitch in a Sundanese *pola lagu*
  (also called *pokok* or *posisi kenong*)

kering in Sundanese gamelan, literally, "dry"; also called *satengah wilet*; medium-fast
  tempo section of a Cirebonese *topeng* dance

ketawang Central Javanese colotomic form

kethuk a small knobbed gong; in Central Javanese gamelan, a small horizontal gong hit
  with a padded stick (*see also ketuk*)

ketipung in Central Javanese gamelan, a small *kendhang*; small Sundanese double-head
  barrel-shaped drum (also called *gendang leutik* and *kulanter*)

ketuk a small knobbed gong; in *gamelan sekaten*, a small, horizontal gong (*see also kethuk*)

ketuk tilu literally, three *ketuks*; a generic term for Sundanese participatory dance
  traditions, often accompanied by an ensemble featuring a three-*ketuk* gong chime

keturunan Indonesian term meaning family lineage or ancestry

keupat Sundanese walking dance movement

khaen Lao mouth organ

khawng Cambodian gong chimes

kinanthi a poetic form associated with Central Javanese poetry

kirata folk etymology in which each syllable of a target word is said to derive from
  a different source word; when arranged in order, the source words provide some
  philosophical insight into the target word's meaning and significance

klasik classical

kliningan Sundanese performances featuring *gamelan salendro* and singing

kluncing metal triangle in the Eastern Javanese (Osing) *gandrung* ensemble

kobongan a Sundanese mode or *surupan* (also called *pelog degung* or *mataraman*)

kocak Sundanese adjective meaning "amusing"

kokuang large, one-row gong chime in Sundanese *goong renteng*; also called *bonang
  renteng* or *koromong*

kolibit idiochord tube zither from the Philippines

kolintang *see kulintang*

koma Sundanese dance gesture; also called *cindek*

konkurs Sundanese term (derived from Dutch) for competition

korng tauch circular gong chime in Cambodian *pinn peat* ensemble

korng thomm circular gong chime in Cambodian *pinn peat* ensemble

koromong large, one-row gong chime in Sundanese *goong renteng*; also called *bonang
  renteng* or *kokuang*

kostim a Sundanese aristocrat's personal dance character and song

kotekan Balinese interlocking parts

kotekan empat type of Balinese interlocking part in which four distinct pitches emerge
  in the combination of the two parts

kraton Javanese or Cirebonese royal palace

kroncong hybrid Indonesian musical genre characterized by gamelan-like textures
  played on Western-derived string instruments such as guitar, mandolins, and cellos
  in conventional Western diatonic tunings

kubing jaw harp from the Philippines

kulanter small Sundanese two-head barrel-shaped drum; also called *gendang leutik* and *ketipung*

kulintang southern Philippine gong chime, as well as ensembles involving a *kulintang* gong chime

ladrang Central Javanese colotomic form

lagu in Indonesian, Sundanese, and Javanese, a word that means "tune" or "song"; in Sundanese *ketuk tilu*, the main part of a dance piece

lagu alit "small pieces" in the Sundanese gamelan repertory; also called *lagu leutik*, *sekar alit*, *rancagan*, or *rerenggongan*

lagu ekstra metrical song at the end of a series of Sundanese *tembang* songs; also called *panambih*

lagu gede "great pieces" in the Sundanese gamelan repertory; also called *sekar ageung*

lagu klasik core, classical pieces in the Sundanese *degung* repertory

lagu leutik "small pieces" in the Sundanese gamelan repertory; also called *lagu alit*, *sekar alit*, *rancagan*, or *rerenggongan*

lagu tengahan "middle pieces" in the Sundanese gamelan repertory

lam generic Lao term for vocal music with flexible melodies

lam klawn Lao dialogue songs with *khaen* accompaniment

lam nithan Lao epic storytelling tradition based on stories about the Buddha

lancaran Central Javanese colotomic form

latihan Indonesian word for practice or rehearsal session

lingkung seni (LS) arts circle; Sundanese performing arts troupe, typically run by a charismatic and business-savvy artist

liwung a Sundanese pitch name in *pelog* (equivalent to *bungur*)

loloran a Sundanese pitch name (equivalent to *kenong* or *lorloran*)

lorloran *see loloran*

ludruk Eastern Javanese theatrical form

macapat Javanese term for a set of poetic forms (equivalent to Sundanese *pupuh* meters)

madenda a Sundanese mode or *surupan* (also called *sorog*)

mak yong Melayu theater form from eastern Sumatra, the Malaysian peninsula, and the Riau islands

mandala sacred representation of the universe, often in the form of a diagram consisting of concentric circles

mapag Sri Cirebonese agricultural ceremony to welcome the rice goddess as the crop matures

mapag tambra Cirebonese agricultural ceremony held after planting and weeding

mataraman a Sundanese mode or *surupan* (also called *pelog degung* or *kobongan*)

mega mendung a Cirebonese *batik* motif with stylized rain clouds

meko gong ensemble from the eastern Indonesian island of Roti

menak Sundanese aristocratic class

merong the first of the two sections of a Central Javanese *gendhing*

metallophone generic term for a percussion instrument with tuned metal keys arranged in a row; can also refer to any metal percussion instrument

mincid Sundanese walking dance movement

mincid rangkep doubletime *mincid* in Sundanese *jaipongan*

ngala genah final drum pattern in *bajidoran* drumming's standard pattern; also called *ala genah*

ngampil in Sundanese, to carry a symbolic object solemnly

ngremo opening dance for an Eastern Javanese *ludruk* performance

ngunjung Cirebonese ceremony giving thanks to Allah and to ancestral spirits

nyered special Sundanese *ketuk tilu* drum pattern that begins and ends pieces; also called *nyorong*

nyorong *see nyered*

octave the musical distance between two pitches when one pitch vibrates exactly twice as fast as the other

odap in Toba Batak *gondang sabangunan*, a large drum

ogel Sundanese comic entertainment form in which four performers provide their own accompaniment on *dog-dog*; also called *reog*

ogung in Toba Batak *gondang sabangunan*, gong chime with four suspended gongs

ombak Javanese, Sundanese, and Indonesian word meaning "waves"; undulating quality of sound, often applied to large knobbed gongs

oncor three-wick standing oil lamp that illuminates a nighttime Sundanese *ketuk tilu* performance

opat wilet four *wilet* (*see wilet*)

oray-orayan men-only dance in Sundanese *ketuk tilu* events

orkes melayu Malay orchestra featuring Western instruments such as guitars, keyboards, and a transverse flute called *bangsing*

ostinato short rhythmic and/or melodic pattern or phrase that is repeated over and over

pakaian adat Indonesian word for traditional clothing

panambih metrical song at the end of a series of Sundanese *tembang* songs; also called *lagu ekstra*

pancer Javanese and Sundanese musical process in which a note is inserted between each of the melody's existing notes

panelu a Sundanese pitch name

panempag second-smallest *dog-dog* in a Sundanese *reog* ensemble

panerus in Sundanese *degung*, fourteen-key metallophone (also called *demung*); in Sundanese *gamelan salendro*, six- or seven-keyed metallophone, one octave lower than *saron*

pangkat introductory phrase in a Sundanese gamelan piece

pangkur a *macapat* poetic meter associated with Central Javanese poetry

panglima large gong chime in Sundanese *goong renteng*

panjang jimat a Cirebonese ceremony for *sekaten* in which palace heirlooms are washed

pantun Sunda Sundanese epic storytelling tradition from West Java, Indonesia

paparikan light Sundanese poetic form

pasinden Sundanese female singer

pasyon lowland Philippine epic storytelling tradition based on Christian stories

pathet Central Javanese musical system in which different configurations of pitches are associated with different moods, feelings, or sections of *wayang* performances

pathet barang one of three Central Javanese *pelog pathet*

pathet lima one of three Central Javanese *pelog pathet*

pathet manyura one of three Central Javanese *slendro pathet*

pathet nem one of three Central Javanese *slendro* or *pelog pathet*

pathet sanga one of three Central Javanese *slendro pathet*

pathetan a type of instrumental Central Javanese piece with no regular beat (*see also sulukan*)

patokan most common *pola lagu* pieces in the Sundanese gamelan repertory

peking in Central Javanese gamelan, the highest-pitched member of the *saron* family (also called *saron panerus*); in Sundanese *degung*, fourteen-key metallophone (also called *titil* or *cempres*); in Sundanese *gamelan salendro*, metallophone similar to *saron* but tuned an octave higher

pelog a Javanese, Sundanese, and Cirebonese seven-pitch non-equidistant tuning system

pelog degung a Sundanese mode or *surupan*; also called *kobongan* or *mataraman*

pelog jawar a Sundanese five-pitch subset of *pelog* with the pitches *barang*, *kenong*, *panelu*, *bem*, and *singgul*

pelog liwung a Sundanese five-pitch subset of *pelog* with the pitches *barang*, *kenong*, *bungur*, *bem*, and *singgul*

pelog sorog a Sundanese five-pitch subset of *pelog* with the pitches *petit*, *barang*, *kenong*, *panelu*, and *bem*

pemade gangsa one octave higher than the *ugal* in a Balinese *gong kebyar* ensemble

penca silat Sundanese martial arts

penclon *see pencon*

pencon gamelan instruments composed of bossed or knobbed gongs; also the name of the raised boss of such an instrument; also called *penclon*

pendopo Cirebonese, Javanese, or Sundanese pavilion with open walls

perunggu Indonesian word for bronze

pesantren Islamic school

pesindhen in Central Javanese gamelan, a female vocalist

petit a Sundanese pitch name in *pelog* (equivalent to *sorog*)

phleng pün ban Thai "songs of the village" sung by men and women in isolated villages to the accompaniment of hand-clapping or percussion instruments

phleng thao Thai music genre that exploits the elasticity of underlying cycles

pi Thai double-reed wind instrument

pi phat Thai gong-chime ensemble

pinn peat Cambodian court music gong-chime ensemble

pitch the characteristic of sound that depends on how fast or slowly something vibrates to produce the sound that is perceived as high and low

pokok Balinese term for main melody; a main pillar pitch in a Sundanese *pola lagu* (also called *posisi kenong* or *kenong*)

pola ibing Sundanese *bajidoran* and *jaipongan* drumming's standard pattern

pola lagu pitch framework for a Sundanese piece or song; also called *tugu lagu* or *arkuh lagu*

polos one of the interlocking parts in Balinese *kotekan*

polyphonic stratification an approach to simultaneous variation in which musical lines are layered on top of each other like strata of rock so that each layer remains distinct

pongdut Sundanese musical hybrid combining *jaiPONGan* and *dangDUT*

posisi kenong a main pillar pitch in a Sundanese *pola lagu*; also called *pokok* or *kenong*

pupuh Sundanese term for a set of poetic forms; *see macapat*

rabab Persian-Arabic bowed instrument (probably prototype for various Southeast Asian bowed spike fiddles)

ramai Indonesian word for "lively, crowded, full of bustle"

ramé Sundanese word for "lively, crowded, full of bustle"

ranat Thai xylophones

rancagan "small pieces" in the Sundanese gamelan repertory; also called *lagu alit*, *lagu leutik*, *sekar alit*, or *rerenggongan*

rebab Javanese, Cirebonese, Balinese, and Sundanese two-string bowed string instrument with two brass strings and a skin-covered resonator

rebana Indonesian single-head frame drum; also called *terbang*

rendo Baduy bowed lute; also called *tarawangsa*

rengkong rice bundles carried on a pole to make a sort of musical instrument in Sundanese rice harvest festivals

reog Sundanese comic entertainment form in which four performers provide their own accompaniment on *dog-dog*; also called *ogel*

rerenggongan "small pieces" in the Sundanese gamelan repertory; also called *lagu alit*, *lagu leutik*, *sekar alit*, or *rancagan*

reyong higher-pitched one-row gong chime played by four musicians in a Balinese *gong kebyar* ensemble; also the four hand-held gongs in a Balinese *beleganjur* ensemble

rincik in Sundanese gamelan, gong chime similar to *bonang* but tuned an octave higher

roneat dek keyed metallophone in Cambodian *pinn peat* ensemble

roneat ek xylophone in Cambodian *pinn peat* ensemble, higher in pitch than *roneat thung*

roneat thung xylophone in Cambodian *pinn peat* ensemble, lower in pitch than *roneat ek*

ronggeng Sundanese female singer-dancers

salendro a Sundanese five-pitch equidistant tuning system (equivalent to Javanese *slendro*)

sampak a type of Central Javanese piece

sampho drum in Cambodian *pinn peat* ensemble

sanggar Sundanese private teaching studios; Balinese music clubs

sangsih one of the interlocking parts in Balinese *kotekan*

saron in Central Javanese gamelan, a generic term for a family of six- or seven-keyed metallophones; in Sundanese gamelan, six- or seven-keyed metallophone

saron barung in Central Javanese gamelan, the medium-pitched member of the *saron* family

saron demung in Central Javanese gamelan, the lowest-pitched member of the *saron* family

saron panerus in Central Javanese gamelan, the highest-pitched member of the *saron* family; also called *peking*

sarune in Toba Batak *gondang sabangunan*, double-reed wind instrument

sasandu tube zither from the eastern Indonesian island of Roti

satengah wilet one-half *wilet* (*see wilet*); also called *kering*

saw Northern Thai repartee songs

sawilet one *wilet* (*see wilet*)

scale a theoretical arrangement, in pitch order, of pitches within a tuning system

sekar ageung "great pieces" in the Sundanese gamelan repertory; also called *lagu gede*

sekar alit "small pieces" in the Sundanese gamelan repertory; also called *lagu alit*, *lagu leutik*, *rancagan*, or *rerenggongan*

sekaten festival marking the birthday of the Islamic Prophet Muhammad

selukat metallophone with many keys in Sundanese *goong renteng*; also called *gangsa*

sembah Javanese, Sundanese, and Cirebonese gesture of greeting

sidekah bumi Cirebonese ceremony of blessing of earth before the farmers begin to work in the fields

sila in Sundanese dance and etiquette, sitting cross-legged

simultaneous variation performing concurrently two or more melodic lines, each of which is recognizable as a variant of the same basic tune

sinden female singer-dancers for Sundanese *bajidoran*

singgul a Sundanese pitch name

sisindiran light Sundanese poetic form

siter in Central Javanese gamelan, a zither with metal strings; also called *celempung*

siyem in Central Javanese gamelan, a hanging gong (smaller than *gong ageng*); also called *gong suwukan* or *gong siyem*

skor thomm drum in Cambodian *pinn peat* ensemble

slendro a Javanese five-pitch equidistant tuning system; equivalent to Sundanese *salendro*

slenthem in Central Javanese gamelan, the lowest-pitched member of the *gender* family, with six to eight keys

sorog a Sundanese mode or *surupan* (also called *madenda*); a Sundanese pitch name in *pelog* (equivalent to *petit*)

sralai double-reed wind instruments in Cambodian *pinn peat* ensemble

srepegan a type Central Javanese piece

suling Javanese, Cirebonese, Sundanese, or Balinese bamboo flute; in Central Javanese gamelan, a vertical bamboo flute with four (*slendro*) or five (*pelog*) holes

suling degung in Sundanese *degung*, a four-hole bamboo flute

suling gambuh in Balinese *gamelan gambuh,* a large bamboo flute

suling miring in Cirebon, often a transverse (side-blown) flute

suling panjang in *tembang Sunda*, a six-hole bamboo flute

sulukan a type of vocal Central Javanese piece with no regular beat (*see also pathetan*)

surupan various Sundanese modes and the practice of using them

tabla small, bongo-like double drum used in *dangdut*; also called *calti*

taganing in Toba Batak *gondang sabangunan*, a set of five tuned drums

talempong Minangkabau gong-chime ensemble from West Sumatra

tanji Sundanese music performed on Western brass instruments

taphon Thai drums in *pi phat* ensemble

tarawangsa Baduy (Sundanese) bowed lute; also called *rendo*

tari klasik Sundanese classical dance

tari kursus Sundanese solo male dance based on *tayub* dancing; also called *ibing keurseus*

tarikh selampit epic storytelling tradition from Kelanten, Malaysia

tarling Cirebonese ensemble featuring guiTAR and suLING

tarompet double-reed wind instrument in a *kendang penca* ensemble

tatalu instrumental overture to a Sundanese *ketuk tilu* performance

tayuban Cirebonese and Javanese men's social dancing; Sundanese aristocratic men's social dancing and dance events with gamelan accompaniment

tembang in Sundanese usage, a formal style of singing refined poetry; traditional form of Central Javanese poetry

tembang Sunda Sundanese sung poetry; also called *Cianjuran*

tengahan medium tempo section of a Cirebonese *topeng* dance

tepak sound of drums; in Sundanese *penca silat*, a specific drum *ostinato* pattern

tepak kocak humorous Sundanese drum patterns

tepak melem florid, subtle style of Sundanese hand drumming for instrumental music or vocal accompaniment

terbang single-head frame drum; also called *rebana*

tilingtit smallest *dog-dog* in a Sundanese *reog* ensemble

timbre quality or "tone color" of a sound

titil in Sundanese *degung*, fourteen-key metallophone; also called *peking* or *cempres*; in *gamelan sekaten*, a small, high-pitched keyed metallophone

topeng Javanese, Sundanese, Cirebonese, or Balinese performance involving masks

tortor dance that accompanies Toba Batak *gondang sabangunan*

tremolo minute variations in volume

triping fast, agitated drum pattern in Sundanese *bajidoran* that accompanies slow, swaying movements (from the English word "tripping")

trompong lower-pitched one-row gong chime played by one musician in Balinese gong *kebyar* ensemble

tugu a Sundanese pitch name (equivalent to *barang*)

tugu lagu pitch framework for a Sundanese piece or song; also called *pola lagu* or *arkuh lagu*

tumbuk a pitch that two Indonesian tuning systems have in common

tuning system the interval relationships between all the pitches available on an instrument or an ensemble

ugal lead *gangsa* in Balinese *gong kebyar* ensemble

upacara Indonesian word for "ceremony"

upacara adat in general, any traditional ceremony; in modern Sundanese usage, a special kind of performance for a wedding (also called *upacara khusus*)

upacara khusus *see upacara adat*

vibrato minute variations in pitch

wali sanga the nine saints of legend and history who brought Islam to Java

wanda anyar "new style" approach to Sundanese dancing characterized by continuous movement

wanda klasik classic (traditional) approach to Sundanese dancing characterized by alternating stillness with dynamic drumming and movement

wangsalan light Sundanese poetic form

wawayangan ketuk tilu dance performed by ronggeng

wayang Javanese, Sundanese, Cirebonese, and Balinese term for theatrical forms based on particular epic stories, including puppet theater

wayang golek Sundanese, Javanese, and Cirebonese rod puppet theater

wayang kulit Cirebonese, Balinese, and Javanese shadow puppet theater

wela omitted *kempul* stroke in a Javanese colotomic form

wilahan gamelan instruments with slab keys

wilet Sundanese term for expanding and contracting *pola lagu* pieces; the more *wilet*, the more time between pillar pitches. Possibilities include *satengah wilet* (one-half *wilet*), *sawilet* (one *wilet*), *dua wilet* (two *wilet*), *opat wilet* (four *wilet*), and *dalapan wilet* (eight *wilet*)

wiraswara male vocalist in a Sundanese gamelan; also called *juru alok*

xylophone generic term for percussion instrument with wooden keys arranged in a row

zaman kaset period in the 1970s and 1980s when local Sundanese recording companies released many commercial cassettes of traditional Sundanese music; golden age of cassette recordings

Additional Resources

Further Reading

Books on Southeast Asia in general

Brandon, James. 1967. *Theater in Southeast Asia*. Cambridge, MA: Harvard University Press.

> Despite its age, this compendium of theatrical forms of Southeast Asia remains an excellent introduction to this rich topic.

Foley, Kathy, ed. 1992. *Essays on Southeast Asian Performing Arts: Local Manifestations and Cross-Cultural Implications*. Center for Southeast Asia Studies, Occasional Paper No. 18. Berkeley: University of California at Berkeley Centers for South and Southeast Asian Studies.

> This volume includes essays on music, dance, and theater from Indonesia and the Philippines. Contributors include Ricardo Trimillos, Kathy Foley, Sue Carole DeVale, Benjamin Brinner, and Jody Diamond. Foley's article on Cirebonese *sintren* (a kind of trance performance) and Trimillos's piece on lowland Philippines *pasyon* (a Christian passion performance) are of particular interest because they illuminate topics covered nowhere else in the literature.

Ghulam-Sarwar, Yousof. 1994. *Dictionary of Traditional South-East Asian Theater*. Kuala Lumpur: Oxford University Press.

> A laudable but uneven effort to compile all sorts of information about Southeast Asian music, dance, and theater into one volume, this dictionary includes brief descriptive entries for terms and genres as well as many black-and-white photographs. It is especially strong in its coverage of Malaysian topics.

Lockard, Craig A. 1998. *Dance of Life: Popular Music and Politics in Southeast Asia.* Honolulu: University of Hawai'i Press.

Lockard compiled virtually everything ever written in English about popular music in Southeast Asia to prepare this book. Each Southeast Asian country is allotted a single chapter. The best chapter is on the Philippines, the area where Lockard has the most personal experience. The other chapters are quite good, however, and the bibliography is truly exceptional.

Manuel, Peter. 1988. *Popular Musics of the Non-Western World.* New York: Oxford University Press.

The sections on Southeast Asia in this perennial favorite are less comprehensive and considerably more out of date than Lockard's *Dance of Life,* but the concise discussions nevertheless provide a quick introduction to many Southeast Asian popular music genres.

Miettinen, Jukka O. 1992. *Classical Dance and Theater in South-East Asia.* Singapore: Oxford University Press.

Miettinen's introductory chapter provides a concise introduction to the layers of influences that have shaped Southeast Asian music, dance, and theater. In subsequent chapters she provides overviews of theater and dance in Burma, Thailand, Java, Bali, mainland Southeast Asia, and Vietnam, illustrated with many beautiful photographs.

Miller, Terry E., and Williams, Sean, eds. 1998. *The Garland Encyclopedia of World Music,* Vol. 4: *Southeast Asia.* New York: Garland.

Probably the most comprehensive single work on Southeast Asian music, this volume includes not only articles covering the musical traditions of each of the countries in the region, but a host of introductory articles presenting Southeast Asian geography, history, and cultural traits as well. The comprehensive guides to publications, recordings, films, and videos are particularly useful. A single CD, with some otherwise difficult-to-find musical examples, accompanies the volume

Reid, Anthony. 1988. *Southeast Asia in the Age of Commerce, 1450–1680,* Vol. 1: *The Lands Below the Winds.* New Haven, CT: Yale University Press.

For those intrigued by Southeast Asian history, Reid provides a fascinating account of many facets of Southeast Asian life around the time that Europeans first came to the area. The chapter "Festivals and Amusements" includes accounts of music, dance, theater, and sports from all over Southeast Asia, drawn from a variety of primary sources.

Sadie, Stanley, ed. 2001. *The New Grove Dictionary of Music and Musicians,* 2nd edn. London: Macmillan. Also available by subscription online; see http://www.grovemusic.com.

This most recent edition of the venerable *New Grove Dictionary* includes an article devoted to Southeast Asian music in general, substantial articles covering each of the individual countries of Southeast Asia, and a variety of brief biographies of important Southeast Asian musicians. Each article includes a bibliography. As the standard musical reference work in the English-speaking world, this excellent resource is available in most libraries; online access also is available in many places. If the second edition (published in 2001) is not available, the first edition of 1980 includes good coverage of Southeast Asia as well.

Taylor, Eric. 1989. *Musical Instruments of South-East Asia*. Singapore: Oxford University Press.

This slim volume opens with brief chapters covering the cultural, historical, and musical background of the region. The rest of the book names and describes a host of Southeast Asian musical instruments. There are some particularly striking color plates, and quite a few black-and-white photographs as well.

Books on Indonesia

Cribb, R. B. 2000. *Historical Atlas of Indonesia*. Honolulu: University of Hawai'i Press.

Cribb makes accessible the complications of the history of Indonesia and surrounding areas by presenting the movements of peoples, religions, technologies, and empires in a series of colorful maps accompanied by well-written text.

Holt, Claire. 1967. *Art in Indonesia: Continuities and Change*. Ithaca, NY: Cornell University Press.

Holt focuses on plastic arts (sculpture and painting), but spends considerable time examining performing arts traditions of Java and Bali, and, to a lesser extent, other parts of Indonesia. Her historical overview of Indonesian art, as well as her succinct summaries of the Byzantine plots of the various Indonesian epic stories, including the *Ramayana* and *Mahabharata*, are particularly useful.

Sutton, R. Anderson. 2002. *Calling Back the Spirit: Music, Dance, and Cultural Politics in Lowland South Sulawesi*. Oxford: Oxford University Press.

Sutton describes how musical activities in Sulawesi enact a dialogue between local meanings and Indonesian nationalist hegemony by analyzing the activities and work of several prominent musicians and dancers. His up-to-date summaries of Indonesian nationalist ideas about the performing arts as well as current ethnomusicological thinking about issues of authenticity are helpful for any student of Indonesian music. The book includes a CD with representative tracks from the artists covered in the text.

Books on Khmer/Cambodian music

Sam, Sam-Ang, and Patricia Shehan Campbell. 1991. *Silent Temples, Songful Hearts: Traditional Music of Cambodia*. Danbury, CT: World Music Press.

Sam-Ang Sam and his family are prominent Cambodian artists living in the United States. The book introduces, in simple language aimed at grade-school audiences, Cambodian and Khmer history, language, culture, and musical instruments. The heart of the book is fourteen "guided listening experiences," coordinated with an accompanying cassette tape, that provide readers with some in-depth information about specific Cambodian pieces from a variety of genres.

Books on Thai music

Dhanit Yupho. 1952. *Thai Musical Instruments.* 2nd edn., translated by David Morton. Bangkok: Fine Arts Department.
> After an extremely questionable five-page historical overview of Thai music history (which doesn't even mention Thai music's debt to Khmer music), the author provides an exhaustive catalogue of Thai musical instruments, grouped into percussion, wind, and string instruments, illustrated with line drawings.

Morton, David. 1968. *The Traditional Music of Thailand: Introduction, Commentary, and Analyses.* Los Angeles: Regents of the University of California.
> This substantial booklet served as the liner notes for a recording of Thai classical music released in the 1970s by the Institute of Ethnomusicology at UCLA. It includes a succinct and useful essay on Thai classical music (illustrated with many black-and-white photographs) as well as commentary on and transcriptions of the individual pieces included on the recording.

Morton, David. 1976. *The Traditional Music of Thailand.* Berkeley: University of California Press.
> Morton approaches Thai classical music quite systematically, first attending to fundamentals (tuning systems, melody, and rhythm), then moving on to musical instruments, then discussing his own ideas about modes in Thai music, and finally addressing forms and compositional techniques. Morton's work is outdated, but his comprehensive documentary approach to the Thai classical music scene of the 1950s and 1960s is still quite useful.

Myers-Moro, Pamela. 1993. *Thai Music and Musicians in Contemporary Bangkok.* Berkeley: University of California at Berkeley Centers for South and Southeast Asian Studies.
> Myers-Moro focuses on the social institutions around Thai classical music in modern Thailand, including how music is taught and learned, and modern Thai contexts for classical music. She also covers musical instruments, ensembles, repertories, and music theory.

Wong, Deborah, guest editor. 1991. *Balungan*, Vol. 5, No. 1.
> This issue of *Balungan* (published by the American Gamelan Institute) is devoted to performing arts of mainland Southeast Asia and includes articles on Thai music by Deborah Wong and Pamela Myers-Moro and an interview with Sam-Ang Sam by Jarrad Powell, as well as descriptions of some Thai music study groups at Kent State and Southwestern Universities.

Wong, Deborah. 2001. *Sounding the Center: History and Aesthetics in Thai Buddhist Performance.* Chicago: University of Chicago Press.
> Deborah Wong uses the Thai ritual (called *wai khruu*) that honors music and dance teachers as an entry point for understanding the power of Thai classical music and dance as it is articulated in discourse about music as well as in musical activities.

Along the way she dispenses a wealth of technical and cultural details about classical Thai music as it is practiced in modern Thailand.

Books on Philippine kulintang *music*

Asian Music (Journal of the Society for Asian Music), Vol. 27, No. 2, 1996.

Almost the entire spring/summer 1996 issue of *Asian Music* is devoted to *kulintang* traditions of the southern Philippines. The various articles cover both musical and cultural topics. Maguindanaon *kulintang* music receives especially good coverage, with articles by Danongan S. Kalanduyan, Karen Posner, Scott Scholz, and Yoshitaka Terada. Articles by Usopay Cadar, Robert Garfias, and Steven Otto treat Maranao *kolintang* music, and Usopay Cadar contributes a piece on *kolintang* in the United States.

Bañas y Castillo, Raymundo. 1969. *Philipino Music and Theater*. Quezon City, the Philippines: Manlapaz Publishing Co.

Bañas y Castillo devotes a scant two pages to southern Philippine gong chime music in this comprehensive study of Western-influenced music in the Philippines.

Maceda, Jose. 1998. *Gongs and Bamboo: A Panorama of Philippine Music Instruments*. Diliman, Quezon City, the Philippines: University of the Philippines Press.

Maceda opens with a short introduction to musical styles of the northern and southern Philippines (except the musical traditions of mainstream Christian Philippines society), including a comparative explication of a variety of southern Philippine *kulintang* ensembles. The bulk of the book is black-and-white photographs of indigenous Philippine musical instruments (including almost thirty pages of *kulintang* photographs from various regions).

Pfeiffer, William R. 1976. *Filipino music: Indigenious* [sic], *Folk, Modern*. Dumaguete City, the Philippines: Silliman Music Foundation.

Pfeiffer spent a lifetime lovingly collecting information about music from the Philippines; this book contains most of his life's work. The coverage is quite uneven, especially with regard to southern Philippine topics, but the book contains much useful information.

Books on Java in general

Hood, Mantle. 1980. *Music of the Roaring Sea*. Wilhelmshaven, the Netherlands: Edition Heinrichshofen.

Hood, Mantle. 1984. *Legacy of the Roaring Sea*. Wilhelmshaven, the Netherlands: Edition Heinrichshofen.

Hood, Mantle. 1988. *Paragon of the Roaring Sea*. Wilhelmshaven, the Netherlands: Edition Heinrichshofen.

Mantle Hood was among the first Western ethnomusicologists to examine Javanese music; this trilogy represents the culmination of his life's work. The "Roaring Sea" of this trilogy's titles is the three-pitch heirloom *gamelan munggang* in the *kraton* Yogyakarta which bears the proper name Kangjeng Kyai Guntur Laut (Roaring Sea). The first volume, after an introductory essay on modern Indonesia, explores Javanese prehistory to posit a fanciful origin story for gamelan instruments in Java. The second volume speculates about medieval developments in gamelan music. The final volume lays out Hood's ideas about Javanese modes and improvisation.

Kunst, J. 1973. *Music in Java*. The Hague, the Netherlands: Martinus Nijhoff.
> Jaap Kunst spent many years in Java in the early part of the twentieth century; this book is an encyclopedic compendium of all the data he collected during that time. The 1973 edition was updated by Ernst Heins and includes a very comprehensive bibliography up to that date. Much of Kunst's time in Java was spent in West Java; nevertheless, the bulk of the book focuses on Central Javanese court traditions. Despite its age, Kunst's book remains a classic; its pre-Independence perspective is especially useful for those undertaking historical research into Javanese music.

Books on Cirebonese music

Materials in English on Cirebonese performing arts are rare and difficult to obtain. Scholars who have produced materials in English include Pamela Rogers-Aguiñiga, Michael Wright, Richard North, Endo Suanda, and Matthew Cohen. General introductions to Cirebonese music, dance, and theater are available in the *New Grove Dictionary of Music and Musicians*, 2nd edn. (written by Matthew Cohen) and the *Garland Encyclopedia of World Music*'s Southeast Asia volume (contributed by Endo Suanda). Both of these articles include bibliographies that can direct a reader to some additional resources. In addition, the following books are available in many libraries.

Abdurachman, Paramita R., ed. 1982. *Cerbon*. Jakarta: Yayasan Mitra Budaya Indonesia, Sinar Harapan.
> This collection of essays, written by Indonesian scholars and experts and presented in the Indonesian language with reasonably accurate English translations, covers a variety of topics about Cirebonese history, culture, arts, and even cuisine. The short chapter on music by Bernard Suryabrata briefly addresses *sekaten*, gamelan, and *wayang*.

North, Richard, guest editor. 1988. *Balungan*, Vol. 3, No. 3.
> This entire issue of the periodical *Balungan* (published by the American Gamelan Institute) is devoted to Cirebonese performing arts and represents one of the only sources of information in English on these topics. It includes articles on gamelan and *wayang* by Richard North, an article on *topeng* dancing by Endo Suanda, and a description of *tarling* by Michael Wright.

Books on Central Javanese music

Western scholars who focused on Javanese music in the first half of the twentieth century include Jaap Kunst and Mantle Hood. A host of more recent scholars have produced plentiful materials in English covering Central Javanese gamelan-related topics. The introductory articles in the *New Grove Dictionary of Music and Musicians*, 2nd edn. (written by several authors) and the Southeast Asia volume of the *Garland Encyclopedia of World Music* (by R. Anderson Sutton) include excellent bibliographies that can direct a reader to many appropriate resources. The books by Jennifer Lindsay and Neil Sorrell described below are introductory texts aimed at general readers; the remaining books are more specialized investigations of specific topics.

Arps, Bernard. 1992. *Tembang in Two Traditions: Performance and Interpretation of Javanese Literature.* London: School of Oriental and African Studies.
    Arps covers Central and Eastern Javanese traditions of *tembang*—sung poetry in *macapat* meters—in great detail, focusing on performance practice in the areas around the cities of Yogyakarta and Banyuwangi. His goal is to come to an understanding of how this literary and performance tradition has meaning for its participants.

Becker, Judith. 1973. *Traditional Music in Modern Java: Gamelan in a Changing Society.* Honolulu: University Press of Hawai'i.
    The background and works of two innovative Central Javanese composers (Ki Narto-sabhdo and K. R. T. Wasitodipuro) provide a framework for Becker to explore what constitutes "tradition" in the context of Javanese gamelan music.

Becker, Judith, ed. 1984. *Karawitan: Source Readings in Javanese Gamelan and Vocal Music*, Vol. 1. Ann Arbor: University of Michigan Center for South and Southeast Asian Studies.
Becker, Judith, ed. 1987. *Karawitan: Source Readings in Javanese Gamelan and Vocal Music*, Vol. 2. Ann Arbor: University of Michigan Center for South and Southeast Asian Studies.
Becker, Judith, ed. 1988. *Karawitan: Source Readings in Javanese Gamelan and Vocal Music*, Vol. 3. Ann Arbor: University of Michigan Center for South and Southeast Asian Studies.
    This three-volume compendium of translations of papers by important Javanese musicians, theorists, and aestheticians, translated by gamelan-savvy ethnomusicologists, provides a valuable peek into the aesthetics of Javanese gamelan as perceived by insiders. The first two volumes present important essays, mostly from the twentieth century; the third volume provides a glossary, notations of the pieces mentioned in the texts, biographies of the Javanese authors, a bibliography, and an index.

Becker, Judith. 1993. *Gamelan Stories: Tantrism, Islam, and Aesthetics in Central Java.* Monographs in Southeast Asian Studies. Program for Southeast Asian Studies, Arizona State University.
    In this esoteric study, Becker digs deep into Javanese history, philosophy, mysticism, and religious attitudes to interpret the manifold meanings of the Central Javanese court dance called *bedhaya*.

Brinner, Benjamin. 1995. *Knowing Music, Making Music: Javanese Gamelan and the Theory of Musical Competence and Interaction.* Chicago: University of Chicago Press.
    Brinner outlines a general methodology for examining how musicians interact during

performance and a framework for understanding musical competence. He illustrates most of his points with examples drawn from Central Javanese gamelan, providing a rich and detailed look at Javanese aesthetics and musical style along the way.

Brinner, Benjamin. 2008. *Music in Central Java: Experiencing Music, Expressing Culture*. New York: Oxford University Press.
Brinner's entry into Oxford's Global Music Series of textbooks provides many fresh perspectives on Central Javanese gamelan music. His detailed yet simple and clear explanations of the roles of drumming and singing in gamelan music—topics often glossed over in introductory texts—are especially welcome. The CD that accompanies the book includes several complete pieces as well as many helpful excerpts that illustrate the sounds of particular instruments or clarify how Central Javanese musical processes work.

Keeler, Ward. 1987. *Javanese Shadow Plays, Javanese Selves*. Princeton, NJ: Princeton University Press.
In this classic study, Keeler convincingly demonstrates that Central Javanese *wayang kulit* (shadow puppet theater) models Javanese ideas about power, status, and interpersonal relationships. The book is rich in ethnographic detail about *dalang* (puppeteers), musicians, and the contexts in which *wayang* performances take place.

Lindsay, Jennifer. 1979. *Javanese Gamelan*. Kuala Lumpur: Oxford University Press.
Lindsay's slim volume provides a good general introduction to Central Javanese court gamelan, with emphases on instruments and cultural context.

Sorrell, Neil. 1990. *A Guide to the Gamelan*. Portland, OR: Amadeus Press.
This brief introduction focuses on aspects of gamelan that will interest fans of music composed by Westerners for gamelan instruments as well as of traditional Indonesian gamelan music. It begins with an overview of gamelan music in Europe and North America, and provides apt Western analogies for Javanese musical and cultural concepts. There is a good overview of instruments, basics of gamelan musical rudiments (such as form, tuning, and rhythm), as well as detailed explanations of various instrumental parts. The book provides only a few pages of cultural and historical background, however.

Sumarsam. 1995. *Gamelan: Cultural Interaction and Musical Development in Central Java*. Chicago: University of Chicago Press.
Sumarsam, who is both a *kraton*-trained Javanese musician and a US-trained ethnomusicologist, takes readers on a breathtaking tour of the history of Javanese musicians' interactions with Western modes of thought; he ultimately argues that modern Central Javanese gamelan music, despite its distinctly non-Western sound, was profoundly influenced by European musical thinking.

Sutton, R. Anderson. 1993. *Variation in Central Javanese Gamelan Music: Dynamics of a Steady State*. Monograph Series on Southeast Asia Special Report No. 28. DeKalb: Northern Illinois University Press.

Sutton explores the processes that allow musical variation and lead to stylistic changes in Central Javanese court-style gamelan. Along the way he provides excellent and detailed insights into the cultural context of gamelan music, the structure of gamelan pieces, and the particulars of how individual musicians go about creating their own realizations of gamelan pieces.

Books on Eastern Javanese music

Only a few scholars have produced books and articles on Eastern Javanese music. A general introduction to music, dance, and theater in Eastern Java is available in the *New Grove Dictionary of Music and Musicians*, 2nd edn. (written by Michael Crawford).

Purwacarita, Sarib. 1998. *Released from Kala's Grip: A Wayang Exorcism Performance from East Java*. Translated and with an introduction by Victoria M. Clara van Groenen-dael. Jakarta: Lontar Foundation.
  The bulk of this book is a transcription and translation of a Javanese *wayang kulit* play performed by *dalang* Sarib Purwacarita in Kediri, East Java. Groenendael's introduction outlines some similarities and differences between Central and Eastern Javanese *wayang* conventions and discusses the significance of *ruwatan* (exorcism) performances.

Sutton, R. Anderson. 1991. *Traditions of Gamelan Music in Java: Musical Pluralism and Regional Identity*. New York: Cambridge University Press.
  Sutton discusses regional styles in Javanese music traditions, with coverage not only of the court cities of Yogyakarta and Surakarta, but of two Eastern Javanese regions (Semarang in northeastern Java, and the Banyuwangi area at the eastern end of the island). Although there is a pervasive influence from the Surakarta style throughout Central and Eastern Java, Sutton makes a case for the ongoing cultivation of regional styles as well.

Books on Balinese music

The arts and culture of the island of Bali have captured the interest of Western scholars for over a century; among the early generation of scholars writing about Bali are illustrious names such as Gregory Bateson, Clifford Geertz, and Margaret Mead. Writers on music from this early period include Colin McPhee and Walter Spies. Many more recent scholars of Balinese music have published plentiful materials in English. General introductions to Balinese music, dance, and theater are available in the *New Grove Dictionary of Music and Musicians*, 2nd edn. (written by Lisa Gold) and the *Garland Encyclopedia of World Music's Southeast Asia* volume (by David Harnish).

Bakan, Michael B. 1999. *Music of Death and New Creation: Experiences in the World of Balinese Gamelan Beleganjur*. Chicago: University of Chicago Press.
  Bakan begins and concludes the book with stories about his own involvement with Balinese music, letting his readers benefit from his own process of coming to understand music in a Balinese way by learning to play (and to hear) *beleganjur* music. In

the middle chapters, he introduces the musical style and cultural context of the *bel-eganjur* ensemble, as well as how both the context and the style have responded to changes in Balinese society, including modernization, the rise of the tourist industry, and feminism.

Belo, Jane, ed. 1970. *Traditional Balinese Culture*. New York: Columbia University Press.
This collection includes a variety of essays on music, dance, and theater by some of the first Western scholars to take an interest in Balinese culture in the early twentieth century, including Katharane Mershon, Gregory Bateson, Margaret Mead, Colin McPhee, Beryl de Zoete, and Walter Spies. Their observations and ideas have helped shape Western views of Balinese culture (and even have affected how Balinese view themselves).

Gold, Lisa. 2005. *Music in Bali: Experiencing Music, Expressing Culture*. New York: Oxford University Press.
Lisa Gold's entry into Oxford's Global Music Series of textbooks provides a detailed yet approachable entry point into the world of Balinese music. She grounds her musical analyses firmly in Balinese cultural contexts to present a balanced picture of a dynamic music culture. As with the other books in the series, the accompanying CD provides a wealth of short excerpts that illustrate various concepts and processes.

Herbst, Edward.1997. *Voices in Bali: Energies and Perceptions in Vocal Music and Dance Theater*. Hanover, NH: University Press of New England.
Herbst investigates the way that performers in Bali learn and improvisationally perform the "pickup" theatrical genres called *topeng* and *arja*, with ample focus on the spiritual and mystical sides of Balinese performance. The book includes a CD with musical examples not generally available on commercial releases.

McPhee, Colin. 1946. *A House in Bali*. New York: The John Day Company.
This engaging volume, in which the author relates his adventures setting up a household in Bali and studying music, reads like a novel yet includes excellent descriptions of musical ensembles, styles, activities, aesthetics, and contexts.

McPhee, Colin. 1966. *Music in Bali: A Study in Form and Instrumental Organization in Balinese Orchestral Music*. New Haven, CT: Yale University Press.
McPhee's magnum opus is a detailed survey of Balinese musical styles and contexts as he experienced them in the 1930s. McPhee's detailed transcriptions and analyses provide a look at Balinese music as it was during the period before the advent of tourism and Indonesian nationalism.

Tenzer, Michael. 1998. *Balinese Music*, revised and updated edition. Hong Kong: Periplus Editions.
This beautifully illustrated book (originally published in 1991), clearly and systematically introduces neophytes to Balinese gamelan music. Chapters on history, instruments and tunings, and basic musical processes provide a background for subsequent discus-

sions of one complete piece (music for the Baris dance), other gamelan ensembles, and the place of music in Balinese society. Tenzer's beautiful prose is a joy to read, and the luscious color photographs are a treat for the eyes.

Tenzer, Michael. 2000. *Gamelan Gong Kebyar: The Art of Twentieth-Century Balinese Music*. Chicago: University of Chicago Press.
Tenzer's prizewinning investigation of *gong kebyar* in Bali delves deeply into the history, development, formal structure, and meaning of this dynamic musical style. The detailed analyses of *kebyar* pieces are not for the faint of heart, but there is something for everybody in this massive, well-organized, and well-written treatise. The book comes with two CDs that illustrate the sound examples.

Vitale, Wayne, guest editor. 1990. *Balungan*, Vol. 4, No. 2.
This issue of *Balungan* (published by the American Gamelan Institute) is devoted to Balinese performing arts. It includes an informative article on *kotekan* by Wayne Vitale and an interview with Balinese musician and dancer I Wayan Dibia.

Books on Sundanese music and dance

Scholars who focus on Sundanese performing arts have authored quite a few theses, dissertations, and journal articles on many Sundanese topics, but readily available books cover only *tembang Sunda* and *wayang golek*. General introductions to Sundanese music, dance, and theater are available in the *New Grove Dictionary of Music and Musicians*, 2nd edn. (written by Simon Cook) and the *Garland Encyclopedia of World Music*'s Southeast Asia volume (by Sean Williams); both of these articles include excellent bibliographies that can direct a reader to many appropriate resources. In addition, the following books are available in many libraries.

Foley, Kathy, guest editor. 1993. *Balungan*, Vol. 5, No. 2.
This issue of *Balungan* (published by the American Gamelan Institute) is devoted to Sundanese performing arts. It includes articles on *pantun Sunda* by Andrew Weintraub, *tembang Sunda* by Cary Young and Marcus Kaufman, on traditional learning by Sean Williams, and interviews by Kathy Foley with *dalang* Asep Sunandar, dancer Irawati Durban Arjo, and scholar Endo Suanda, as well as a score and analysis of Nano S.'s gamelan piece "Warna" by Linda Burman-Hall.

Herbert, Mimi, with Nur S. Rahardjo. 2002. *Voices of the Puppet Masters: the Wayang Golek Theater of Indonesia*. Honolulu: University of Hawai'i Press.
Mimi Herbert explores the world of Sundanese *wayang golek* rod puppet theater by telling the life stories of several performers and artists involved in the *wayang* world. The text is not deep, but is accurate for the most part. The book's chief value lies in its profusion of lavish photographs of musicians, *dalang*, and puppets.

Weintraub, Andrew N. 2004. *Power Plays: Wayang Golek Puppet Theater of West Java*. Athens: Ohio University Press.

As part and parcel of his overall project of explicating the significance of Sundanese *wayang golek* puppet theater in modern West Java, Weintraub provides excellent descriptions of several genres of Sundanese music as well as keen analyses of the cultural institutions within which the performing arts operate in Indonesia. The CD-ROM that accompanies the book is of special interest to those new to Sundanese performing arts; it includes not only MP3 audio recordings, but a multimedia introduction to Sundanese gamelan music and *wayang* puppet theater. The video clips and explanations provide an easy-to-grasp introduction to Sundanese gamelan style and supplement the explanations in the present volume quite well.

Williams, Sean. 2001. *The Sound of the Ancestral Ship: Highland Music of West Java.* Oxford: Oxford University Press.

Williams uses one musician's reference to the *kacapi* (and, by extension, the music) as a vessel that carries its listeners into a nostalgic past as a metaphor to frame her discussion of the social and musical meaning of *tembang Sunda*. Although her book does not have the encyclopedic breadth of information of Wim van Zanten's book on the same topic, it is more approachable, easier to read, and comes with a CD.

Zanten, Wim van. 1989. *Sundanese Music in the Cianjuran Style: Anthropological and Musicological Aspects of Tembang Sunda.* Dordrecht, the Netherlands: Foris Publications.

Zanten includes practically every piece of information about *tembang Sunda* he ever discovered in this musical and cultural examination of the genre, which covers poetic forms, musical instruments and techniques, history, and extremely technical details about tuning systems and modes. An appendix includes several *tembang* song texts in the original Sundanese with fine English translations.

Further Listening

Recordings of Indonesian music in general

Music of Indonesia series (Smithsonian Folkways Recordings)

Ethnomusicologist Philip Yampolsky recorded, compiled, and annotated this astonishing series of twenty compact discs; the series includes many tracks from Indonesia's lesser known islands and cultures. Each CD comes with a comprehensive and authoritative booklet which provides impeccably researched historical, contextual, and bibliographic information available nowhere else. Smithsonian Folkways has also produced an inexpensive sampler CD which contains selected cuts from all of the releases in the series.

Some of the CDs are of particular interest to readers of this book on gamelan music because they include recordings of songs or genres discussed in the various chapters. Vol. 1: *East Java 1* features *gandrung* music (as discussed in Chapter Two). Vol. 2: *Indonesian Popular Music* contains some examples of *dangdut* songs composed by Rhoma Irama (as discussed in Chapter Four). And Vol. 4: *Music of Nias and North Sumatra* includes Toba Batak *gondang* music (as discussed in Chapter 1). Sound samples, brief descriptions, lyrics transcriptions, and supplemental notes for each CD in the series are available on the Internet by following the "Indonesia Series" link at: http://www.folkways.si.edu/. The twenty volumes in the series are listed below.

Vol. 1: *East Java 1—Songs Before Dawn: Gandrung Banyuwangi* (SFW 40055, 1991)

Vol. 2: *Indonesian Popular Music—Kroncong Dangdut and Langgam Jawa* (SFW 40056, 1991)

Vol. 3: *Music from the Outskirts of Jakarta: Gambang Kromong* (SFW 40057, 1991)

Vol. 4: *Music of Nias and North Sumatra: Hoho, Gendang Karo, Gondang Toba* (SFW 40420, 1992)

Vol. 5: *Betawi & Sundanese Music of the North Coast of Java* (SFW 40421, 1994)

Vol. 6: *Night Music of West Sumatra: Saluang, Rabab Pariaman, Dendang Pauah* (SFW 40422, 1994)

Vol. 7: *Music from the Forests of Riau and Mentawai* (SFW 40423, 1994)

Vol. 8: *Vocal and Instrumental Music from East and Central Flores* (FW 40424, 1994)

Vol. 9: *Vocal and Instrumental Music from Central and West Flores* (SFW 40425, 1994)

Vol. 10: *Music of Biak, Irian Jaya: Wor, Church Songs, Yospan* (SFW 40426, 1996)

Vol. 11: *Melayu Music of Sumatra and the Riau Islands* (SFW 40427, 1996)

Vol. 12: *Gongs and Vocal Music from Sumatra* (SFW 40428, 1996)

Vol. 13: *Kalimantan Strings* (SFW 40429, 1997)

Vol. 14: *Lombok, Kalimantan, Banyumas: Little-known Forms of Gamelan and Wayang* (SFW 40441, 1997)

Vol. 15: *South Sulawesi Strings* (SFW 40442, 1997)

Vol. 16: *Music from the Southeast: Sumbawa, Sumba, Timor* (SFW 40443, 1998)

Vol. 17: *Kalimantan: Dayak Ritual and Festival Music* (SFW 40444, 1998)

Vol. 18: *Sulawesi: Festivals, Funerals, and Work* (SFW 40445, 1999)

Vol. 19: *Music of Maluku: Halmahera, Bura, Kei* (SFW 40446, 1999)

Vol. 20: *Indonesian Guitars* (SFW 40447, 1999)

Rough Guide to the Music of Indonesia (World Music Network in association with Rough Guides, NCOS and New Internationalist, RGNET 1055 CD, 2000)

Rough Guide CDs generally feature world music in a pop vein; this release is no different. It includes a variety of fine tracks culled mostly from CDs released commercially in Indonesia, with a particular emphasis on songs from West Java. Of special interest to readers of this book are the *dangdut* tracks from Rhoma Irama and Elvy Sukaesih, and the Sundanese *degung*, *kacapi-suling*, and *tembang Sunda* tracks. The liner notes, unfortunately, provide no enlightening information at all.

Sampler: Indonesia South Pacific: Music from the Nonesuch Explorer Series (Nonesuch 79794, 2003)

The venerable Nonesuch Explorer Series includes a number of recordings of Javanese, Balinese, and Sundanese music; this sampler includes representative tracks from several recordings. Not all of the choices are among the best the series has to offer, but it does include at least some favorite Javanese tracks (*ketawang* "Puspawarna" and *bubaran* "Udan Mas"), a wonderful Sundanese cut ("Tonggeret"), and a few good Balinese examples.

Recordings of Toba Batak/Gondang music

Batak of North Sumatra (New Albion Records NA 046 1992)
These tracks are recordings of a Sumatran troupe that toured the United States in 1990; they include feature examples of Toba (*gondang sabangunan* and *gondang hasapi*), Karo, and Mandailing music.

Music of Nias and North Sumatra: Hoho, Gendang Karo, Gondang Toba, Music of Indonesia, Vol. 4: (Smithsonian Folkways 40420, 1992)
Gongs and Vocal Music from Sumatra, Music of Indonesia, Vol. 12: (Smithsonian Folkways 40428, 1996)
These two volumes from the Music of Indonesia series provide excellent recordings (with excellent liner notes) of gong ensemble music from several Sumatran ethnic groups. Vol. 4: *Music of Nias and North Sumatra* features the Toba Batak *gondang sabangunan* and *gondang hasapi* ensembles described in Chapter 1.

Sumatra (Indonésie): Musiques des Batak Karo, Toba et Simalungun (Inédit W 260061, 1995)
This excellent CD features a multiethnic Batak troupe performing five different Sumatran ensembles; the recording was made while the group toured France. It features musical styles from three different Batak ethnic groups, including the Toba Batak *gondang sabangunan* ensemble described in Chapter 1.

Recordings of Khmer/Cambodian music

Homrong: The National Dance Company of Cambodia (Real World 2–91734, 1991)
This recording of the musicians of the National Dance Company is a testament to the revival of the Cambodian National Dance Company. It features a variety of songs with *mohori* (string ensemble) accompaniment. The liner notes feature helpful transcriptions and translations of song lyrics.

Mohori: Khmer Music from Cambodia (Latitudes LAT50609, 1997)
The Sam Ang-Sam Ensemble includes Cambodian musicians and dancers now living in the United States. *Mohori* is the string instrument ensemble.

The Music of Cambodia: 9 Gong Gamelan Music (Celestial Harmonies 13074–2, 1993).
The Music of Cambodia: Royal Court Music (Celestial Harmonies 13075–2, 1994)
The Music of Cambodia: Solo Instrumental Music (Celestial Harmonies 13076–2, 1994).
Celestial Harmonies has released several recordings of Southeast Asian music, collected and produced by David and Kay Parsons. The first CD of this three-disc set devoted to Cambodian music includes six tracks of the *pinn peat* ensemble described in Chapter 1 as well as other gong chime music (the misnamed "nine-gong gamelan"

is a *korng skor* ensemble, played for Cambodian funerals). The disc is rounded out with non-gong music as well. The second CD includes recordings of the *pinn peat* ensemble as well as the string ensemble called *mohori*. The third CD includes a variety of solo instruments recorded in Phnom Penh.

Les Musiques du Ramayana: Vol. 2: *Cambodge* (Ocora C 560015, 1990)
  This CD, from a set of three CDs that presents versions of the *Ramayana* from India (Vol. 1), Cambodia (Vol. 2), and Indonesia (Bali and West Java, Vol. 3), features an hour's worth of music from a Reamker dance performance, accompanied by *pinn peat* ensemble and performed by the Cambodian Royal Dance Company. This 1964 Paris recording predates the worst of the political turmoil that led to fall of the Cambodian monarchy and the decimation of Cambodian court musicians and dancers.

Recordings of Thai music

The Nang Hong Suite: Siamese Funeral Music (Nimbus NI 5332, 1991)
Royal Court Music of Thailand (Smithsonian-Folkways SF 40413, 1994)
  This excellent recording features musicians from the Thai government Fine Arts Department performing *piphat*, *krueng sai*, and *mahori* music.

Siamese Classical Music series (Marco Polo)

  Vol. 1: *The Piphat Ensemble before 1400 AD* (8.223197, 1994)
  Vol. 2: *The Piphat Ensemble 1351–1767 AD* (8.223198, 1994)
  Vol. 3: *The String Ensemble* (8.223199, 1994)
  Vol. 4: *The Piphat Sepha* (8.223200, 1994)
  Vol. 5: *The Mahori Orchestra* (8.223493, 1994)
  The Sleeping Angel: Thai Classical Music (Nimbus NI 5319, 1991)

All the above CDs feature the well-known Fong Naam ensemble performing various repertories of Thai classical music on *piphat* (gong-chime), *khruang sai* (string), and *mahori* (mixed) ensembles.

Recordings of Cirebonese music

The Gamelan of Cirebon (King Records World Music Library KICC-5130, 1991)
  Features several well-recorded cuts of modern Cirebonese gamelan, including a *topeng* dance accompaniment for the "Panji" dance as performed by Sujana Arja.

Recordings of Central Javanese music

Java: Historic Gamelans (UNESCO collection, Musical sources, Art music from South-East Asia; IX-2, Philips 6586 004, released on LP in the 1970s)
  Although it has yet to be rereleased on CD, this recording is worth seeking out to hear a variety of Central Javanese heirloom palace gamelan ensembles, including the very old ceremonial ensembles *sekaten*, *kodok ngorek*, and *carabalen*, as well as more modern-style ensembles.

Nonesuch Explorer series (Elektra-Nonesuch)

> *Java: The Jasmine Isle: Gamelan* (79717, released 1969; rereleased on CD 2003)
> *Java: Court Gamelan* (79719, released 1971; rereleased on CD 2003)
> *Java: Court Gamelan II* (79721, released 1977; rereleased on CD 2003)
> *Java: Court Gamelan III* (79722, released 1979; rereleased on CD 2003)

Court Gamelan, Court Gamelan II, and *Court Gamelan III,* all recorded by Bob Brown, feature well-recorded selections from three of the four Central Javanese *kraton* (Paku Alaman, Mangkunegaran, and Kraton Yogyakarta, respectively). *The Jasmine Isle* (recorded by David Lewiston), on the other hand, includes tracks that are not particularly representative of either Central Javanese or Sundanese gamelan music.

The Sultan's Pleasure: Javanese Gamelan and Vocal Music (Music of the World CDT-116, 1994)

Ethnomusicologist Roger Vetter put together this excellent sampling of music that is broadcast over the radio from the Yogyakarta *kraton* every thirty-five days to celebrate the Sultan's "birthday." It includes a diverse range of musical styles and sounds that represent a specifically Yogyakarta palace approach to gamelan music.

World Music Library Javanese gamelan recordings (King Records)

> *The Javanese Gamelan* (King Records World Music Library KICC-5129, 1987)
> *Klenengan Session of Solonese Gamelan I* (King Records World Music Library KICC-5185, 1994)
> *Langendriyan—Music of Mangkunegaran Solo II* (King Records World Music Library KICC-5194, 1995)
> *Music of Mangkunegaran Solo I* (King Records World Music Library KICC-5184, 1994)

Although not as extensive as their Balinese releases, these World Music Library CDs of Javanese music are similarly well-recorded (especially the later ones). Unfortunately, the bulk of the liner notes is in Japanese, and the English translations are not always particularly good.

Gamelan of Central Java (Yantra Productions)

This new series of CDs features lovingly produced recordings of many different styles and genres of Central Javanese music. The new recordings of archaic gamelan music on Vol. II: *Ceremonial Music* are an especially welcome addition. The producers plans to release more recordings; their website (http://www.gamelan.to/) has an up-to-date list of the releases. The titles to date are:

> I *Classical Gendings* (fy 8041, 2001)
> II *Ceremonial Music* (fy 8042, 2002)
> III *Modes and Timbres* (fy 8073, 2004)
> IV *Spiritual Music* (fy 8074, 2004)
> V *Gaya Yogyakarta* (fy 8075, 2005)

VI *Kraton Surakarta* (fy 8103, 2005)
VII *Edge of Tradition* (fy 8104, 2005)
VIII *Court Music Treasures* (fy 8119, 2006)
IX *Songs of Wisdom and Love* (fy 8120, 2006)

Lokananta Remastered Series (Polosseni)
Indonesia's national recording company, Lokananta, released a host of excellent cassettes of traditional music during the 1960s and 1970s; a selection of these have been remastered from the original studio tapes and released to the international market on CD. More information about the CDs (including liner notes) are available at the Polosseni website (http://www.polosseni.com/mastering/lokananta.html). The CDs include Central Javanese gamelan and Sundanese *degung* music. The CDs are:

Upacara Pengantin (from Lokananta cassette acd 004)
Gambir Sawit (from Lokananta cassette acd 101)
Beber Layar (from Lokananta cassette acd 042)
Ibu Pretiwi (from Lokananta cassette acd 007)
Lumbung Desa (from Lokananta cassette acd 127)
Klenengan Gobjog (from Lokananta cassette acd 001)
Klenengan (from Lokananta cassette acd 002)
Gending Soran (from Lokananta cassette acd 010)
Onang-Onang (from Lokananta cassette acd 014)
Rangu-Rangu (from Lokananta cassette acd 015)
Rampak Sekar (from Lokananta cassette acd 018)
Jamuran (from Lokananta cassette acd 037)

Recordings of Eastern Javanese music

Music of Indonesia Series, Vol. 1: *East Java 1—Songs Before Dawn: Gandrung Banyuwangi* (Smithsonian Folkways SFW 40055, 1991)
The first volume of Smithsonian Folkways' excellent Music of Indonesia series provides excerpts of Eastern Javanese *gandrung* music; Philip Yampolsky's detailed liner notes provide meticulously researched background information and an excellent bibliography.

Music of Madura: Java, Indonesia (ODE Records ODE 1381; 1991)
Madura is technically part of the province of East Java, but is home to a variety of musical traditions unique to the island. This disc features an extensive sampling of vocal and instrumental genres (including several gamelan ensembles); each track is well recorded, but unfortunately the liner notes are not very extensive—a serious liability because information about Madurese music is not readily available.

Recordings of Balinese music

Because of its status as an international tourist destination, there are quite a few recordings of Balinese music readily available. Listeners should beware of recordings that appear to have been put together by producers with little knowledge of Balinese music or culture; usually a cursory examination of the liner notes will help determine whether a recording is credible or not. Below are a few recordings that are reliable.

Bali: Roots of Gamelan (World Arbiter 1999)
   This fascinating release makes readily available a scattering of old 78 rpm recordings of Balinese music released in the 1920s; the rest of the disc features performances of Colin McPhee's transcriptions (for piano, mostly) of Balinese music.

Music of the Gamelan Gong Kebyar, Vol. 1 (Vital Records VR 401, 1996)
Music of the Gamelan Gong Kebyar, Vol. 2 (Vital Records VR 402, 1996)
   Wayne Vitale, an American composer and the director of California's eminent Sekar Jaya ensemble, compiled these CDs devoted to *gong kebyar* repertory. Vol. 1 features the musicians of the Indonesian government-sponsored music academy (STSI Denpasar), directed by I Wayan Beratha. Vol. 2 features compositions by I Nyoman Windha.

Nonesuch Explorer series (Elektra-Nonesuch)

   Bali: Music from the Morning of the World (79714, 1967, rereleased 2002)
   Bali: Golden Rain (79716, 1967, rereleased 2002)
   Bali: Gamelan and Kecak (79814, 1987, rereleased 2003)
   Bali: Music for the Shadow Play (79718, 1970, rereleased 2003)
   Bali: Gamelan Semar Pegulingan: Gamelan of the Love God (79720, 1972, rereleased 2003)

All five of the groundbreaking Nonesuch recordings of Balinese music have been rereleased on CD. The earlier Nonesuch Explorer series recordings of Balinese music are tantalizing samplers of the many ensembles, styles, and genres that Balinese music encompasses, recorded by David Lewiston. *Music from the Morning of the World* (recorded in 1966), includes *gong kebyar, kecak, angklung*, and a vocal solo. *Gamelan and Kecak* includes well-recorded examples of a variety of *beleganjur, angklung, gong kebyar*, as well as some non-gamelan genres, including a *kecak* excerpt. *Golden Rain* has a much longer *kecak* excerpt as well as some gamelan tracks. Bob Brown's contributions to the series are a bit more focused: *Music for the Shadow Play* includes only music for *gender wayang* (the quartet of metallophones that accompanies Balinese shadow puppet theater), and *Bali: Gamelan Semar Pegulingan: Gamelan of the Love God* is devoted to the seven-tone gamelan revived with the help of Colin McPhee.

World Music Library recordings of Balinese music (King Records)

   Music in Bali (KICC-5127, 1991)
   The Gamelan Music of Bali (KICC-5126, 1991)
   Kecak and Sanghyang of Bali (KICC-5128, 1991)
   Gamelan Gong Gede of Batur Temple (KICC-5153, 1992)
   Gamelan Gong Kebyar of "Eka Cita," Abian Kapas Kaja (KICC-5154, 1992)

Gender Wayang of Sukawati Village (KICC-5156, 1992)
Jegog of Negara (KICC-5157, 1992)
Gamelan Semar Pegulingan of Binoh Village (KICC-5155, 1992)
Gamelan Joged Bumbung "Suar Agung," Negara (KICC-5158, 1994)
Gamelan Semar Pegulingan "Gunung Jati," Br. Teges Kanginan (KICC-5180, 1994)
Gamelan Selonding "Guna Winangun," Teganan (KICC-5182, 1994)
Geguntangan Arja "Arja Bon Bali" (KICC-5183, 1994)
Golden Rain: Gong Kebyar of Gunung Sari, Bali (KICC-5195, 1995)
Saron of Singapadu (KICC-5196, 1995)
Baleganjur of Pande and Angklung of Sidan, Bali (KICC-5197, 1995)

Most of these releases focus on a particular Balinese genre and ensemble; although the recording quality of the earlier releases is spotty, the later ones are generally quite good. Unfortunately, the bulk of the liner notes is in Japanese, and the English translations are not always particularly good.

Recordings of Sundanese music

Classical Tembang Sunda: Music from West Java (Celestial Harmonies 13134–2, 1996)
There is some fine *tembang Sunda* performed by Ida Widawati on this CD, including many of the best-known songs in both *pelog* and *sorog* tuning systems. The liner notes are quite good (except for the peculiar opening essay by Barbara Crossette).

Gamelan Degung: Classical Music of Sunda, West Java (Pan 2053, 1996)
Ernst Heins recorded the musicians of Jugala performing a number of classical *degung* pieces. One track features Euis Komariah singing two beautiful songs ("Kembang Bungur" and "Reumbeuy Bandung") in *degung kawih* style; two other tracks include vocal solos by Ida Widawati.

Indonesia: Music from West Java (UNESCO D 8041, 1970, rereleased on CD in 1994).
Java: Sundanese Folk Music (UNESCO D 8051, 1972, rereleased on CD in 1994).
These two samplers of Sundanese music include quite a variety of genres and styles. The first features two lovely, old-fashioned tracks of *gamelan salendro* music, along with *kacapi-suling* and *degung* pieces, rounded out with a sample of *wayang golek* (accompanied by *gamelan salendro*). The notes, unfortunately, are riddled with errors. The second is a rich resource for non-gamelan music from West Java, including non-diatonic *angklung* ensemble music, a *ketuk tilu* cut, and music to accompany *penca silat*. The liner notes are informative and accurate.

Indonesia: Wayang Golek: The Sound and Celebration of Sundanese Puppet Theater (Multicultural Media. MCM3019/24 2001)
Six compact discs, with a forty-four-page booklet and an enhanced CD with complete text transcription and translations. Recorded, edited, and annotated by Andrew N. Weintraub.
This six-CD set presents a complete performance of Sundanese *wayang golek*

purwa (rod puppet theater) performed by West Java's best-known and most popular *dalang*, Asep Sunandar Sunarya. The substantial liner notes include a pithy history of *wayang golek*, a rich description of the social context of *wayang*, an excellent general introduction to the art of *wayang* and the gamelan music that accompanies it, as well as specific details of this particular performance and a biography of Asep Sunandar Sunarya. In addition, a complete transcription and translation of the dialogue and song texts is provided in Adobe's Portable Document Format (PDF). The scene-by-scene (and track-by-track) performance flowchart in the liner notes makes it quite simple to match up the recordings with the text transcription and translation, enabling non-Sundanese speakers to follow and understand the performance.

Lolongkrang: Gamelan Degung Music of West Java (Sakti 33, 1994)
Pusaka Sunda: Samagaha (Sakti 34, 1999)
   The renowned *suling* player Burhan Sukarma leads an ensemble of American gamelan musicians in renditions of classical *degung* compositions and modern compositions.

The Sound of Sunda (Globestyle CDORB 060, 1990)
Jaipongan Java: Euis Komariah with Jugala Orchestra (Globestyle CDORB 057, 1990)
   These two excellent CDs feature the velvet voice of Euis Komariah accompanied by the peerless musicians of Jugala. *Jaipongan Java* features *gamelan salendro* and a variety of *jaipongan* and *kliningan* selections. *The Sound of Sunda* features both *gamelan salendro* and *degung* accompaniments.

Trance 3: Zen Shakuhachi, Mbira Spirit Ceremony, and Sacred Tembang Sunda (Ellipsis Arts 4330, 1999)
   Although *tembang Sunda* is not "trance" music by any stretch of the imagination, this trance sampler features some excellent recordings of one of West Java's most renowned *tembang* singers (Euis Komariah). The Japanese *shakuhachi* (bamboo flute) and Zimbabwean *mbira* ("thumb piano") tracks are quite nice, too.

Udan Mas Tembang Sunda: Ida Widawati (Pan 4004, 1996)
   Recorded live in 1974 at concerts in Amsterdam, this recording captures one of *tembang Sunda*'s most celebrated performers at the very beginning of her illustrious career. Although there are some awkward moments on the recording, it is a good sampler of the *tembang* repertory, and includes songs in all three of the major *tembang Sunda* tuning systems.

West Java: Sundanese Jaipong and Other Popular Music (Nonesuch Explorer Series 79815, 2003)
   This collection of songs was originally released under the title "Tonggeret"; it contains several excellent *jaipongan* tracks sung by Idjah Hadidjah, who was one of the most famous and popular singers recording for the Jugala studio under the direction of Gugum Gumbira during the 1980s. "Daun Pulus/Keser Bojong" remains a *jaipongan* standard. Some of the tunes, for which the drumming is not quite so exuberant, are perhaps better classified as *kliningan*.

Recordings of dangdut *and other popular Indonesian music*

Dari Sunda: Women of the World, Vol 6: *Detty Kurnia* (Riverboat TUGCD1011, 1997)
Detty Kurnia: Coyor Panon (Timbuktu FLTRCD519, 1993)
   Detty Kurnia's substantial background as a performer of Sundanese traditional
   music is apparent in her global-pop-tinged versions of old and new Sundanese- and
   Indonesian-language songs. The accompanying tracks on both these CDs include
   synthesized gamelan sounds as well as excellent *rebab, gendang*, and *suling* playing, all
   of which enliven the more conventional guitar-keyboard-drum grooves.

Music of Indonesia 2: Indonesian Popular Music—Kroncong, Dangdut and Langgam Jawa
(Smithsonian-Folkways SFW 40056, 1991)
   Along with some *kroncong* and *langgam* selections, this CD includes four Rhoma
   Irama *dangdut* songs, along with transcriptions and translations of the lyrics.

The Rough Guide to the Music of Indonesia (World Music Network 1055, 2000)
   Includes two Rhoma Irama songs, one performed by Rhoma Irama, and one by Elvy
   Sukaesih; unfortunately the notes do not include any lyrics or translations.

Further Viewing

Videos and DVDs on Southeast Asia in general

JVC Video Anthology of World Music and Dance (Victor Company of Japan, 1990)
   This monumental 30-tape collection of video excerpts from around the world
   includes five volumes featuring Southeast Asian performances. The quality of the material is very uneven, as is the coverage; because many of the excerpts were recorded
   when national arts troupes toured Japan, there is a "pot-luck" quality to the selection
   of traditions, genres, pieces, and performers included in the collection. The copious
   notes that accompany the tapes are similarly uneven; although they are mostly accurate, they do not always tell the viewer much that is interesting or relevant about the
   taped examples. Nevertheless, by virtue of its comprehensiveness and its wide avail-
   ability, the JVC video series is a useful resource. It is worthwhile to consult some of
   the comprehensive reviews of the series before investing too much time in the individual selections. One exhaustive review essay, published in the journal *Asian Music*
   (Vol. 24, No. 2, 1993: 111–88), features detailed commentary from experts in each of
   the performing traditions that the series covers; Deborah Wong's essay in the journal
   Ethnomusicology (Vol. 39, No. 3, 1995: 529–38) is much easier to digest but still alerts
   its readers to most of the series' significant problems (Miller, Dilling, et al. 1993;
   Wong 1995).

Southeast Asia I—Tape 6: *Vietnam and Cambodia*
   The Vietnamese selections are not well contextualized, either on the video or in the
   accompanying booklets, but they do provide a window into some Vietnamese performing traditions. According to Sam-Ang Sam, the four Cambodian excerpts are

"partial and not representative. I would not even recommend showing them to a class" (Miller, Dilling, et al. 1993: 141).

Southeast Asia II—Tape 7: *Thailand and Myanmar (Burma)*
The Thai examples were performed by musicians and dancers from the Thailand Department of Fine Arts on tour in Japan and feature samples of *piphat*, *mahori*, and *khruang sai* ensembles. The Burmese selections, too, feature a national troupe on tour in Japan.

Southeast Asia III—Tape 8: *Malaysia and the Philippines*
Most of the Philippines examples are staged examples of indigenous music from the uplands of the northern Philippines. The two examples featuring *kulintang* ensemble accompaniment are not particularly satisfying. The Malaysian examples feature the courtly Malaysian version of a gamelan ensemble (based on Javanese models), supplemented by one string instrument duet performed in a studio by Kenyah musicians from Sarawak.

Southeast Asia IV—Tape 9: *Indonesia 1: Bali*
The six selections were all filmed outdoors in the courtyard of a Balinese temple, giving some semblance of an appropriate context, but without an audience. Nevertheless, the performances are adequate for demonstration purposes, and some of the dancing is quite good.

Southeast Asia V—Tape 10: *Indonesia 2: Bali and Java*
This volume includes several selections by a Sundanese troupe on tour in Japan, including *degung*, *tembang Sunda*, *pantun*, and *celempungan* (an ensemble featuring zithers, gongs, drums, *rebab*, and singers which plays *gamelan salendro kliningan* repertory). These performances are quite good, although their "in the studio" ambience makes them seem a bit stiff. The *pantun* performance in particular seems inappropriately staged, performed by a *tembang* singer who accompanies himself on a *tembang*-style *kacapi*. The *celempungan* selection includes some excellent close-up footage of *rebab* fingering for the *sorog* tuning. The sole Central Javanese clip (an excerpt from a *wayang kulit* performance), however, leaves much to be desired. Also on the tape is a long excerpt from a rather unconventional, but fascinating, Balinese *kecak* performance.

Videos on Indonesia in general

Traditional Dances of Indonesia (Berkeley: University of California Extension Center for Media and Independent Learning, 1990)

> *Dances of West Sumatra: Tari Piring; Tari Alang Tari Jawa* (37961)
> *Dances of Surakarta, Central Java: Bedoyo Elo Elo* (37950)
> *Dances of Surakarta, Central Java: Bedoyo Pangkur* (37951)
> *Dances of Yogyakarta, Central Java: Bekasan Menak* (37955)
> *Dances of Yogyakarta, Central Java: Langen Mandra Wanara* (37957)

Dances of Yogyakarta, Central Java: Lawung Ageng (37956)
Dances of Bali: Baris Katekok Jago; Kebyar Duduk (37959)
Dances of Bali: Barong (37960)
Dances of Bali: Legong Kraton (37958)
Dances of Surakarta, Central Java: Menak Konchar (37954)
Dances of Surakarta, Central Java: Srimpi Anglir Medung (37953)
Dances of Surakarta, Central Java: Srimpi Gondokusomo (37952)

This series of twelve videos was filmed in the 1970s; each provides video documentation of a particular Central Javanese, Balinese, or Sumatran dance.

Videos on Khmer/Cambodian music and dance

Dancing through Death: The Monkey, Magic and Madness (Filmakers [sic] Library, 1999)
This video focuses on one Cambodian refugee who finds purpose and meaning in Cambodian dance to explore the effect of the murderous Khmer Rouge on Cambodian performing arts. It includes interviews with performers in Cambodia and the United States, and documents the process of reconstructing and reviving classical dance traditions in Cambodia and abroad.

Khmer Court Dance: Cambodian Royal Court Dances (Multicultural Media, 1995)
The video presents five Cambodian court dances, replete with dramatic costumes, performed to the accompaniment of mostly prerecorded music. The video features performances by Sam-Ang Sam, Chan Moly Sam, and other fine Cambodian artists living in the United States (some of whom performed both as dancers on the video and musicians in the prerecorded sound track). Each dance is introduced on the video by Paul Cravath, who provides useful background information.

The Tenth Dancer (Women Make Movies, 1993)
Em Theay was among the few Royal Court Ballet dancers to survive the Khmer Rouge assault on Cambodian arts; this documentary tells the story of her attempts to rebuild the troupe with the help of a former student.

Video on Thai music

Two Faces of Thailand: A Musical Portrait (Shanachie, 1994)
Originally released in 1983, this documentary followed a troupe performing Luk Tung (a genre which mixed Thai and global pop styles) as it toured rural Thailand.

Videos on Cirebonese music and dance

Penca and Topeng Babakan from Sunda, Indonesia (Performing Arts Program of the Asia Society, 1977)
The Asia Society sponsored a tour of the US by *dalang topeng* Sujana Arja with Cirebonese and Sundanese musicians from Slangit and Bandung. The video features

explanations of the music and dance by Beate Gordon and performances of *penca silat* as well as Cirebonese *topeng*.

Topeng Babakan: Solo Masked Dance of West Java (KT Films, 1984)
This ten-minute video describes the artistic and social world of *dalang topeng* Sujana Arja from the village of Slangit near Cirebon. Unfortunately, the music on the soundtrack is not synchronized with the dance footage, giving a rather false impression of the form.

Videos on Central Javanese music and dance

Copper, Tin and Fire: Gongsmithing in Java (Sam Quigley, 1989)
Ethnomusicologist Sam Quigley produced this documentary that follows the process of forging a small gong in the smithy of Tentrem Sarwanto in Surakarta.

Gambyong Pangkur: Traditional Javanese Court Dance from Solo (Resonance Media, 1993)
The Prosperity of Wibisana: A Performance of Wayang Kulit (Resonance Media, 1995)
The Prosperity of Wibisana: A Study Guide and Analysis of Javanese Wayang Kulit (Resonance Media, 1995)
These three well-produced videos feature Lewis and Clark College gamelan ensemble (Portland, OR), directed by Widiyanto S. Putro (also known as Midiyanto), and guest artists. *Gambyong Pangkur* is a Central Javanese court-style dance, here performed by Sri Endah Wahyuningsih. *The Prosperity of Wibisana* is a one-and-a-half hour *wayang kulit* performance (with Midiyanto as the *dalang*), presented mostly in English, accompanied by the college gamelan ensemble (with a few expert musicians sitting in). The *Study Guide and Analysis* video has Midiyanto explicating many aspects of *The Prosperity of Wibisana*'s plot, the puppets, and music.

Gamelan Music of Java (East West Center, University of Hawai'i, 1983)
The University of Hawai'i gamelan ensemble systematically introduces the instruments and idioms of Central Javanese gamelan music. The video also features interviews with the eloquent Hardja Susilo, and a dance performance by the late Ben Suharto.

Wayang Kulit: Shadow Theater of Java (Baylis Glascock Films, 1997)
A performance by the *dalang* Oemartopo provides the opportunity for some excellent and extensive footage of Central Javanese *wayang kulit* and gamelan. The video also places the *wayang* performance within a Javanese cultural context.

Videos on Balinese music and dance

Bali: The Mask of Rangda (Hartley Film Foundation, 1975)
This film develops a rather convincing Freudian interpretation of Balinese masked and trance dances and includes some good footage of the *barong* dance.
Dance and Trance of Balinese Children (Filmmakers Library, 1995)
This video updates Mead's, Bateson's, and Belo's earlier documentaries on Balinese

dance. It features interviews with Balinese dance teachers and also explores the role of trance dancing in modern Bali as well as internationally.

The Great Ceremony to Straighten the World (University of California Extension Media Center, 1994)
This video contextualizes Balinese ritual, music, and dance in the lives of Balinese.

Island of Temples (Jeffrey Norton Publishers, 1992)
Originally produced in 1973, this film is quite dated, but features some good footage of a *kecak* performance as well as the *barong* dance.

Shadowmaster (Shadowlight Productions, 1981)
This charming movie weaves together fascinating images of many Balinese performing arts (filmed by John Knoop) into a compelling story about two young Balinese men who must find a way to reconcile modernity with traditional Balinese culture. Director C. L. (Larry) Reed brought his prodigious knowledge of Balinese *wayang kulit* to bear in making the film, which provides an excellent introduction to Balinese arts.

Kawitan: Creating Childhood in Bali (Berkeley: University of California Extension Center for Media and Independent Learning 38281, 2002)
Documents rituals marking a child's growth.

Kembali: To Return (Berkeley: University of California Extension Center for Media and Independent Learning 38220, 1991)
A documentary of the American group Sekar Jaya as they perform in Bali as the first Western ensemble to perform Balinese music there.

Learning to Dance in Bali (Pennsylvania State University, Audio-Visual Services, 1991)
Trance and Dance in Bali (Pennsylvania State University, Audio-Visual Services, 1991)
Filmed by Jane Belo, Gregory Bateson, and Margaret Mead in the late 1930s, these black-and-white films provide an historic look at Balinese dance. *Trance and Dance*, filmed in Pagoetan, presents a trance ritual involving masked dancers portraying Rangda (a witch) and the Barong (a mythical beast). *Learning to Dance* demonstrates how Balinese children learn dance by being moved by their teacher as well as by watching and imitating.

Video on Sundanese music, dance, and theater

Wayang Golek: Performing Arts of Sunda (West Java) (BBC, Open University, Insight Media, 1999)
Produced with the help of Simon Cook, this excellent video provides glimpses into the lives of *dalang* Atik Rasta and his father Otong Rasta as it examines Sundanese *wayang golek* and *gamelan salendro* music. The second part of the video provides an instrument-by-instrument breakdown of the *gamelan salendro* piece "Bendrong" that clarifies the musical structure of *gamelan salendro* style.

Further Web-surfing

The Internet's World Wide Web is an ever-shifting source of information about just about anything, including Indonesian music. The sites listed below are only a few of the hundreds that address Indonesian musical topics; criteria for their inclusion in this volume include (1) they are relatively stable and unlikely to disappear soon, (2) they provide information or services that are difficult to find elsewhere, and (3) they are reliable and accurate. Most of the sites listed below include updated lists of other useful links to relevant websites. Not included in the list are the home pages of the myriad American and European gamelan clubs that maintain an Internet presence; these sites are often the source of much useful general information about gamelan music.

http://listserv.dartmouth.edu/Archives/gamelan.html
This archive contains all the messages ever posted to the "Gamelan List," an online mailing list for those interested in Indonesian performing arts, since its inception in 1994.

http://mysite.freeserve.com/gamelan/
Simon Cook's site focuses on his own Sundanese music groups based in London, UK, but it also includes general information about Sundanese music.

http://web.grinnell.edu/courses/mus/gamelans/
Grinnell College hosts this amazing site introducing the heirloom gamelan ensembles of the Kraton Yogyakarta, with excellent and detailed text by Roger Vetter, as well as many beautiful photographs and sound clips.

http://www.arts.cornell.edu/gamelan/aski.htm
This site, hosted by Cornell University, contains quite a few Real Audio files of recordings of gamelan music made at ASKI (now STSI) Surakarta in 1971. These are substantial performances of interesting repertory.

http://www.calarts.edu/~drummond/gendhing.html
Barry Drummond, an expert on Central Javanese music, maintains this page that features an enormous collection of notation for Central Javanese gamelan pieces in PDF format as well as a useful "Introduction to Gamelan" written by Sumarsam and a detailed glossary of Javanese musical terms.

http://www.gamelan.org/
The American Gamelan Institute is a source for purchasing difficult-to-find recordings, musical scores, and publications about Indonesian music. It also includes many valuable links to other relevant websites. One resource maintained by the Institute is a list of gamelan ensembles active in the United States.

http://www.indonesianmusic.com/
The Indonesian Music Shop is an online store featuring a large selection of Indone-

sian traditional and popular music recordings and VCDs ("Video CDs," a format for video in Southeast Asia that is compatible with some American DVD players and computers).

http://www.joglosemar.co.id/index.html
Joglosemar Online, a non-profit foundation that promotes interest in and tourism to Central and Eastern Java, sponsors this compendium of information about Central and Eastern Javanese culture from the cities of Yogyakarta, Surakarta, and Semarang, including music, theater, and ceremonies.

http://www.cirebonart.com
Richard North's website devoted to the arts of Cirebon offers North's essays about Cirebonese culture, many fine photographs, as well as an annotated bibliography and many helpful World Wide Web links relating to Cirebon.

http://www.kulintang.com/
The Palabuniyan Kulintang Ensemble's home page features photographs, video samples, and audio clips.

http://www.marsudirarasa.org/gamelan
Geert Jan van Oldenborgh has made samples of many of the keys and gongs from the nineteenth-century gamelan on display in the Museum Nusantara Delft in the Netherlands; this web page lets visitors hear the samples; in some cases, users can click on pictures of the gamelan instrument keys/pots to hear the sampled sounds.

http://www.monkeyc.org/play.html
Monkey C bill themselves as an "alternative gamelan" from Santa Barbara, California; this part of their website features interactive gamelan instruments that sound quite good and are easy to play.

http://www.research.umbc.edu/efhm/cambodia/index.htm
Noted Cambodian-American scholar Sam-Ang Sam has put together an array of resources to introduce interested Web-surfers to Cambodian culture. The music and dance links are especially rich; the materials include sound clips and virtual instruments that visitors to the site can play with mouse clicks.

http://www.seasite.niu.edu/Indonesian/Budaya_Bangsa/Gamelan/Main_Page/main_page.htm
This site, hosted by the Center for Southeast Asian Studies at Northern Illinois University, provides basic introductions to Central Javanese and Balinese gamelan styles; it includes many RealPlayer sound files to demonstrate tunings, instrument timbres, and styles.

http://www.seasite.niu.edu/thai/music/classical/thaiensemble/pi_phat_ensemble.htm
Hosted by the Center for Southeast Asian Studies at Northern Illinois University, this

site provides a basic introduction to the *pi phat* ensemble through text, pictures, and sound clips.

http://www.wcsmusic.org.uk/

Visitors to this site may download a technologically sophisticated interactive educational module aimed at elementary-school children that introduces Indonesian culture in general and Central Javanese gamelan in particular; the module includes a virtual Javanese gamelan, which allows users to try playing some instruments with strokes on the computer keyboard.

Listening Guide

The compact disc that accompanies this book features recordings drawn from commercial and field recordings that are intended to illustrate and amplify the book's descriptions of musical styles and processes. The listening notes below provide background information about the performers and analytical information about the selections.

There also is a timeline for each track on the CD that precisely locates notable musical features (in a minutes:seconds format) within the recording for listeners who monitor the CD player's timing display. In most cases, the timeline is set up in a sort of outline format; indented subentries do not indicate another successive event, but rather further amplify the notable feature(s) to which they are subordinate.

Track 1

Music culture: Toba Batak
Genre: gondang sabangunan
Piece title: "Gondang Si Monang-Monang"
Performers: Musicians from Parondang, North Sumatra: Ama ni Hallasson Tamba (*tag-aning*); Ama ni Jontiar Manik (*sarune bolon*); Ama ni Rudi Simarmata (*gordang*); Ama ni Saria Situmorang, Hallasson Tamba, Ama ni Ronald Simarmata, and Ompu Ramlan Sihaloho (*ogung*); Ama ni Resta Turnip (*hesek*).
Source: Track 10 from Music of Indonesia Vol. 4: *Music of Nias and North Sumatra* (Smithsonian-Folkways SF 40420).

Philip Yampolsky recorded this *gondang sabangunan* ensemble outdoors in Parondang, North Sumatra, in 1991. "Monang" translates as "to be victorious," suggesting that this piece is associated with warfare; in current practice it might be played for either a secular or ritual function.

The colotomic foundation of the piece is provided by *ogung* (set of four gongs) and *hesek,* on which musicians perform the cycle of ostinato patterns notated in Figure 1.6 (on p. 19). According to Philip Yampolsky's liner notes, this performance of "Gondang Si Monang-Monang" includes six statements of a melody; each statement occupies twenty-four gong ostinato cycles (except for the first statement, in which one of the melodic motifs is repeated a couple of extra times and occupies a total of twenty-six cycles). The melody includes five slightly different melodic motifs, each of which takes two gong cycles to play and each of which is repeated two or four times.

The simultaneous variations of the melody, played on the *sarune* (double-reed wind instrument) and *taganing* (set of tuned drums), are very clear in this performance. The *taganing*'s pitches are not the same as those of the *sarune,* but the *taganing* melody's overall contour—how it rises and falls—tracks the *sarune* melody quite closely. When the *sarune* player sustains a note for a while, the *taganing* player creates a similar effect by rapidly beating on a single drum.

Timeline for "Gondang Si Monang-Monang"

0:00–0:13	introductory phrase
0:00	drums set the pulse for the musicians
0:02	*ogung* and *hesek* join in, performing a fairly fast version of the cyclic ostinato pattern (see Figure 1.6); each repetition of the cycle takes about 1½ seconds.
0:04	*sarune* (double-reed wind instrument) and *taganing* (set of tuned drums) join in
0:13–0:42	first statement of melody
0:42–1:27	second statement of melody
1:27–2:01	third statement of melody
2:01–2:34	fourth statement of melody
2:34–3:08	fifth statement of melody
3:08–3:43	sixth statement of melody
3:43–end	ending phrase

Track 2

Music culture: Cirebon
Genre: Village-style gamelan for *topeng* accompaniment
Piece title: "Gonjing/Sarung Ilang/Gonjing" (for "Rahwana" dance)
Performers: Members of the Panji Asmara troupe (led by *dalang topeng* Sujana Arja)
Source: Field recording made by Michael Ewing on April 9, 1993 at a *mapag Sri* village festival in the village of Cangkring near Cirebon.

This lively music accompanies the final character dance ("Rahwana" or "Klana") of a Cirebonese village-style *topeng* (masked) dance performance. This particular performance was commissioned by the village of Cangkring for *mapag Sri* (a village ceremony that welcomes the rice goddess as the rice crop matures). The *dalang topeng* is the late

Sujana Arja, who came from a prominent family of *dalang topeng* from the village of Slangit (Sujana Arja's father was a *dalang topeng*, as are several of his siblings; he in turn taught one son and other members of his extended family the art of *topeng*). Sujana Arja's troupe was called Panji Asmara and included musicians whose ancestors played music for Sujana Arja's forebears. The gamelan that accompanies him is tuned to a *slendro*-like tuning system that Cirebonese musicians call *prawa* (*topeng* may also be accompanied with gamelan in the *pelog* tuning system).

"Rahwana" is the last dance in the sequence of five character dances that Sujana Arja typically performed for a complete *topeng* performance. It often is the shortest dance as well. This performance is quite short at thirteen minutes; although it includes all four of the main sections of a *topeng* dance (from slowest to fastest: *dodoan, tengahan, kering,* and *deder*), the first two sections are quite short.

The primary piece for accompanying Rahwana, called "Gonjing," is a very short and simple melody. The colotomic form of the version of "Gonjing" that is played by the Panji Asmara musicians from the village of Slangit is notated in Figure 3.13 on p. 65; the melody is notated below using Sundanese cipher notation:

$$1 \; (2) \; 3 \; 4 \; 3 \; 4 \; 1 \; (2)$$

Each of the four sections of the Rahwana accompaniment is based on this same basic melody; the melody is transformed in each section, however, to portray a significantly different mood and provide a different colotomic form. The *dodoan* section of the dance, for example, is accompanied by a very stretched out version of the piece "Gonjing." The musicians insert an additional *pancer* and reiterate each short phrase to create a much longer and more convoluted tune; each note in the tune is allowed four beats for elaboration to further expand the piece. The character of this new melody is further altered by moving the gong stroke to the midpoint of the piece (on pitch 4):

$$1 \; 2 \; 1 \; 5 \; 1 \; 5 \; 1 \; 2 \; 1 \; 2 \; 1 \; 5 \; 1 \; 5 \; 1 \; (4) \; 1 \; 4 \; 1 \; 3 \; 1 \; 3 \; 1 \; 4 \; 1 \; 1 \; 1 \; 5 \; 1 \; 5 \; 1 \; (2)$$

In this performance, the *dodoan* version of "Gonjing" is played twice.

For the *tengahan* section, the piece is made exactly half as long by halving the number of beats devoted to each of the notes in the *dodoan* section's expanded melody. The musicians give this version of the tune a unique character by playing a tuneful elaboration in unison for much of the gong phrase. This *tengahan* version includes only one gong stroke per cycle. In this version, this section is played only twice before moving on to the *kering* section via a special transition phrase.

The *kering* section's accompaniment, too, is derived from the original "Gonjing" melody. This time the musicians take four beats to elaborate each of the melody notes. They typically call this version of the piece another name—"Sarung Ilang"—however. This version includes ten iterations of "Sarung Ilang." The final section of the dance is accompanied by "Gonjing" played without too much elaboration; one of the *saron* players plays the tune over and over again, while the other instrumentalists provide changing variations. This is the longest section of the dance; the musicians repeat "Gonjing" sixty-four times, with seemingly infinite variations in tempo, dynamics, and elaborations.

The drums and *kecrek* play the most dramatic variations because they are following the dancer's movements, providing appropriate sonic accents for the dancer's gestures. The Rahwana dance involves dramatic and sudden changes in energy flow, which help portray the Rahwana character's excessiveness; the loud drumming contributes enormously to the success of the portrayal.

A careful listener will be able to hear subtle differences in the drum patterns as the drummer accentuates the dancer's different choreographic patterns. The performance opens with a brief introduction to "Gonjing" before slowing down to the *dodoan* accompaniment; after the dance is over, the musicians seamlessly transition to an ending piece ("Jiro") to let the audience know that the performance has ended.

Timeline for "Gonjing"

0:00–0:07	*buka* (introductory phrase played by one of the *saron* players)
0:07–0:26	"Gonjing" and transition to *dodoan*
0:26–2:25	"Gonjing" for *dodoan* section
0:26–1:05	first gong phrase
1:05–1:34	second gong phrase
1:34–2:01	first gong phrase
2:01–2:25	second gong phrase
2:25–3:32	"Gonjing" for *tengahan* section
2:25–2:58	gong phrase
2:41	tuneful elaboration of the main melody begins
2:58–3:19	gong phrase
3:10	dramatic tempo increase to signal transition to "Sarung Ilang"
3:19–3:32	transition to "Sarung Ilang"
3:32–5:42	"Sarung Ilang" (10 iterations) for *kering* section
3:32–3:36	short gong phrase
3:36–3:49	long gong phrase
5:33–5:42	"Sarung Ilang" cycle, transition to the *deder* version of "Gonjing"
5:38	drum plays signal; other instrumentalists quickly follow suit
5:42–12:46	"Gonjing" for *deder* section (64 iterations)
5:42–5:48	"Gonjing" (two gong phrases)
5:42–5:43	first gong phrase
5:43–5:48	second gong phrase
12:11–12:21	slow down to *rangkep* (in which instrumentalists play double patterns)
12:21–12:32	*rangkep* cycle
12:32–12:46	ending phrase with transition to Jiro
12:46–13:07	"Jiro" (ending piece)

Track 3

Music culture: Central Java; Sundanese
Piece title: Pelog and *slendro* (*salendro*) scales

The first excerpt is the seven pitches of a *pelog* scale, played from low to high (on one of the *pelog demung* from Kyahi Udan Mas, a Central Javanese *gamelan* owned by the University of California at Berkeley). The second excerpt of the track is the five pitches of a *slendro* scale, played from low to high (on one of the *saron* from the *gamelan salendro* set owned by the author).

0:00	*pelog*
0:00	Javanese 1/Sundanese 5
0:01	Javanese 2/Sundanese 4
0:03	Javanese 3/Sundanese 3
0.05	Javanese 4/Sundanese 3–
0:06	Javanese 5/Sundanese 2
0:08	Javanese 6/Sundanese 1
0:10	Javanese 7/Sundanese 5+
0:15	*slendro (salendro)*
0.15	Javanese 1/Sundanese 5
0:17	Javanese 2/Sundanese 4
0.20	Javanese 3/Sundanese 3
0:22	Javanese 5/Sundanese 2
0.25	Javanese 6/Sundanese 1
0:27	Javanese 1/Sundanese 5

Track 4

Music culture: Central Java
Genre: Court-style gamelan
Piece title: Ladrang "Pangkur" *pelog barang*
Performers: Saptobudoyo Group from Surakarta, Indonesia, under the direction of Saptono (the musicians' formal titles and names are provided in parentheses when appropriate): Saptono (K. R. T. Saptodipuro, *kendhang*); Teguh (R. T. Widododipuro, *gender*); Supanggah (K. R. T. Prof. Dr. S. Kar., *rebab*); Muryono (*slenthem*); Dalimin (M. Ng. Purwopangrawit, *bonang barung*); Sagimin (M. Ng. Haropangrawit, *bonang panerus*); Karno (M. Ng. Karnopangrawit, *saron demung*); Marsono (Drs. Marsono M. S. (*saron barung*); Kamso (*saron panerus*); Wardi (M. Ng. Wardipangrawit, *kenong*); M. Ng. Santopangrawit (*gong*); Tarnopangrawit (R. T. Mloyodipuro, *suling*); Suwito (M. Ng. Suwitodiprojo, *gambang*); Sigit (Sigit S. Kar., *siter*); Mulyani (Nyi Lurah Cendanilaras, *pesindhen*)
Source: Recording session conducted by Alex Dea in Surakarta, Indonesia, November 16, 2003.

Ethnomusicologist/composer Alex Dea arranged to have the distinguished musician Saptono convene his group of gamelan musicians to record this rendition of *ladrang*

"Pangkur" especially for this book. The ensemble includes a who's who of musicians in Surakarta, many of whom are associated with the two *kraton* (palaces) in Surakarta, the radio station (RRI Surakarta), the government-sponsored arts academy (STSI Surakarta), or the troupes of famous *dhalang* (puppeteers).

They present a version of "Pangkur" in the *pelog* tuning system, in *pathet barang* ("Pankgur" also is often performed in *slendro pathet manyura* or *slendro pathet sanga*). In this performance, the musicians treat "Pangkur" in a variety of ways to illustrate some of the sonic variety that different musical treatments bring to a single piece. The excerpt begins with a *buka* (introductory phrase) played on the *rebab* (two-stringed fiddle); this phrase is specifically associated with "Pangkur." The drummer and the *gender* player join in toward the end of the introductory phrase, reinforcing for the other musicians the exact moment of their first entrance and the first gong stroke.

The rendition technically begins in rhythmic treatment called *irama lancar* (also referred to as *irama I*), in which the *balungan* part moves fairly quickly; however, the drummer immediately cues the musicians to slow down to *irama dados* (*irama II*). The *balungan* parts move somewhat more slowly in *irama II* and become much quieter, creating sonic space for the soft-style instrumental parts to come through in the texture. By the time the first *kempul* stroke occurs, the musicians have settled into *irama II* and the *pesindhen* (female vocal soloist) begins to sing. She is joined by the *gerong* (male chorus) in the second iteration of "Pangkur." The *gerong* sing a unison melody, using a standard set of words that can be used for any *ladrang* in *irama II*. The *pesindhen* sings the same words, but with her own free-flowing melody and rhythm. Like many Javanese song texts, this verse is a sort of riddle in which the first two lines give clues to words and the second two lines play with the words suggested by the first two lines to create a moral. (See Chapter 4 for an explanation and translation of the first verse.) The second verse follows a similar pattern: The first two lines describe the wife of a king, and the second two lines warn that playing around with women has its dangers.

Parabe sang smarabangun
sepat domba kali Oya
aja dolan lan wong priya
geremeh nora prasaja

Garwa Sang Sindura prabu
wicara mawa karana
aja dolan lan wanita
tan nyata asring katarka

At the end of the third *irama II* phrase, the drummer speeds up slightly and then turns from the set of two drums (*kendhang kalih*) he has been playing up to this point and switches to a medium-sized drum called *ciblon*, which signals the musicians to switch to the lively *kebar* style of playing. In *kebar*, many of the soft-style instruments (such as *rebab* and *suling*) drop out completely, the *kendhang* player provides a much more intricate part, the *kempul* player plays a slightly more elaborate pattern than usual, and the *gerong* (male chorus) sings spirited *alok* (wordless vocalizations), while the *pesind-*

hen sings her own florid melody. The *balungan*, played on instruments in the *saron* and *demung* section, is quite loud and strident and moves at a fairly brisk clip, and the *bonang barung* and *bonang panerus* players perform fancy interlocking (*imbal*) figurations.

After a few repetitions of the *kebar* treatment, the drummer signals a transition back to *irama II*. The end of *kebar* doesn't occur until after the gong stroke, however. Once back in *irama II*, the drummer continues to slow down, which lets the musicians know that they won't linger in *irama II*, but will slow down again into *irama wilet* (or *irama III*), a rhythmic treatment in which approximately twice as much time elapses between each *balungan* note as in *irama II*, providing time for the elaborating instrumentalists to play longer patterns.

It becomes quite difficult for neophyte listeners to follow the *balungan*, in part because the *balungan* actually changes, and in part because it is obscured by the increasingly florid and prominent melodic parts played on the *rebab*, *suling*, and other elaborating instruments, as well as from the *gerong*'s and *pesindhen*'s vocal lines. The distinctive timbres of the colotomic instruments (*gong, kempul, kenong,* and *kethuk*), however, easily cut through the dense texture to provide a clearly audible framework for the music (the timings for the strokes of each colotomic instrument are provided in the timeline below). The musicians play one complete cycle of "Pangkur" in *irama III*; at the appropriate moment during the second cycle of *irama III*, the drummer signals a transition to yet another rhythmic treatment: *irama rangkep*. In *irama rangkep*, the balungan part moves still more slowly (although not quite half its *irama III* speed). The extra time gives the elaborating instrumentalists time to play extremely rapid figurations; they fit twice as many notes into the time between *balungan* notes as they did in *irama III*. The result is a kind of controlled freneticism which contrasts the stately, ponderous movement of the *balungan* and the colotomic form with dizzyingly rapid elaborating figurations.

Just before the end of the cycle, the drummer signals that the musicians should transition back to *irama III* at the gong stroke. *Irama III* sounds almost simple after the complexities of *irama rangkep*; at the end of a full cycle of *irama III*, the drummer signals the musicians to return to the *kebar* treatment after the upcoming gong stroke. The quick-moving *balungan* melody once again emerges from the texture, lending a sense of return and familiarity leading to some kind of closure.

After a few more cycles of *kebar*, the drummer speeds up and changes back to using the *kendhang kalih* (set of two drums) to direct a cycle of a quick *irama I*. At the appropriate moment, he gives the signal to end, to which the musicians respond by beginning a gradual slowing down, delaying their inexorable arrival at the final *gong* stroke. The *gong* player creates one last moment of tension by delaying his final stroke for a moment or two, leaving the listeners hanging, waiting for that final note. When he finally plays the ending *gong* stroke, the other musicians quickly follow with their last note, and the release of built-up tension and the sense of closure are quite satisfying.

This rendition of "Pangkur" systematically explores the various rhythmic expansion techniques. The musicians stretched the time of each "Pangkur" cycle from about twenty-seven seconds in *kebar* to almost one minute in *irama II*, to two minutes in *irama III*, to over two and a half minutes in *irama rangkep*.

Timeline for "Pangkur"

0:00–0:16	*buka* (introductory phrase)
0:00	*rebab* begins "Pangkur"-specific *buka* melody
0:10	drum begins the cue that reminds the musicians to play the parts appropriate for *ladrang*
0:12	*gender* joins in before the gong stroke
0:16–2:46	"Pangkur" in *irama II* (four cycles)
0:16–1:04	first gong phrase in *irama II*
1:04–2:00	second gong phrase in *irama II*; *gerong* (and *pesindhen*) sing the *salisir* verse that begins "Parabe sang" (see Chapter 4)
2:00–2:46	third gong phrase, which begins in *irama II* but ends in *kebar*
2:46–4:34	"Pangkur" in *kebar* (four cycles), in which *gerong* sings *alok* (stylized vocalizations), *kendhang* player performs lively drum patterns on *ciblon* (medium-sized drum), *bonang barung* and *bonang panerus* perform interlocking figurations (*imbal*), and *kempul* player adds extra strokes
2:46–3:15	first *kebar* phrase
3:15–3:42	second *kebar* phrase
3:42–4:09	third *kebar* phrase
4:09–4:34	fourth *kebar* phrase
4:34–5:25	gong phrase that begins in *kebar*, transitions through *irama II* to end in *irama III*
5:25 –11:58	three gong phrases in *irama III* and *irama rangkep*
5:25–7:23	phrase in *irama III*
5:25–5:52	first *kenong* phrase
5:30	*kethuk* stroke
5:37	*wela*
5:44	*kethuk* stroke
5:52	*kenong* stroke
5:52–6:21	second *kenong* phrase
5:59	*kethuk* stroke
6:06	*kempul* stroke
6:14	*kethuk* stroke
6:21	*kenong* stroke
6:21–6:52	third *kenong* phrase
6:29	*kethuk* stroke
6:37	*kempul* stroke
6:44	*kethuk* stroke
6:52	*kenong* stroke
6:52–7:23	fourth *kenong* phrase
6:59	*kethuk* stroke
7:07	*kempul* stroke
7:14	*kethuk* stroke
7:23	*kenong*/gong strokes

7:23–10:06	gong phrase that begins in *irama III* and transitions to *irama rangkep*
7:45	drummer signals that musicians should slow down to *irama rangkep*
7:50	musicians playing elaborating instruments double the density of their patterns for *irama rangkep*
10:02	drummer confirms the end of *rangkep* just before the *gong* stroke with a signal
10:06–11:58	another gong phrase in *irama III*
11:47	drummer speeds up to indicate a change in rhythm after the *gong* stroke
11:52	drummer signals musicians that the rhythm change will be to *kebar*
11:58–13:34	four more phrases in irama kebar
11:58–12:23	first *kebar* phrase
12:23–12:48	second *kebar* phrase
12:48–13:13	third *kebar* phrase
13:13–13:34	fourth *kebar* phrase
13:25	drummer speeds up to signal a change to *irama I* after the gong stroke
13:30	drummer changes to *kendhang kalih* (set of two drums) to confirm change to *irama I*
13:34–14:05	phrase in *irama I*, slows down to end (*suwuk*)
13:42	drummer begins signal to end; musicians slow down
14:02	gong player delays the last gong stroke
14:03	other musicians play their final note slightly after the final gong stroke

Track 5

Music culture: Bali
Genre: gamelan beleganjur
Piece title: Music for *memukur* procession
Performers: Sekehe Gong Werdhi Suara of Banjar Kedaton, Kesiman, Bali
Source: field recording made by Michael B. Bakan in 1995 in Denpasar, Bali (track 18 from the CD accompanying his book, *Music of Death and New Creation: Experiences in the World of Balinese Gamelan Beleganjur* [1999]).

In this excerpt, a *gamelan beleganjur* is marching in a *memukur* procession. *Memukur* is the final rite of purification for the dead in Bali. The climax of the week-long ritual involves a procession to the sea, where an effigy representative of the soul of the deceased is thrown into the water; a *gamelan angklung* leads the procession, and a *gamelan beleganjur* brings up the rear (Bakan 1999: 75–77).

In the recording, we hear the *gamelan beleganjur* as it passes us by on the road. The excerpt begins with the ensemble approaching from the distance. Each of the different groups of musical instruments is clearly audible as they pass by in sequence.

Timeline for music for memukur procession

0:00	even in the distance, the colotomic instruments and the main melody are evident
0:30	the drums signal the *cengceng* (cymbal) players to be silent
0:43	the *reyong* players' elaborations are quite clear as they draw near and pass by
0:54	the *cengceng* players join in with their own interlocking pattern (see Figures 4.14 and 4.15 on p. 94)
1:32	the drums signal an intensification in the *cengceng* part, followed by another rest
1:58	the *cengceng* players join in again, this time with a start–stop elaboration pattern
2:49	the *gamelan beleganjur* fades out as it continues toward the sea
3:17	the *cengceng* players' next pattern change is barely audible

Track 6

Music culture: Bali
Genre: Gong kebyar
Piece title: Jaya Semara
Composer: I Wayan Beratha (b. 1924)
Performers: Gamelan Sekar Jaya (Wayne Vitale, director)
Source: Balinese Music in America (track 1) produced by Gamelan Sekar Jaya, 6485 Conlon Avenue, El Cerrito, CA 94530 (1995).

I Wayan Beratha is a prominent Balinese composer and one of the pioneers of the *gong kebyar* style. According to ethnomusicologist Michael Tenzer, Beratha composed "Jaya Semara" in 1964, and it is loosely based on an older piece called "Kapi Raja"; it remains a fixture of *gong kebyar* repertory into the present (Tenzer 2000: 326). Here it is performed by Gamelan Sekar Jaya, a California-based group (founded by Michael Tenzer, Rachel Cooper, and I Wayan Suweca in the 1970s and currently directed by Wayne Vitale) that focuses on studying and promoting Balinese music in the United States.

Like many *gong kebyar* pieces, "Jaya Semara" follows a three-section formal outline. The first section (*kawitan*, also called *kebyar* or *gineman* in the context of *gong kebyar*) serves as an introduction; it is a patchwork quilt of short snippets of musical ideas and textures. The second section (*pengawak*) provides the main body of the composition— a relatively slow, cyclical musical structure repeated a number of times with variations. The third section (*pengecet*) is a faster concluding section.

The introductory (*kawitan*) section of "Jaya Semara" features some of the *gong kebyar*'s instrumental sections playing alone, and thus provides an excellent opportunity to hear what the ensemble's instrumental resources sound like in isolation. In the second section (*pengawak*) the *kempli*'s timekeeping beat, as well as a colotomic framework, are quite clear.

In the second section (*pengawak*), the *calung* play a simple melody (notated below using Western solfège syllables) that is easily heard within the texture of the rest of the ensemble; the relationship of the strokes on the *gong*, *kempur*, and *kemong* that outline the colotomic form of the piece to the *calung* melody is very straightforward:

calung (pokok melody)	mi	do	so	fa	mi	do	so	fa
kemong				m				
kempur		p				p		
gong								G

In this main section, the *kempli* beat and strokes of the *gong*, *kempur*, and *kemong* (outlining colotomic form) are quite clear. A *suling* (bamboo flute) is added to the texture. Each cycle of the *pengawak* section is about three seconds long. The cycles are grouped into larger sections (each six cycles long) that are shaped by dynamics and varying instrumentation and end with an *angsel* (a special variation that begins with an increase in the dynamic level and involves leaving some notes out of the melody).

In the concluding section (*pengecet*), the tempo seems to increase wildly; the *kempli* drops out, and there is no longer a regular colotomic form underlying the figurations. The ending gesture involves the *gangsa* players executing a dramatic back-and-forth glissando on their instruments, in which they swipe their mallets rapidly across the keys to create a loud, chaotic cluster of tones that slowly fades out.

Michael Tenzer covers "Jaya Semara" in great detail in his book *Gamelan Gong Kebyar: The Art of Twentieth-Century Balinese Music* (2000), including excellent transcriptions (in Western staff notation; pp. 327–31) and analysis (scattered throughout Chapter Eight).

Timeline for "Jaya Semara"

0:00–2:35	introductory section (*kawitan/kebyar/gineman*)
0:00	"Jaya Semara" begins with dramatic opening from the entire ensemble
0:07	*reyong* "solo" (four musicians playing interlocking *kotekan* parts)
0:17	*kendang* "solo" (two drummers playing interlocking parts)
0:24	entire ensemble
0:33	*reyong*
0:53	entire ensemble
0:58	*gangsa* (*gangsa* section playing interlocking *kotekan* parts)
1:13	*reyong*
1:38	*kendang* (drums), *cengceng*, *kempur*, gong
1:53	*ugal* (lead *gangsa*) player cues the entire ensemble
1:58	*calung* and *jegogan* (low-pitched, slow moving *gangsa*-family instruments) followed by the rest of the ensemble

2:11	extended *kendang* "solo" (two drummers playing interlocking parts) leading into the main section
2:35–4:41	main section (*pengawak*)
2:35–2:56	the first six-cycle section ending with an *angsel*
2:35–2:45	three repetitions of the cycle at a relatively quiet dynamic level
2:45	drum signal lasting one cycle cues the musicians that they will begin an *angsel*
2:49	*angsel* begins and occupies two cycles; in the first cycle, the ensemble section plays louder
2:53	the dramatic moment of the *angsel* when most of the instruments drop out for a moment, leaving the *kempli* and the colotomic instruments playing alone until the end of the cycle
2:56–3:17	after the *angsel*, another six-cycle section begins; at its beginning, the *gangsa* section's interlocking parts are emphasized
3:06	drums cue another *angsel*
3:17–3:37	after the *angsel*, another six-cycle section begins; at its beginning, the *reyong* section's interlocking parts are emphasized
3:27	drums cue another *angsel*
3:37–3:58	after the *angsel*, another six-cycle section begins; at its beginning, the *gangsa* section's interlocking parts are emphasized
3:48	drums cue another *angsel*
3:58–4:20	after the *angsel*, another six-cycle section begins; at its beginning, the *reyong* section's interlocking parts are emphasized
4:09	drums cue another *angsel*
4:20–4:41	after the *angsel*, the *reyong* and *gangsa* interlocking parts are equally prominent
4:30	drums cue another *angsel*, which ends with a transition to the concluding section (*pengecet*)
4:41–5:27	concluding section (*pengecet*)

Track 7

Music culture: Sundanese
Genre: gamelan salendro to accompany *wayang golek*
Piece title: "Sinyur"
Performers: LS Giri Harja III (Asep Sunandar Sunarya, *dalang* and director)
Source: Wayang Golek: The Sound and Celebration of Sundanese Puppet Theater, CD 4, tracks 3–4, recorded and annotated by Andrew Weintraub, released by Multicultural Media (2001).

In this excerpt from a Sundanese *wayang golek* performance, *dalang* Asep Sunandar Sunarya first makes one of his puppets perform dance. He uses his *campala* (a wooden knocker held in his right hand and knocked against the wooden chest in which he keeps his puppets) to signal the *gamelan* to start.

Even without seeing the puppet, a *wayang* fan would know what kind of character was dancing from the sound of the drum patterns that accompany the dance—in this case, the drumming clearly identifies Aradea as a *satria* (knight) character; the *gamelan*'s rhythmic treatment (*sawilet*—one *wilet*) is appropriate for this type of character as well. The singers further enliven the dance accompaniment music by singing short *sisindiran* verses. After the dance is over, the *dalang* plants the puppet firmly into the banana log stage so that the character can undertake a meditation. The *dalang* uses this break in the action to take a cigarette break of his own. He signals the *gamelan* to slow down to *opat wilet* (four *wilet*) so that the singers (two *pasinden* and a *wiraswara*) can sing an extended musical interlude. In four *wilet*, the *pasinden* have plenty of musical space to show off their virtuosity; they also take the opportunity to insert into their sung texts the names of prominent members of the audience as well as the names of patrons who sent notes, monetary gifts, or requests to the singers (such names are usually prefixed with the honorific title "Bapa," roughly equivalent to "Mr."). When the *dalang* is ready to resume the dramatic action, he again signals the gamelan to speed up to *dua wilet* (two *wilet*) and end. The gamelan plays in the *salendro* tuning system while the singers' melodies are in *sorog*.

After the musical interlude is over, and before beginning with the narration and subsequent action, the *dalang* sings a *kakawen* (mood song) to set the scene. There is a whole repertory of stock *kakawen* from which the *dalang* can choose to create the appropriate mood; in this case, "Nurcahaya" ("A Ray of Brilliance") suggests that Aradea's meditation is indeed powerful. In the timeline for this piece, below the timing for each gong cycle are the words each singer performs during that cycle, along with a translation. The translations were first published in *Jabang tutuka/The Birth of Gatotkaca: A Sundanese Wayang Golek Purwa Performance from West Java Performed by Asep Sunandar Sunarya and Giri Harja III* (1998: 54–5, 191–4), and are reprinted here with permission from Lontar Press and Andrew N. Weintraub.

Timeline for "Sinyur"

0:00	*campala* cue from *dalang*, followed by *pangkat* (played on *saron*)
0:05–0:17	cycle 1 of "Sinyur" in one *wilet*

Aradea: Ama. Mudah-mudahan we putra tatapa teh aya
dinakakiatan, Ama . . .
I pray and hope that my meditation will be strong . . .

0:17–0:26	cycle 2 of "Sinyur" in one *wilet*
0:26–0:40	cycle 3 of "Sinyur" in one *wilet*; the musicians add interlocking vocalizations called *senggak* to enhance the dance's liveliness

wiraswara: Belut sisit saba darat
A scaly eel arrives on shore
Kapiraray siang wengi
appearing both day and night

0:40–0:54	cycle 4 of "Sinyur" in one *wilet*; dynamic dance drumming for Aradea's dance begins

pasinden 1: Sapanjang urang gumelar
As long as we live
Ulah kendat nya ihtiar
do not give up hope

0:54–1:02	cycle 5 of "Sinyur" in one *wilet*

Elmu tungtut dunya siar
strive for knowledge to achieve wealth
Nu perlu kudu disinglar
What must be avoided—

1:02–1:11	cycle 6 of "Sinyur" in one *wilet*

Ka batur ulah takabur
to others do not be rude
Kalakuan nu teu jujur
That is not right

1:11–1:18	cycle 7 of "Sinyur" in one *wilet*

Hirup anu kudu akur
Our lives must be controlled
Titisan urang sakujur
our skills fortified

1:18–1:26	cycle 8 of "Sinyur" in one *wilet*

wiraswara: Aya manuk dina haur
A bird on a bamboo
Eunteup dina luhur pager
perched atop a fence

1:26–1:34	cycle 9 of "Sinyur" in one *wilet*

Hirup anu jadi paur
a life full of worries
Laku lampah nu teu bener
behavior that is not right

1:34–1:42	cycle 10 of "Sinyur" in one *wilet*

pasinden 2: Ka Bojong ka Purwakarta
To Bojong, to Purwakarta
Neangan jalan ka desa
looking for a village road

1:42–1:51   cycle 11 of "Sinyur" in one *wilet*

Bati bengong ka panutan
Startled by his girlfriend
Neangan pujaan rasa
looking to calm his heart

1:51–1:59   cycle 12 of "Sinyur" in one *wilet*

Keur ngabela rumah tangga
To protect one's household
Milih rabi jeung utama
find the right person

1:59–2:06   cycle 13 of "Sinyur" in one *wilet*

Mungguhing jalmi utami
because for the best person
Sagala kedah utama
everything must be right

2:06–2:12   cycle 14 of "Sinyur" in one *wilet*

wiraswara: Melak saga palintangan
Plant the saga bush as a sign
Babalean pangalusna
of the best place to sleep

2:12–2:21   cycle 15 of "Sinyur" in one *wilet*

Sanaos dikantun ngaran
Although you've gone home
Kasaean moal musnah
your goodness is not forgotten

2:21–2:31   cycle 16 of "Sinyur" in one *wilet*

pasinden 1: Nayaga anu nyarengan
Musicians playing together

2:31–2:39   cycle 17 of "Sinyur" in one *wilet*

Sadaya ngaturkeun lagu
all presenting musical pieces

2:39–2:49   cycle 18 of "Sinyur" in one *wilet*; dance ends, the tempo slows, and the volume drops in preparation for the *dalang*'s narration

Nyanggakeun tambih lumayan
to the best of their ability
Ka sadaya kaum dangu
for all the spectators

2:49–3:02   cycle 19 of "Sinyur" in one *wilet*

narration: Raden Aradea aniprek tatapa sareng puasa
Prince Aradea sits in meditation and fasts

3:02–3:15   cycle 20 of "Sinyur" in one *wilet*

nyaeta nampi pancen ti guruna
as fulfillment of his vow to his guru
Watek wantos satria gentur tapana
The diligent knight meditates

3:15–3:34   cycle 21 in one *wilet* (slowing down to four *wilet*)
  3:23   signal to slow down and transition to four *wilet*

wiraswara: Ka Bojong ka Purwakarta
To Bojong, to Purwakarta
Neangan jalan ka desa
looking for a village road
Bati bengong ka pandita
startled by the priest
Neangan pujaan rasa
looking to calm his heart

3:34–4:13   cycle 1 of "Sinyur" in four *wilet*

pasinden 1: Melak saga, dunungan, palintangan
Plant a saga bush as a sign
Lah . . . melak saga palintangan
Yes, plant the saga as a sign
Babalean, Pa Jajang, pangalusna
of the very best place to sleep

4:13–4:55   cycle 2 of "Sinyur" in four *wilet*

> Sanaos mah, Pa Anton, dikantun mulang
> *Although Mr Anton may have gone home*
> Lah . . . kasaean moal musnah
> *his goodness will not be forgotten*
> Kasaean moal musnah
> *No, his goodness will not be forgotten*

4:55–5:39   cycle 3 of "Sinyur" in four *wilet*

> Salajeng ka Sukapakis, Kapinis ka Sindanglaya
> *Salajeng to Sukapakis, Kapinis and to Sindanglaya*
> Saleuheung lamun sapikir, kumaha lamun sulaya, A Dedi
> *it is good to be of one mind. What about the promises you made,*
>   *Dedi?*
> Kumaha lamun sulaya
> *What about your broken promises?*

5:39–6:22   cycle 4 of "Sinyur" in four *wilet*

> Buntiris paranjang leutik, ngala hurang dikorangan
> *Legumes, both long and small, take the shrimp to the pond*
> Abong titis tulis diri tunggara abdi sorangan, tunggara A Dedi,
>   abdi sorangan
> *My fate is to suffer, Dedi, for I am all alone*

6:22–7:05   cycle 5 of "Sinyur" in four *wilet*

> **pasinden 2**: Seungit hurang tunggal seni manis rupa, Bapa Heru
>   Suparta
> *Shrimp flavor like the sweetness of the arts, Mr Heru Suparta*
> Manis rupa ranjang rupa
> *Like the sweetness of sleep*
> Sok hoyong mah sok hoyong tacan laksana, teu weleh mah
> *Full of desire, an unrequited love*
> Ari teu weleh tacan laksana
> *always unrequited*

7:05–7:49   cycle 6 of "Sinyur" in four *wilet*

> Srimanganti bumi asih, Bapa Sutiono
> *The entrance to this beloved place, Mr Sutiono*
> Tepangan para dina latar
> *Is found in the backyard*

Sangkan Gusti welas asih, dadasarna kedah sabar
So that God will love us, we must be patient
Dadasarna kedah sabar
we must be patient

7:49–8:34   cycle 7 of "Sinyur" in four *wilet*

Sangkan ku sisi laun
Take things slowly
Ku pamugi gamelan kedah
Hopefully the gamelan will follow
Ulah tanggung unggal taun geuning teundeun neang jaman
Don't suffer alone each year, face the passing of time with a
     loving attitude
Bapa Endang Budi Asih
Mr Endang Budi Asih
Jadi teundeun neang jaman
Face the passing of time

8:34–9:20   cycle 8 of "Sinyur" in four *wilet*

Da pamadeg lampah jalan
Of one mind and one pathway
Iwal ti bangsa sorangan
Except among one's own people
Cinta kana kabudayaan sami cinta kabangsaan, Bapa Sunaryo
Love your culture and your people, Mr Sunaryo
Sami cinta kabangsaan
Yes, love your people

9:17   cue from *dalang's campala* just before the *goong* stroke to signal *wilet*
            change and end
9:19   *campala* and drums lead the *gamelan* from four *wilet* to two *wilet*
9:20–9:40   penultimate gong phrase; gamelan speeds up to transition from four
            wilet to two *wilet*
9:40–9:55   final *goong* phrase in two *wilet*
9:51   *campala* and drum signal to end at the next *goong* stroke
9:55   Kakawen Pondok "Nurcahaya," *laras sorog/salendro*

dalang: Nur cahaya sesekarning wang cahaya gilang gumilan
   A ray of light, bright and brilliant
   Cahaya gilang gumilang, gumilang. Lawan . . .
   Radiance bright and brilliant and . . .

Track 8

Music culture: Sundanese
Genre: Degung
Piece title: "Ujung Laut/Sinyur"
Performers: Pusaka Sunda (Burhan Sukarma, director; Undang Sumarna, *gendang*)
Source: Lolongkrang (track 7) produced by Sakti Productions (1994).

Burhan Sukarma's *suling* style for *tembang Sunda, kacapi-suling,* and *degung* set the standard for Sundanese *suling* playing in the 1970s and 1980s; he became particularly famous for his soaring and soulful improvisations. Since moving to the United States in the late 1980s, Burhan has led a group of American musicians called Pusaka Sunda ("Sundanese heirloom") in playing both traditional pieces and Burhan's own new compositions (the author is among those Americans performing in Pusaka Sunda).

"Ujung Laut" is a *lagu klasik* piece from the early days of *degung* at the beginning of the twentieth century; its composition is often attributed to *degung* pioneer Idi. Its phrase structure and style are discussed in some detail in Chapter 6. The various bronze instruments play the melody together, each with its own particular idiom, to create a texture of simultaneous variations. The *suling* player provides a particularly florid version of the melody. The drumming style is austere and simple, featuring only a few simple strokes performed with a padded stick.

In current *degung* practice it is common to follow a *lagu klasik* piece with a *panambih*—an "extra" song. In this selection, the second piece is "Sinyur." In theory, it is the same "Sinyur" as that discussed in Chapter 5; its sound, however, is quite different because it is performed in the *degung* tuning instead of in *salendro*. Pusaka Sunda's rendition is instrumental, but the *panambih* also might feature a solo singer or a group of singers. In *panambih* style, most of the instruments improvise parts based on the pillar pitches of "Sinyur"; this rendition features the addition of fast interlocking *saron* parts to fill out the texture.

Timeline for "Ujung Laut/Sinyur"

0:00	*pangkat* (played on the *bonang*)
0:11–2:08	first iteration of "Ujung Laut"
0:11–0:40	phrase 1
0:40–1:15	phrase 2
1:15–2:08	phrase 3
2:08–4:02	second iteration of "Ujung Laut"
2:08–2:37	phrase 1
2:37–3:10	phrase 2
3:10–4:02	phrase 3
4:02–4:33	third (incomplete) iteration including Phrase 1 only
4:23	drummer switches to *tepak melem* (restrained hand drumming) and signals a transition to "Sinyur"
4:33–5:19	first complete iteration of "Sinyur"

4:33–4:56	first gong phrase of "Sinyur"
4:56–5:19	second gong phrase of "Sinyur"
5:19–7:29	three more iterations of "Sinyur" (for a total of four)
7:16	drum signal to end

Track 9

Music culture: Sundanese
Genre: Ketuk tilu
Piece title: "Sinur"
Performers: Candra Puspita: Samin (*wiraswara* [male singer] and director); Arliani (*juru kawih* [female singer]); Lili Suparli (*rebab*); Tosin Muchtar (*gendang*); Dedy S. Hadianda (*goong* and *ketuk*).
Source: Celempungan and Ketuk Tilu: Candra Puspita, produced by Florence Bodo and Dedy S. Hadianda (n.d.).

This example, "Sinur" (n.b. not to be confused with "Sinyur" in tracks 7 and 8), was performed for a recording session by some well-known Bandung musicians who are more famous for their work in other genres. The late Samin was renowned as *wiraswara* (male singer) for all sorts of genres and as a repository of knowledge about obscure musical genres; the late Tosin Muchtar's tasteful *gendang* playing can be heard on literally hundreds of commercial recordings; Lili Suparli and Arliani are staff musicians for the Bandung branch of the government-sponsored college-level school of performing arts (Sekolah Tinggi Seni Indonesia [STSI]). Samin and Tosin were once associated with the Bandung branch of the Indonesian national radio station, Radio Republik Indonesia (RRI), where they revived some of the *ketuk tilu* repertory for broadcast, learning the ins and outs of the pieces from older musicians then on the staff. Although this performance was not made for dance accompaniment, the music was played as if there were dancers present.

A *ketuk tilu* ensemble provides all four layers of a *gamelan*-like musical texture with very few instruments: a three-pot gong chime and a gong provide a colotomic foundation; a *rebab* player and singers provide a basic melody and elaborations; a *gendang* player provides the drumming.

Each of the gong chime's three pots has a different pitch; the actual pitches vary somewhat from ensemble to ensemble, but there always is a lower-pitched pot, a higher-pitched pot, with the third pot's pitch falling somewhere in between (i.e., a medium-pitched pot). One musician plays all three pots; the most typical pattern is the following (M = medium, L = low, H = high, and <rest> = no stroke):

M L M H M L M <rest>

This eight-pulse pattern (with the accent falling on the rest at the end) serves as a kind of holding pattern that outlines the basic rhythmic unit for most *ketuk tilu* songs. In the course of performance, however, the *ketuk* player frequently varies the pattern both rhythmically and with regard to pitch.

The cycle of the song "Sinur" includes two main phrases: the first phrase consists of eight of the eight-pulse units, with a stroke of the *goong* falling on the rest of the final unit; the second lasts four eight-pulse units, again with a *goong* stroke falling on the fourth unit's ending rest. There is an optional *goong* stroke in the middle of the second phrase, that is, on the final pulse of the second unit.

The colotomic phrase structure is notated below; each of the eight-pulse units is represented with the symbol "–"; an eight-pulse unit that ends with a gong stroke is represented with "–g"; an eight-pulse unit that sometimes ends with a gong stroke is represented –[g].

$$– – – – – – – – –g$$
$$– – [g] – –g$$

Because its phrase lengths are unequal, the cycle of "Sinur" has something of an asymmetrical character; in this sense, *ketuk tilu* phrases are comparable to *degung lagu klasik* tunes.

For the first six units of the first phrase, the drummer plays one of several repeating patterns; the dancers move in a way that looks and feels to them the way the drum pattern sounds, choosing different foot, arm, hand, and head gestures to mimic the drumming. For the last two units, the drummer plays a special cadential pattern that leads up to the gong stroke; it is typical for these patterns to stop with a dramatic accent just before the gong stroke. The *ketuk* player may deviate from the usual ostinato during these cadential patterns to enhance the drumming's drive toward the gong stroke.

For the second phrase, the drummer plays one of several more complicated, less repetitive patterns. For these patterns, the *ketuk* player follows the drumming's rhythm, and, again, the dancers perform gestures that look like the patterns sounds, paying special attention to where the gong strokes fall.

There are *ketuk tilu* songs in most of the Sundanese scales and modes, including *sorog* and *salendro* (see Chapter 5). Because the accompanying instruments are not tuned to any particular scale, the ensemble can quite easily accompany any Sundanese mode. The vocal melody of "Sinur" (also played on the *rebab*) is cast in *pelog degung*. The melody occupies an entire cycle, encompassing both the long and the short phrase. In this performance, the female singer performs two cycles in a row, then lets the *wiraswara* (male singer) take a cycle, creating a "metacycle" three cycles long. The metacycle is repeated four times.

For each cycle of "Sinur," the singers utilize a single verse in a poetic form called *paparikan*; *paparikan* is one of several poetic forms collectively known as *sisindiran*. A verse of *paparikan* consists of two couplets; the first lines of the two couplets rhyme, as do the second lines of the two couplets. The first couplet is the *cangkang* ("shell" or "rind"), and the second couplet is the *eusi* ("filling" or "content"). Generally, the shell's content has little do with the content's meaning. Because the melody has more than four melodic phrases, the singers often repeat one of the couplets to fill out the tune.

There is no specific theme that ties all of the *paparikan* together in this performance of "Sinur"; most of the *paparikan* provide advice on proper Sundanese values and behavior. Some of these *paparikan* verses are well-known among Sundanese. The transcription and translation of these *paparikan* verses was provided by Tati Haryatin, who warns readers that because of the hidden meanings and complex allusions in these verses, it is not always possible to translate them into another language; her goal in these translations was to give a sense of what the verses are trying to convey.

As is typical for a *ketuk tilu* song, this rendition of "Sinur" begins and ends with a special drum and *ketuk* pattern called *nyered*. Dancers stand still during *nyered* and prepare to begin or end their dancing appropriately. In many cases (but not in this rendition) the *nyered* would serve as a transition to another *ketuk tilu* song, which would accompany the all-male *oray-orayan* dance.

Timeline for "Sinur"

0:00	*pangkat* from the *rebab*, drums join in
0:06	first *goong* stroke
0:06–0:17	*nyered*
0:17–0:25	transitional phrase
0:25–2:26	first "metacycle"
0:25–1:08	first cycle sung by female singer
0:25–0:55	first phrase

pasinden: Harepan mah geuningan kembang ermawar
I am hoping for roses
pacampur mah jeung kaca piring
mixed with gardenias
Sumeblak loba kakelar
My heart is sick with worry
tagiwur mah Bapa teu ngeunah cicing
tossing and turning uncertainty

0:55–1:08 second phrase (with an "optional" gong stroke at 1:01)

Kembang wera geuningan da daun turi
Hibiscuses and sesbanias
hayang leuleuweungan bae
always grow in the forest

1:08–1:48 second cycle sung by female singer

pasinden: Lamun teu era, era, era ku diri
If I'm not ashamed of myself

wiraswara: (spoken) Rek kumaha karep teh, Nyi?
What are you going to do, Miss?

pasinden: hayang reureujeungan bae
I want always to be together (with my love)
Lamun teu era ku diri
If I'm not ashamed of myself
hayang reureujeungan bae
I want always to be together

1:48–2:26   cycle sung by male singer

wiraswara: Manuk piit jeung kapinis
Sparrows and swallows
di lebak keur nyaratuan
feeding down below
Sapapait samamanis
Together for better or worse
nu disebut persatuan
that's what's called unity

2:26–4:14   second "metacycle"

pasinden: Japati mah geuningan da ti Situ Aksan
Doves from Situ Aksan
sukuna kenging mulasan
their feet painted
Babakti ku kamonesan
We are devoting ourselves
seni Sunda ieung da ngadeuheusan
to preserve Sundanese art
Surawung mah geuningan sarana pahang
Basil is pungent
gedangna mah geuningan dipiringan
as papayas are on a plate
Mun aya nu salah, salah paham
If there are misunderstandings
ku urang mah bapa kudu elingan
we have to correct one another

wiraswara: Mawa peti dina sumbul
Carrying a box in a basket
dibawa ka Nusa Jawa
carrying it to Java
Pangarti mah teu beurat ngandung
Knowledge is not just something you carry around
kabisa teu beurat mawa
and the ability to do anything is useful

4:14–5:51   third "metacycle"

> **pasinden**: Kulah di pipir pipir ti dapur
> *Small pond behind the kitchen*
> dipelakan lalasunan
> *planted with a hedge*
> Ulah sok raresep nganggur
> *Don't you sit around doing nothing*
> matak nungtun ieuh da lalamunan
> *as it leads you to uncertain musings*
> Halimun mah geuningan aya di imah
> *A thin mist comes down around the house*
> ulah di kana batukeun
> *don't let it touch the stones*
> Lamun aya nu teu ngeunah
> *If there is anything unpleasant*
> ulah osok geuningan dikabaturkeun
> *don't give it to someone else*

> **wiraswara**: Motongkeun dahan kanyere
> *Breaking off a branch of berries*
> dadago rek moro subuh
> *waiting for the break of dawn*
> Tembongkeun ahlak nu sae
> *Show everyone good conduct*
> dina jero hirup kumbuh
> *in living your life*

5:51–7:15   fourth "metacycle"

> **pasinden**: Itu saha geuningan da nungtun munding
> *Who is it leading a buffalo by a rope?*

> **wiraswara**: (spoken) mana nyai?
> *where, Miss?*

> **pasinden**: digantelan saputangan
> *with a handkerchief about the neck*
> Itu saha ginding-ginding teuing
> *Who is it all dressed up*
> sing horeng mah ieung batur sorangan
> *it turned out to be a friend of mine*

> **wiraswara**: (spoken) Tobat . . .
> *Mercy . . .*

pasinden: Rek rancana geuningan da meser meser madu
Planning to go and buy some honey
dilogoder kikinciran
but I have so many things to do
Sadayana ulah bendu
Please everyone don't be angry
ngan sakadar geuning da sisindiran
it's only a sisindiran

wiraswara: Sing getol nginum jajamu
Drink jamu [traditional medicinal concoctions] frequently
ambeh jadi kuat urat
so you'll be strong and healthy
Sing getol neangan ilmu
Learn anything industriously
gunana dunya aherat
it will come handy sometime

7:15–7:24   *nyered* to end

wiraswara: (spoken) Mundur, mundur, mundur!
Back off!

Track 10

Music culture: Sundanese
Genre: gamelan salendro to accompany *jaipongan* dance entitled "Renggasmara"
Piece title: "Lindeuk Japati"
Composer: Nano S. (also known as Nano Suratno, b. 1944)
Performers: The late Tati Saleh, accompanied by LS Gentra Madya (directed by Nano S.)
Source: Top Jaipong: Lindeuk Japati, track 1, SP Record.

The noted Sundanese composer Nano S. wrote "Lindeuk Japati" in 1986; although he is better known for his *pop Sunda* hits, Nano's foray into *jaipongan* achieved considerable success in the 1980s and continues to sell well into the present. Nano S. engaged the most famous *jaipongan* drummer of the time, Suwanda from Karawang (who also played on most of Jugala's most successful recordings), to play the *gendang* on the recording. Nano also collaborated with the prominent Bandung-based singer and dancer Tati Saleh for the recording; she provided the choreography (entitled "Renggasmara") for the piece.

The background of the song is a basic *patokan* piece called "Banjaran," whose pillar pitches can be notated:

1 ② 1 ④

Like most *jaipongan* songs, the *patokan* is performed in two *wilet*, and each of the instrumentalists fills out the pillar pitches by inserting *pancer* tones and plays appropriate idiomatic figurations based on the pillar pitches to create his or her part.

Nano composed the song's melody to fit into the tonal framework provided by "Banjaran." As is typical for *jaipongan* tunes, the piece opens with a fast introductory section, which features a careful arrangement (*arensemen*) of instrumental parts that show off the individual instrumentalist's dexterity as well as the ensemble's skill at playing together. After the fast introduction, the tempo slows down to a speed that is appropriate for *jaipongan* dancing. The entire composition (the "metacycle") of the main section takes six iterations of the two-gong-phrase cycle of "Banjaran" to complete; four of the iterations feature Tati Saleh singing the official text of the song (see Figure 7.14 on p. 191 for the song text and translation); the remaining two cycles feature the extemporized singing of a *wiraswara* (male singer; on this recording, Atang Warsita). The entire melody is cast in the *sorog* tuning system, which clashes euphoniously with the gamelan's *salendro* tuning system.

The drumming is meant to accompany a specific dance choreography, created by Tati Saleh, entitled "Renggasmara." Like all *jaipongan* recordings, however, other dancers feel free to improvise or rehearse their own movements according to the drumming. The timeline below provides a phrase-by-phrase accounting of the choreography using the terms introduced in Chapter 7 for the various types of *jaipongan* drum/dance phrases: *pola ibing* (the standard pattern that features five flurries of drumming activity with silence in between), *mincid* (continuous walking pattern), and alternating patterns (which involve special phrases repeated several times within a single gong phrase). The choreography requires two and a half metacycles to complete.

Careful listeners will notice that the *kempul* player's part is quite lively and animated (in stark contrast to that instrument's typically static, sparse idiom as a colotomic instrument). For *jaipongan* accompaniments it is common for the *kempul* player to follow the drumming; he plays particular patterns for each drum flurry in the *pola ibing* as well as a frenetic syncopated pattern for *mincid*. This ensemble also features a *kecrek* player who, for the most part, follows and reinforces the *gendang* parts.

Timeline for "Lindeuk Japati"

0:00	fast introduction: *ketuk tilu*-like opening leading to first gong stroke at 0:08
0:08–0:40	first Banjaran gong phrase with *arensemen* ends with gong 2
0:40–1:11	second *arensemen* phrase ends with gong 4
1:11–1:25	transition phrase (ends with gong 4)
1:25–4:17	First "metacycle" (female singer goes through song, plus answer from *wiraswara*)
1:25–1:52	first gong phrase of song; drummer plays holding pattern
1:52–2:20	second gong phrase of song; drummer plays partial standard pattern
2:02	*jalak pengkor*
2:08	*capang*

2:14	*cindek*
2:17	*ngala genah*
2:20–2:48	third gong phrase of song; drummer plays complete standard pattern
2:24	*bukaan*
2:31	*jalak pengkor*
2:35	*capang*
2:42	*cindek*
2:45	*ngala genah*
2:48–3:18	fourth gong phrase; drummer plays an alternating pattern
3:18–3:48	fifth gong phrase (sung by *wiraswara*); drummer plays standard pattern
3:48–4:17	sixth gong phrase (sung by *wiraswara*); drummer plays an alternating pattern
4:17–7:10	Second metacycle
4:17–4:46	drummer plays standard pattern in which *bukaan* and *jalak pengkor* are slightly varied
4:46–5:14	drummer plays varied version of standard pattern again, this time with a variation of *capang* that slides directly into *cindek*
5:14–5:43	drummer plays *mincid*
5:18	drum transition to *mincid*
5:21	*mincid* begins
5:43–6:13	*mincid* continues
6:13–6:42	fourth gong phrase (sung by *wiraswara*); drummer plays a variation of the standard pattern
6:42–7:10	fifth gong phrase (sung by *wiraswara*); drummer plays a variation of the standard pattern
7:10	Third (incomplete) metacycle
7:10–7:42	first gong phrase of song; drummer plays standard pattern
7:42–8:06	second gong phrase of song; drummer plays standard pattern
8:06–8:36	third gong phrase of song; drummer plays *mincid rangkep* and signals piece's ending
8:10	transition to *mincid*
8:13	*mincid* begins
8:27	ending signal begins

Appendix
Ensemble Instrumentation

The following lists summarize the instrumentation of the various ensembles discussed in the text.

Gondang sabangunan (Toba Batak, Sumatra; see Chapter 1)
  taganing a set of five tuned drums
  gordang large drum
  odap large drum
  ogung gong chime with four suspended gongs
  hesek rattle
  sarune double-reed wind instrument

Pinn peat (Cambodia; see Chapter 2)
  sralai double-reed wind instruments (ensemble includes two of different sizes)
  roneat ek xylophone
  roneat thung xylophone
  roneat dek keyed metallophone
  korng tauch circular gong chime
  korng thomm circular gong chime
  chhing pair of small cymbals
  skor thomm drum
  sampho drum
  vocalists

Pi phat (Thai gong-chime ensemble; see Chapter 2)
  pi double-reed wind instrument
  ranat xylophones

khawng gong chimes
ching cymbals
taphon drums

Maguindanao kulintang (southern Philippines gong-chime ensemble; see Chapter 2)
agung pair of hanging gongs with deep flanges
gandingan set of four hanging gongs
babandil single hanging gong
dabakan goblet-shaped drum

Gamelan sekaten (Cirebonese; see Chapter 3)
gong large hanging gongs (two)
bonang large one-row gong chime
ketuk or *kajar* small, horizontal gong
demung larger, lower-pitched keyed metallophones
titil smaller, higher-pitched keyed metallophone
beri, *cret*, or *kecrek* flat, unbossed gong
bedug large drum

Central Javanese court-style gamelan (see Chapter 4)
gong ageng extremely large hanging gong
gong siyem (or *gong suwukan*) hanging gong (smaller than *gong ageng*)
kenong horizontal gong chime
kethuk small horizontal gong
kempyang small, high-pitched *kethuk*-like gong, or a pair of such little gongs
kempul gong chime consisting of several small hanging gongs
saron generic term for a "family" of six- or seven-keyed metallophones
saron demung lowest-pitched member of the *saron* family
saron barung medium-pitched member of the *saron* family
saron panerus (or *peking*) highest-pitched member of the *saron* family
bonang generic term for a family of horizontal gong chimes with ten to fourteen pots arranged in two rows
bonang barung lower-pitched horizontal gong chime
bonang panerus higher-pitched horizontal gong chime
gender generic term for a "family" of keyed instruments with thin keys suspended over resonating tubes
slenthem lowest-pitched member of the *gender* family, with six to eight keys
gender barung medium-pitched member of the *gender* family, with fourteen keys
gender panerus highest-pitched member of the *gender* family, with fourteen keys
gerong male chorus
pesindhen female vocalist
rebab two-string fiddle
suling vertical bamboo flute with four (*slendro*) or five (*pelog*) holes
gambang xylophone with eighteen to twenty-one wooden keys
celempung (or *siter*) zither with metal strings

bedug large barrel-shaped drum with skin heads attached at each end with large wooden pegs
kendhang two-headed barrel-shaped drums with heads secured with rawhide laces
kendhang gendhing large *kendhang*
ketipung small *kendhang*
kendhang kalih "two drums"—combination of *kendhang gending* and *ketipung*
ciblon (or *batangan*) medium-sized *kendhang*-style drum

Gandrung ensemble (Eastern Java, Osing; see Chapter 4)
    various gongs and gong chimes
    pair of violins
    kluncing metal triangle

Gong luang (Bali; see Chapter 4)
    saron bar metallophone (two)
    gangsa gender-family metallophone (two)
    trompong large gong chime played by several musicians
    gong ageng large hanging gong
    cengceng cymbals
    bedug small drum

Gamelan gong beleganjur (Bali; see Chapter 4)
    cengceng cymbals
    reyong four small, hand-held gongs, each played by a different musician
    ponggang two medium-sized hand-held gongs, two players
    kajar (or *kempluk*) medium-sized hand-held gong
    kempli similar to *kajar*
    bende large hanging gong with a sunken boss
    kempur large hanging gong
    gong lanang "male" large hanging gong (smaller than *gong wadon*)
    gong wadon "female" large hanging gong (larger than *gong lanang*)
    kendang lanang "male" drum (lighter, higher-pitched)
    kendang wadon "female" drum (heavier, lower-pitched)

Gamelan gong kebyar (Bali; see Chapter 4)
    gong ageng large hanging gong
    kempur smaller hanging gong
    kemong tiny hanging gong
    kempli small gong laid horizontally on a frame
    jegogan lowest-pitched *gender*-family instrument
    calung second-lowest-pitched *gender*-family instrument
    gangsa family of *gender* with multiple octaves of keys
    ugal lead *gangsa*
    pemade gangsa one octave higher than *ugal*
    kantilan gangsa one octave higher than *pemade*

trompong lower-pitched one-row gong chime played by one musician
reyong higher-pitched one-row gong chime played by four musicians
cengceng set of six or more cymbals played by a single player

Goong renteng (Sundanese; see Chapter 5)
goong large gong (two)
gangsa (or *selukat*) *saron*-like instrument with many keys
beri non-bossed gong
bonang (or *koromong*, or *kokuang*, or *renteng*) large, one-row gong chime
cecempres *saron*-like instrument
panglima large gong chime
tarompet double-reed wind instrument

Gamelan salendro (Sundanese; see Chapter 5)
goong large gong
kempul smaller gong suspended from the same frame as *goong*
saron six- or seven-keyed metallophone (two)
panerus six- or seven-keyed metallophone, one octave lower than *saron*
bonang horizontal gong chime with ten to fourteen small knobbed gongs
gambang xylophone with eighteen to twenty-one wooden keys
gendang set of two-headed, barrel-shaped drums.
rebab spike fiddle with two brass strings and a skin-covered resonator
pasinden female vocalist
kenong horizontal gong chime with one to six large, high-pitched gongs
jengglong horizontal gong chime with three to six gongs, flatter and tuned an octave lower than *kenong*
peking metallophone similar to *saron* but tuned an octave higher
rincik gong chime similar to *bonang* but tuned an octave higher
kecrek stack of iron plates hit with a wooden hammer
ketuk small gong laid horizontally and hit with a padded stick

Kendang penca (Sundanese ensemble to accompany *penca silat* martial arts; see Chapter 5)
kendang set of drums (two)
tarompet double-reed wind instrument
goong small hanging gong

Degung (Sundanese; see Chapter 6)
bonang fourteen-pot horizontal gong chime arranged in one row on a V- or U-shaped frame
panerus (or *demung*) lower-pitched fourteen-key metallophone
titil (or *peking* or *cempres*) higher-pitched fourteen-key metallophone
goong large hanging gong
jengglong gong chime with six low-pitched gongs, suspended vertically or arranged horizontally

suling four-hole bamboo flute
gendang set of two-headed barrel-shaped drums

Reog or ogel ensemble (Sundanese; see Chapter 7)
tilingtit smallest *dog-dog* in a *reog* ensemble
panempag second-smallest *dog-dog* in a *reog* ensemble
jongjrong second-largest *dog-dog* in a *reog* ensemble
bangbrang largest *dog-dog* in a *reog* ensemble

Ketuk tilu (Sundanese; see Chapter 7)
goong large hanging gong
ketuk gong chime with three small horizontal gongs
gendang set of two-headed, barrel-shaped drums.
rebab spike fiddle with two brass strings and a skin-covered resonator

References

Adams, Monni. 1981. "Instruments and Songs of Sumba, Indonesia: A Preliminary Survey." *Asian Music* 13(1): 73–84.

Amelia, Lia. 1996. *Jenis tari rakyat dalam kategori ketuk tilu: Kajian teknik dan bentuk terhadap pertunjukan ronggeng gunung, bangreng dan doger*. Research report. Bandung, Indonesia: STSI.

Anderson, Benedict. 1972. "The Idea of Power in Javanese Culture." In C. Holt, ed., *Culture and Politics in Indonesia*, pp. 1–69. Ithaca, NY: Cornell University Press.

———. 1991. *Imagined Communities: Reflections on the Origin and Spread of Nationalism*. London: Verso.

Anon. 1996. "Dampak ecstasy pada tubuh." *Kompas Online* (July 14, 1996). Electronic source, URL http://www.kompas.co.id/9607/14/iptek/damp.htm, accessed December 6, 2000.

Anon. 2003. "Maguindanao." Electronic source, URL http://www.mindanao.org/cm/overview/ka1.htm, accessed May 16, 2003.

Atmadibrata, Enoch. 1980. "Indonesia VI, 3: West Java: Dance." In S. Sadie, ed., *New Grove Dictionary of Music and Musicians*, Vol. 9, pp. 211–15. London: Macmillan.

———. 1996. "West Java: Ketuk Tilu and Tayuban." In E. Sedyawati, ed., *Indonesian Heritage: Performing Arts*, pp. 80–1. Singapore: Archipelago Press.

———. 1998. *Dari ibing tayub ke ibing keurseus: Sumber berbagai kemungkinan pengembangan tari*. Bandung, Indonesia: STSI.

Azis, Abdul, and Nandang R. Barmaya. 1983–4. *Tari ketuk tilu sebagai materi kuliah tari rakyat*. Bandung, Indonesia: Proyek Pengembangan Institut Kesenian Indonesia.

Bakan, Michael B. 1999. *Music of Death and New Creation: Experiences in the World of Balinese Gamelan Beleganjur*. Chicago: University of Chicago Press.

Bancroft, Hubert Howe. 1893. *The Book of the Fair*. Chicago: The Bancroft Co.

Barrow, Sir John, Pieter Jan Truter, and Kenneth E. Hill. 1806. *A Voyage to Cochinchina, in the Years 1792 and 1793*. London: T. Cadell and W. Davies.

Basile, Christopher. 1998. *Troubled Grass and Crying Bamboo: The Music of Roti* (album liner notes). Victoria, Australia: Indonesian Arts Society.

Basile, Christopher, and Janet Hoskins. 1998. "Nusa Tenggara Timur." In T. E. Miller and S. Williams, eds., *The Garland Encyclopedia of World Music*, Vol. 4: *Southeast Asia*, pp. 786–803. New York: Garland.

Bateson, Gregory. 1963. "Bali: The Value System of a Steady State." In M. Fortes, ed., *Social Structure: Studies Presented to A. R. Radcliffe-Brown*, pp. 35–53. New York: Russell & Russell.

Becker, Judith. 1968. "Percussion Patterns in the Music of Mainland Southeast Asia." *Ethnomusicology* 12(2): 173–91.

———. 1979. "Time and Tune in Java." In A. L. Becker and A. Yengoyan, eds., *The Imagination of Reality: Essays in Southeast Asian Coherence Systems*, pp. 197–210. Norwood, NJ: Ablex Publishing Company.

———. 1980. "A Southeast Asian Music Process: Thai Thaw and Javanese Irama." *Ethnomusicology* 24(3): 453–64.

———. 1988. "Earth, Fire, Sakti, and the Javanese Gamelan." *Ethnomusicology* 32(3): 385–91.

Belo, Jane. 1970. "Introduction." In J. Belo, ed., *Traditional Balinese Culture*, pp. xi–xxvii. New York: Columbia University Press.

Brandts-Buys, J. S. n.d. "Krantenartikelen over Javaanse dans." Folder H 972. Archives of the KITLV, Leiden.

Bratawidjaja, Thomas Wiyasa. 1990. *Upacara perkawinan adat Sunda*. Jakarta, Indonesia: Pustaka Sinar Harapan.

287

Broughton, Simon, Mark Ellingham, David Muddyman, and Richard Trill, eds. 1994. *World Music: The Rough Guide*. London: Rough Guides.

Cadar, Usopay H. 1996. "The Role of Kolintang Music in Maranao Society." *Asian Music* 27(2): pp. 81–103.

Canave-Dioquino, Corazon. 1998. "The Lowland Christian Philippines." In T. E. Miller and S. Williams, eds., *The Garland Encyclopedia of World Music*, Vol. 4: *Southeast Asia*, pp. 839–67. New York: Garland.

Cook, Simon. 2007. "Indonesia V. West Java 1. Sunda e. Gamelan Ensembles," *Grove Music Online*, ed. L. Macy. Electronic source, URL http://www.grovemusic.com, accessed December 6, 2007.

Cribb, Robert B. 1984. *Jakarta in the Indonesian Revolution, 1945–49*. London: University of London Press.

———. 2000. *Historical Atlas of Indonesia*. Honolulu: University of Hawai'i Press.

Dahlan, Mas Nana Munajat. 1996. "Bajidor: Dalam pertunjukan klininganbajidoran di Kabupaten Subang." Thesis for the degree of S-1, STSI Bandung.

Dapperen, J. W. van. 1933. "Moeloeddagen te Cheribon." *Djawa* 13: 140–65.

Day, Tony. 1996. "Ties that (Un)Bind: Families and State in Premodern Southeast Asia." *Journal of Asian Studies* 55(2): 384–409.

DeVale, Sue Carole. 1977. "A Sundanese Gamelan: A Gestalt Approach to Organology." PhD dissertation, Northwestern University.

Diamond, Jared. 1999. *Guns, Germs, and Steel: The Fates of Human Societies*. New York: Norton.

Dris, Jose Arnaldo. 2003. "Maguindanao." Electronic source, URL http://litera1no4.tripod.com/maguindanao_frame.html, accessed May 16, 2003.

Durban Ardjo, Irawati. 1998. *Perkembangan tari Sunda: Melacak jejak Tb. Oemay Martakusuma dan Rd. Tjetje Somantri*. Bandung, Indonesia: Masyarakat Seni Pertunjukan Indonesia (MSPI).

Dyck, J. Z. van. 1922. *Garoet en omstrenken: Zwerftochten door de Preanger*. Batavia: G. Kolff.

Ekadjati, Edi S. 1995. *Kebudayaan Sunda (Suatu Pendekatan Sejarah)*. Jakarta, Indonesia: Pustaka Jaya.

Encyclopaedia Britannica. 2003a. "Mandala." *Encyclopaedia Britannica Online*. Electronic source, URL http://www.search.eb.com/eb/article?eu=51701, accessed May 17, 2003.

———. 2003b. "Southeast Asia, History of." *Encyclopaedia Britannica Online*. Electronic source, URL http://www.search.eb.com/eb/article?eu=120876, accessed May 17, 2003.

Eringa, F. S. 1984. *Soendaas–Nederlands woordenboek*. Dordrecht, the Netherlands: Foris Publications.

Fajaria, Ria Dewi. 1996. *Ketuk tilu dalam konteks tari pergaulan*. Research report. Bandung, Indonesia: STSI.

Falla, Jonathan. 1985. "Gate-Crashing the Kraton." *New Statesman* 109 (April 5): 38.

Foley, Kathy. 1979. "The Sundanese Wayang Golek: The Rod Puppet Theater of West Java." PhD dissertation, University of Hawai'i.

———. 1989. "Of Gender and Dance in Southeast Asia: From Goddess to Go-Go Girl." In *Proceedings of the 20th Anniversary CORD Conference*, pp. 57–62. New York: Congress on Research in Dance.

Frederick, William H. 1982. "Rhoma Irama and the Dangdut Style: Aspects of Contemporary Indonesian Popular Culture." *Indonesia* 34: 103–30.

Frick, Christoph. 1929. *Voyages to the East Indies*. London: Cassell and Company.

Geertz, Clifford. 1973. *The Interpretation of Cultures*. New York: Basic Books.

Hardjana, Suka. 1996. "Keroncong and Dangdut." In E. Sedyawati, ed., *Indonesian Heritage: Performing Arts*, pp. 128–9. Singapore: Archipelago Press.

Harnish, David. 1998. "Bali." In T. E. Miller and S. Williams, eds., *The Garland Encyclopedia of World Music*, Vol. 4: *Southeast Asia*, pp. 729–61. New York: Garland.

Harrell, Max Leigh. 1974. "The Music of the Gamelan Degung of West Java." Ph.D. dissertation, University of California at Los Angeles.

———. 1975. "Some Aspects of Sundanese Music." *Selected Reports in Ethnomusicology* 2(2): 81–101.

Hatch, Martin. 1985. "Popular Music in Indonesia." In D. Horn, ed., *Popular Music Perspectives 2: Papers from the Second International Conference on Popular Music Studies, Reggio Emilia, September 19–24, 1983*, pp. 210–27. Göteborg, Sweden: IASPM.

———. 1997. "Classroom Indonesia: Music." Southeast Asia Program at Cornell University. Electronic source, URL http://www.einaudi.cornell.edu/SoutheastAsia/outreach/resources/ProjectIndonesia/Music.htm, accessed October 28, 2003.

Heine-Geldern, R. 1942. "Conceptions of State and Kingship in Southeast Asia." *Far Eastern Quarterly* 2: 15–30.

Heins, Ernst. 1975. "Kroncong and Tanjidor: Two Cases of Urban Folk Music in Jakarta." *Asian Music* 7(3): 20–32.

———. 1977. "Goong Renteng: Aspects of Orchestral Music in a Sundanese Village." PhD dissertation, University of Amsterdam.

Herdiani, Een. 1996. *Ketuk tilu dalam konteks upacara*. Research report. STSI Bandung.

Hermantoro, Dwiono. 1991. *Garap lagu kiliningan: materi kuliah karawitan Sunda di STSI Surakarta*. Research report Penelitian. Surakarta, Indonesia: STSI.

Heyden, Johan van der. 2007. *GeoHive: Global Statistics*. Electronic source, URL http://www.geohive.com/cntry/indonesia.aspx, accessed December 9, 2007.

Higham, Charles. 1989. *The Archaeology of Mainland Southeast Asia: From 10,000 BC to the Fall of Angkor*. New York: Cambridge University Press.

——. 1996. *The Bronze Age of Southeast Asia*. Hong Kong: Cambridge University Press.

Hinton, Harold C. 1976. *Far East and Southwest Pacific*. Washington, DC: Stryker-Post.

Hobsbawm, Eric. 1983. "Introduction: Inventing Traditions." In Eric Hobsbawm and Terence Ranger, eds. *The Invention of Tradition*, pp. 1–4. Cambridge, UK: Cambridge University Press.

Hood, Mantle. 1980. *Music of the Roaring Sea*. Wilhelmshaven, the Netherlands: Edition Heinrichshofen.

Hood, Mantle, and Hardja Susilo. 1967. *Music of the Venerable Dark Cloud: Introduction, Commentary, and Analyses* (notes to recording of same name, IER-7501). Los Angeles: Institute of Ethnomusicology, UCLA.

Junengsih. 1997. "Bajidoran Subang: Tinjauan khusus sekarannya." Thesis for the degree of S-1, STSI Bandung.

Kalanduyan, Danongan S. 1996. "Magindanaon Kulintang Music: Instruments, Repertoire, Performance Contexts, and Social Functions." *Asian Music* 27(2): 3–18.

Kartodirdjo, Sartono. 1982. "The Regents in Java as Middlemen: A Symbolic Action Approach." In G. Schutte and H. Sutherland, eds., *Papers of the Dutch-Indonesian Historical Conference held at Lage Vuursche, the Netherlands, 23–27 June 1980*, pp. 172–95. Leiden/Jakarta: Bureau of Indonesian Studies.

Kartomi, Margaret J. 1990. *On Concepts and Classifications of Musical Instruments*. Chicago: University of Chicago Press.

——. 1998. "Sumatra." In T. E. Miller and S. Williams, eds., *The Garland Encyclopedia of World Music*, Vol. 4: *Southeast Asia*, pp. 598–629. New York: Garland.

Koentjaraningrat, R. M. 1972. "Sundanese." In Frank M. LeBar, ed., *Ethnic Groups of Insular Southeast Asia*, pp. 54–6. New Haven, CT: Human Relations Area Files Press.

——. 1975. *Introduction to the Peoples and Cultures of Indonesia and Malaysia*. Menlo Park, CA: Cummings.

Kunst, Jaap. 1973 [1934]. *Music in Java*, 3rd enlarged edn, ed. E. L. Heins. The Hague, the Netherlands: Martinus Nijhoff.

Kunst, J., and C. J. A. Kunst-van Wely. 1923. "Over Toonschalen en Instrumenten van West-Java." *Djawa* 3(1): 26–40.

Lansing, J. Stephen. 1995. *The Balinese*. Fort Worth, TX: Harcourt Brace.

Lindsay, Jennifer. 1979. *Javanese Gamelan*. Kuala Lumpur and New York: Oxford University Press.

Lockard, Craig A. 1995. "Integrating Southeast Asia into the Framework of World History: The Period before 1500." *History Teacher* 29(1): 7–35.

——. 1998. *Dance of Life: Popular Music and Politics in Southeast Asia*. Honolulu: University of Hawai'i Press.

Logan, J. R. 1853. "Journal of an Excursion to the Native Provinces on Java in the Year 1828, during the War with Dipo Negoro." *Journal of the Indian Archipelago and Eastern Asia* 7: 1–19, 138–57, 225–46, 358–78.

Lubis, Nina H. 1998. *Kehidupan kaum ménak Priangan 1800–1942*. Bandung, Indonesia: Pusat Informasi Kebudayaan Sunda.

——. 2000a. "Perlukah Jawa Barat Ganti Nama?" *Pikiran Rakyat* (December 13, 2000), p. 8.

——. 2000b. *Sejarah Kota-Kota Lama di Jawa Barat*. Sumedang, Indonesia: Alqaprint Jatinangor.

Lysloff, René, and Deborah Wong. 1998. "Popular Music and Cultural Politics." In T. E. Miller and S. Williams, eds., *The Garland Encyclopedia of World Music*, Vol. 4: *Southeast Asia*, pp. 95–112. New York: Garland.

Maceda, José, and Harold C. Conklin. 1955. *Hanunóo music from the Philippines* (album liner notes). New York: Folkways Records.

Manuel, Peter. 1988. *Popular Musics of the Non-Western World*. New York: Oxford University Press.

Manuel, Peter, and Randall Baier. 1986. "Jaipongan: Indigenous Popular Music of West Java." *Asian Music* 18(1): 91–110.

Matusky, Patricia. 1998. "Island Southeast Asia: An Introduction." In T. E. Miller and S. Williams, eds., *The Garland Encyclopedia of World Music*, Vol. 4: *Southeast Asia*, pp. 594–7. New York: Garland.

Matusky, Patricia, and James Chopyak. 1998. "Peninsular Malaysia." In T. E. Miller and S. Williams, eds., *The Garland Encyclopedia of World Music*, Vol. 4: *Southeast Asia*, pp. 401–43. New York: Garland.

Miller, Terry E. 1998a. "Culture, Politics, and War." In T. E. Miller and S. Williams, eds., *The Garland Encyclopedia of World Music*, Vol. 4: *Southeast Asia*, pp. 87–94. New York: Garland.

——. 1998b. "Laos." In T. E. Miller and S. Williams, eds., *The Garland Encyclopedia of World Music*, Vol. 4: *Southeast Asia*, pp. 335–62. New York: Garland.

——. 1998c. "Thailand." In T. E. Miller and S. Williams, eds., *The Garland Encyclopedia of World Music*, Vol. 4: *Southeast Asia*, pp. 218–334. New York: Garland.

Miller, Terry E., and Sean Williams. 1998. "Waves of Cultural Influence." In T. E. Miller and S. Williams, eds., *The Garland Encyclopedia of World Music*, Vol. 4: *Southeast Asia*, pp. 55–86. New York: Garland.

Miller, Terry E., Margaret Walker Dilling, J. Lawrence Witzleben, Lu Guang, Phong Nguyen, Sam-Ang Sam, et al., 1993. "Review Essay." *Asian Music* 24(2): 111–88.

Morton, David. 1980. "The Music of Thailand." In E. May, ed., *Musics of Many Cultures: An Introduction*, pp. 63–82. Berkeley: University of California Press.

Muda, Mas Nanu. 1999. "Erotis sinden yang bikin heboh." *Pikiran Rakyat* (June 10), p. 14.

Myers, Douglas. 1992. "Jaipongan: A Seed Takes Root." *The Archipelago* (5): 44–6.

Myers-Moro, Pamela. 1991. "Teachers on Tape: Innovation and Experimentation in Teaching Thai Music." *Balungan* 5(1): 15–20.

Natapradja, Iwan D. 1972. "Karawitan Sunda." Unpublished manuscript.
——. 1975. "Sundanese Dances." *Selected Reports in Ethnomusicology* 2(2): 103–8.
North, Richard. 1982a. "Degung: My Search for the Ancient Gamelan of Sunda." Unpublished manuscript.
——. 1982b. Letter from R. North to Michael Wright.
——. 1988. "An Introduction to the Musical Traditions of Cirebon." *Balungan* 3(3): 2–6.
——. 2002. Phone conversation, March 31, 2002.
——. n.d. "Traditions: A Brief History of the Sundanese Degung." Unpublished manuscript.
Notosusanto, Nugroho, and Sarah Weiss. 1995. "Tayuban." *Review of Indonesian and Malaysian Affairs* 29(1 and 2): 119–24.
O'Connor, Richard A. 1995. "Agricultural Change and Ethnic Succession in Southeast Asian States: A Case for Regional Anthropology." *Journal of Asian Studies* 54(5): 968–96.
Osborne, Milton. 1985. *Southeast Asia: An Illustrated Introductory History*. Sydney, Australia: George Allen & Unwin.
Panitia Kamus, Lembaga Basa, and Sastra Sunda. 1969. *Kamus Umum Basa Sunda*. Bandung, Indonesia: Tarate.
Pemberton, John. 1994. *On the Subject of "Java."* Ithaca, NY: Cornell University Press.
Perris, Arnold B. 1971. "The Rebirth of the Javanese Angklung." *Ethnomusicology* 15(3): 403–6.
Pfeiffer, William P. 1976. *Filipino Music: Indigenious [sic], Folk, Modern*. Dumaguete City, the Philippines: Silliman Music Foundation.
Purba, Kornelius. 2003. "Yogyakarta's Spirit Could Be Model for the Nation." *Jakarta Post Online* (July 17, 2003). Electronic source, URL http://www.thejakartapost.com, accessed March 5, 2004.
Purba, Mauly. 2002. "Gondang Sabangunan Ensemble Music of the Batak Toba People: Musical Instruments, Structure, and Terminology." *Journal of Musicological Research* 21: 21–72.
——. 2003. "Adat ni Gondang: Rules and Structure of the Gondang Performance in Pre-Christian Toba Batak Adat Practice." *Asian Music* 34(1): 67–109.
Reid, Anthony. 1988. *Southeast Asia in the Age of Commerce, 1450–1680, Vol. 1: The Lands Below the Winds*. New Haven, CT: Yale University Press.
——. 1999. *Charting the Shape of Early Modern Southeast Asia*. Chiang Mai, Thailand: Silkworm Books.
Ricklefs, M. C. 1993. *A History of Modern Indonesia since c. 1300*. Stanford, CA: Stanford University Press.
Rouffaer, Gerret Pieter, and Jan Willem t. I. Jzerman. 1915. *De Eerste Schipvaart der Nederlanders naar Oost-Indie onder Cornelis de Houtman, 1595–1597*. The Hague, the Netherlands: MartinusNijhoff.
Rukmana, Deden. 2007. *Indonesia's Urban Studies*. Electronic source, URL http://indonesiaurbanstudies.blogspot.com/2007/03/jakarta-as-indonesias-primate-city.html, accessed December 9, 2007.
Ruswandi, Tardi. 2000. *Koko Koswara: Pencipta Karawitan Sunda yang Monumental*. Bandung, Indonesia: STSI.
Sam, Sam-Ang, and Patricia Shehan Campbell. 1991. *Silent Temples, Songful Hearts: Traditional Music of Cambodia*. Danbury, CT: World Music Press.
Sam, Sam-Ang, Panya Roongrüang, et al. 1998. "The Khmer People." In T. E. Miller and S. Williams, eds., *The Garland Encyclopedia of World Music*, Vol. 4: *Southeast Asia*, pp. 151–217. New York: Garland.
Santos, Ramón P. 1998. "Islamic Communities of the Southern Philippines." In T. E. Miller and S. Williams, eds., *The Garland Encyclopedia of World Music*, Vol. 4: *Southeast Asia*, pp. 889–912. New York: Garland.
Sastramidjaja. 1978. "Goong Renteng di Sukabumi." *Kawit* 17(V-II): 23–5.
Sedyawati, Edi and Yulianti Parani, 1995. *Ensiklopedi tari Indonesia*. Jakarta, Indonesia: Departemen Pendidikan dan Kebudayaan.
Shelley, Judith. 2002. "Interview with Bpk Ismet Ruchimat from Sambasunda." Australia Indonesia Arts Alliance. Electronic source, URL http://www.aiaa.org.au/news/news11/ismet.html, accessed September 7, 2003.
Sjamsuddin. 1992. *Menuju Negara Kesatuan: Negara Pasundan*. Jakarta, Indonesia: Departmen Pendidkar dan Kebudayaan.
Skog, Inge. 1993. *North Borneo Gongs and the Javanese Gamelan: Studies in Southeast Asian Gong Music*. Stockholm, Sweden: Akademitryck.
Soeharto, M. 1992. *Kamus Musik*. Jakarta, Indonesia: PT Gramedia.
Soekanda. 1991. "Mengenang Bapak Ojo 'Tokoh Degung Purbasaka.'" *Kawit* 43(5-V): 88–93.
Soepandi, Atik. 1976. "Gamelan Sekaten Kanoman Cirebon." *Buletin Kebudayaan Jawa Barat* 8 (II–II): 25–6.
——. 1977. "Jenis-Jenis Gamelan di Jawa Barat." *Kawit* 13 (I-II-III): 37–8.
——. 1985. *Kamus istilah karawitan Sunda*. Bandung, Indonesia: Satu Nusa.
Soepandi, Atik, and Enoch Atmadibrata. 1976. *Khasanah Kesenian Daerah Jawa Barat*. Bandung, Indonesia: Pelita Masa.
Soepandi, Atik, Enip Sukanda, and Ubun Kurbarsah, 1996. *Ragam cipta: Mengenal seni pertunjukan daerah Jawa Barat*. Bandung, Indonesia: CV Beringin Sakti.
Solihin, Asep. 1986. *Perbendaharaan tabuh reog buhun pada perkumpulan seni Reog Mitra Siliwangi Bandung*. Bandung, Indonesia: ASTI.
Somawijaya, Abun. 1990. *Perkembangan ketuk tilu buhun hingga jaipongan: Salah satu materi pelajaran pada ASTI Bandung*. Research report. Bandung, Indonesia: ASTI.
Sorrell, Neil. 1990. *A Guide to the Gamelan*. Portland, OR: Amadeus Press.

Spiller, Henry. 1993. "Sundanese Dance Accompaniment: The Career of Pa Kayat." *Balungan* 5(2): 15–18.

——. 1996. "Continuity in Sundanese Dance Drumming: Clues from the 1893 Chicago Exposition." *World of Music* 38(2): 23–40.

Stowitts, Hubert Banner. n.d. "The Key to the Culture of Java." Unpublished manuscript.

——. 1930. "Where Prime Ministers Dance." *Asia* 30(1): 699–703.

Suanda, Endo. 1988. "Dancing in Cirebonese Topèng" *Balungan* 3(3): 7–15.

——. 1999. "Cirebon (Java)." In T. E. Miller and S. Williams, eds., *The Garland Encyclopedia of World Music*, Vol. 4: *Southeast Asia*, pp. 685–99. New York: Garland.

Suganda, Her. 1996. "Tjetjep Supriadi, kerisauan wayang golek." *Kompas* (June 14), Jakarta, p. 10.

——. 1998. "Bajidor dan sinden." *Kompas Online* (March 8, 1998). Electronic source, URL http://www.kompas.co.id/kompas%2Dcetak/9903/08/dikbud/baji20.htm, accessed December 6, 2000.

——. 1999. "Cicih 'Cangkurileung,' Tancap Gas Terus . . ." *Kompas* (March 8, 1999). Electronic source, URL http://www.kompas.co.id/kompas%2Dcetak/9903/08/naper/cici12.htm, accessed March 5, 2004.

——. n.d. "Deded . . . deded-deng: Ritme gendang Sundan yang seolah menyampaikan dialog." *Kompas* (date unknown), Jakarta, p. 8.

Sugiharwati, Tutty. 1980. "Ketuk tilu Ujungberung sebagai tari rakyat." Thesis for the degree of Sarjana Muda Tari, ASTI Bandung.

Suhaeti, Etty. 1986. "Perkembangan gerak-gerak tari ketuk tilu di Bandung." Thesis for the degree of Sarjana Seni Tari, Institut Seni Indonesia (ISI).

Sujana, Anis. 1993. "Tayuban di kalangan bupati dan priyayi di Priangan pada abad ke-19 dan ke-20." Thesis for degree of S-2, Universitas Gadjah Mada.

Sukarya, Chandra. 1997. "Penyajian karya seni wanda kendang ketuk tilu." Diploma 3 thesis, STSI Bandung.

Sukerta, Pande Made. 1998. *Ensiklopedia Mini Karawitan Bali.* Bandung, Indonesia: MSPI.

Sumardjo, Jakob. 1999. "Nenek Moyang Kita yang Porno." *Kompas Online* (August 28, 1999). Electronic source, URL http://www.kompas.com/kompas%2Dcetak/9908/28/opini/nene04.htm, accessed March 5, 2004.

Sumarsam. 1975. "Inner Melody in Javanese Gamelan Music." *Asian Music* 7(1): 3–13.

——. 1980. "The Musical Practice of the Gamelan Sekaten." *Asian Music* 12(2): 54–73.

——. 1995. *Gamelan: Cultural Interaction and Musical Development in Central Java.* Chicago: University of Chicago Press.

Sunarya, Asep Sunandar. 1998. *Jabang tutuka/The Birth of Gatotkaca: A Sundanese Wayang Golek Purwa Performance from West Java Performed by Asep Sunandar Sunarya and Giri Haraja III*, translated and with an introduction by Andrew N. Weintraub. Jakarta, Indonesia: Lontar.

Supandi, Atik. 1970. *Teori Dasar Karawitan.* Bandung, Indonesia: Pelita Masa.

Supanggah, Rahayu. 2003. "Campur Sari: A Reflection." *Asian Music* 34(2): 1–20.

Surjodiningrat, R. M. Wasisto. 1971. *Gamelan Dance and Wayang in Jogjakarta.* Jogjakarta: Gadjah Mada University Press.

Sutherland, Heather. 1979. *The Making of a Bureaucratic Elite: The Colonial Transformation of the Javanese Priyayi.* Singapore: Heinemann Educational Books (Asia) Ltd.

Sutton, R. Anderson. 1991. *Traditions of Gamelan Music in Java: Musical Pluralism and Regional Identity.* Cambridge: Cambridge University Press.

——. 1999. "Central and East Java." In T. E. Miller and S. Williams, eds., *The Garland Encyclopedia of World Music*, Vol. 4: *Southeast Asia*, pp. 631–85. New York: Garland.

Sweeney, Amin. 1974. "Professional Malay Story-Telling." In *Studies in Malaysian Oral and Musical Traditions*, pp. 48–99. Ann Arbor: Center for South and Southeast Asian Studies, University of Michigan.

Swindells, Rachel. 2004. "Klasik, Kawih, Kreasi: Musical Transformation and the Gamelan Degung of Bandung, West Java, Indonesia." PhD dissertation, City University, London.

Tamsyah, Budi Rahayu, Purmasih, Tati Prumawati, and A. R. Supratman, 1998. *Kamus Sunda-Indonesia.* Bandung, Indonesia: Pustaka Setia.

Taruskin, Richard. 1995. *Text and Act.* New York: Oxford University Press.

Tenzer, Michael. 1991. *Balinese Music.* Berkeley, CA: Periplus.

——. 2000. *Gamelan Gong Kebyar: The Art of Twentieth-Century Balinese Music.* Chicago: University of Chicago Press.

Thunberg, Charles Peter, MD. 1795. *Travels in Europe, Africa, and Asia Made Between the Years 1770 and 1779.* Vol II. London: F. and C. Rivington.

Tim Yayasan Mitra Budaya Indonesia. 1982. *Cerbon.* Cirebon, Indonesia: Yayasan Mitra Budaya Indonesia.

Tirasonjaya, Gugum Gumbira. 1988. "Jaipongan, Tari." In Anon., ed., *Ensiklopedi nasional Indonesia*, p. 293. Jakarta: Cipta Adi Pustaka.

Tisana, Herlia. 1997. "Tinjauan musikologis terhadap bentuk penyajian gamelan degung dalam fungsinya sebagai sarana upacara mapag panganten adat Sunda." Thesis for the degree of Sarjana Seni, STSI Bandung.

Tjarmedi, Entjar, Deded Suparman, Entis Sutisna, and Asep Resmana. 1997. *Pedoman Lagu-Lagu Klasik dan Kreasi Gamelan Degung Jawa Barat.* Bandung, Indonesia: CV Satu Nusa.

Toth, Andrew F. 1975. "The Gamelan Luang of Tangkas, Bali." *Selected Reports in Ethnomusicology* 2(2): 65–79.

Vetter, Roger. 2001. "More than Meets the Eye and Ear: Gamelans and their Meaning in a Central Javanese Palace." *Asian Music* 32(2): 41–92.

Vitale, Wayne. 1990. "Kotekan: The Technique of Interlocking Parts in Balinese Music." *Balungan* 4(2): 2–15.

Weintraub, Andrew N. 1990. "The Music of Pantun Sunda: An Epic Narrative Tradition of West Java, Indonesia." MA thesis in music, University of Hawai'i.

——. 1993. "Theory in Institutional Pedagogy and 'Theory in Practice' for Sundanese Gamelan Music," *Ethnomusicology* 37(1): 29–39.

——. 1997. "Constructing the Popular: Superstars, Performance, and Cultural Authority in Sundanese Wayang Golek Purwa of West Java, Indonesia." PhD dissertation, University of California, Berkeley.

Wessing, Robert. 1978. *Cosmology and Social Behavior in a West Javanese Settlement.* Athens: Ohio University Center for International Studies.

Williams, Sean. 1989–90. "Current Developments in Sundanese Popular Music," *Asian Music* 21(1): 105–36.

——. 1998. "Java: Sunda." In T. E. Miller and S. Williams, eds., *The Garland Encyclopedia of World Music*, Vol. 4: *Southeast Asia*, pp. 699–727. New York: Garland.

Wolbers, Paul Arthur. 1986. "Gandrung and Angklung from Banyuwangi: Remnants of a Past Shared with Bali." *Asian Music* 18(1): 71–90.

Wong, Deborah. 1995. "Video Reviews: The JVC Video Anthology of World Music and Dance, Vols. 1–15." *Ethnomusicology* 39(3): 529–38.

Wright, Michael Richard. 1978. "The Music Culture of Cirebon." PhD dissertation, University of California at Los Angeles.

Yampolsky, Philip. 1987. *Tonggeret* (album liner notes). New York: Elektra Nonesuch/Icon Records 79173–2.

——. 1994a. *Betawi and Sundanese Music of the North Coast of Java: Topeng Betawi, Tanjidor, Ajeng* (album liner notes). Washington, DC: Smithsonian/Folkways Recordings: SFW 40421.

——. 1994b. *Musik Populer Indonesia: Kroncong, Dandut, Langgam Jawa* (album liner notes). Bandung, Indonesia: MSPI: 10083620.

——. 1996. *Melayu Music of Sumatra and the Riau Islands* (album liner notes). Washington, DC: Smithsonian/Folkways Recordings: SFW 40427.

——. 1997. *Musik dari Nias and Sumatera Utara* (album liner notes). Bandung, Indonesia: MSPI: 10083620.

Zanten, Wim van. 1995. "Aspects of Baduy Music in its Sociocultural Context, with Special Reference to Singing and Angklung." *Bijdragen tot de taal-, land- en volkenkunde* 151(4): 516–43.

——. 1997. "Inner and Outer Voices: Listening and Hearing in West Java." *World of Music* 39(2): 41–9.

Zoetmulder, P. J., S. O. Robson, Darusuprata, and Sumarti Suprayitno, 1995. *Kamus Jawa kuna-Indonesia.* Jakarta, Indonesia: PT Gramedia Pustaka Utama.

Index

Page numbers for illustrations are in italics.